REAL ESTATE BROKERAGE MANAGEMENT

Third Edition

Bruce Lindeman

Professor of Finance and Real Estate
H. Clyde Buchanan Professor of Real Estate
University of Arkansas at Little Rock

Regents/Prentice Hall, Englewood Cliffs, New Jersey 07632

Library of Congress Cataloging-in-Publication Data

Lindeman, Bruce.
    Real estate brokerage management / Bruce Lindeman. -- 3rd ed.
        p.   cm.
    Includes bibliographical references and index.
    ISBN 0-13-763459-5
    1. Real estate business--United States--Management.   I. Title.
HD255.L55 1993
333.33'068--dc20
                                                      93-17156
                                                      CIP

Production Editor: *Eileen O'Sullivan*
Acquisitions Editor: *Mark Moscowitz*
Prepress Buyer: *Ilene Sanford*
Manufacturing Buyer: *Ed O'Dougherty*
Editorial Assistant: *Mark Cohen*
Cover Design: *Laura Ierardi*

 1994 by REGENTS/PRENTICE HALL
A Division of Simon & Schuster
Englewood Cliffs, New Jersey 07632

Printed in the United States of America

10   9   8   7   6   5   4   3   2   1

ISBN: 0-13-763459-5

Prentice-Hall International (UK) Limited, *London*
Prentice-Hall of Australia Pty. Limited, *Sydney*
Prentice-Hall Canada Inc., *Toronto*
Prentice-Hall Hispanoamericana, S.A., *Mexico*
Prentice-Hall of India Private Limited, *New Delhi*
Prentice-Hall of Japan, Inc., *Tokyo*
Simon & Schuster Asia Pte. Ltd., *Singapore*
Editora Prentice-Hall do Brasil, Ltda., *Rio de Janeiro*

CONTENTS

PREFACE

There are tens of thousands of real estate brokerage firms in the United States; it is one of the most popular small business endeavors in the country. However, since many large firms employing hundreds of people also exist, it is a business which has excellent potential for growth and success.

To most people, real estate brokerage appears to be concerned largely with salesmanship, with success depending upon the listing and selling capabilities of the sales force. While this is true, it is not the whole truth. Real estate brokerage is a business, and to be successful, a brokerage firm has to be properly operated. There may have been a time when selling ability alone was enough, but in today's competitive market the ability to operate a brokerage firm as an efficient business is just as significant as the quality of the service the firm provides. In today's successful brokerage firm, the management personnel (principal brokers, sales managers) spend little or no time on direct listing or selling because the company's organization, control and finances require their full-time attention. It is this aspect of the real estate brokerage business that this book addresses.

These pages contain little about the mechanics of listing and selling, sales techniques, or negotiating. Rather, we are concerned with the management of the business: planning, organization, control and financial well-being. A great many new firms are created every year and most of them eventually fail. While the reasons for failure are many, much of the time it is because of improper management and the confusion, inefficiency, and money troubles that result. Many brokerages that survive do so far below their potential for the same reason.

This book is arranged as a text, but it is not intended for classroom use only. The working broker and sales manager will be able to find it of use and value. Furthermore, anyone considering owning and/or operating a real estate brokerage business should be aware of the concepts and ideas contained here. Approaching the operation of a full-fledged brokerage firm armed only with the skills and knowledge of the selling process is a very risky venture. However, since most states require that an individual's broker's license be preceded by a certain period of licensure as a salesperson, we can assume with reasonable safety that someone interested in the independence of a brokerage operation will have acquired some knowledge of the selling process itself. This frees us to concentrate upon the management and organizational aspects of the real estate brokerage business.

ORGANIZATION OF THE BOOK

This book is oriented to the practical application of management techniques and organizational form as they apply to the real estate brokerage business. The specific characteristics and necessities of the brokerage business are given full emphasis, and brokerage-related examples are used throughout the discussion. Every effort has been made to produce a book that will cover all aspects of the management of the real estate brokerage enterprise.

The book incorporates a number of special features. Case experiences are included in most of the chapters. These are real-life incidents and situations that illustrate particular points. While they may have been edited slightly to make them more suitable to the book's direction and tone, the significant aspects of the actual experiences they relate have been left intact. Illustrations, graphics, tables, and other material have been chosen to augment the text discussion and should be read and examined along with it. Discussion questions, also provided at the ends of the chapters, will direct the reader or student to examine particular topics in further detail.

Two chapters are devoted to the legal situation of the brokerage firm: contract, agency and licensing law are emphasized. The hearing records of the states' real estate licensing regulatory agencies show that most complaints they hear concern improper practice by licensees in these areas. Also, the emerging field of consumer advocacy regularly seeks potential paydirt in the area of proper and legal performance by real estate licensees who ignore or are unaware of all of the law under which they operate.

Chapter 1 introduces the study of real estate brokerage and provides a preview of the study pattern of the book and its subject matter. This chapter also presents an overview of the real estate brokerage business and its function in our modern society and economy. The brokerage process and its methods are reviewed, and professional approaches to the business are discussed.

Chapters 2 and 3 are devoted to the legal framework within which the real estate brokerage business operates. Chapter 2 discusses licensing and agency law. Chapter 3 concerns other important legal effects upon the real estate brokerage business, especially contract law.

Chapter 4 introduces the basic concepts of management that come into play in the brokerage industry. Organization of the firm, patterns of management, and the functions of management are discussed. This chapter also includes the initial discussion of personnel selection and management.

Chapter 5 considers the arrangements and contracts that exist between the brokerage firm and its personnel. The very important features and requirements of the independent contractor relationship with sales personnel are given particular emphasis. Specific discussion of the requirements of legal agreements between brokerages and salespeople is also included.

Chapter 6 presents the methods and problems of personnel selection by the real estate brokerage firm. Sources of potential salespeople, the recruitment process, the selection process, and the choice of sales personnel are presented.

Chapter 7 is devoted entirely to discussion of the firm's policy manual: the statement of policy and goals each firm should have and make available to its personnel. An example of such a manual is included.

Chapter 8 considers the firm's policy with respect to the listing of real estate for sale. The design and use of a proper listing contract form is discussed, followed by consideration of the legal means of assuring the firm's right to a commission upon the sale of listed property. Other important uses of the various kinds of listings, accumulation of information on listed property, and setting the proper commission fee to be charged also are discussed. This chapter concludes with a discussion of the dissolution of listing contracts.

Chapter 9 discusses the firm's policy in the process of selling listed property. The sale contract and its form introduce the discussion, which is followed by consideration of the offer and acceptance procedure. Specific topics of concern in this area are discussed. These include cooperation with other brokerage firms, multiple listing, franchising, information services and the settlement process. A final word is devoted to the firm's policies with respect to default of contract by buyer, seller, or both.

Chapter 10, "Real Estate Finance and Appraisal", is new to this edition. It was added in response to requests from many users of the book. Great changes in the world of real estate finance and appraisal in the past few years demand that the brokerage professional be up-to-date. Also, dealing with appraisers and answering clients' questions about finance and appraisal are important functions of today's real estate brokerage firm and its licensees.

Chapter 11 considers the compensation of the salesperson. Means and policies of commission sharing are discussed, along with incentive pay plans. This chapter also looks at the use of company referrals and company listings as compensation, and various other means of nonmonetary support to the salesperson.

Chapter 12 discusses sales management. The various procedures of controlling, training, and motivating the sales force are considered. Marketing procedure policy is given considerable attention, as is the use by the firm of property advertising. The chapter also considers finding financing for buyers, broker liability, and proper performance.

Chapter 13 discusses the proper administration of the firm's financial resources and obligations. The concepts of costs, cash flow, the company dollar, financing, and cost control are presented in a framework devoted to their significance in the brokerage business.

Chapter 14 considers the physical space and equipment needs of the firm and sales force. Office layout, equipment, and location are discussed, along with the needs of the individual salesperson.

Chapter 15 concludes the book. It discusses the problems of establishing a successful brokerage business and considers the important topic of marketing the brokerage firm itself to the public in a competitive business environment.

The reader is assumed to have at least a reading knowledge of any of the widely used texts on the principles of real estate. I have made a conscious effort to eliminate unnecessary material from the discussion. While it is tempting for an author to increase the thickness of a book with frequent rehashes of the same material, irrelevant tables and illustrations and the like, my goal has been to avoid such tactics and concentrate upon a clear and readable presentation of the subject matter.

CHANGES FOR THE THIRD EDITION

The real estate brokerage business is not characterized by frequent upheavals and wholesale change. As I write this, the second edition is beginning its fifth year. Though its acceptance has been most gratifying, and has increased year by year, there have been substantial changes in the business environment of the real estate brokerage business in the United States. The bailout of the thrift industry, newly required state certification of appraisers, and the collapse of high-flying residential and nonresidential markets throughout the country all have occurred since the second edition was written. Interest rates have settled into what appears to be a much lower range than prevailed throughout most of the 1980's. The ubiquitous "middle class", that huge group of households which supports the housing industry, is facing uncertainties of employment and income which were unheard of a few years ago. I have tried to incorporate these changes into this edition.

A number of other additions and changes have been made. All of the chapters in the book have been edited and, where necessary, rewritten to be clearer and easier to read and understand. The result, I would hope, is a book which is clearer and more readable. Some important changes and additions of substance will be found in this edition. Chapter 1 now incorporates, more concisely, the material contained in the second edition's Chapters 1 and 2, and the very long Chapter 3 from that edition has been split into what are now Chapters 2 and 3. As mentioned above, a new chapter 10 ("Real Estate Finance and Appraisal") has been added. In addition to presenting rudimentary discussion of mortgage lending and appraisal, this new chapter also discusses FIRREA, appraiser certification and new appraisal standards. What were Chapters 10 to 14 in the second edition now are Chapters 11 to 15. The discussion of computers in Chapter 14 has been updated. New to this edition is discussion of broker and seller disclosure which has been added to Chapters 3 and 12.

I also have done some cutting. I have thinned out the end-of-chapter "References." Nearly all users of the book tell me that they make little use of this section which, over the life of an edition, tends to get badly out of date anyway. Where I do list references, they are well-known or very significant to the topic, and not likely to become outdated. Also, I no longer reprint the REALTORS® Code of Ethics. This is not because I don't think it's relevant, but because it is frequently amended and updated, so a copy in the book soon will become outdated. Instead, I encourage readers to get a current copy of the Code of Ethics from their local REALTORS® Association.

There is one other change for this edition which, I hope, is not easily apparent and, yet, which marks a significant evolution in the way books are being produced. I wrote the manuscript for this book using a desktop computer and word processing software. I also did the page layouts and composition; what you see here is exactly what I saw on my computer screen and printed on my laser printer, except for the graphics, which were inserted by the publisher. Allowing for my innate capacity for monumental procrastination, this procedure saved a lot of time and expense. It also let me arrange the book the way I wanted to see it, and will let me produce the next edition "on the fly" over the next few years. (For the technically inclined: I used Lotus Amí Pro 2.0 and 3.0, operating under Microsoft Windows 3.1. Since my 300dpi printer does not produce the resolution needed for publishing, I sent the publisher encapsulated Postscript disk files of the manuscript; these were downloaded to a high-resolution printer which produced the camera-ready copy. Significantly, I think, I did *not* use desktop publishing software; today's word processing software is plenty powerful enough.)

No textbook is perfect. It is normal practice for an author to acknowledge the many people who assisted in the preparation of a book, and I do so below. It is also normal practice for the author to take responsibility for all errors that may remain in the work, and I do so now. However, since I also did the layout for this book, I suppose I have to take the blame for typos and other errors of composition as well.

Therefore, I earnestly solicit comments and suggestions from readers, who may write to me in care of the publisher.

ACKNOWLEDGEMENTS

I would like to thank several people for their help on this book. My editors during the overly long time that I took to prepare this edition were Bob Kern, Ed Francis and Mark Moscowitz. In addition to being invaluably helpful, Gloria Schaffer, Mr. Kern's assistant, and Eileen O'Sullivan, my production editor, cheerfully tolerated an astounding and varied stream of excuses for my tardiness. Helene Messer proofread the initial version of the manuscript, and Bonnie Neuman proofread the final version. Both did wonderful jobs. And special thanks to Henry Harrison, Forms & Worms, Inc., New Haven, Connecticut, for permission to reproduce the Uniform Settlement Statement (Chapter 9) and Uniform Residential Appraisal Report (Chapter 10).

Many users of the book have provided helpful suggestions, and I thank them all. Most of these dealt with detail, another gratifying indication that the second edition hit its target pretty well.

BRUCE LINDEMAN

April, 1993

A SPECIAL NOTE TO READERS

Please note that when you read "he," "his," or "him" in this book, that they are being used in their grammatical sense and refer to women as well as men.

ONE

INTRODUCTION

The Brokerage Business

The Management Approach to Real Estate Brokerage

Characteristics of the Real Estate Brokerage Business

The Brokerage Process

Professionalism

The Scope of Our Study

The real estate brokerage business is one that offers many people the promise of a fascinating and exciting career. It offers the opportunity to rely on one's own abilities, in a business which can start as small as one that can be run in the owner's home, but has the potential to grow to great size. The real estate broker can have a significant impact upon his home community and, as the years pass, can point with pride to a great many highly visible and lasting results of his work.

To someone who isn't familiar with it, the real estate business seems deceptively easy and lucrative. After all, doesn't a broker just put a sign in someone's yard, show people around the house a few times, make the sale – and collect a handsome commission every time? Of course, the experienced real estate salesperson knows there's much more to it than that. Nonetheless, each year several hundred thousand people sit for real estate licensing examinations so that they may join this lucrative business. And each year nearly as many others, people who have already obtained licenses and tried their luck, drop out of the business. Perhaps one licensee in ten manages to make a decent living, but his success attracts thousands of others who want to try it.

Success in the real estate brokerage business demands many qualities. Successful real estate brokers must be at ease with people and be able to convince them of their sincerity and reliability. They must have an excellent knowledge of the law, even though they cannot practice law. Brokers must be able to manage their personal lives to accommodate odd working hours and an irregular, commission-based income.

The real estate broker confronts a large number of business risks. He is at the mercy not only of the fluctuations of his local real estate market, but also of financial markets, local and national economic fluctuations, etc. When mortgage money is scarce or when economic conditions shrink the demand for real estate, he must tighten his belt and work harder than ever to get a decent share of the business available. When times are good, he finds that practically everyone else seems to be licensed and competing for business. He usually has no regular salary to fall back on and so must handle his personal finances very carefully. In compensation, he usually can hold onto his job (since he is, in effect, the creator of his job), but in bad times he may find that although he doesn't lose it, the job can just dwindle away unless he works hard.

As in any business, the successful broker must be an expert in his chosen work. He must know his community, its practices, and its preferences. His customers expect him to be aware of property value trends and neighborhood developments. They feel free to ask him practically anything, and expect to get a proper and informative answer. The broker has to have the psychological instincts to be able to shepherd nervous buyers and sellers whose transactions, to them, are of vital and overriding importance. The broker is expected to bring these transactions to successful conclusions that satisfy all parties.

All these things may not be apparent to those who watch a competent broker going about his business. They see "large" commission rates, and FOR SALE and SOLD signs, but not the immense amount of work and experience necessary to get these results. In this book we will examine this work and show some of the things necessary for it to be successful.

THE BROKERAGE BUSINESS

Real estate brokerage is a service business. Brokerage firms provide a wide variety of services to their clients. Most people think of the business as selling houses, but all kinds of real estate can be handled in a brokerage business. Many firms specialize in certain kinds of real estate, or certain activities. However, the largest number of real estate brokerage firms concentrate on *residential sales* (the selling of houses). Usually they will deal both in *new* homes, being sold by builders, and in *resales:* existing homes being sold by owner-users rather than builders.

Beyond residential sales, real estate brokers can deal with the sale and rental of all other kinds of properties, each with its own features, problems, and required knowledge. There is a full range of *investment property*, from the very small to the very large: from duplex structures to apartment projects, shopping centers, office parks and buildings, industrial properties and more. Brokers handle *land sales*: from parcels of "raw," undeveloped land to building sites, entire subdivisions, downtown commercial sites, and *plottage*: assembling large tracts of land, for a variety of purposes, by combining the purchases of smaller parcels. Some brokers sell entire businesses, as well as the buildings and land they occupy. Others specialize in the sale of *farms, recreational properties* and other specialized properties.

In addition to sales, brokers handle *real estate leasing.* Some handle only the transaction of leases, but the field of property management can include handling for a property owner all transactions associated with investment property such as maintenance, hiring personnel (janitors, resident managers, etc.), recordkeeping and more. Many brokers expand their businesses to include the provision of *related services* such as property insurance, mortgage brokering, and investment analysis and advisement. Also, many brokers engage directly in such activities as *land development* and *construction.* Clearly, the real estate brokerage field is considerably more far-reaching and involved than is apparent to the casual observer.

Function of Brokerage

In essence, the real estate broker is hired by the owner of a property to arrange a sale of the property or to arrange for one or more tenants to rent it. The broker signs a *listing contract* with the property owner, in which the terms of the broker's employment are spelled out. Normally, the broker's compensation is in the form of *commission*: a certain percentage of the sale price or rental value of the property. He is paid when he has done his job. In a sale arrangement, he usually collects his commission at the time title to the property is transferred to the buyer and the sale becomes an accomplished fact. In a rental arrangement, he either collects a certain sum when the lease begins or takes a percentage of each of the tenants' rent payments. Sometimes the commission is arranged so that he does both. (Under the law of many states, the broker actually *earns* the commission *before* the transaction is consummated, even though he is not paid until then. This point is discussed more thoroughly in Chapter 2.)

The Brokerage Process

Once he has secured a *listing* (signed a listing contract with a property owner), the broker begins marketing the property. He advertises it, contacts potential buyers, and usually advises other brokers that the listing exists. As potential buyers appear, he screens or *qualifies* them, determining that they are indeed potentially capable buyers of the particular property. To do so, he examines their needs and their financial situation. If the property is not what they need or if they cannot afford it, there is no point in showing them the listed real estate. However, even though a particular interested buyer turns out not to be a good *prospect* for a certain property, the broker does not lose interest. Instead, he tries to find the buyer a more suitable purchase. In this manner brokers may show a variety of properties to buyers who originally responded to the marketing of real estate they were not actually qualified to buy.

When a qualified prospect appears to be interested in a property, the broker arranges to *show the property*. He takes the prospect to see and inspect the property. The broker has to be intimately acquainted with all the features and drawbacks of the property properly if he is to describe it and to answer all the prospect's questions. If the prospect remains interested after the showing, the broker tries to solicit an *offer*. If an offer is made, the broker takes it to the seller and they discuss it. Sometimes it is accepted, but more likely it is not entirely satisfactory to the seller. A *counteroffer* is made from the seller to the prospective buyer. The transaction is now in the *negotiation stage*, and buyer and seller may offer and counteroffer several times before either a final arrangement is concluded, or it is decided that no common ground exists. In the latter case, the broker tries to find another prospective buyer, and this process continues until the sale is made. At that point, a *contract of sale* will exist between the seller and the buyer; but the broker's job is by no means over.

The contract of sale is an agreement that buyer and seller will *transact* the sale at some time in the future; in the meantime they prepare for the transaction. The buyer may need to get *financing*, often with the assistance of the broker. Many other activities also must be carried out during this period, including appraisals, surveys, termite inspections, other inspections, preparation of documents (deeds, mortgages, and the like), and a number of other arrangements. The broker often handles or arranges many of these. Finally, at the *closing*, all papers are signed and all other arrangements are concluded, and the buyer receives a *deed* from the seller.

Many brokers find it useful to enlist the aid of other brokers in transactions. One broker will arrange with other brokers that if they find buyers for his listings, he will split the commission he earns from the sellers with them. Usually, he also is assured that if he or his staff sell listings of the other brokers, they in turn will split their commissions with him. In some areas these arrangements are informal, while in others they are formalized through an arrangement called a *multiple listing service*, or *multilist*.

What we have described are elements of a "typical" brokered transaction. But it should not be inferred that all transaction arrangements are the same for the broker. While brokers usually are employed and paid by owners of properties to be sold or rented, they also are employed by prospective buyers or tenants to help them find suitable quarters. (Many states require that brokers employed by sellers disclose their agency relationship to prospective buyers. See the discussion in Chapter 3.) In most states it is legal for a broker to be paid by both parties under certain circumstances, but this commonly occurs only in cases when real estate properties are exchanged rather than sold. Brokers need not accept only commissions as payments; they can contract to receive a flat fee if they wish. They may choose to receive payment in a noncash form, such as a percentage of ownership of the brokered property.

The Broker's Contribution

While many people think of the real estate broker only as a salesperson, perhaps his most important functions are resolving differences in negotiations, and dealing with unexpected events that threaten a transaction. In residential sales, especially, the participants in the transaction – the buyer and the seller – often are inexperienced. They don't know much about the alternatives available to them. They know how to place classified ads, put signs in their yards, and to inquire at the bank about loans. They may even know enough to hire a lawyer or other professional to handle the technical details of the transaction. Many do this to avoid paying brokers' commissions, and some are successful. However, most of them can't perform these functions with anything like the efficiency and confidence of a professional real estate broker. They waste enormous amounts of time and energy, and many nonbrokered deals fall through because of unanticipated problems.

The broker sells his *knowledge*, *expertise*, and *experience*. This becomes of inestimable value as he assists in arranging a well-conceived transaction, foreseeing the common risks, avoiding the common mistakes, and providing satisfaction to all parties. A good broker understands the implications of each deal and explains them thoroughly to the parties involved so that they are fully aware of them and know what to expect. He can tailor each transaction to fulfill everyone's needs, and he should be ready to handle any and all problems that may arise by giving proper, considered advice and by proposing and arranging the necessary solutions. More than everything else, even more than ability as a salesperson, he sells *professionalism* and experience, and it is this that constitutes by far the most valuable part of his service to his customers.

THE MANAGEMENT APPROACH TO REAL ESTATE BROKERAGE

Real estate brokerage is a business, and for a brokerage business to succeed it must be *managed* properly. Indeed, the prime cause for business failure in all aspects of commerce is the failure of management to do its job properly. Management's function is to get things done by an *organization*. Particularly, management should seek the best way of accomplishing the goals and objectives of the firm involved. Management should not be confused with the actual activities that most of the firm's employees engage in; rather, management should see to it that those things get done, and properly, by the people who are supposed to do them.

The Importance of Management

It wouldn't be hard to fill a good-sized bookcase with literature describing the techniques of successful and profitable listing and selling of all kinds of real estate. However, finding information on the proper operation of a business whose goals are to do those things is much harder to do. There is a need for this information. Somehow, the successful salesperson who sets up a business for himself often finds that for some reason the expected profits do not materialize, and at every turn new and unexpected problems arise, problems with no easy solutions.

The majority of new real estate brokerage firms eventually fail, many within a short time. It takes more than knowing how to list and sell real estate well to operate a real estate brokerage business. It takes *management*. The brokerage firm's *sales force* must be able to list and to sell real estate in a profitable manner that fits in with the company policy. The *management* of the firm has the responsibility of directing the sales force to accomplish this goal, and to provide the proper business environment for this success. In a small firm, management may consist of only one person: the broker-owner. He may devote much of his time to listing and selling activities, and may do management only on a part-time basis. Nonetheless, this management is necessary if the firm is to operate efficiently and profitably and it is to have a good chance to succeed.

Therefore, we must distinguish between *management* of a brokerage firm and its *sales activity*. In our discussion in this book we will look much harder at the management function than at sales activity. This means that we have no chapters that discuss the "secrets" of successful listing, or tell how to wangle a reluctant prospect into making an offer. The reasons for this approach are important to understand.

First, management is the key to long-term success. A firm with competent employees but poor management is much less likely to survive than a firm with good management but poor employees. In the first case, management will give the employees the wrong things to do by misreading the market and having employees produce the wrong mix of goods and services for the market. Good employees eventually will leave the firm for more secure and lucrative positions at better managed firms. In the second case, good management can take effective steps to improve the quality of poor employees by providing additional training and a more suitable working environment, and by replacing poor performers with better ones.

A second reason for emphasizing the management approach is individuals seeking to enter the real estate brokerage business must *already* have had at least minimal experience in the selling or leasing aspects of the business. The states' real estate licensing laws require applicants for broker licenses to have held a salesperson's license for some minimum length of time. Though newly licensed brokers will have had some experience in sales work, most will not have had any experience at all in the problems associated with properly managing the business. Simply because someone has a successful record of listing, selling, and/or leasing real estate doesn't mean that person will be competent and successful at operating and managing a real estate brokerage business.

Organization of the Brokerage

Just like any other business, a brokerage firm must be managed properly in order to succeed. In any except a one-person operation, some kind of chain of command must be set up. The duties of each person in the organization must be defined so that everyone knows who does what and all the functions of the business are handled efficiently. Brokerage personnel can be classified in three categories: *management personnel, sales force*, and *support staff*. We must remember, though, that in many firms, especially smaller ones, an individual may perform functions in more than one category.

Management personnel are in charge of operating the business and seeing to it that everyone else does his job properly. Management determines the goals, objectives, and scope of the firm; hires and fires personnel; and determines their duties. The sales force is the group that actually performs the brokerage's main business functions of listing and selling real estate. They are the ones who produce the company's income. Support staff are nonmanagement personnel who perform the nonsales duties that assist management and the sales force. These employees are secretaries, receptionists, accountants, lawyers, and others whose services are necessary to the proper functioning of the brokerage, but who do not engage directly in sales activity or management.

Licensing

Sales personnel and management personnel in the real estate brokerage business are required to be licensed by the states in which they live and work in order to be able to carry out their jobs legally. The states have two types of licenses, those for *brokers* and those for *salespersons*. The exact nomenclature for these licenses varies slightly from state to state, but each type of license has essentially the same attributes nationwide.

A *broker's license* entitles the holder to establish an independent brokerage business. A *salesperson's license* entitles the holder to engage in the real estate business, but under the supervision and responsibility of a licensed broker. Although state licensing laws do not specifically refer to it in this way, it might be thought that the salesperson is a sort of apprentice, qualified to engage in some selling activity but not yet considered qualified to act fully on his own and assume full responsibility for what he does.

The broker's license is issued directly to the broker. The salesperson's license actually is issued to the broker who will *hold* that license, and for whom the salesperson will work. Therefore, a licensed salesperson can work for only a single broker, and that broker assumes legal responsibility for everything the salesperson does in the course of business.

The broker has the opportunity to set up his own business, while the salesperson represents someone else's brokerage firm. A licensed broker with his own business is required to fulfill certain requirements in the organization of the firm. He must establish certain trust accounts for the handling of other people's money, and he is responsible for seeing to it that all transactions handled by his firm are properly done. He must also make sure that unlicensed employees do not engage in any sales activity and that his licensed salespeople do business properly and within the law. All this requires careful supervision, since it is dictated by law and especially since the sales force by its very nature operates independently. The broker can rarely be physically present every time a salesperson solicits a listing, solicits an offer, or shows a property.

CHARACTERISTICS OF THE REAL ESTATE BROKERAGE BUSINESS

In a very few words, real estate brokerage can be described as a business devoted to providing the service of *finding buyers or renters for real estate properties*. It is a complex business, however, and a more thorough description is necessary for our purposes. Real estate is a varied commodity. While most observers see real estate brokerage as essentially the selling of peoples' houses for an apparently lucrative fee, few are aware of the complexities involved in even that limited enterprise. Real estate does not sell itself; each transaction is different, with its own set of problems to be solved. Buyers must be matched to properties, and a considerable amount of additional facilitative service usually is provided by the broker. He advertises, screens buyers, negotiates the final transaction to everyone's satisfaction, and usually is responsible for closing the transaction, seeing to it that all papers are properly drawn and recorded and that all monies are properly paid to those entitled to receive them.

Real estate brokerage is a very competitive and highly localized business. It is not difficult for a conscientious and dedicated person to acquire a sales or brokerage license, although applicants for broker's licenses are required to have spent time (varying from state to state) as licensed salespersons. New brokerages are constantly being formed, and within the business competent salespersons are in great demand and so have frequent opportunities to leave one firm to work for another. Therefore, the successful brokerage must not only be able to get its share of the listing and selling business, but must also be organized to retain productive salespersons.

Ease of Entry

Real estate brokerage is one of the most popular small businesses in the United States, partly because it is very easy to enter. (*Staying* in it, however, is another question altogether, and is the main thrust of this book.) The cash investment can be quite small: a few hundred dollars for license exam courses, examinations, license fees, business licenses and taxes, and some signs and business cards. The family car and a desk in the corner of a bedroom can function as an "office." One may even be extravagant and install a separate "business" telephone in the home.

The Local Character of Real Estate Brokerage

Most real estate brokerage firms list and sell properties located in their own immediate vicinities, neighborhoods, towns, or cities. In large cities, firms frequently specialize in particular areas, and do little activity outside familiar geographic confines. The reason is that a successful brokerage has to have an intimate knowledge of the real estate market it operates in, and the larger the market area, the harder it is to keep up with. Also, since brokers and salespeople *show* properties to interested buyers, they are limited in their geographic scope by the time and effort it takes to make a trip to a given location for a showing.

Competition and Cooperation

Within the real estate brokerage business, individual firms both compete and co-operate with one another. On the one hand, firms compete to list properties and to find buyers for listed properties. At the same time, in most localities it is common practice for brokerage firms to allow other firms to find buyers for their listings. Usually there is a local industrywide pattern by which such *cooperating brokers* arrange to allow one ano-ther to show their listed properties and to share the selling commission. When these arrangements exist, a broker who finds a buyer for another's listing knows that the listing broker will pay to the "selling broker" an agreed portion of the commission received from the seller.

Many localities have an arrangement within the brokerage industry that formalizes such cooperative action. Usually it is called a *multiple listing service*, or *multilist* program. It is an organization composed of member brokers who have agreed to share some or all of their listings. The multilist agreement spells out the procedures for includ-ing listed properties in the multilist inventory, and the manner in which selling commis-sions are split between the broker who listed the property ("listing broker") and the one which found the buyer for it ("selling broker").

The states' real estate licensing laws and regulations have provisions that govern the manner in which brokers must respect one another's listings. This recognizes the fact that cooperative selling often occurs.

The Brokerage Firm and Its Markets

The real estate brokerage is a firm that deals in *services*. It produces no goods, but instead offers to the public the ability of its sales force to bring about and fulfill real estate transactions. Since it is a business that assists sales, it may be said to operate in two sepa-rate markets. First, it offers its services to potential *buyers*, *sellers*, *lessors*, and *lessees* of real estate. In this market it seeks its customers and competes with other, similar firms. Second, it operates directly in the market for real estate itself when its services are used. The first market we can refer to as the *brokerage market*; the second is the *real estate market*.

We must always keep clear the distinction between these two markets. In the brokerage market, the firm sells or markets itself in the form of the services it can provide to others who want to operate in the real estate market. We often refer to the firm as marketing property in the real estate market, but it must be remembered that in its real estate market operations, the brokerage is selling and/or buying on behalf of *someone else*, and it is these others who, properly speaking, do the actual buying, selling, and renting. However, if they use the services of a brokerage firm, they normally expect considerable assistance and expert advice from the brokerage in return for the fees they pay. Therefore, the competent brokerage firm must maintain a continuously updated accurate knowledge of the forces at work in the real estate markets in which they operate.

Since most real estate sales involve the use of borrowed money (usually in the form of mortgage loans), it is essential that the broker be aware of the trends in a *third* market: the *money market*. Although the broker may offer a wide range and variety of services in a single transaction, often one of the most significant is to assist in arranging the financing the buyer needs in order to complete a transaction negotiated by the broker. Indeed, in times of tight money, the broker who knows where the mortgage money can be found, or who has had the foresight to make early arrangements with lenders to keep funds flowing to his customers, will have a formidable competitive edge over those who have not paid the necessary attention to this crucial market. Since the broker is usually neither lender nor borrower in mortgage transactions, and generally is not agent for either party, we do not consider him an active operator in this market. Nevertheless, we must understand the vital importance of knowing the financing markets to the success of the brokerage business.

THE BROKERAGE PROCESS

The brokerage business is dominated by *contracts*. We might even say that the broker's stock in trade is the ability to arrange advantageous contracts for clients. The broker usually is hired by a property owner to find a buyer or a tenant for the owner's real estate. The broker most often is paid in the form of a *commission* – when he succeeds. The commission is based on the proceeds (sale price or rental) that the owner gets as a result of the transaction negotiated with the assistance of the broker.

Brokers are *agents*. Agency is a status defined by a large body of law (discussed in the next chapter). Since the broker usually is employed by the property owner, the broker is the owner's agent, and has a legal obligation to look out for the owner's best interests. This means that the broker cannot do anything that would be thought of as opposed to the owner's interests. Potential buyers often assume, when they contact a broker to show them the property, that the broker is working for *them* and will advise *them* and look out for *their* interests. In fact, the broker is acting only as the agent for the potential seller. The next chapter, in its discussion of licensing and agency law, elaborates on these points.

What we are discussing here is the most common way of doing things in the brokerage business. This doesn't mean that less familiar ways of operating do not exist. A broker can be hired by a buyer to find suitable property; in such a case, the broker is in fact the buyer's agent and has the responsibility to look out for his interests alone. Furthermore, brokers don't have to work only on commission. They may choose to charge a flat fee, or some other form of compensation for their work. However, in the large majority of broker-assisted transactions, particularly in the residential brokerage field, the broker is employed by the property owner and is paid a commission based on the dollar price that the property sells for. Unless specifically directed otherwise, the reader should assume this kind of arrangement to be the case throughout the discussion in this book.

The brokerage process is illustrated in Figure 1-1, which shows the typical steps the broker takes in a brokered residential transaction. Our discussion will concentrate upon residential sales brokerage for several reasons. One is that a huge proportion of brokerage activity is devoted to sales of houses. Also, more firms specialize in home sales than in all other forms of real estate combined. Much of the essence of brokerage activity can be explained in the context of a firm specializing in residential sales; nonresidential sales tend to be more complicated, and require more sophisticated approaches. Finally, such transactions probably are more familiar to readers. However, since our basic discussion is devoted to the study of proper management of a real estate brokerage business, most basic principles developed will be applicable to any kind of brokerage firm, regardless of its specialty.

Listing

Before a brokerage firm can sell property, it must obtain *listings*. Listing contracts are agreements between property owners (sellers) and brokerage firms. The broker agrees to make his/her best efforts to solicit a satisfactory purchase offer for the seller's real estate. The seller in turn agrees to pay the brokerage firm a *commission* (a percentage of the selling price) if the broker succeeds in getting a satisfactory offer for the listed real estate.

Soliciting listings is a key element of long-term success for a real estate brokerage firm. A new firm may start out by trying to sell the listings obtained by other brokers, through cooperative deals or multilist. However, long-term survival requires the firm to develop its own listing program, and successful firms vie for the services of salespeople known to be "good listers".

When a potential seller is ready to list the property, the listing contract is entered into. This contract, as well as subsequent ones in the transaction, may actually be negotiated by a salesperson; legally, however, the contract is between the *broker* and the seller. All contracts negotiated by sales staff ultimately are the legal responsibility of the broker. Our discussion concerning the broker can sometimes be construed to include the entire sales staff where appropriate, but remember that legal responsibility for the accuracy and proper handling of these contracts rests ultimately with the broker. The brokerage firm, therefore, must have within its organization the proper means of controlling and supervising the drawing up of such contracts.

Most states require that the listing contract be written. A few allow verbal listings, but a professional broker should insist that all listings taken by his firm be in writing no matter what local law may permit. Listings are the source of the firm's livelihood, and they should be treated with proper respect and not left to the inaccurate memories of the parties involved. Listings are discussed in more detail in Chapter 8.

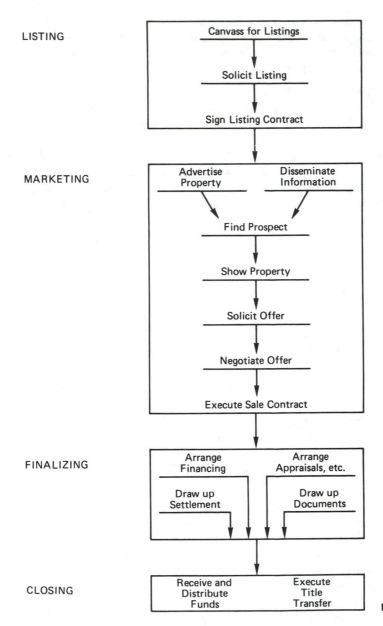

LISTING

MARKETING

FINALIZING

CLOSING

Figure 1-1. The Brokerage Process

Marketing the Property

Once the listing contract is signed, the broker begins to solicit potential buyers. A FOR SALE sign usually is placed on the property. The broker advertises the property, and makes other brokers aware of the listing. Prospective buyers are shown the property.

A very important service provided by the broker to the seller is the *qualifying of prospects*, or potential buyers. Qualification of prospects consists of a number of things: weeding out those who aren't really serious, who can't afford the property, or for whom it is unsuitable. Also, buying prospects should be interviewed to find out just what they are looking for, what they want and don't want. As the experienced broker interviews prospects and shows them various properties, he listens to their comments and uses the information gained to refine his perception of their needs. Often prospects themselves do not really know what it is that they will be happiest with, and the skilled broker often finds that by leading them to the right property he does them a useful service, in addition to selling his employer's property. Owners trying to sell their property on their own have little skill in buyer qualification, and often they miss out on a chance to sell to someone who would have bought, had a professional broker been involved.

After an offer has been solicited, the broker presents it to the owner. At this point the broker can offer very useful advice concerning the advisability of accepting, declining, or *countering* the offer. Countering is the process of turning down the offer received from the buyer, and simultaneously presenting to the buyer an offer (to sell) from the seller. This *counteroffer* is a sale proposal that is more suitable to the seller. Here the broker's knowledge of the market and of the particular situations of the parties involved is critical. If he does his job well, he not only arranges a transaction that benefits all parties, but also manages to convince all concerned of the facts.

The Sale Contract

Once an offer is accepted, a *contract of sale* exists. This contract gives certain rights and responsibilities to both buyer and seller. The property has not yet actually changed hands (that happens at the *closing*, or *settlement*, when the *deed* is given by the seller to buyer), but both parties are obligated to complete the sale at some time in the future. The contract of sale spells out the terms and conditions under which the sale will take place. It is rare that the parties involved will have the experience or knowledge to anticipate all possible problems and solve them at the outset within the contract.

Here is an area where the broker's expert knowledge can make the difference between a clean, mutually beneficial transaction and one that results in one headache after another. The objective of any sale contract should be to arrange a transaction that everyone involved can live with comfortably, and that all are able to go through with. The broker, with his experience, knows where the potential pitfalls are and can explain them at the very beginning, when there is ample time to anticipate them. He can suggest solutions at a time when no one is under pressure to act. Furthermore, if unanticipated difficulties arise later, the broker can make suggestions and arrangements that can lead to an acceptable solution.

Next to the sale price itself, the *terms of the sale* are the most important parts of the contract of sale. These include all *contingencies*: conditions or performance that have to be satisfied before the transaction can occur. Typical contingencies are that the buyer can find suitable financing, that the buyer be able to sell his own house before completing the current sale, etc. The role of the broker looms large here in assuring not only that the right conditions are included, but also, in the interest of a clean, smooth deal, that improper or inconsequential conditions may be excluded.

Settlement

Once buyer and seller have agreed to transact, the broker begins preparations for the transaction itself: this is called the *settlement*, or *closing*, of the sale. Between the time of the sale contract and the settlement the broker may have to "shepherd" both buyer and seller through some of the process, and to make sure that all paperwork is being expedited properly.

It used to be customary that real estate brokers actually handled the settlement process themselves. They had to arrange preparation of the necessary documents (deeds, mortgages, etc.) and make sure that both buyer and seller met all the special conditions specified in the contract. At the closing, when the transfer of the property ownership actually took place, brokers had to make sure that all required payments were properly made by everyone concerned, that all documents were recorded and delivered to the proper recipients, and that everyone signed and understood everything. Finally, they had to provide a settlement statement to all parties in the transaction, showing where all money involved came from, and how it was distributed.

Nowadays, settlements usually are handled either by the institution which provides the buyer's mortgage loan, or by agencies which specialize in settlement (*title companies, abstract companies, escrow agents*, etc.). Even so, buyer and seller usually turn to the broker when they have questions or need advice in this process.

The Broker's Services

Clearly, the broker has a lot to do, even in the simplest of sale transactions. By employing a competent broker, the seller can go about his daily business while the broker handles all the work of arranging and concluding the sale. The preceding description concerned a simple sale of a home by one person to another; imagine the additional complexity of more involved transactions. Sales of commercial or other rental properties require financial analyses to be made before serious buyers will consider the property. Arrangements concerning existing leases, handling of rent money during the transaction period, and detailed breakdowns of incomes and expenses must be made. Many deals involve purchase and/or sale by more than one party, adding complexity to the transaction. Successful brokerage, then, requires much more than merely finding sellers willing to list and buyers willing to buy.

PROFESSIONALISM

Some people feel that the word "professional" can only be used to describe someone who practices a job that requires a high level of education and very specialized knowledge and skills and is greatly recognized and respected by everyone. These jobs might include medicine, the law, the ministry, and the like. It is evident that the real estate brokerage field is not viewed by the public in this same hallowed light. However, if we define a professional as one who is talented and knowledgeable in his work, is respected by those who deal with him as a competent and reliable person, and takes considerable pride in doing a good job every time he has the opportunity to practice his chosen work, then we certainly can consider professionalism as something all real estate brokers and licensees should strive for.

The professional real estate broker is most easily noticeable for pride in his work, competence, desire for recognition for his chosen field, and continuing to improve his abilities. This book will assume that the brokerage business should be peopled by this kind of professional and will discuss the brokerage business in this light.

Several organizations exist whose purpose is to promote professionalism in the brokerage field and recognition by the public of the service, high qualifications, and ability of its members. The most prominent of these is the National Association of REALTORS® and the many organizations affiliated with it in various ways. These include, among others, the Appraisal Institute, the Institute of Real Estate Management, the REALTORS® National Marketing Institute, and State Associations in all fifty states. These organizations speak for their members on a variety of public issues of interest to them, provide many kinds of training programs and classroom sessions designed to improve their skills, and provide professional designations to members who meet the rigorous sets of standards that identify them as being recognized by their peers as highly competent professionals.

All members of REALTORS® organizations must meet certain qualifications, including proper licensure and recommendation by other members. They are also required to subscribe to and conform to the REALTORS® Code of Ethics. Its concern is with the sound ethical business practice that will make the REALTORS® member a valued and recognized contributor to the welfare of his community, state, and nation. The reader is urged to contact his/her local REALTORS® organization for a copy of the latest edition of the REALTORS® Code of Ethics.

The reader should note that the term REALTOR® is a federally registered identifying term. It cannot be used by anyone who is not a member of a board of REALTORS® that is affiliated with the National Association of REALTORS®. It is improper to refer to a real estate broker as a REALTORS® unless he is such a member, although many uninformed members of the public do just that. Most successful, ethical and respected real estate brokers and their associates are members of the local board of REALTORS®. They find that the recognition and the contributions to their profession are well worth it. The term REALTORS® should always be written as it appears in these pages: in capital letters and using the registered trademark (®) sign.

Membership in a REALTORS® organization is highly advantageous to any ethical real estate broker and the members of the firm. In addition to its concern for proper recognition of the real estate business and the wide variety of educational opportunities in the real estate field that the organization offers, it is the best available source of continuing information likely to be of interest to real estate brokerage professionals. Its magazine, *Real EstateToday*, publishes articles on matters of interest, and other newsletters and publications that can keep the real estate professional informed and supplied with useful ideas.

The National Association of REALTORS® is a large organization. There are close to 2,000 local Boards of REALTORS® with a total membership exceeding 700,000. These numbers are growing every year, not only as the real estate brokerage industry expands, but also as more and more licensees recognize the obvious advantages of membership and as the business as a whole strives for higher and higher standards of professional excellence.

THE SCOPE OF OUR STUDY

Real estate brokerage firms come in all sizes. A great many are very small: a broker-owner operating alone or with a few associated salespeople. At the other end of the scale are large concerns with several branch offices and salespeople numbering in the hundreds. Especially in California, real estate brokerage firms exist that have over 100 branch offices and well over 1,000 salespeople. Our concern here will be the small- to medium-sized residential firm (under 100 salespeople) that is so typical of the industry nationwide.

Our objective will be to examine the management techniques and practices that apply to these small and medium sized residential firms. We will consider the problems associated with setting up a firm and getting it under way. We will look very hard at personnel practices (selection, training, and retaining of good salespeople and other necessary personnel) since a topnotch sales force is a key element to success. We will examine organizational patterns that contribute to the most efficient operation of the sales force. We will consider the marketing problems the firm faces, particularly with regard to marketing the firm's services. We will study the management practices necessary for the continued successful operation of the firm: the establishment of management policy, goals, and objectives; financial controls and planning; dealing with liability; and operating in a competitive environment. It is important, therefore, that we understand at the outset that our objective is to study real estate brokerage as a business, and not as a personal endeavor. We won't spend a lot of time examining how an individual becomes a better salesperson or a more effective procurer of listings. Instead, we will examine the real estate brokerage firm as a business and describe the techniques and management skills necessary to make it thrive in today's economic and social environment.

An important feature of this text is the *Case Studies*, the first of which appear at the end of this chapter. Taken from actual experiences (with names changed), they illustrate features of the brokerage business.

Previous Preparation

We make certain assumptions about the background of the reader, particularly since real estate is a complex field that we cannot hope to describe in detail in just this single volume. While many readers may already be licensed salespersons and so may have had some practical experience in the field, we do not assume that every reader has such a history. Most states require some sort of educational background in real estate principles and practices for salesperson licensees, and we will assume that the reader, whether licensed or not, has at least the minimum educational background required by most licensing laws. That would be the equivalent of a single introductory college level course in real estate, though we emphasize that this equivalent need not actually have been obtained at a college or university. In most states, excellent private schools, business schools, and specialized real estate schools offer such courses. For the purposes of this book, a reading knowledge of any good text in real estate principles and practices ought to be sufficient.

Readers will find some overlap between this book and those suggested above for prior reading. There are several reasons for this. First, there are some topics included in an introductory course or text that we must examine in greater detail. Second, some repetition of introductory material will be necessary to provide a more logical and sensible discussion here. Further, it will be necessary to repeat some introductory material in order to present it in the context of the brokerage business, rather than from the general viewpoint.

DISCUSSION QUESTIONS AND PROJECTS

1. Approximately how many brokerage firms exist in your local area? How many of these would be classified as large? Small? Does it appear that a relatively few firms seem to have a large part of the total business among them? Why or why not?

2. Describe the essentials of the process a brokerage firm goes through as it handles a transaction from beginning to end.

3. Of the procedures you described in the answer to (3), which are most interesting to you? Why? Which seem least interesting? Why?

4. From newspaper articles and other sources, try to find out how effective the zoning process in your area has been. What are its objectives? Can you point out any parts of your city or town where these procedures have failed to work as hoped? What caused the failure?

5. Find out from your state REALTORS® association what fraction of the state's brokerage firms belong to the organization. What kinds of services does it offer?

6. Interview three or four brokers whose firms are REALTORS® members. Find out from them what they consider to be the major advantages of membership.

Case Studies

PREPARING FOR SUCCESS IN REAL ESTATE BROKERAGE

1. Robert V. had been a part-time real estate salesperson for a number of years, working occasional weekends, holidays and vacations. once a year or so he secured a successful listing, usually because he happened to be in the right place at the right time. His brokerage firm paid him about half of the commission revenues he brought in.

One day he wondered why he continued to work for someone else: "Why shouldn't I get my own brokerage license? That way, I would get to keep the entire share of the commission, and I would make almost twice as much money for the same work!" So he took a couple of courses, applied to take the broker's license examination and, on the third try, passed it.

He set up an "office" in his basement recreation room, printed up some business cards and waited for the business to roll in. It didn't. Potential buyers had come to him or been referred to him because of his association with his previous firm, and now he managed to obtain only an occasional prospect referred to him by someone he had previously done business with. Even then, he found it difficult to get the larger firms in town to cooperate with him on the sales of their listings. He got no listings at all himself; potential sellers went elsewhere as soon as they learned that his was a one-man operation.

At the end of the year he discovered that he had worked harder and made less money than he had before. Unhappily, he closed down his business and went back to work as a salesman for another firm. He never understood exactly what had happened. He knew that he was competent at selling real estate, and that considering the time he was able to put in, he did well as a salesman for another firm. But as an independent broker he just had not made it.

2. Louise J. had been a highly successful full-time salesperson for one of the town's major firms for nearly twenty years. She was very active in local and state industry groups and was well-known and highly regarded by her peers in the business. For several years before she finally started her own business, others had suggested such a move to her. Even her broker admitted that. Although he would be very unhappy to lose her, he knew she had what it took to operate her own successful business.

Louise knew that, too. But she also had learned that a real estate brokerage business involves a lot more than the ability to sell and list property if it is to succeed. She discussed the business with her own broker and sales manager, and made a point of getting all the information she could from the managers of the other respected firms in her city. Initially she decided that while she loved real estate and the brokerage business, she did not have the necessary management knowledge and experience. She enrolled at the local university on a part-time basis and took several courses in management and accounting. She attended a number of seminars related to the management of the real estate business. When her sales manager went on vacation, she asked her broker to appoint her to fill in for him. That experience taught her more about the nature of business, and that she worked well with people and enjoyed administrative duties. She consulted with bankers to determine how much money she would need to start a business, and how easily she would be able to secure the funds.

Finally she felt she was ready. She breezed through the licensing examination and set up her firm. She was realistic enough to realize that it would take her some time to get it going at the level she desired, and she made sure she had the resources to last her until it did. Several good salespeople expressed interest in affiliating with her, and she was able to assemble a good sales force of seven people at the very beginning. Her new business was prospering well before the deadline she had set for herself.

A Case Study

NATIONAL BROKERAGE FIRMS

Although real estate brokerage firms are localized by nature, there has been a trend during the 1970s and 1980s toward national identification of "chains" of realty firms. Foremost among these are the national "franchise" firms. While these companies have a national image, the individual member "offices" actually remain separate, locally owned and operated entities. They are owned by the people who run them, and affiliate with the national franchise organization.

Franchiser firms offer name identification, national advertising, media advertising and other features of nationally-oriented businesses which are well beyond the means of local small businesses to afford. Also, these companies of ten provide training services, information networks, referral exchanges and other facilities which are useful to many real estate brokerage firms.

There have been attempts by other national firms, especially stock brokerages and other investment houses, to establish their own chains of company-owned and -controlled realty office systems. Many of these have encountered serious problems. First, state license laws make it very difficult for real estate brokerage companies to be controlled in a centralized manner. Second, many of these companies have discovered that in spite of their success in marketing in other investment areas, they often turn out to be lacking the experience and knowledge to operate a successful realty business. As a result, many originally ambitious plans for such nationwide chains have been abandoned or severely scaled down. Those which survive have relatively few branches, and tend to concentrate on "big-ticket" investment properties. They compete very little in the residential, owner-occupied real estate area which is the mainstay of most real estate brokerage firms.

A Case Study

EDUCATION AND THE REAL ESTATE PROFESSIONAL

For decades, one important objective of the real estate brokerage business has been to increase the professional image of licensees as well as to increase their professional knowledge and capacity. A key element in this process has been the growing requirement in state licensing laws for certain educational standards for licensees.

Educational accomplishment as a prerequisite to licensure has been common for a long time. By the 1970s almost all states required at least a minimal real estate education experience for anyone applying for a salesperson's license. Most states require additional education for broker's license applicants. Also, all states require at least the equivalent of a high school education, and some are requiring some college-level general education as well. Overall education requirements still vary greatly among the states, from a minimum of 24 to 30 clock hours of real estate education for salesperson's license applicants in some states, to 300 or more clock hours of specialized real estate education for broker's license applicants in some others. Most states also specify the content of the required real estate education, as well as the length required.

A trend which has emerged in recent years has been the additional requirement of continuing education for those who already have real estate licenses. In the growing number of states with this provision in their license law, the education requirement does not stop once a person is licensed. In order to retain the license, the licensee must satisfactorily complete an additional specified amount of real estate education every year or two. Some states which do not require continuing education do offer a series of seminars which licensees are encouraged to take on a voluntary basis.

Other requirements which extend beyond those mentioned also are under consideration. One is to require periodic re-examination for licensees. Another is the designation of additional license categories. An example would be different licenses for residential, commercial, investment, appraisal, etc.

One thing is certain: As time passes, the general nationwide trend will be to require more and more education and other evidence of competence from real estate licensees. While some may object, most professionally-oriented real estate people may applaud this trend and, indeed, are among the prime movers in bringing it about in their respective states. The end result will be a continually improving population of real estate professionals to serve the nation's real estate brokerage needs.

REFERENCES

HARWOOD, BRUCE, AND CHARLES JACOBUS, *Real Estate: An Introduction,* 6th edition. Englewood Cliffs, NJ: Prentice-Hall, Inc., 1993. A widely used basic textbook used largely in license examination preparatory courses. Periodically updated in new editions.

HARWOOD, BRUCE, AND CHARLES JACOBUS, *Real Estate Principles,* 6th edition. Englewood Cliffs, NJ: Prentice-Hall, Inc., 1993. One of the most popular college-level textbooks. Periodically updated in new editions.

LINDEMAN, BRUCE, AND JACK P. FRIEDMAN, *Barron's How to Pass Real Estate Licensing Examinations: Salesperson and Broker,* 4th edition. Hauppauge, NY: Barron's Educational Series, Inc., 1991. A good, inexpensive, basic review of real estate principles with emphasis upon material required for licensing. Also contains about principles with emphasis upon material required for licensing. Also contains about 1,000 questions and several sample examinations to aid in study. Periodically updated in new editions. Makes a wonderful gift, and I should know, because I wrote it. Buy several.

Anyone interested in the real estate brokerage business ought to obtain and read the latest versions of the following:

REALTORS® Code of Ethics. Chicago, IL: National Association of REALTORS®. Periodically updated.

NATIONAL ASSOCIATION OF REALTORS®, *Interpretations of the Code of Ethics*. Chicago, IL: National Association of REALTORS®. Periodically updated.

TWO

LICENSE AND AGENCY LAW

Vulnerability to Legal Action

Licensing

License Law

Broker and Salesperson

Infractions of License Law

Agency Law

The real estate brokerage business is covered by a large body of law. Licensing law establishes standards in each state that real estate salespeople must meet. Agency law describes the responsibilities of the brokerage's function as an agent for its customers. Contract law covers much of the business activity of the brokerage firm. Other laws deal with specific factors of the business and business practice.

The intelligent broker cannot hope to function efficiently without a thorough understanding of his legal position and the legal framework that governs him. This need is becoming more and more important every day; the broker's customers and clients cannot any longer be expected to take whatever he dishes out without any protest. Dissatisfied customers in all areas of business are discovering very rapidly that the law is often on their side, and that they have recourse to a great many legal remedies. In nearly every state, the branch of state government that supervises and enforces real estate licensing law is becoming much more vigorous in seeking out and punishing violators of the law.

To the ethical broker, this trend is welcome, for it rids the profession of undesirable members, and helps to create in the public mind a better and more favorable attitude toward brokerage. Any professional likes to take pride in his work and to be proud of his membership in his chosen profession. The real estate business is one in which the public's attitude toward the entire profession is easily affected by poor behavior and performance of a few of its members.

VULNERABILITY TO LEGAL ACTION

This is the age of the consumer. To the business operator, however, it is more important to recognize that this is the age of the consumer's lawyer. There is no question that our legal system and its interpretations are undergoing a transformation in favor of the consumer, the buyer and user of products. It used to be, so it is thought, that the rule of *caveat emptor* – "let the buyer beware" – prevailed in purchase situations. Actually, buyers have long had many legal rights and expectations, but in recent years they appear to have become more aware of their rights, and all levels of government have been busy passing new laws defining more strictly just what these rights are and just what responsibilities sellers have.

In the past few years the news has featured stories of spectacular awards to consumers in cases where sellers of products and services have been held responsible for damage suffered by their customers. Faulty gasoline tanks on automobiles, disintegrating power lawn mowers, and dubious insurance selling practices are among the many cases that have been brought to public attention. It may not seem that this consumer attitude has spread into the real estate business, but it has, and it will spread further. Every year, in every state, licensed brokers and salespeople are required to pay large sums in damages, and even lose their licenses, their businesses, and their livelihoods because of improper practice of their profession.

Of course, cases arise where the broker's improper performance leads consumers into unfortunate situations, and in such cases the broker usually can be held legally liable for damages to the injured parties and may be in jeopardy of having his license suspended or revoked as well. But even the blameless broker may find himself defending his actions in court; irate customers may try to make him a scapegoat. Sometimes they can find an attorney who is willing to take their money to press a spurious case; sometimes they do not tell their attorneys the true facts.

Regardless of whether or not a suit against him has merit, the broker will incur some expense defending against it, and it is one of the characteristics of the business that such things will happen. They cannot be avoided, but the broker who keeps up with the law, and who understands how it affects his business, can keep those unhappy events to a minimum. And, of course, by doing so he also eliminates the risk that he will be assessed substantial damage judgments or lose his license, because he will be assured that he is always working within the law.

There is more detailed discussion of broker liability in Chapter 12.

LICENSING

Every state requires that real estate brokers and salespersons be licensed. There are two categories of licensees: brokers and salespersons. The salesperson may function in the brokerage business only if his license has been issued to a licensed broker: He is under the supervision of a broker in his work, and the broker is legally responsible for what his licensed salespeople do in the course of business. Whereas all states refer to the primary license of the independent operator as a real estate broker's license, the salesperson's nomenclature differs among the states: most call it a salesman's license, but such terms as salesperson or associate broker also are encountered.

Qualifications

The applicant for a license must meet a number of qualifications. Nearly all states require a minimum general education, such as the equivalent of a high school education, and most have minimum age requirements. Applicants must generally be able to show that they are of good character. Those who have been convicted of certain crimes, for example, may be disqualified. Some states will run credit checks and other investigations to substantiate the applicant's worthiness. Most states require a minimum level of educational attainment in the real estate area for one or both licenses, and the majority of states will not allow an applicant for a broker's license to take the qualifying examination until he has served at least a minimum amount of time as a licensed salesperson.

Licensing Examination

Every state has a qualifying examination the applicant must pass before he can be issued a license. The examination concentrates upon knowledge of the features of the real estate business, the brokerage business, ethics, contract law, real estate contracts, real estate mathematics and, especially, license law and real estate practices of the state giving the examination. Examinations vary from state to state, although there are two national examinations, one or the other being used, at least in part, in about forty states. In other states, the examination is prepared by or for the arm of state government that supervises and regulates real estate licensing.

Variations among States

Real estate licensure is regulated entirely at the state level; there are practically no federal laws or regulations that influence real estate licensure as such. However, the broker should be aware that a lot of other federal laws affect him, even though it may not be directly related to licensing. Examples are fair housing laws, truth-in-lending laws, tax laws, environmental protection laws, land use regulation laws, and regulations affecting federally supported financing such as FHA, VA, etc., and a maze of other laws and regulations as well.

Since licensure is a state operation, we will find variations in the laws of the fifty states. Most of these are in details, while the general thrust of all of these laws remains the same from state to state. The reader should contact his state's real estate licensing authority for information about its law and regulations, and should examine it for details of its nature and enforcement. Variation occurs most often in such areas as administration of examinations, qualifications for licensure, fees charged for licenses and examinations, and the like. The following discussions, therefore, will have to be general in nature, and will concentrate (except where indicated) on those aspects of licensing law that are generally uniform among the states.

LICENSE LAW

This is not the place to engage in an elaborate discussion of license law, because license applicants are required to study their state's license law carefully if they hope to pass the examinations. Readers of this book either already have studied their state's law, or will have to do so in order to be licensed to put this book's information to use in business. And, as we have mentioned, it is wise for any person in the real estate brokerage field to have a thorough knowledge of state laws and practices.

License laws originated early in this century as a means of controlling what at that time appeared to be widespread abuses and improper practices in the real estate business. Today, their purpose is to protect the public by assuring the real estate salespeople will have met certain minimum standards of ability and knowledge and by providing a set of rules, laws, and regulations governing the business. Licensing standards vary from state to state, but there is a strong nationwide trend under way to make the qualifications for licensure increasingly rigorous.

For example, some states require that newly licensed real estate brokers will have to have taken and passed a course of study equivalent to as many as 200 or more clock hours of classroom work in the various areas of real estate. In addition, many states require some amount of continuing education of licensees in order to keep the license once it is earned. The amount, quality, and subject matter will vary among the states, but as time passes it can be expected that these requirements will become more rigorous and will spread to additional states.

Licensure and Exemption

Usually, anyone who sells, rents, buys, or leases real estate belonging to others, and who does so for pay, must hold a license before he can engage in any aspect of the business. This goes so far as to render illegal the actions of someone who intends to seek a license but who, before it is issued, begins to line up people with whom he will do business once he is licensed. Several exceptions to the law are provided for.

Attorneys may be exempted from licensure since they are presumed to be expert in law anyway, and they are licensed and regulated by other branches of state government, usually even more rigorously than real estate salespeople. One who has an owner's power of attorney to act for him may be exempted, though most states will not permit someone to circumvent the law by getting powers of attorney on a regular basis. Trustees, executors, government employees acting in the course of their duties (for example, employees of the state highway department who conduct negotiations for the purchase by the state of highway right-of-way land), and some others who are acting in special capacities are also exempted. Resident managers of apartment projects may not have to be licensed, even though they sign leases and sometimes negotiate on behalf of the owner. Generally, no one has to be licensed to sell real estate that he owns himself; however, some states restrict even this privilege by requiring licenses for owners of large subdivisions if they wish to sell them on a lot-by-lot basis. These latter provisions, which are fairly new in license law, were a response to customer complaints involving speculative subdivisions and, more particularly, rapid increases in the growth of sales of undeveloped land lots accompanied by overenthusiastic sales efforts.

In some states, an employee of a real estate owner may sell that owner's real estate while unlicensed, provided that it is part of the employee's full time job with that owner, and that the employee sells real estate for no one else but that owner. A provision like this would allow a homebuilding company to hire an unlicensed sales force, provided that they were employed only by that company. But other states specifically require that such employees be licensed.

Administration of License Law

The majority of states have a *real estate commission* that administers the real estate license law. In those that do not have a separate real estate commission, the law is administered by another branch of state government such as the department of state or branch that is set up to handle most or all professional licenses the state issues.

Real estate commissions usually are made up of appointed members who have the responsibility of administering the law. Most often they are required to be members of the real estate business and to hold licenses issued by the state. Many states also require that commission members from other walks of life, such as a consumer representative, be included. Generally the commission will have a staff that handles its day-to-day business, since it is rare that the commissioners themselves hold their positions on an exclusive, full-time basis. Staff members are concerned with handling the paperwork, administering the examinations, and arranging for commission business such as hearings, examination reviews, and the like.

In states that have no commissions, staffs handle much of the work in the same way described above; however, they may be concerned with more than real estate licensure. In these states there may or may not be representation of the real estate brokerage business in a decision-making capacity similar to the commissioners in other states. Most states require their real estate commissions, departments, or divisions, if they have them, to be self-supporting from the fees and other charges they collect. Fees are charged for license examination (sometimes an additional fee is charged for administrative matters such as changes of address or transfers of salespersons to different brokers).

Financial Responsibility

Most states require that the licensee have some sort of financial responsibility to protect the public in case he causes loss to someone. Some require that he post a bond wronged customers can claim against. Many states have instituted what usually is called a Real Estate Recovery Fund. These are funds set up and administered by the state government, and aggrieved parties may claim against them if they provide proper proof that a licensee has caused them loss. The fund is supplied by assessments against all active licensees in the state.

The exact manner and requirements of these assessments vary from state to state, but the effect is to provide a fund of money, supplied by the brokerage industry itself, against which claims can be made. The exact nature of the fund, and the manner in which monies are paid in and claimed against usually is somewhat complex. The interested reader should consult his own state's law to determine if such a fund exists in his state, and how it operates.

Violation and Penalties

In most states, violating the license law is a misdemeanor, and the penalty is a fine or imprisonment. A violation would include any infraction of license law by a licensee (in which case the licensee could also be subject to suspension or revocation of his license), as well as any activity by an unlicensed person for which the law requires licensure (in which case the unlicensed person may jeopardize his eligibility to be issued a license in the future). If there is reason to believe that a licensee has violated the law, a hearing will be held. The licensee will be notified of the charges, and given an opportunity to defend himself against them in the hearing. He is usually allowed to have an attorney present, but in most states hearings do not follow the rigid rules of courtroom procedure and so tend to be more informal in that sense. As a result of the hearing, a decision can be made as to whether or not the licensee's license will be suspended for a period of time or revoked outright.

Of course if it is decided that the licensee is blameless, no action against him will result. Actual prosecution for the criminal offense of violating the law or license regulations generally is up to the state's prosecuting attorney or other similar official. Even though a licensee has suffered the loss of his license, he still is subject to possible criminal penalties if he is prosecuted successfully. In addition, he suffers a third jeopardy: Those who have suffered because of his action may sue him in a civil case to recover damages.

Generally, decisions made in license law violation hearings may be appealed by the licensee to the regular court system. It frequently happens that a license is suspended or revoked, and the licensee is required to fulfill certain conditions to get it back. A frequent condition is that the former licensee must retake the licensing examination. Sometimes brokers who are found in violation of license law are prohibited from holding broker's licenses for a period of time during which they are allowed to apply for salesperson's licenses and work, once again, under the supervision of another broker. A decision may require that the former licensee take and pass courses in certain areas of the real estate field before he can apply for reinstatement of his license.

License Valid Only in Issuing State

Every state requires that in order for anyone to operate as a real estate broker or salesperson in any way within the state, the person must hold a daily issued license from that state. Unlike driver's licenses, therefore, real estate licenses usually are valid for use only within the state that issues them. Thus, a broker who wishes to do business in more than one state must secure licenses from each of the states in which he wishes to operate. To allow for this, most states will issue nonresident licenses to nonresidents of the state.

Normally, the nonresident applicant must fulfill at least the same requirements (except residence location) that are required of a resident licensee, including coming to an examination site in that state to take the licensing examination. A few states do not issue nonresident licenses. To operate in those states a resident broker of another state usually is required to operate in cooperation with a resident broker of that state. In most states, any kind of real estate brokerage activity by nonresidents requires licensure, even the act of selling out-of-state property by mail to residents of that state.

A few states have a limited form of reciprocity with neighboring states, particularly with regard to large metropolitan areas that overlap state boundaries. However, even this is the exception rather than the rule. The only other form of reciprocity exists among some of the states that use the same "national" licensing examination. Some will allow licensees from other states using the same examination to take only the state law and practices portion of the licensing examination, since they have already passed the general portion of the examination in another state.

BROKER AND SALESPERSON

As we have seen, license law requires anyone engaging in certain real estate selling activities for pay to be licensed; the license law will have a long section in which all these activities are spelled out in detail. Every state provides for two types of licenses, that of the broker and that of the *salesperson*.

Broker

A broker is a licensee who is permitted to act independently. He may operate his own business and has certain responsibilities and duties outlined in the law. He must prepare (and take responsibility for the preparation of) certain documents, such as sale contracts and leases, and must arrange the settlement of transactions in which he is an agent. The law, or some other source, will have a long list of rules and regulations that govern the conduct of the broker with respect to his clients and customers and the other licensees with whom he may operate.

The broker generally is considered by the law to be legally responsible for anything that is done by his business and his employees. This responsibility extends to anything done in the course of his business by licensees whose licenses the broker holds. Most states require that if a brokerage firm has more than one office, a licensed broker or salesperson with a certain amount of experience must be in charge of each branch. Salespeople's licenses must be held and displayed at only one branch office per salesperson, although they usually would be allowed to operate out of other branches as well. The broker, in addition, takes all responsibility for trust monies coming into possession of the firm.

Salesperson

The salesperson, regardless of what he may be called in the laws and definitions of the various states, is allowed most of the activity permitted to the broker, with certain exceptions. Generally, he cannot conduct closings, unless the broker supervises; he cannot handle trust monies, except to transport them directly to his broker; he cannot act as an independent entity. His license is held by a broker, and he is considered to be an employee of that broker. Normally, the brokerage's advertisements must feature the name of the broker, although the salesperson who is involved may have his own name and telephone number included. Everything he does, he does in the name of the broker, for as we have seen the broker takes the legal responsibility for the salesperson's actions in business.

This sales license may be likened to an apprenticeship, although no state law refers to it as such. However, the gist of the law is to imply that the salesperson is an apprentice. The law usually states that he must be under the constant supervision of a broker, and most states will not allow anyone to apply for a broker's license without having spent a certain length of time as a licensed salesperson.

Commission Payments

License law regards the salesperson as hired by, and the responsibility of, one broker and one broker only. Normally, a salesperson may be paid commission by only his own broker. In the case of cooperative sales, where a salesperson finds a buyer for property listed by a broker other than his own, the seller of that property will pay the entire commission to the listing brokerage. That brokerage firm then pays an agreed upon share of the commission to the selling brokerage. Then each broker individually pays the proper portion of his share of the commission to his own salesperson involved in the deal.

The exact nature of the manner in which a broker shares commissions with his salespeople depends upon the arrangements between broker and salesperson. It is not determined by the license law. In fact, the actual commission arrangement between the property owner and the broker is always a matter of negotiation. License law does not specify any particular rate of payment or commission for real estate brokers. Indeed, commission schedules drawn up by local organizations of brokers have come under fire from the Antitrust Division of the U.S. Department of Justice. Therefore, recent revisions in license law often mention that actual commission rates are a matter of negotiation in each transaction.

Handling Money

A real estate broker frequently comes into possession of money rightfully belonging to others. He is *custodian* of the money, but the money does *not* belong to him. The sources of such money are earnest money payments, rents the broker collects, and a wide variety of other collections he makes. At settlement, the broker is required to disburse all the money involved in the transaction to the parties entitled to it.

A considerable portion of license law rules and regulations is devoted to discussion of the manner in which the broker handles this money. Normally, he is required to set up at least one bank account into which all of this money is deposited, and from which he withdraws the money when it is time to disburse. Some states call this a trust account, and the broker is regarded in the state law as a trustee. In other states it is called an escrow account, and the broker is regarded as the escrow agent. But whatever the nomenclature, the intent of the law is the same. The broker is entrusted with money belonging to others and has to take special steps to ensure that the money is not jeopardized. The broker must keep scrupulous records of these accounts, the money that goes into them (and from whom it came and why), and the money that is disbursed (to whom and why).

License law enforcement agencies are extremely sensitive on this matter because improper handling of trust (or escrow) monies is a frequent subject of license law violation hearings. In most of these cases there is no malicious intent on the part of the offending broker, only ignorance or sloppy recordkeeping. However, this is small consolation to the broker who finds himself without his license or his business because his records were not kept properly.

It is not enough that the broker himself knows where the money came from or where it went. It is not enough that no money ever actually got lost or misappropriated or even mishandled. The states have rigorous laws and regulations concerning the record-keeping itself, and if they are not followed scrupulously and to the letter, the broker is in violation of the law and can rarely expect to find sympathy when he is called to explain his lapse.

Generally, the license laws and regulations will explain in some detail just how the records are to be kept; also, the state's license law enforcement agency will provide detailed instructions to brokers concerning the exact method of keeping the records, and brokers are expected to be fully aware of them, and to abide by them. This is particularly important because the state's inspectors have the right to enter any brokerage office in the state whenever they please and demand to see the trust account records, and they do it, too. The reasons are obvious. The handling of money is the most delicate and sensitive of the broker's duties, and a licensing agency will be very careful to assure that it is done properly by all.

The account the broker keeps this money in is a special type of account that identifies the money as being in the custody of the broker, but not actually his own. This is critically important. If the broker should go bankrupt or have a judgement entered against him, his trust accounts are immune from claims, since they do not represent any assets of his own. Thus, the owners of the money are protected from changes in the broker's personal or business financial position.

Because of this protection, two specific rules must be followed to the letter. First, the broker must never put any of his own money into the trust accounts. (Some states allow him to keep a minimum balance of his own personal funds for the specific purpose of avoiding or reducing service charges banks impose.) Second, he must never keep trust money anywhere but in such accounts. Any violation of these rules is considered *commingling*; that is, the broker is keeping his own money and trust monies together, and that is a cardinal sin of trusteeship or escrow agency. Further, he usually is required to deposit all trust monies coming into his possession into such an account as soon as possible; many states allow him only until the close of business day following the receipt of the money. Therefore, salespersons who collect such money are required to give it to the broker as soon as possible. Some brokers even give the salespeople deposit slips to the account to use for the proper deposit of these funds to avoid the time delay of bringing them back to the office. Other brokers insist on having the trust monies delivered to them by salespeople immediately so that the broker can personally supervise their proper handling.

INFRACTIONS OF LICENSE LAW

License laws and the accompanying rules and regulations contain lists of specific offenses that are defined as violations of the law. These lists should not be interpreted as being exclusive in that they are the only possible infractions; the laws are full of phraseology allowing much broader interpretation. Frequently a catchall category is written in to include "any other behavior or practice which constitutes unethical, fraudulent or dishonest dealing." This kind of definition would enable inclusion of just about anything that might be considered detrimental to the licensing purpose.

Following is a list of specific business practices usually included as particular infractions of the law. It should be noted that the law can be violated in many other ways, also, such as by acting while unlicensed, improperly paying licensing fees, improper responses to requests to appear at hearings, and so on.

Mishandling Trust Monies

1. Commingling trust monies with personal funds.
2. Not remitting trust monies to a trust account within a reasonable time.
3. Salesperson not remitting trust monies to the broker quickly.
4. Accepting noncash payments on behalf of a principal without the principal's knowledge and agreement. (This is a particularly knotty problem. It is required that trust monies be in the form of cash or check; if they are in any other form, such as a postdated check, a note, etc., then they cannot be deposited immediately and so are not money in hand. If a broker submits an offer in which the earnest money is in such a form, the broker's employer must know of it, and approve.)

Misrepresentation and Fraud

1. False advertising.
2. Intentionally misleading someone.
3. Acting for more than one party to a transaction without the knowledge and permission of all affected parties.
4. Using trademarks or other identification of a firm or organization, such as REALTORS®, of which one is not a member.
5. Not identifying oneself as a licensee in a transaction to which one is also a party (this is often not necessary if the licensee does not share in any way in the commission).

6. Taking kickbacks, referral fees, placement fees, and the like without the employer's knowledge. An exception would be taking referral fees or commissions from financing companies, since the act of getting financing for a buyer cannot be thought of as damaging to a seller.

7. Guaranteeing future profits. Most state license laws or regulations forbid the licensee to promise a potential buyer that he will prosper in any particular financial way.

8. Pretending to represent owners by whom one is not actually employed.

9. Failing to identify the broker in all advertising. Many states specifically prohibit "blind ads," which are advertisements by brokerage firms but which appear to have been placed by individuals.

Improper Business Practice

1. Salesperson pretending to be a broker, or pretending to be employed by a broker other than the one he actually works for.

2. Offering property on terms other than those specifically authorized by the broker's employer.

3. Failing to submit all offers to the broker's employer. The broker is usually hired to solicit offers; even silly or ridiculous offers must be submitted to the broker's employer for his consideration. This must also be done when the employer already is considering other offers. Only after the employer has accepted an offer and so created a sale contract, may offers be withheld. However, a broker may be instructed by the employer to turn down offers below a certain price, or lacking some other requirement of the seller's, but these instructions must be *specific*.

4. Attempting to thwart another broker's exclusive listing. When a broker has an exclusive agency or exclusive right-to-sell listing, the law requires that any other broker who comes across an offer on the listed property must submit it to the listing broker and may not deal directly with the owner. Also, it is generally illegal for a broker to attempt to convince an owner to fire his current broker and hire him instead. This provision often goes so far as to prohibit contact with owners who have listings that are about to expire; the competing broker must wait until the listing has expired before contacting the owner.

5. Inducing someone to break a contract.

6. Accepting a net listing. (Some states prohibit net listings, but in states where they are allowed this practice would not be a violation. See Chapter 8 for description of net listings.)

7. Failing to put an expiration date in a listing.

8. Putting the brokerage's sign on listed property without the owner's permission. In most states, the creation of a listing between an owner and a broker does not automatically give the broker the right to post his sign; this must be agreed to specifically.

9. Blockbusting or discrimination. *Blockbusting* is the practice of soliciting listings by pointing out the "undesirables" (i.e., persons of another race, creed, color, national origin) are moving into the neighborhood, and the owner would be advised to get out while the getting's good. *Discrimination* refers to any action denying the right to buy or sell to someone for the same reasons.

Failure to Impart Required Information

1. Failing to leave copies of relevant contracts with all parties involved.

2. Failing to deliver a closing statement to all parties entitled to one.

3. Failing to inform all parties of relevant closing costs.

4. Failing to impart any other required information. Various states have differing requirements here. Some have none; others may require disclosure of (a) the broker's agency relationship with the seller, and/or (b) certain characteristics of the offered property, such as significant structural defects, liens against the property, and so on. The broker should check his own state law to see what the requirements are in his jurisdiction. Sometimes local law will affect this area as well.

Improper Handling of Commissions

1. Paying a commission to an unlicensed person. Many states allow a broker to pay a small referral fee to unlicensed persons, but generally this is limited to referral only, and the unlicensed person may not have engaged in any other aspect of effecting the listing and/or sale except to refer the broker to a possible client or customer.

2. Paying a commission to a licensee not in the broker's employ.

3. Salesperson receiving a commission payment from someone other than the employing broker. License law is very specific about (2) and (3). A broker may share a commission with another licensed broker with whom he has cooperated on a deal. However, in no other case may he share commissions with anyone other than the licensees who work for him.

4. Collecting a higher commission from an employer than agreed upon, unless the employer agrees to the new arrangement.

Other

1. Being convicted of certain crimes.

2. Making false statements on license applications.

3. Violating any part of license law.

4. Any other evidence of incompetence, unworthiness, dishonesty, and the like.

We point out that not all of these provisions may be found in the law of each state, and that each state is likely to have additional provisions not listed here.

AGENCY LAW

In addition to abiding by his state's specific laws governing real estate licensees, a broker is legally an agent, and comes under the broad category of the legal system called agency law. Whereas brokerage and licensing law generally is well codified and conveniently described, agency law has its roots in history and has developed over the years as a part of the common law as well as specifically legislated and codified law. Many aspects of agency law are included within licensing law, but it is wise to have some basic knowledge of the generalities of agency law itself, since it affects the broker just as much as any other law he must abide by.

An *agent* is employed by his principal (usually the property owner in the case of the real estate broker). The broker's function is to deal with third parties (prospective buyers or tenants) on behalf of his principal.

A *general agent* has broad powers, including the right to commit his principal in business and financial transactions. A real estate broker, however, is a *special agent* because his agency powers are quite *limited*. Essentially they include little more than publicizing and presenting the principal's property to prospects, and soliciting offers from them. The broker normally cannot commit his principal to anything; it is the principal who decides how to respond to offers. In some instances a principal will grant a broker additional agency powers, but these are special arrangements that are not typical of the business as a whole.

The principal may even refuse to deal with anyone the broker brings to him, although he still may be liable to pay the broker a commission. This is because the broker has been hired to solicit offers. The existence of a listing is not construed by the law as an offer to sell, but merely as a solicitation of offers to buy. Even though an offer may agree specifically with all the conditions the owner spelled out in the listing, the owner is not legally compelled to accept the offer. But this refers only to any responsibility he may have to someone who makes him an offer.

His contract with the broker is another matter entirely. If a broker has brought someone to make a *bona fide* (genuine and in good faith) offer that meets or exceeds the conditions put in the listing by the owner, then the broker has done what he was hired to do: to solicit an offer meeting certain conditions. Therefore, the broker normally would be considered to have earned his commission. Even if the owner refuses to accept the offer, he must pay the broker the agreed upon commission.

Duties of the Parties

The agent is an employee of the principal, and must follow his principal's instructions implicitly. Furthermore, he has a duty to act in his employer's best interests, even when doing do means that he cannot act in his own favor. More specifically, agency law requires that the agent abide by the following obligations to his principal:

He must obey the principal's instructions. (Except, of course, when he is instructed to do something illegal.)

He must be loyal to his principal's interests.

He must act in good faith.

He is expected to be able to use his own professional judgement, skill, and ability in his actions. This is particularly so in the case of licensed agents such as real estate brokers, because they are assumed to have met certain standards by virtue of qualifying for licensing.

He must be able to account for all money belonging to others that comes into his possession. Real estate brokers often collect rents, earnest money payments, and other money on behalf of parties other than their principals; by doing so they also develop responsibility to these other parties for the proper handling of their money.

He must perform his duties in person. Normally, this would mean that he could not delegate his duties to anyone else unless the principal approved of the arrangement. Because of the nature of the real estate brokerage business and the establishment of the broker-salesperson relationship by all state licensing laws, a real estate broker has the implied right to delegate his function to duly licensed salespersons and brokers in his employ.

He must keep his principal fully informed as to developments affecting their relationship. In the case of a real estate broker, he should report all offers made on the principal's property, as well as all other information he acquires that may affect the principal's property, price, etc.

The principal also has responsibilities to the agent. He must compensate the agent for his services and reimburse expenses the agent makes on his behalf. However, selling expenses (such as advertising, signs, property-showing, etc.) usually are paid by the agent out of the commission which the principal pays him. The principal also should make the agent fully aware of his duties and inform him about anything that will affect his performance.

The fact that the broker as agent is responsible to his employer and must remain loyal to him creates some significant problems in the proper conduct of the brokerage business. Most important, it must be remembered that in most transactions, there is no such thing as the buyer's agent. All agents involved usually will be paid by sharing in the commission that the seller will pay; therefore they all are the seller's agent. In brokerage practice, it is certainly prevalent that buyers themselves assume that the agents they work with are working for them. (We are not saying that buyers *never* employ agents; sometimes they do. Also, a recent trend has been the emergence of brokerage firms which work only with buyers, and do not take listings; see the discussion in Chapter 9. But still, in most transactions and especially residential sales, the agent is employed exclusively by the seller.)

Even among brokers and in license law, it is considered unethical practice for a broker to bypass another agent in order to deal with that agent's client. In brokerage terminology, a *client* is a potential buyer to whom a broker is showing property in an effort to make a sale. Certainly, clients are absolutely necessary to the operation of the business, but all agents must be especially careful to make sure that nothing they do while they work with a client could be thought of as detrimental to the interests of a seller and must protect his interests, and not the buyer's.

DISCUSSION QUESTIONS AND PROJECTS

1. From the agency in your state that regulates and licenses real estate brokers and salespeople (Real Estate Commission, Licensing Agency, Real Estate Department, etc.), secure a copy of your state's licensing law and review it thoroughly.

2. From the same source, find out how many people apply to take real estate licensing examinations each year, how many pass, and how many appear to remain in the business on a career basis.

3. From the same source, find out the most common violations for which complaints are received and   hearings held concerning real estate licensees.

4. What are the penalties in your state for violation of license law?

5. Describe the legal differences between a broker and a salesperson.

6. What are the procedures that your state law requires a broker to follow in the handling of trust (escrow) monies?

7. Describe a situation in your experience in which a real estate licensee violated agency law. What would have been the proper procedure? Did anyone suffer from his actions?

8. Describe three situations in which you think a real estate licensee would be tempted to violate license or agency law. Why are they tempting? What would be the proper procedure to follow in each instance?

Case Studies

LICENSE LAW

1. Elwood R. was a licensed real estate salesperson; his license was held by a licensed broker, James G.

Elwood's wife became ill with cancer. After hospitalization and surgery she was cured, but the cost of her treatment came to over $20,000. Since she was employed by a firm which provided medical benefits as part of its fringe benefits package, Elwood had not included her in the medical insurance policy he had on himself. However, it turned out that her employers had made an error in their insurance coverage and, in fact, Mrs. R. had not been covered. She and Elwood were liable for the full extent of her medical bills.

The result for them was financial disaster. Elwood tried to make ends meet, but he was unable to do so, and eventually he did something illegal. He negotiated a contract of sale involving Mr. and Mrs. L., who paid $1000 earnest money payment toward the purchase of a house. However, without their knowledge, Elwood altered the contract to read that the deposit was $100, and pocketed the other $900. Naturally, he intended to pay it back somehow before the transaction closed, but he wasn't able to. When Mr. and Mrs. L. found out what had happened, they went to James G., Elwood's broker, and demanded that he refund the $900. He refused to do so, saying that he had no knowledge of what had happened, and that he was not responsible for his salesperson's activity. Mr. and Mrs. L. appealed to the State Real Estate Commission.

The Commission held a hearing at which the facts were presented. They pointed out to Broker G. that license law specifically stated that he was responsible for all activity by his sales force in the course of business, and required him to refund the $900. They also revoked broker G.'s license, as well as Elwood's.

2. Jane R. and Ben M. passed the broker's license examination and set up a real estate brokerage business in May of 1988. Shortly afterward they secured a listing on a large tract of land offered at $300,000, with a 10% selling commission. In August they negotiated a full-price sale of the land. Naturally they were pleased; when the deal closed they would get a commission of $30,000. However, they overlooked one thing. The buyer had given them an earnest money check for $25,000, but had dated the check October 15, 1988, which was the contracted date of closing. He explained that he did not have the ready cash, but by the closing date he would be able to make it good.

Brokers R. and M. did not disclose that the earnest money deposit was a postdated check; they simply wrote into the contract that a check for $25,000 had been received. They put it into their office safe, but their seller naturally assumed it had been deposited and cleared. Of course, the obvious happened. On the closing date the buyer did not show up and attempts to contact him were fruitless. The brokers deposited the earnest money check; however, it was returned unpaid because of insufficient funds.

The seller demanded his share of the forfeited earnest money. When the brokers told him what had happened, he sued them for his share and complained to the State Real Estate Commission. The court awarded the seller a judgement for $15,000, plus court costs. The Real Estate Commission revoked the brokers' licenses.

If the brokers had notified the seller that the deposit was in the form of a postdated check, and if he had accepted the offer on that basis, they would have been blameless. By concealing the fact, they lost their licenses, their business, and several thousand dollars.

REFERENCES

The reader should consult the *Real Estate Licensing Law* of his/her state, as well as literature concerning his/her state's licensing examinations, which is provided by the state's licensing authorities.

THREE

THE LEGAL ENVIRONMENT OF REAL ESTATE BROKERAGE

The Brokerage and the Law

State and Local Legislation

Federal Legislation

General Contract Law

Requirements of Contracts

Duress, Misrepresentation, and Fraud

Discharge and Breach of Contract

Disclosure by Seller

Disclosure by Broker

THE BROKERAGE AND THE LAW

The real estate brokerage firm operates in a situation in which legal requirements and arrangements are a constant factor. Brokers and salespeople are licensed by all states. They are legal agents and so are covered by agency law. They draw up contracts, and so must have a knowledge of the basics of contract law and detailed familiarity with the particular contracts they use. Each of these contracts is discussed in subsequent chapters. The previous chapter provided a general coverage of license, agency, and contract law. Here we will discuss briefly some other elements of state, local and federal laws the broker should be familiar with.

It must be emphasized that the possession of a real estate license does not entitle its holder to practice law! Most states allow brokers and salespeople to assist in the preparation of sales and listing contracts that they use, but complicated or confusing questions always should be referred to a competent attorney. Legal advice should *never* be given by licensees.

STATE AND LOCAL LEGISLATION

States and localities throughout the country have passed a large variety of laws that in one way or another affect real estate marketing practices. Most of these occur at the local level, although some states have adopted significant legislation, other than licensing law, that may apply statewide. In these pages, some of the more significant examples will be covered.

Land Use Regulation

Land use regulation has been in existence since early in this century. It usually is applied at the local level, although in most states the actual authority to develop and enforce these regulations had to be given to local government. These laws specify minimum standards of construction and development and, in the case of zoning, prohibit certain uses of land in specified areas. Usually zoning laws or ordinances are sweeping in nature, designating the entire geographical area under consideration as various kinds of development zones. Then what usually follows is a long series of *variances* from the law that are granted to petitioners who convince the responsible authorities that their building and development plans will not significantly affect surrounding area growth and development and will be of advantage to the community. These variances apply to specific parcels of property. By requiring developers to get variances before undertaking *nonconforming* land use, the authorities manage to retain some kind of control over the manner in which development takes place.

Since prohibiting or permitting certain kinds of uses for a given parcel of land can materially affect its usefulness, and consequently its market value, licensees should be aware of these restrictions and their effects. Furthermore, since it usually is possible, to some degree, to obtain the necessary permissions and variances to put land to more profitable use than current zoning and other restrictions dictate, licensees should be aware of the possibilities when they deal in properties that might be so affected. In fact, a few firms in the country actually specialize in such properties, and part of their service includes going through and orchestrating the steps necessary to obtain required permissions. Frequently a buyer will make an offer on a piece of property subject to proper rezoning. In such cases the licensee should make sure that the sale contract contains language which properly and fully explains this contingency.

Sign Ordinances

For various reasons, some localities have passed ordinances that restrict or prohibit the use by real estate brokerage firms of the familiar FOR SALE signs. The constitutional legality of these laws often is challenged, and in some cases these laws have been overturned. However, it is generally legally accepted that properly drawn ordinances and statutes can survive the scrutiny of the courts. The reasoning behind such laws varies from purely aesthetic ("the signs are ugly and mar the appearance of the neighborhoods") to attempts to prevent panic selling in changing neighborhoods.

Some sign ordinances merely restrict the size or appearance of FOR SALE signs without actually prohibiting their use. They may also restrict the length of time that a sign may be in place and the length of time that a SOLD sign may stand. They may permit FOR SALE signs but prohibit SOLD signs. Many local laws, in the interest of safety, prohibit such signs from being installed within a certain distance of roadways and sidewalks. All licensees should be fully aware of any sign restrictions that may be in effect in the areas in which they operate and abide by them accordingly.

Implied Warranty

An ancient precept of law states that the buyer must assure himself of the quality, quantity, and usefulness of goods that he buys and that the seller is under no obligation to reveal any information of this nature unless he is asked. In modern law this view is gradually being changed, and in the past decade or two considerable legislation at all levels has been passed that requires sellers of goods to recognize that the buyer may infer that certain warranties and guarantees exist, even if he has not bargained for them. One area in which states in particular have been very active has been that of real estate. Here we are concerned with the physical quality of the real estate, rather than the quality of title.

There is an enormous variation in treatment of this matter from state to state, and some still adhere to the doctrine that the buyer is still totally responsible. But be warned that the trend is turning very strongly to favor the buyer. Licensees should make special efforts to keep up to date in this area, because the changes are occurring rapidly and in many states each session of the legislature makes alterations.

This matter is important to the real estate broker because he is the seller's agent and the law frequently is interpreted to hold the broker as well as the seller liable for violations of implied warranty.

FEDERAL LEGISLATION

It would take a book ten times the size of this one just to give marginally adequate coverage of all federal laws, rules, and regulations that might be of concern to a real estate brokerage business. We can consider only a few here. Some affect the everyday pattern of doing business, and others will affect business only occasionally. We will attempt to deal with these in order of importance to the brokerage firm.

Fair Housing

Title VIII of the Civil Rights Act of 1968, and subsequent refinements, made it illegal to discriminate in the sale of housing with respect to race, sex, creed, color, or national origin. There are exceptions to the law, the major one being that an owner selling the property unassisted may be exempt from all or part of the law. The effect, then, is that the law covers mainly brokerage practices, and almost all enforcement attempts and suits have been aimed directly at real estate brokerage firms for alleged violations of the law.

This matter is important to the real estate broker because he is the seller's agent, and the law is frequently interpreted to make the broker, as well as the seller, liable for violations of implied warranty. When this is the case, it is absolutely necessary for the broker to be certain of the physical condition of the property sold to insure that all necessary legal notifications of this condition have been made to the buyer, preferably in writing as part of the sale contract.

Violation of this law can be assumed from the actions of a brokerage firm, and not just from specifically published or elucidated policies. Several firms have been successfully prosecuted and sued not because they specifically refused to show certain people houses in certain areas, but simply because their practice appeared to take some people to certain areas and others to different ones, apparently based on racial characteristics.

All brokerages should display the poster illustrated in Figure 3-1, which is a statement that the firm abides by fair housing laws and also briefly explains those laws. State license laws also contain provisions that make this kind of discrimination in selling practice a specific violation of license law.

Credit and Lending

A number of recent federal laws aim at preventing discrimination and unfair practices in the allocation of credit. While brokerage firms themselves are rarely lenders

**EQUAL HOUSING
OPPORTUNITY**

We Do Business in Accordance With the Federal Fair Housing Law

(Title VIII of the Civil Rights Act of 1968, as Amended by
the Housing and Community Development Act of 1974)

IT IS ILLEGAL TO DISCRIMINATE AGAINST ANY PERSON BECAUSE OF RACE, COLOR, RELIGION, SEX, OR NATIONAL ORIGIN

- In the sale or rental of housing or residential lots
- In advertising the sale or rental of housing
- In the financing of housing
- In the provision of real estate brokerage services

Blockbusting is also illegal

An aggrieved person may file a complaint of a housing discrimination act with the:

U.S. DEPARTMENT OF HOUSING AND URBAN DEVELOPMENT
Assistant Secretary for Fair Housing and Equal Opportunity
Washington, D.C. 20410

Figure 3-1. Fair Housing Poster

as well, they work closely with lenders in order to facilitate mortgage loans for buyers. Since borrowed money is so important to successful real estate sales, brokers should be aware of the regulations surrounding this industry. They then will be prepared to answer some of the questions prospective buyers are likely to ask with respect to the availability of loans.

Regulation Z   *Regulation Z* of the Federal Reserve System implements the Truth in Lending Act of 1969, which requires lenders to disclose certain facts and charges surrounding loans and lending policies. A particular requirement is that interest rates be stated as an *annual percentage rate* (usually abbreviated *APR*) in order to make comparison of terms from one loan to another easier and more standardized.

Brokers should always use the APR term and its methods of calculation in advertisements that state the interest rate available on loans to be used for the purchase of property, whether the loan is to be assumed or negotiated as a new loan. A significant consideration is that the APR should take into account variations from the loan's "face" rate of interest that may be caused by the use of loan discounts, points, or other charges by the lender that have the effect of materially altering the net rate of interest he receives.

The Equal Credit Opportunity Act of 1974 and later amendments prohibit certain practices that have the effect of favoring certain people for credit while denying it to others – discrimination purely on the basis of race, creed, color, national origin, sex, or marital status. The major effect of this legislation has been to restrict practices which made it difficult for women to obtain loans. The practice had been to pay scant attention to income provided by a working wife when calculating the ability of a couple to pay a loan (on the theory that the wife could become pregnant or for other reasons choose not to work in the future); similarly, the incomes of single or divorced women often make little impression because they might remarry or quit working. To a lesser extent, the elderly were discriminated against because they might die or retire before a loan was fully paid. The effect of the legislation was to make this kind of discrimination illegal.

Land Sales

Certain land sales are regulated by the Interstate Land Sales Full Disclosure Act of 1968, which was passed in response to complaints about selling practices associated largely with interstate sales of land in certain Sunbelt and resort areas. The law requires considerable disclosure to be provided to prospective buyers of land in the affected subdivisions. This information and the answers to a number of specific questions required by the U.S. Department of Housing and Urban Development (HUD) is contained in a handout called the property's *HUD Report*, which must be given to all prospects.

These regulations usually do not cover most subdivisions in which brokers may operate, unless a substantial number of sales are made to out-of-state buyers. If there is doubt as to whether or not compliance with these regulations is required, efforts should be made to ascertain whether it is or is not necessary. A broker involved in sales practices that violate this law can be prosecuted and held liable for damages.

RESPA

The Real Estate Settlement Procedures Act of 1974 (RESPA) was designed to assure that buyers received, at settlement, the proper information as to the disposition of monies involved and the charges assessed against them. A particular function of the law is to assure full disclosure of the itemized costs involved. Costs must be disclosed in advance, a uniform settlement statement must be used (see Chapter 9), and a booklet prepared by HUD must be given to all applicants for loans secured by real estate. There are some exceptions to this law, but its provisions generally apply to all normal sources of third-party loans except for totally private arrangements among friends, relatives, business associates, etc.

While the prime responsibility for abiding by the law rests with the lenders themselves, brokers whose service includes handling of closings and settlements should make certain that proper procedures are followed, even though they are not directly responsible for the actual lending of the money.

GENERAL CONTRACT LAW

The average American has a little familiarity with contracts; usually enough to inspire fear, but not understanding. A wide belief is that contracts must be filled with obscure, legalistic language and a lot of fine print, and that only someone with a lot of training can hope to be able to write them and understand and interpret them properly. This really is not so, because all the law requires of a contract is that it clearly state what it is supposed to. At the present time, there is an admirable trend under way to simplify the language in contracts, making it easier for them to be understood by laymen.

Real estate brokerage involves a great many contracts. Brokers and salespeople must be totally familiar and comfortable with all of them. They must be able to explain them to the people they work with and, in most states, take the responsibility for actually drawing up many contracts that will affect the actions and responsibilities of others. Therefore, it is imperative that real estate brokers and salespeople understand them. But one word of warning: a real estate agent is *not* an attorney! He may not give legal advice. In any discussion of contracts he should make a point of emphasizing that he is not practicing law and that any significant questions concerning contracts must be referred to a qualified attorney.

Nature of Contracts

A contract is an agreement between two or more parties, in which each promises to do, or is shown to have done, something benefitting the others. Benefit can take many forms; one is the payment of money, although contracts involving no money can be perfectly valid. Since each party must benefit, contracts must involve exchanges of benefits. Jones gives up something to Smith, in return for which Smith gives up something to Jones. One example is a purchase: A gives up money to B and B gives up the thing A is buying. A valid contract that doesn't involve money might be swapping a car for a lawn mower. Or, two people could agree that neither will build ugly structures where the other could see them.

While there are other requirements that must be met, the critical test of the validity of a contract is whether or not the parties can be shown to benefit from it. So, if you and I sign an agreement which says simply that I will give you my automobile next Tuesday, we don't have a contract because no benefit to *me* appears in it. However, if our agreement says that I will give you my car next Tuesday in return for some benefit to me from you (money, your car, etc.), then a contract could exist.

Enforcement of Contracts

A valid contract has the force of law among the parties to it. It is as if they had agreed to enact a law among themselves and promised to abide by it. However, when someone violates the provisions of a contract, the law will do nothing about the dispute until one of the injured parties petitions the courts to intervene. At that point, the law requires the affected parties to appear and present their arguments. Then the court (a judge or jury) makes a decision as to what is to be done, and by whom. All parties to contracts have the inherent right to request the court to render judgement if they feel that other parties to the agreement are not living up to it. (This description, of course, is somewhat simplified. Resolving a contract dispute in court often consumes a lot of time and expense. Many violated contracts never reach court because the offended parties do not want to bother with it.)

Generally, one who brings a contract to court has two remedies available. First, he can ask that the court require specific performance of the offending party. This means he wants the court to order the other party to live up to the agreement. By the time a contract dispute reaches court, it often is too late for mere performance to do any (or enough) good. In such a case, the injured party may seek damages, claiming that he had suffered a loss due to the other party's violation of the contract, and asking that the court order the violator to make the loss good.

Once the court has reached a decision, parties to the dispute are required by law to abide by it. If they do not, they are in contempt of court and can be fined or jailed; thus every contract carries the threat of court action against violation, backed up by potentially severe penalties.

REQUIREMENTS OF CONTRACTS

A contract cannot be considered by a court unless it is a proper and valid contract. Some kinds of contracts have additional requirements for validity, but all must show the following:

1. Mutual agreement
2. Consideration
3. Legally competent parties
4. A legal purpose
5. Legal form

Mutual Agreement

Mutual agreement (often referred to as *"offer and acceptance," "realty of consent," "mutual assent," "meeting of the minds,"* and similar phrases) means that all parties recognize that an offer has been made and has been accepted by the others. All agree to the nature of the requirements made of each. Generally, the parties will agree to do, or not to do, some thing or things in return for some kind of obligation from the others.

Provided that the other essentials of a contract are present, once an offer has been accepted, a contract exists. The parties' actions creating the contract must be intentional and deliberate. Generally their signatures to a written contract are evidence of this, provided that no fraud, misrepresentation, duress, or mistake occurred. However, many kinds of contracts need not be written; in such cases the testimony of the affected parties provides the evidence that an agreement exists.

Consideration

Consideration refers to the benefit received by the parties. It can take many forms; all that must be shown is that each party received something of use to him and that he was willing to oblige himself in some way in order to get it. Payment of money is always consideration, as is the transfer of ownership of anything that can be shown to have a market value. In addition, some transfers of rights are consideration also; as an example, a lease transfers rights to use property, but not ownership of the property. Some further examples are:

1. X pays $50,000 to Y. Y transfers ownership of his house to X.
2. X pays Y $300 per month. Y gives X the right to use an office for each month for which X pays.
3. X agrees not to hang his laundry outside where Y and Z can see it. Y agrees not to hang his laundry outside where X and Z can see it. Z agrees not to hang his laundry outside where X and Y can see it.
4. R agrees to try to find a buyer for S's house. S agrees to pay R a commission of 8% of the sale price if R finds a suitable buyer.
5. J agrees to pay K $80,000 in 30 days, at which time K will transfer ownership to J of a certain building now owned by K.
6. A transfers ownership of his house to B. B transfers to A the ownership of his parking lot, four albums of rare stamps, two sets of dishes, and a mongrel dog.
7. M transfers to his son (M, Jr.) the ownership of a building in return for the "love and affection" which M, Jr. has given to M in the past.
8. N lends Q $10,000. Q gives L the right to have Q's house sold if Q defaults on his debt to N.

All of these include legal consideration. Some involve money, but in 3 and 6, no money changes hands. In most, the consideration involves the parties performing some act; in 3, however, the parties agree not to do something. Examples 2, 3, and 8 include the exchange of rights; 4 includes the exchange of services, and the others involve the exchange of ownership of things.

All of the examples are real estate contracts. Example 2 is a *lease*, 3 is a *restrictive covenant*, 4 is a *listing*, 5 is a *contract of sale*; 8 is a *mortgage*, and 1, 6, and 7 are *deeds*.

Good and Valuable Consideration   In all except Example 7 we have *valuable consideration*, which is anything that would be of value to practically everyone and thus could be sold for money. Money itself is valuable, as is ownership of things, receipt of someone's services, receipt of various kinds of rights, and so on. However, things like friendship, love, and affection are not valuable consideration because their worth is subjective. You may set a very high value upon the love you receive from your spouse, but to most of the rest of us it is valueless since we don't even know him or her. Also, someone's affection is not a transferable benefit, in that it can't be sold. Friendship and love are of value to the one who receives them, and if he agrees to transfer benefit in return for them he can be held to his bargain. However, these are called *good consideration* to distinguish them from marketable value consideration.

The law does not require that *equal* consideration accrue to all parties, only that some consideration exist. There is only one exception: The courts will not enforce a contract requiring only the simultaneous exchange of different sums of money.

Competent Parties

Competent parties are persons whom the law allows to enter into contractual arrangements. Not all legal persons are human. Corporations, partnerships, trusts and some other organizations are legal persons, and can be parties to contract. One can contract to purchase an automobile from XYZ Auto Sales, Inc., although the firm is not a living being. Furthermore, not all people are competent to contract; some are legally unable to, and many others may do so only under carefully defined circumstances.

Nonhuman Parties   Usually the law requires each party to a contract to ascertain the other's legal competence. While the law places few restrictions upon the contracting ability of corporations and some other organizations, they may operate under self-imposed restrictions. A corporation's charter can permit or forbid it to enter certain kinds of contractual arrangements, and it may require that some or all of the permitted functions be carried out in certain ways. A person contracting with an organization must assure himself that it may engage in such a contract, and that the contract is executed and carried out consistent with its limitations and prescribed methods.

People   Among people, there are two important categories of incompetent parties, *infants* and *insane persons*, and several lesser ones, such as drunkards, convicts, and others.

INFANTS *Infants* (or *minors*) are people who have not yet attained the age of majority, which, in most states, is eighteen. While one may doubt that a hulking seventeen-year-old football star could be incompetent at anything, the law says he is. One who is immature, foolish, or naive in business judgement can be considered by the law to be quite capable of assuming responsibility for his actions providing he has attained the age of majority.

Contrary to what most people think, minors are *not* prohibited from contracting. No law is broken if a minor signs a contract. However, the minor can *void* the contract later on, if he wishes, while adult parties to the contract do not have that privilege. The minor may not void (or *disaffirm*) only part of the contract; he must abandon it entirely. If he agrees to buy property from an adult, he has the right to void the agreement anytime before it is carried out. The adult, however, must honor the contract unless and until the minor actually disaffirms it. The minor cannot, for example, disaffirm the part of the contract that specifies that he must pay for the property while at the same time requiring the adult to transfer it to him anyway; he must abandon the entire contract. Furthermore, if he disaffirms it after the adult party has provided him some benefit under it, he may have to pay for what he had already received by the time he decided to void the contract.

The whole idea behind legal incompetence is a matter of *protection.* We know that people can be too young to make binding commitments requiring mature judgement. Some age has to be chosen to represent the limit of protection, and that is why each state has an age of majority. Once a person attains this age he loses the protection of legal infancy, but he is given a reasonable time beyond the attainment of majority to decide whether or not he will disaffirm any contracts he had entered into as a minor.

INSANE PERSONS *Insane persons* are another important category of legal incompetence. Unlike infancy, insanity is a state that can come and go. One who is sane can become insane, and one who is insane can be cured and become sane again. Also, a person under severe stress or other temporary disturbance can become so disoriented that the law may extend the protection of incompetence to him during the episode.

Legal protection of an insane person takes two forms. If he has had a guardian appointed by the court, then all "contracts" he enters into are *void*. He has no capacity to contract at all. If he has no guardian, his contracts usually are voidable, like those of minors. He has the choice to require that his bargains with others be carried out or to disaffirm them.

OTHER INCOMPETENCY Certain other forms of incapacity earn one the legal protection of incompetency. Contracts made by a person who is severely intoxicated with alcohol or is under the dominating influence of drugs known to affect judgement might later be considered voidable. Felon prisoners usually have no right to contract; this situation is described by the rather grim term of *civilly dead*. Usually when the sentence has been served, and sometimes at the time parole is secured, most rights are restored.

Necessaries Not all contracts by incompetents are voidable; generally courts will enforce contracts for *necessaries*, which are things such as food, clothing, shelter, and sometimes others such as contracts for employment or education. Here again the law extends protection, acknowledging that in today's world some contracts are so important that they take precedence over other protection. A known incompetent may be at a serious disadvantage if his personal circumstances *require* him to contract, so the law allows some incompetents what amounts to a limited competency. For things that are necessary to them, they are allowed to create binding contracts that they cannot disaffirm and that a court can enforce against them. This gives other competent parties the protection *they* seek in any contractual arrangement, and removes any reluctance they may have to deal with an incompetent.

Lawful Purpose

A contract requiring any of its parties to violate the law is usually void. However, if a contract's basic purpose can be saved, a court will uphold the contract but strike out that part requiring an illegal act. For example, the Federal Open Housing Act of 1968 declared illegal certain deed covenants that required some home buyers to agree that they would resell only to people of particular racial or cultural backgrounds. Many deeds to homes contained such clauses, but their prohibition had no effect upon the main purpose of the deeds, which was to transfer title to realty in return for consideration. However, if someone had created a special separate contract only for the purpose of restricting the racial or cultural background or purchasers of certain real estate, then that entire contract would have been voided by the enactment of the law. If this kind of agreement came into being after the law was passed, then it would be void from the beginning and would *never* be a contract.

Legal Form

Some contracts are required to follow a certain form or be drawn in a certain manner. For example, deeds and contracts of sale require that legal descriptions of the property be included; without them they are invalid. However, much of the wordy, archaic language that frequently appears in contracts is not required by any law and appears only by tradition.

Statute of Frauds   For most real estate contracts, there is one critical requirement with respect to form. In most states, all real estate contracts (except leases of one year or less) *must be written*. Each state has a law called the Statute of Frauds, which requires that all contracts of certain types be written if legal enforcement is to be possible. Included are all contracts in which land or an interest in land is sold and contracts that cannot be performed within one year.

A listing contract is a contract of *employment*, which is a category not usually covered by the Statute of Frauds. However, many states, in their real estate licensing laws, require or imply that listings must be in writing.

The definition of "land or an interest in land" is very specific and quite broad. It includes future interests, so in addition to deeds, contracts of sale must be written. It includes partial interests, so mortgages must be written. It includes improvements to land

and all attachments to it, so contracts involving purchase of buildings or growing plants must be written, even if the actual land beneath is not part of the transaction. However, once an attachment to land is severed from it (such as trees being cut down or crops being reaped) it becomes personal property and is no longer subject to that part of the Statute of Frauds covering realty. This law usually covers much more than just realty contracts, so it is quite possible that many other non-realty contracts can also be required by law to be written.

DURESS, MISREPRESENTATION, AND FRAUD

All parties to a valid contract must have entered into it willingly and without having been misled about significant matters. Thus, a person who points a gun at someone else to force him to sign a contract cannot expect much sympathy from the courts. Nor could he if he had (deliberately or unintentionally) misled others so that they agreed to contracts based on false information. The former situation is *duress*; the latter is either *misrepresentation* or *fraud*.

Duress

Duress can take many forms. When circumstances force someone to do something against his will he could say duress exists, but the law does not always see it that way. Duress caused by one who benefits under the contract usually will be recognized by the court; this would include forcing someone's assent by threatening him illegally. If duress is caused by one's own actions, the court is reluctant to recognize it. If you buy a new house and thereby become desperate to sell your own home, that is pretty much your own fault. If you create your own "duress," you usually have to suffer with it.

Misrepresentation and Fraud

Misrepresentation is loosely defined as unintentional giving of false information, whereas fraud is *deliberate*. There is another difference, too: fraud is a *crime* as well as a civil wrong. A victim of either fraud or misrepresentation is entitled to compensation for what he was misled into losing. Fraud victims may also receive *punitive* damages, which is a form of extra payment required of the culprit, as a kind of punishment. Finally, the perpetrator of a fraud may be prosecuted in criminal court and may end up being convicted, fined, and/or imprisoned.

Proving Misrepresentation or Fraud A victim must prove three things to show that misrepresentation or fraud exists: (a) that the incorrect information was relevant to the contract he is disputing – that is, it was *material*; (b) that it was *reasonable to rely* upon this false information; and (c) that this *reliance led him to suffer some loss* as a result.

Some Information Must Be Divulged   For some kinds of contracts, the law requires that certain information be provided by at least some of the parties. If it is not, then misrepresentation or fraud may exist. For example, most licensing laws require that brokers inform other parties if they are acting as principals in the contract as well as agents. Also, most states require a broker to disclose which party he is acting for, especially if more than one party to a transaction is paying him a commission.

DISCHARGE AND BREACH OF CONTRACT

Contractual arrangements can be terminated in two general ways. *Discharge* of a contract occurs when no one is required to perform under it any longer. *Breach of contract* occurs when one party makes performance impossible, even when other parties are willing, by preventing discharge of the contract in some way.

Discharge

Most often discharge occurs by *performance: this* means that everyone has done what was promised, and nothing more is required of anyone. Other forms of discharge involve agreement to terminate a contract, for one reason or another, before it would have been discharged by performance. Sometimes the parties may decide to terminate one agreement by substituting another one for it. Discharge can also occur when the parties simply agree to abandon the contract without substituting anyone or any other for it. It is advisable that any agreement discharging a contract for reasons other than performance or limitation be in writing. Under some situations (particularly when some, but not all parties have performed or begun to perform under the contract), an agreement discharging an existing contract *must* be in writing.

Statute of Limitations   The law limits the time in which a contracting party may take a dispute to court for settlement. This law is the *Statute of Limitations,* and it varies from state to state not only in the length of time allowed, but also with respect to types of contracts, which are allowed various lengths of time for challenge. Once the time limit has expired, a dispute will not be heard in court unless it can be shown that extraordinary circumstances prevented a more timely filing. Therefore, once the time limit has expired, a contract can be said to have been discharged, since legal remedy is no longer available.

Breach

Breach occurs when a party violates a contract's provisions. Often this action can be considered serious enough to terminate the contract by making it impossible, or very disadvantageous, for the other parties to continue the arrangement. The injured parties must seek remedy from the courts, unless they and the violating party or parties can come to some agreement discharging the contract. If breach is successfully proved, the injured parties are entitled to a judgement for damages or for specific performance. A judgement is a ruling by the court that the offending party must perform in some way, or be in contempt of court.

There are several ways of proving breach. Failing to perform completely as specified in a contract is breach; so is the declaration by the offending party that he does not intend to fulfill his obligations under the contract. It is also a breach if a party makes it impossible, by his actions, for one or more of the other parties to continue to perform under the contract; one who has breached a contract cannot have that agreement held good against other parties.

Following are some common forms of breach that occur in real estate contracts that brokers often deal with.

LISTING CONTRACTS: *Breach by broker* includes (a) failing to advertise and market the property as specified; (b) misrepresenting the buyer's capacity to perform; and (c) subverting the agency responsibility by acting to the benefit of buyer against the principal's interest. *Breach by principal* includes (a) failing to pay a commission earned by the broker; (b) failing to allow the broker to market, show, and sell the property as specified; and (c) misrepresenting pertinent facts about the property to the broker.

SALE CONTRACTS: *Breach by seller* includes (a) failure to provide the deed when the buyer has performed and tendered payment as specified in the contract; and (b) failure to perform to other specifications of the contract (i.e., provide termite bond, abstract, etc.). *Breach by buyer* includes (a) failure to conclude the transaction when the seller performs and tenders deed; and (b) failure to perform under other specifications (i.e., make good faith efforts to acquire financing, etc.).

Injustice

The courts will not enforce a contract if it appears that by doing so it will aid an obvious injustice. This does not mean that someone can get out of a bad bargain on this basis, but only that the court will not enforce the contract if, in its judgement, there is a gross injustice involved. As an example, if Jones freely agrees to buy Smith's property for $50,000 and later discovers that it is worth only $40,000, he cannot claim injustice if he cannot show that Smith or his agent misled him into paying the higher price. Suppose, however, that Green and Brown orally agree that Green will buy land from Brown. After paying for the land, Green builds a house on it. At that point Brown goes to court saying that since the purchase agreement was oral and not written it has no validity, and Green must vacate, thus allowing Brown to take over the house and land at no cost to him. Here the court will award title to Green even though no written sale agreement exists and no written deed exists. First, there is a principle of law that recognizes such transactions when the buyer "substantially improves" the property. Second, if Brown had engineered the whole scheme specifically in order to take advantage of Green, the court would be legalizing fraud by recognizing Brown's continued claim to the title.

Outside Circumstances

Contracts can be terminated by events outside the specific terms of the agreement. New legislation may invalidate all or part of a contract. The death of a party can void some contracts; so can illness or injury to the point that the party affected cannot properly discharge his obligations. If the subject matter of the contract is destroyed (such as a house burning down while it is listed with a broker for sale) the contract usually is terminated. Finally, under the doctrine of *realty of consent,* a contract that is the result of a genuine mistake can be void. For example, a seller has two properties for sale, one on 21st Street and the other on 31st Street. A buyer makes an offer on one but the seller thinks he is accepting an offer on the other. There is no contract because, in actuality, the parties have not agreed to the same thing. Regardless of what may be written down and signed, no genuine meeting of the minds has occurred, and so no contract exists.

DISCLOSURE BY SELLER

During the 1980's a trend developed among the states to require sellers to make certain *disclosures* with respect to the property for sale. The impetus for such laws came from an alliance of consumer advocacy groups and the real estate brokerage business itself. Consumer advocates were interested in protecting buyers from possible hidden problems. The real estate business was interested in protecting licensees. Since licensees are agents of the seller, they can be held liable for hidden problems just as a seller can. A growing volume of successful litigation against brokers and salespeople in this regard created the motivation within the brokerage industry to require seller disclosure. As this is being written, six states (California, Kentucky, Maine, New Hampshire, Virginia and Wisconsin) require sellers to complete a disclosure form; about half the remaining states are likely to consider such legislation in the near future. Licensees in all states must know their state's law in this regard.

These disclosure requirements modify the traditional principle of *caveat emptor*: "let the buyer beware." The only disclosure requirement placed on the seller is to notify buyers of "dangerous conditions." What a dangerous condition may or may not be is not well-defined, and often has to be decided on a case by case basis in the courts. The *caveat emptor* principle makes it the buyer's responsibility to find out anything he/she wants to know about a property being considered for purchase. Although the seller isn't required to disclose much, once the buyer asks about something, the seller must give truthful answers. To do otherwise is fraud or misrepresentation.

Disclosure laws vary among the states that have them. Usually they require that a certain specified form be filled out by the seller. This form requires that certain possibly "negative" characteristics of the property be disclosed. These can include such things as presence of hazardous materials (lead-based paint, asbestos, aluminum wiring, etc.), known major defects in construction, equipment, etc., and local hazards such as termites, vulnerability to severe weather, etc.

Seller disclosure is discussed further in Chapter 12.

DISCLOSURE BY BROKER

A thorny issue always has been the public's lack of awareness of the broker's agency relationship with the seller; prospective buyers usually assume that an agent "working" with them also represents their interests. During the late 1980's many states enacted laws requiring brokers and salespeople to disclose to buying prospects that they represent only the seller, and that the buyer, in effect, has no agent. These laws vary from state to state. Many states require a written disclosure, others do not. Some require disclosure as soon as the first contact between buying prospect and agent, others require it only if and when the prospect actually makes an offer.

Late in 1992, in an unusual alliance, the National Association of REALTORS® and the Consumer Federation of America produced a "model" disclosure and began a campaign to have its features adopted by all states. Briefly, the NAR/CFA criteria are that a state-prescribed *written disclosure form* should be used, and that it should be signed by agent and buyer at the first meaningful contact between them. NAR and CFA also advocate that the disclosure form be concise and easy to understand

Texas adopted a disclosure form in 1988 which closely matches these guidelines. It fits on one sheet of paper, and is printed in large type. It advises the buyer that all agents represent the seller, to whom their loyalty is due. It also spells out what the agent legally *may* do for the buyer (provide information, show properties, assist in preparing an offer and obtaining financing, etc.) and what the agent *must* do: treat buyers honestly and fairly, present written offers promptly, disclose material facts that they know about, and offer property without regard to race, creed, sex, religion, etc. The form also advises that buyers may hire brokers to represent them.

When such a form is used, agent and buyer should sign two copies: the agent keeps one, and the buyer keeps the other.

DISCUSSION QUESTIONS AND PROJECTS

1. If a contract is breached, what are the remedies the injured party should seek? Does it make sense to take every dispute to court? Why or why not?

2. What should a salesperson do to make sure that all parties to contracts he negotiates are competent?

3. Give three examples of misrepresentation or fraud in a real estate transaction. How could they have been avoided?

4. Find out exactly what contracts in your state are required by its Statute of Frauds (or similar legislation) to be in writing. Given this information, can you think of any

situations in which verbal contracts would be enforceable in your state in situations a real estate brokerage might encounter?

5. Using one of the contract forms shown on pages 130 and 154-55 of this text, analyze it to make sure that all the required parts of an enforceable contract are present.

6. Does there appear to be evidence in your area that "fair housing" has worked? Are some areas predominantly white and others mostly black? If so, is this due to prejudice or other factors? If other factors are important, what are they?

A Case Study

INCOMPETENCY

Broker Marion C. showed a lovely new home to prospect Janis P. Janis decided that she wanted to buy it, and offered $125,000 for it. The builder accepted the offer, and Janis's earnest money check for $25,000 was deposited. Five days later, Janis drove up in her new Cadillac and discussed some alterations she wanted to have done. The builder agreed to do them, but asked that $20,000 of the earnest money be paid to him to provide the funds he needed to make the changes. This was agreeable to Janis, who signed an agreement instructing Broker C. to release $20,000 of her deposit to the builder and acknowledging that if she defaulted on the deal, her entire earnest money deposit would be forfeited. Broker C. and the builder further agreed, in a separate contract, that if Janis defaulted, Broker C. would keep the remaining $5,000 of the deposit, and would relist the property for sale.

The work began immediately, and for several days Janis would appear at the construction site to observe the work. At all times she was expensively dressed. One day she said that she had to return to her home in South Carolina to make final arrangements to move into her new home.

Ten days after she left, her earnest money check, which had been drawn on a small bank in the same state where she bought her new home, was returned to Broker C. for insufficient funds. The broker called the bank. He was told that they were sorry that it had taken so long to return the check, but that they had been a bit shorthanded. Further investigation by Broker C. revealed that in South Carolina Janis had been undergoing treatment for severe psychosis and a year before had been declared legally incompetent by the courts. When she had returned there, her family had committed her to a mental hospital for treatment.

Broker C. then contacted the builder to get back the $20,000. Legally, the earnest money had been the builder's all along, and Broker C. was only holding it in trust; therefore, he was liable to make good the bad check. However, the building business was poor, and he was in the process of filing bankruptcy. The best Broker C. could do was to secure a lien on the unsold property; however, her lien was low in priority and no payment ever was made.

Naturally, she was upset. By abiding scrupulously by the law (by handling trust monies as instructed by the people it belonged to) she had lost $20,000. As soon as the $25,000 check was returned, she had to make good the deficiency in her trust account; $5000 of the deficiency was due to her anyway, so her net loss was $20,000. She complained to the real estate commission that the law required her, in effect, to take the risk that a deposited check would clear. They were sympathetic but could say only they would look into the matter, and possibly suggest revisions in the law that would lessen brokers' risks in the future.

Marion C. is philosophical about the experience. "If I tried to check the competency of everyone I do business with, I wouldn't have time for anything else. If you run a business you take some chances, and things like this will happen. I'm having my lawyers look into the possibility of rewriting my contracts so I don't have to pay money out of my trust account until checks have cleared, but we have to make sure that it's legal for me to do that."

"Luck runs good and bad. I lost a lot on this deal, but I've had other deals that were so smooth that I've made large commissions with what seems like only a few hours work. I suppose it all evens out."

REFERENCES

FISHER, FREDERICK J., *Broker Beware: Selling Real Estate Within the Law*. Reston, VA: Reston Publishing Company, Inc., 1981.

KRATOVIL, ROBERT, AND RAYMOND J. WERNER, *Real Estate Law*. Englewood Cliffs, NJ: Prentice-Hall, Inc. This is the recognized classic in its field; periodically updated in new editions.

FOUR

BROKERAGE MANAGEMENT CONCEPTS

BUSINESS FUNCTIONS

Compare a business organization to the human body. Both are designed to perform certain functions. The body is controlled by the brain and to a lesser extent by the nervous system; its other parts perform their functions and keep it alive. The vital organs keep the body healthy and consume the food and oxygen it needs, process them, and dispose of the unusable parts. The senses relate to its environment and take account of its surroundings so that it may react to them. The other body parts (limbs, parts of the brain) perform its functions, including physical activities such as walking, hitting a baseball, and writing a letter, or mental activities such as reading and analyzing material, composing music, and speaking. All of the parts operate together smoothly and in excellent coordination, so long as the body is kept healthy and properly stimulated.

Now consider the business organization; the analogy with the body is an apt one. *Management* is the brain of the organization; it directs and motivates the organization to fulfill the objectives it has set. *Lines of communication* link management with *line* and *support* functions, just as the nervous system links the brain and the rest of the body.

The line functions are those parts of the organization that actually perform the actions which are needed for achievement of its objectives. In real estate brokerage these are the activities of the sales force in securing listings and making sales. Support functions are those necessary to keep the business operating smoothly. These include secretarial services, receptionists, data processing, record-keeping, etc. Specialized support functions also may be necessary. These can include legal counsel, accounting assistance, and similar professional assistance that can be contracted on a part time, as-needed basis from outside the firm, although larger brokerages often will have such specialists employed full time in their support staffs.

This doesn't mean that everyone in a firm should be a specialist. Especially in smaller firms, individual personnel may perform a variety of these functions. In a small brokerage firm, the broker-owner may perform all of the management functions as well as being an active member of the sales staff performing. Sales personnel may perform support functions by typing their own contracts, doing their own filing, or doing floor duty that includes answering telephones and receiving visitors. Nonetheless, the differences among the functions of the organization need to be distinguished, even though we realize that they may not necessarily be performed exclusively by certain members of the firm.

Organization

The human body is put together in a certain way, so as to be as efficient as possible in the total performance of its functions, while at the same time keeping itself alive and healthy. Similarly, a business must be organized not only to achieve its objectives, but also to remain a viable, surviving entity. When one's body performs poorly, it becomes ill or infirm. Sometimes it may perform so badly that it dies. When a business performs poorly it also can become "sick," and if the condition lingers and worsens, the firm can "die" by going bankrupt or by being closed down and abandoned.

The purpose of organization is to arrange the business functions so that personnel, and the firm, can perform most efficiently. Organization also allows information to be gathered and processed so that the firm, and its objectives, can be altered and rearranged to reflect changing conditions. Finally, organization allows the management function to direct the business properly. The organizational pattern defines the functions that are to be performed and arranges them so that they complement one another by establishing lines of communication and control. *Control* is administered by management and *communicated* through the organization to line and service personnel. It serves the dual purpose of making the firm's objectives known throughout the system, while at the same time *directing* the firm's activities so that the objectives may be accomplished.

Management

The purpose of management is to direct and control the organization. *Managerial talent* is the ability to accomplish this effectively. Managerial talent is not the same as *technical talent*, which is the ability to perform the actual line and support functions. Management personnel need managerial skills, not technical skills, because they must direct and control and need not actually perform technically. Of course in small organizations the same person may do both, and usually it is useful that a managerial person have some knowledge of technical activity, but it is not always critical. Managerial ability, however, is essential. If it is missing, the organization is likely to fail since only luck and chance can keep it going, and these cannot be trusted to be favorable for very long.

While some business failures can be attributed to bad luck or other outside influences, most are the direct result of poor management. Management makes the decisions: it controls the firm and directs the activities of the line and support personnel. Even if these people are highly skilled and competent technically, they cannot keep the firm going indefinitely if poor management is telling them to do the wrong things. Good and competent management, on the other hand, can keep a business going. It can replace poorly functioning line and support personnel, and to see to it that remaining personnel have the training and motivation to do their work properly.

Line Functions

In a real estate brokerage, line personnel are the *sales force*. These are the people who secure the firm's listings and effect its sales. In larger or specialized firms, these personnel may also list rentals, negotiate leases, and perform similar functions. In essence, the line functions of the brokerage are those that result directly in revenue; that is, they are the services the firm provides to the outside world and for which it is paid.

The technical talent that the sales force needs is the ability to convince sellers and landlords to list their properties with the brokerage firm, and the ability to achieve the results (sales and leases) desired by these customers. Management must provide the sales force with direction, support, and incentive. Direction comes in the form of training, job analysis and description, and management policy. Management supports the sales force by providing work space, contract forms, resolution of conflicts, and the assistance of support personnel. Incentive includes pay as well as recognition and other acknowledgment of skill and ability.

Support Functions

Support personnel are secretaries, receptionists, and other employees who are not directly involved in the sales process. Additional support functions may be performed by people who are contracted by the firm but are not actually a regular part of its organization. For example, all real estate brokerages ought to have at least one competent contract attorney available for consultation, even if it means paying a retainer fee. Accounting assistance and other specialized legal assistance also should be available.

The particular tasks and functions of the support staff are defined by management, and these people report to management unless they have been specifically assigned to the sales staff. For example, a managing broker will need secretarial assistance; he may also hire secretarial help that he specifically directs is to be available to the sales staff. However, the sales staff will rarely hire their own help, relying upon management to provide it for them if it is to be available at all.

Distribution of Functions in the Real Estate Brokerage

We can be very specific about the nature of the various functions within a business, and we can categorize them into management, line, and support functions. However, we must realize that in many organizations we can't be so specific about the *people* themselves. People can and do perform several functions. Generally, though, the larger the firm, the more specialized will be the functions of each individual. In contrast, in the smallest real estate brokerage (one broker-owner with no sales or support staff) we find one person performing all the functions.

In small firms (say fewer than ten members) we find a fairly distinct differentiation between management and the other members, but it is less clear with respect to line and support activity. The broker-owner performs the necessary management functions, although even these may be fairly limited. Such a firm is so small that it may not be able to afford to hire full-time support staff. Sales staff, then, may have to perform support functions. They may do their own filing, type their own contract forms, type their own letters, place their own ads, etc. The broker-owner of the small firm probably does a lot of sales staff work as well. If secretarial or other support staff are hired, their main responsibility will be to the broker-owner, and they will be available to the sales force only if they have spare time.

Larger firms can be more specific in their definition of duties. They can afford to hire a support staff, freeing the sales force to concentrate upon their primary duties. Management will do relatively little sales work because the demands of managing a large organization will require a full time commitment if the firm is to succeed and survive.

Individual staff members in the large brokerage firm are more likely to have the opportunity to specialize in their specific areas of work, and support staff will have more rigidly defined responsibilities.

ORGANIZATION OF BROKERAGE FIRMS

Any group of people assembled to perform some specific group purpose requires *organization* as well as management. If management is defined as the exercise of control over a group of people, then organization can be considered to be the *structure of relationships* that allows this control to be communicated and exercised within the group. It is the organizational pattern that defines various jobs to be performed and determines the controls over each position.

Organization Patterns

Nearly all organizations are *hierarchical*. This means that control is communicated and exercised down a pattern of succeeding layers of operation. Each layer usually is composed of a larger number of people or positions than the one above; each reports to and is supervised by a member of the group immediately above it. If all this sounds very authoritarian and rigid, it usually is. While our American society is democratic, a business must be operated with authority and control.

Organizational patterns usually can be shown graphically by using *organization charts*; these are the pyramid-shaped drawings (Figures 4-1, and 4-2 on page 64) showing the organizational lines of communication and control. At the top of the pyramid will be one person, usually the President, or principal broker. This individual is the one charged with the ultimate responsibility for whatever goes on in the firm. In a small firm, he/she may indeed be the only person with any executive responsibility.

As an organization grows, it becomes more and more difficult, and ultimately impossible, for one person to be aware of, and in charge of, everything of importance that is going on. At this point, some of the direct responsibility must be *delegated* to *subordinates*. These subordinate managers handle the day-to-day management of the particular parts of the firm they have been given responsibility for. They report to the top person and relay to their own subordinates the decisions that the top level makes. A well-established rule of management science is that a given individual cannot adequately supervise more than a certain number of subordinates; the number varies according to the capabilities of the person involved and the kind of work overseen. However, most authorities agree that this number is surprisingly small, if a manager is to supervise with greatest efficiency and productivity. In most typical business environments this number can be as few as three or four and rarely is much more than ten.

Management and Sales Activity

In the real estate business, a sales manager or owner-broker usually can supervise a relatively large number of sales personnel, who act fairly independently in their functions and so are required to do a lot of self-supervision. Nonetheless, a broker-owner who also does a considerable amount of sales work must realize that his capacity for supervision is very limited, particularly since he will not be available to his sales force for his consultation or assistance during the times that he is conducting his own business away from the office. The same would apply to a sales manager who is an active sales-person as well; the capacity to direct and control will be limited to the free time found between appointments and other work.

When a brokerage firm becomes large enough to need a sales manager, a logical choice for the position usually is a member of the existing sales force. The broker-owner must understand that to have any useful effect, a sales manager must be freed from some sales duties. If the new manager has to do just as much selling as before to maintain his income, then he cannot manage adequately. This means that management personnel have to be paid directly for the duties they perform. Often a sales manager will receive an *override* of a small part of the commissions the supervised sales staff brings in. Some-times the firm prefers to pay a straight salary. However it is done, the firm must understand that management isn't free. If it is needed, it also has to be paid for.

Brokerage Organization

Figures 4-1 and 4-2 show typical organizational charts for small and medium-sized real estate brokerage firms. These patterns, of course, are not the only ones that could apply to a given real estate firm, but they provide useful examples for discussion.

Small Firm   The organization of the small brokerage is very simple. The broker-owner is the boss, and the sales force reports to him. We have also given him a secretary-receptionist who might not be there in very small firms. While charts such as these are supposed to clarify and explain relationships within firms, this chart doesn't tell us much. This is because the organization is so simple that there just isn't much to tell.

Large Firm   Figure 4-2 shows the more complex organization of a large residential brokerage firm. Here we have a president of the firm to whom subordinate managers and a personal secretary report directly. The sales manager is in charge of the sales force, and the mortgage division manager is in charge of the firm's mortgage brokerage business. Both will have large numbers of people working directly under them. The accountant and the closing manager head smaller divisions; they even may be divisions composed of themselves and no one else at all.

The sales and mortgage divisions of the firm are line functions; the rest are support functions. Note that a secretarial staff and receptionist are included. They are not part of any one division but are available to all. The receptionist, especially, will report directly to everyone, although the nature of the job limits this to delivering messages and putting through calls.

In this organization there are two levels of management, the president and the four managers who report to him. The division of management authority in the second level is an illustration of *departmentalization*. Each manager is responsible for an important part of the firm's activities, but not for all. In a small firm, all these functions may be handled by a single broker-owner. In the large firm, these responsibilities are too great for one

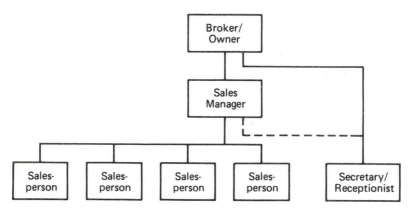

Figure 4-1. Organization of a Small Brokerage

Figure 4-2. Organization of a Large Residential Brokerage

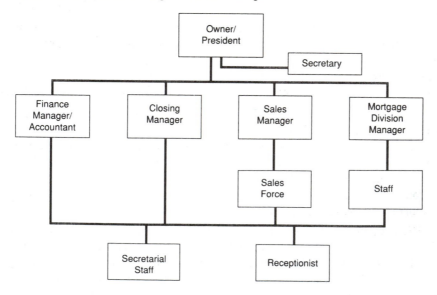

person, so the top manager delegates some or all of them to subordinates. These subordinate managers handle the firm's day-to-day activities, but matters of policy and other important decisions are made or approved by the president.

Different firms will organize in different ways; the illustrations given here are just examples. Some jobs may be divided among two or more managers, and others may be combined under one person. Some also may be held by the president. If the sales force is very large, a sales manager may have one or more assistant sales managers, each in charge of a certain portion of the sales force.

At each level, the people filling the slots report to the person above them, but not always to each other. This doesn't mean that they keep to themselves or don't cooperate or interact. However, they have no specific *authority* over one another. If one feels that the other ought to be doing something, he does not have the direct authority to require such action, but has to convince a higher level of management (the president) that it is necessary.

In a large firm, there is a certain organizational "insulation" between the top person and the people who actually perform the line functions. They are separated by one or more layers of management, and there may be little or no direct communication between top management and the personnel several layers down. This has advantages and disadvantages. Top management's time is freed for more important activities of directing and planning with respect to the entire organization. However, "intimacy" is lost because top management is estranged from the line activity people who actually carry out the firm's functions and achieve its goals. Ideally, however, the organization has both, in that the middle management people (sales manager, etc.) are able to perform the function of motivating the sales staff to do the work required while at the same time giving upper management an accurate picture of their needs and personal objectives.

Communication in the Organization

While direction and control should be exercised from the top down in an organization, communication must flow *both* ways. Management cannot make reasonable and realistic decisions without a full awareness of the abilities, desires, and mood of subordinate personnel. All kinds of information is communicated by subordinates to their managers. Some of it can be dealt with by the manager, especially in the area of day-to-day problem solving. But all the information must be sifted and considered in order to determine what should be communicated to higher levels, what can be ignored, and what should be handled at the manager's own level.

A lot of information won't be communicated at all unless it is asked for specifically. Personnel may be willing to take up a superior's time with information that is critical, but usually won't for things that don't seem so significant. However, this "unimportant" information often is very useful to managers. Therefore, an essential qualification of a good manager is the ability to identify all the information needed from his subordinates, and then to encourage them to pass it on. Also, by encouraging communication they may receive useful information they might not have thought to ask for specifically.

THE MANAGEMENT FUNCTION

The function of management can be described in a very few words: *plan, organize, activate, control*. Planning provides the goals and objectives. Organization provides the structure of relationships and activities needed to accomplish the goals. Activation is the actual process of getting the performance needed from the members of the organization. Control leads to achieving the desired results of the entire activity.

Management requires three essential inputs: *information, resources*, and *money*. Information gives the manager the knowledge needed to perform functions realistically. Resources are what the organization uses to accomplish things. These include *human resources* (the talents and abilities of the people available to the firm) and *physical resources* (paper, pencils, offices and equipment, cars, buildings, etc.). Money is the lubricant that makes it all work, that makes it possible to gather the information and acquire the necessary resources.

The preceding paragraphs make it look pretty simple, but it is not. We cannot expect, in today's world, that a manager always can plan, acquire information and resources, organize them, activate them, and then find that they operate smoothly and indefinitely like some efficient machine. Conditions change all the time, and since the prime resource in a brokerage firm is the human one, we cannot expect consistency day in and day out from the people involved. Management is an ongoing process, and the need for it never diminishes. Some organizations appear to work like well-oiled machines, but this is deceiving: the most efficiently run firms are those in which the management talent is the best and works the hardest.

Planning

Planning determines the firm's *goals and objectives*, as well as some of the *continuing development* that is needed to achieve them. *General goals* might be to provide the best and most ethical brokerage service available. *Specific objectives* could be to sell so many dollars worth of real estate next year, to show a certain level of profit, to expand to a certain size, and so on. General goals and objectives can be very long term, rather like the ideals that must be lived up to continuously. Specific goals and objectives often change. They are meant to be achieved within a shorter time, and good management also will alter them over time as conditions dictate. It is essential that all goals be realistic ones. It makes no sense at all for a small firm composed of a single full-time broker and a couple of part-time salespeople to set a goal of, say, $10 million of sales and listings in the next year when few firms several times as large can accomplish such a feat. Therefore the manager must have the information at hand to determine what is reasonable or not.

General goals are not a great problem, since they tend to be vague to begin with. For example, it is desirable to set a goal of offering ethical and appreciated service, but it is difficult to measure this sort of accomplishment. This kind of goal is a reasonable one. Its effect upon the firm would be to generate interest in the performance of existing sales force members, and to set high standards for the employment of new salespeople. Specific goals require more direct action. "We have to close this transaction within ten days or the buyer will back out." "We at ABC Realty want to generate more business than XYZ Realty."

Information

Required information will concern factors both inside and outside the firm. Outside conditions such as the current state of the real estate market, the projected state of the local economy, and the firm's competitive situation are obvious examples. They set realistic limits of what the firm can expect to do within its market environment. From this information the many goals can be formulated. Opportunities for expansion, taking advantage of poor performance by competitors, and opportunities provided by an expanding economy can be identified. At this point, however, only *potential* has been noted; this is the maximum accomplishment that outside conditions may be expected to make available to an individual firm.

Goals and objectives can't stand alone. They should be accompanied by management's plans for achieving them. Information from inside the firm tells management how goals relate to the firm's own resources, talents, and abilities. Given proper assembly and use of information, and sensible analysis of the resources available, useful goals and objectives can be set. Analysis of the company's own resources probably will reveal weak points, and plans can be made to overcome them. Other plans might be to achieve certain sales levels or other overall goals within a certain time. Actual action plans can be relatively modest or quite sweeping, depending upon the needs. The more sweeping they are, and the more they dictate fundamental changes, the more carefully they should be analyzed and formulated before they become company policy.

Necessary action has to be outlined and anticipated, and steps should be formulated and taken to get them under way. Obviously, these actions should be within the capacity of the firm to perform them; once again analysis of the firm's resources comes into play. Goals that are outside the ability of the firm to achieve are unreasonable, no matter how attractive they may be.

Activation: The Job Description

Achieving objectives requires *action*. Action, to be efficient, must occur in a proper organizational framework so that all the necessary activity can be properly related and integrated. The specific *forms* of action themselves must be described so that those responsible for them will know what to do. Finally, management must exercise the proper control to see to it that everyone is doing what they are supposed to do.

Activation requires definition and description of the jobs which must be done to accomplish goals. Most firms find *job descriptions* a valuable tool in this process, since they can provide documented illustrations of the duties and responsibilities of particular positions. Unfortunately, they often are vague and almost impossible to pin down, full of words like "coordinate," "supervise," "administer," and other language that is easy to use in a meaningless fashion. For example, someone hired to "coordinate supervisory administration of department functions" could end up doing practically anything, and may have no real idea of exactly what to do until someone explains it in English. Figure 4-3 shows a sample job description for a sales manager in a residential brokerage firm.

Job descriptions serve two functions. They tell each person what he is supposed to be doing, and they tell management who is supposed to be doing what. Job descriptions should be specific, to the point, and above all understandable. They should describe the following: (a) exactly what work is to be done, (b) whom the person occupying the job should report to, (c) who reports to the person occupying the job, (d) specific skills and qualifications necessary, and (e) if necessary, what the person occupying the job is *not* supposed to do. It's good practice to include job descriptions in employment contracts.

Job descriptions are useful guides to employees; they are even more so to management as planning and control tools. As the organization develops, good management can remain aware of the tasks to be performed and the best way to allocate them within the structure of the firm. These tasks are logically and reasonably collected into specific jobs which are defined by their job descriptions. The job descriptions then can be used as tools for finding the right personnel to fit each position. Prospective employees can examine them to find if they represent the kind of work desired, while the descriptions will be used by management as the criteria for hiring and assignment decisions.

Control

Control is the management function that involves *supervision* of assigned activity to assure that it is being done properly and is consistent with the established objectives. This is the exercise of *authority* to *make decisions* and to *enforce* them. Control is *not* meddling! It requires management that is capable of honest evaluation of performance and has the ability to leave alone someone whose performance is satisfactory. Control is so fundamental a factor of management that it is discussed in its various forms throughout this text, so specific analysis will not be provided here. As the various aspects of the brokerage business are considered in later pages, the applicable control techniques and objectives will be incorporated into the discussion.

SALES PERSONNEL

Proper selection, training and supervision of personnel is essential to the long-term success of a real estate brokerage business. The selection process should recruit people who will fit into the firm and into its pattern of business performance, its goals, and

DOVER REALTY COMPANY

1776 Twelfth Street, Waltham, Xxxxx 12345   (908) 555-4321

JOB DESCRIPTION: RESIDENTIAL SALES MANAGER

QUALIFICATIONS: Licensed broker, at least one year's successful sales experience, proven managerial ability.

AUTHORITY: All residential sales personnel report to the sales manager. The sales manager reports to the President of the company.

DUTIES: Following policy manual procedures whenever applicable,

(a) Assign floor duty

(b) Assign open houses

(c) Supervise system of keeping track of all sales associates whereabouts.

(d) Directly supervise all contracting activities of beginning sales associates.

(e) Resolve disputes among sales associates. Refer unusual problems to the President of the Company.

(f) Interview all prospective new sales associates; hire with approval of President of the Company.

(g) Keep records of productivity of sales associates. Report these monthly at executive meeting. Terminate associates with approval of the President.

(h) Conduct weekly sales meeting.

(i) Distribute all information on new listings (Company, MLS, Co-op) to sales associates.

(j) Attend weekly executive meetings.

(k) Follow directives of President of the Company only. All disputes with other department heads should be referred to the President.

(l) When in doubt, seek consultation with President of the company. Nobody can be expected to know everything, but a good manager will not keep referring the same kinds of problems over and over again to the President once a determination has been made about dealing with them.

(m) Assume all responsiblities also outlined in policy manual. Policy manual directives and procedures should be used in all situations where they will apply.

Figure 4-3. Sample Job Description for Residential Sales Manager

objectives. Training programs are necessary not only to keep experienced personnel up to date on the techniques of the business and the information they need to be effective, but also to prepare new entrants into the business for successful performance. Supervision assures that all are doing them correctly, and that the manner in which they do their jobs is consistent with the firm's methods, image, and goals. In this discussion we include sales managers and principal brokers in the sales force. They need the knowledge of sales that comes from personal experience to succeed in such positions.

Characteristics

Real estate brokerage is a *service* business, and so is very people-oriented. Behavior, attitude, appearance, and personality are critical to success. Sales personnel require certain types of personalities. They must enjoy real estate dealings, of course, but they also should like dealing with people, be understanding and patient, and have the ability to express themselves well and to inspire confidence in those they deal with. Considering that they will be shepherding people through the most important business and financial dealings of their lives, salespeople must be able to inspire optimism, soothe worries, and convince customers that they are doing the right thing. While many people are attracted to a real estate sales career, relatively few of them will have all that it takes to be able to make a successful career of it. Therefore, it is essential that the brokerage firm have at its disposal the means to determine just who these people are and to tell at the outset which applicants will succeed and which may not.

Transience

Many real estate brokerage firms are plagued by *transience*. This refers to personnel who do not remain on the job very long. Transience requires frequent replacement and training of new people. The ideal person is one who takes the job, learns to do it well and reliably, and stays in the job indefinitely. The objective of management ought to be to have every salesperson fit this model, since it reduces personnel management effort and costs to a minimum and leads to greater efficiency in the firm's operation. This can be done several ways: by hiring people who appear likely to remain with the firm and who show the ability to do the job well, by using procedures that maximize employee satisfaction, and by paying well.

Compensation

Personnel have to be paid, and desirable ones must be paid enough to keep them on the job, if at all possible. At the same time, the firm can't pay so much that it loses money. Compensation, however, often can take forms other than money. Recognition, appreciation, and a desirable work environment are examples of nonmoney compensation, and often these can make a difference when money alone cannot. Successful salespeople tend to be relatively emotional, up-and-down types for whom the right words or actions at the right time can have a profound effect.

Environment

Work environment and working conditions themselves are matters of extreme importance. While management control is necessary, it should not be so impersonal or harsh that personnel dissatisfaction results. Part of the problem can be solved through communication. If people are aware of the purposes of controls and the need for them, they will be more likely to accept them, particularly if they can be made to feel that to some extent they have had a voice in their formulation.

It is particularly important that judgments about employee performance be made using relevant criteria. It is easy to fault someone for being late to work, taking long lunch hours, using too many paper clips. These are things that are easily measured but often tell very little about the actual worth of an employee. The firm should measure performance by *results*. A salesperson who regularly makes the Million Dollar Sales Club should be allowed a considerable amount of leeway in the manner in which he does the job (so long as it doesn't defy the firm's ethics or principles). A firm that is known for a result-oriented attitude is likely to attract more good producers than one that seems to rate its people according to relatively inconsequential standards.

Favoritism

A final problem is that of favoritism. Here we refer to management's apparent preference for some staff members over others, without communicating a valid, understandable reason for it. It is natural for management to bend over backwards to make life easy for star producers; they are the company's bread and butter. But other staff must be made to know, first, that the favors enjoyed by the preferred few are earned and justifiable, and even more important, that all staff members can enjoy these preferences by *earning* them. A final important point here is that less successful staff members should not be made to feel that there are any obstacles to their own achievement of superior status, and that the attainment of it by others will not in any way interfere with the same attainment by themselves.

EVALUATING PERSONNEL NEEDS

Good management constantly evaluates the effectiveness of its personnel, always seeking to improve the productivity and mix of people working in the organization. This sometimes reveals a need to add to the firm's work force, usually because of replacement, growth or expansion. *Replacement hiring* occurs when a position becomes vacant because a member of the staff resigns or is promoted. *Growth* results from the firm doing more and more business. As a firm grows, new positions must be created because more and more people will be needed to handle the larger volume of business. *Expansion* is the result of a decision by the firm to enter a new area of business. Jobs are created in entirely new divisions of the company. These jobs are unlike any that may have existed in the company until that time since they involve business that is new to the firm.

In the real estate brokerage business, growth can occur when a firm's reputation and service secure it more and more business. It also happens when the real estate market itself flourishes; there is more business for everyone. Growth also can be sought by the company as a goal in itself. In such cases, rather than expanding the sales staff in order to be able to handle an increasing volume of business, a firm may expand its sales staff so that the new members will actively seek and bring in the new business that the company wants.

Expansion is a somewhat different matter. Here the firm decides to add a *new* type of business. A residential firm may decide to enter the area of commercial sales or take up property management. It may add a mortgage lending office or a property insurance branch. All of these may require the use of new kinds of personnel who do work which the firm previously did not need.

Whatever the source of the personnel need, once it has been identified and the desired qualifications of the new staff members have been outlined, the firm is able to begin active recruitment. It knows what it wants; it knows the abilities, talents, and skills desired; and it is able now to identify those people who may be best qualified to meet these objectives. The next step is to plan a recruitment program to find the person or people needed. This includes knowing where to look, how to attract the right person, and how to convince him that his best opportunity is with this particular company.

SUPPORT PERSONNEL

Support personnel in a real estate brokerage firm are those who are not directly involved in sales and listing work. They fall into a number of categories, and many of them will have jobs that might also be found in many other businesses. A brokerage firm can need secretaries, receptionists, file and recordkeeping personnel, and accounting and legal assistance. Also, specialized to the real estate business, will be people who handle closings, writing advertisements for listed property, and drawing up contracts and other paperwork associated with the business. At times a real estate firm may want the services of an advertising agent, a real estate appraiser, a property management firm, handymen, specialized repair people, painters, printers, and others.

All of these can be employed on *full-time, part-time* or *when-needed* bases. Full time usually refers to the traditional eight hours per day, five days a week, although in the brokerage business this arrangement often is modified because of the large amount of weekend work. Part-time help generally works a fairly limited schedule, such as during regular busy periods. When-needed help usually is restricted to outsiders who are employed for specific jobs whenever it is necessary.

Dealing with employment for support positions will vary considerably among firms. A small one may have no full-time support personnel. A "bare-bones" operation may try to get by with no support personnel at all, relying upon the licensees in the sales force to take care of all support activity that they need. But most firms eventually will require full-time help. A secretary-receptionist usually is the first support employee to be hired by a growing firm; such a person has the typing skills to prepare much of the paperwork that otherwise will consume valuable sales force time, and can be in the office at all times, freeing the salespeople from most office duties.

Depending upon the nature of the job, varying degrees of training will be needed. At the very least, the new employee will have to meet and get to know the people he or she will be working with, but there is also the need to know exactly what is to be done. If someone of longer standing in the office is assigned to conduct this training, this person should be required to make sure that the training process is effective. Often, new employees are tossed into the office and left pretty much to sink or swim. At the very least, a few minutes advance thought should be given to the kinds of information the new employee will need and a successful effort made to provide it.

Of course, the degree to which this training process is necessary varies with the nature of the particular job, but it should not be ignored. The ideal employee is one who knows what to do and how to do it, and the sooner that is accomplished the more quickly the entire office can return to its normal efficient routing. An employee who continually must ask someone else for advice or assistance is disruptive to the entire office, and it is rare that this cannot be avoided with only a little advanced planning and effort.

DISCUSSION QUESTIONS AND PROJECTS

1. Find a local brokerage firm that will let you develop an organization chart of the firm. Analyze your results.

2. Describe the difference between line and support functions in the real estate brokerage business.

3. Since one of the functions of management is planning, what kinds of plans do you think managers of a real estate brokerage concern should make? Why?

4. Why is communication an important function of the management process?

5. Write a job description for a real estate salesperson.

6. Write a job description for a secretary-receptionist who is the only support service member of a small brokerage firm.

7. Examine the organization and control patterns of a small brokerage firm in your area. How do you think it could improve? What serious problems (if any) presently exist?

A Case Study

PLANNING AND FLEXIBILITY

A long time ago, when we all were much younger and things were a lot simpler (or so we think, now) real estate was a lot more stable. Interest rates were low. Things didn't change much, and when they did it usually was for the better. "Property" always seemed to grow in value – not rapidly, but consistently. Life seemed simpler and easier. So did the real estate brokerage business.

Things changed around 1970. Since then, real estate and the brokerage business has seemed like a gigantic roller coaster ride. Fluctuations in the economy in general and in interest rates in particular have made it a feast-or- famine business. The first serious downturn came in 1969-1970, after over two decades of general prosperity and growth in the business. Many brokerage firms were caught by surprise by the shrinking markets that most of them were experiencing for the first time.

It happened again in 1973-74, only worse. Some firms, after surviving the earlier crisis, had made contingency plans to cope with a repeat, but most managers apparently assumed that it wouldn't happen again. Once more they were faced with unpleasant consequences. Both times were severe shakeouts. A lot of firms went out of business, and many brokers and salespeople left the field entirely.

Experience is sometimes a good teacher. After the 1974 recession, brokerage firms began acting as if other poor markets would occur again. This meant that they had to be prepared to deal with them when they arose, and one of the best ways of preparing was to get better at predicting when they would occur. Many brokerage managers began to study the economy more carefully. In particular, they kept track of the rate of inflation and its effect upon interest rates. Slowly rising inflation in 1977 and 1978 suggested that another bad market could be on the way. Well-prepared firms put off heavy financial commitments that might leave them vulnerable to a bad downturn, and concentrated on building staffs of skilled salespeople who could be expected to weather a bad market more successfully.

By 1979 rising interest rates made it clear that tough times were on the way again. In the early 1980s they reached unprecedented heights, so high that most potential buyers stayed away from the market. The real estate brokerage business fell off considerably; in some areas it dwindled almost to nothing. Although interest rates began to fall in 1982, it was 1985 before they fell far enough to spark a significant increase in home buying. During that time, huge numbers of licensees left the business. By the time good times returned, only the best, most accomplished, and professional licensees remained.

The period from 1985 to 1989 saw an amazing boom in real estate in many parts of the country. Prices soared. The market flourished. The brokerage business took off, and hordes of new licensees found their way into a business which seemed to have no limits. Of course, limits eventually were reached. Beginning around 1989, real estate markets in many parts of the U.S. suffered some of the worst collapses on record. It was most severe in the areas which had prospered the most: the Northeast and the West Coast. In some parts of New England, home prices in 1991 were as little as half what they had been a couple of years before.

The effect on the brokerage business was devastating. Business shriveled, and many less- experienced licensees were unable to cope with markets which now required the highest standards of professional ability for survival. As this is being written (early 1993) interest rates are relatively low. The real estate business is picking up, but more slowly than in similar circumstances in earlier times.

Planning and flexibility are very important for survival in these up-and-down markets. Some of the events which have such a profound effect upon the market cannot be anticipated very easily: who can tell when the economy is about to suffer significant reversal? As a result, *flexibility* has become the watchword in the real estate brokerage business of the 90's. The company which has the flexibility to grow or downsize quickly is the one which stands the best chance of surviving what appears to be a constantly fluctuating up-and-down future.

REFERENCES

HALL INSTITUTE OF REAL ESTATE, *Managing a Real Estate Team*, Ch. 3-5, Appendix E. Hinsdale, IL: The Dryden Press, 1980.

PHILLIPS, BARBARA, "Office Management for Brokers," in *The McGraw-Hill Real Estate Handbook*, ed. Robert Irwin, Ch. 33. New York, NY: McGraw-Hill Book Company, 1984.

Real Estate Office Management: People Functions System, Ch. 1-6, 22.   Chicago, IL: REALTORS® National Marketing Institute, latest edition.

FIVE

EMPLOYMENT
AGREEMENTS

Independent Contractor

Problems with the Independent Contractor Relationship

The Salesperson's Contract

Support Personnel

A properly run brokerage firm will use many kinds of contracts and instructions involving its personnel. This chapter considers the brokerage's employment contracts. These are the agreements which define the duties and responsibilities that exist between the firm and the people working for it. While it may often be legally allowable for these to be verbal, unwritten employment contracts should not be used because they are difficult to pin down, and usually lead to misunderstanding. The sensible rule for *any* contract is to *put it in writing!* This assures that everyone involved will have a clear, unchanging statement of the conditions of the arrangement.

INDEPENDENT CONTRACTOR

The real estate brokerage business extensively uses the *independent contractor* form of employment for sales personnel. This arrangement treats the "employee" as an independent self-employed entity, at least for federal income tax purposes. Because of the importance of this type of contract we must devote considerable discussion to it.

In most businesses, people who work for the firm are considered *employees*. They are assigned jobs to do, directed in those jobs, and paid for their work. By law, the firm must withhold federal, FICA (Social Security) and, when applicable, state and local income taxes from their paychecks. The firm also must pay the employer's share of FICA taxes, and make payments into state-run unemployment insurance funds, workmen's compensation funds, and the like. Many businesses also offer their employees fringe benefits such as partially or fully paid pension contributions, health and life insurance, profit sharing, and so on.

Nature of Independent Contractor

However, there is another kind of "employee," the *independent contractor*. Independent contractors are not regarded by law as "employees," at least not as they are described in the previous paragraph. The independent contractor is looked upon as a *separate, self-employed* business entity who contracts his services to others. His employer pays him for his services, but no more. He pays all his FICA taxes himself. He makes estimated tax payments of his income taxes, because they are not withheld from payments made to him. He is not eligible for unemployment or disability benefits provided by employers; he must pay his own money into such funds, and must buy or pay into pension plans and insurance programs on his own. He doesn't participate in his employers' profit sharing plans or other fringe benefits. He will not be eligible for unemployment coverage or workmen's compensation, unless he pays into these funds himself.

Advantages of the Independent Contractor Relationship

From the point of view of an employer, hiring independent contractors instead of people with employee status appears to be very economical. There is no paperwork and associated cost of withholding income taxes, paying FICA taxes, or contributing to unemployment or compensation funds. Employers don't pay for independent contractors' fringe benefits. Since FICA taxes and other mandatory contributions can come to as much as 10% of total payroll, the savings can be quite substantial, to say nothing of the additional 10% or more that is saved on other employee benefits. There is little wonder that in the real estate business, as in any other, hiring people who can be regarded as independent contractors is very attractive.

There are some sensible reasons for thinking of real estate salespeople as independent contractors. After all, their jobs *do* require them to act on their own quite a lot, make many of their own decisions, and spend much of their working time completely unsupervised. To a considerable degree they must be self-motivated, because most of the time nobody else is around to push them along, or to tell them or show them what to do. In other words, they do seem to have a lot of "independence."

Independent Contractor and U.S. Internal Revenue Service

Given the obvious benefits to the employer of having a work force on independent contractor status, one might wonder why there would be any working people at all on employee status. The answer rests with the legal definitions of the employee and independent contractor, most particularly as they are defined and interpreted by tax law and by the United States Internal Revenue Service (IRS). More taxes can be collected from firms using employees than from those hiring independent contractors. No wonder, then, that a fairly severe body of law and regulation has emerged defining the *exact* circumstances under which independent contractor status will be allowed and recognized.

Definition of Independent Contractor

One significant point here is that the status of independent contractor can only be sustained if, in fact, the actual employment situation fits the IRS definition. It is not enough simply for an employer and employee to agree that independent contractor status exists and to go on from there. To be sure, a necessary condition for such status is that it is recognized to exist by the employer and individual involved, but this is not enough; the duties and responsibilities of the independent contractor also must be consistent with the IRS definition.

The key element of the definition of independent contractor hinges on the word *independent*. In order for one to have independent contractor status, one must be seen to be acting in a largely independent manner, free from much of the direction and control that would normally be associated with the employer-employee relationship. This factor comes directly to bear upon the *control* the employer exerts over the employee. On the one hand, some control over an independent contractor is recognized, since it is necessary to have a definition of the task to be performed and the service for which payment is made. However, the independent contractor is supposed to be largely independent in the *means* used to *perform* the required tasks and *achieve* the specified goals.

Controlling the Independent Contractor

Briefly, control can be exerted over an independent contractor so far as defining the result to be accomplished. However, control *cannot* extend to the means, details, and specific techniques used by the contractor to achieve the desired result. In real estate brokerage, this means that an independent contractor agreement is allowed to specify that the contractor is being hired to list and sell real estate on behalf of the company. Requiring that certain procedures be followed is all right, so long as they are generally accepted courses of action within the industry. Independent contractors can be required to abide by all laws and regulations that apply. They also may be specifically *prohibited* from certain activities; for example, an independent contractor can be hired to list and sell houses, but prohibited from listing and selling commercial property.

All these considerations represent genuine control, but note also the implicit assumption that the independent contractor is a professional who can be trusted to handle the details and many of the methods used to get the required job done. It is control in the area of these *details* which cannot be exerted by the employer of an independent contractor. In a real estate brokerage context, independent contractors cannot be required to hold open house every so often, to handle a certain listing in a particular way, to be at any particular place at any particular time. Firms can't require that independent contractor salespeople do floor duty, attend sales meetings, wear certain uniforms, use a certain kind of car. They may do so *voluntarily*, of course, but they can't be forced to do so, as a condition of employment. The firm may not control independent contractors' hours of work and cannot require them to attend training sessions, professional or other meetings. The broker may not have any substantial control over priorities the contractor assigns to listings, prospects, clients, and customers that he is working on.

The IRS Definition of Independent Contractor

Current law specifies five conditions that will allow a real estate salesperson to qualify as an independent contractor under the U.S. Internal Revenue Code. The salesperson, and his/her employment situation, must meet all five conditions. If they don't, the person will be considered an *employee* for federal income tax purpose. The conditions are:

1. The independent contractor must have absolute control over the number of hours worked and the manner in which they are scheduled.

2. The independent contractor must have a written contract with the broker, and the broker must provide the contractor written information describing the contractor's self-employment and income tax obligations.

3. The independent contractor must maintain a separate place of business; OR

   at least one-third of the value of the contractor's service must be due to property provided by the contractor; OR

   the independent contractor must be a licensed real estate agent, a licensed insurance agent, or a direct seller.

4. At least 90 percent of the contractor's income must be related to sales rather than to the number of hours worked.

5. The broker employing the services provided by the independent contractor must file the legally required information tax returns.

Provision 3 defines a real estate licensee as an independent contractor, provided that the other four conditions are also met. Provision 5 requires the broker to file periodic returns with the IRS showing how much was paid to each independent contractor; however, no withholding or employer-related taxes will have to be paid by the broker. Provision 2 assures that the independent contractor is aware of his/her status, and that there is a written agreement available that defines this independent contractor status. Provision 4, in effect, requires that the independent contractor's income be earned from commissions and not from salary paid for hours worked.

Provision 1 is the most significant. By requiring that the contractor have absolute control over time and scheduling of work, his/her independence is assured. This means that brokers are not able to schedule independent contractors to work assigned floor duty, open houses, or other duty unless they specifically agree to it.

Provisions 2 and 4 pose no serious problems, since they relate directly to the manner in which the brokerage business currently is conducted. Employment contracts can be written to include the necessary information required by provision 2. Virtually all real estate licensees qualify under provision 4, anyway, since practically all of their income *is* from sales commissions. However, this provision is likely to generate scrutiny of any kind of *draw arrangements* with independent contractors. Draws are payments made toward future commission income, and are supposed to be paid back when the commission income actually is earned. If a draw of some kind is used, the contract defining it should be airtight. The draw must be a *legally collectable loan*, and it is preferable if there were no mention at all of future commissions being used to pay it off. Otherwise, the IRS may contend that by requiring the future commissions be used to pay off the loan, a disguised form of salary has been created. A better arrangement would be to provide a specific repayment date for the loan, regardless of commissions paid by the contractor.

Employee Status

So far as the law is concerned, an "employee" is anyone who works for someone else, and who does not qualify as an independent contractor. Outside of salespeople, practically no one in a real estate brokerage firm could so qualify. Support people are salaried, supervised, often told what to do and how to do it, and work specified hours. Management personnel usually are salaried, and almost certainly are controlled and supervised by superiors.

Compensation of the Independent Contractor

It is essential that an independent contractor *not* be paid in any manner that might be construed as *salary*. Normally, all payments should be earned commissions. It is usually all right for some form of *incentive* to be used. An example is a bonus or larger commission split, once a certain level of commission income has been reached. However, incentives must be based entirely upon the performance of the individual independent contractor. This rules out any form of profit sharing. Some sales-oriented businesses pay a small salary, supplemented by commissions; this can't be done in an independent contractor arrangement and isn't a common practice in the real estate brokerage industry.

Expenses

The independent contractors must pay their own expenses. They must pay their own license fees, professional dues, and other fees, although an employer may supply them to people on employee status. They cannot be provided with company cars or other business equipment. Providing them with office space is permitted so long as it is clear that the space is there to be used or not, as the independent contractor wishes. Providing office space can't be construed as *requiring* the salesperson to spend any particular amount of time in it. Nor should it imply that all or most of the independent contractor's function is performed in the employer's office. This isn't much of a problem with real estate salespeople, since they have to spend so much time out on their own soliciting listings and showing property.

Independent contractors may be provided with office services, such as secretarial service and telephone availability, so long as they aren't *required* to use it. Any expenses of this nature that accumulated outside the broker's office cannot be reimbursed. The independent contractor cannot be given the usual run of fringe benefits that an employee might expect, such as pension plans, group insurance plans, sick pay, or paid vacations. All of these are defined by the IRS as benefits available only to employees. Contractors' vacation time cannot be controlled by the broker either; they must be left free to schedule working hours, days, and weeks as they see fit.

Information

Finally, the broker is entitled to *information* from the independent contractor only so far as it pertains directly to the conduct of business. Brokers may require that listings and sale contracts be submitted in a timely manner and in certain form. They may require any information needed to assure that the salesperson is abiding by the law.

PROBLEMS WITH THE INDEPENDENT CONTRACTOR RELATIONSHIP

The key determinant of independent contractor status "is not what you *say*, but what you *do*." Anyone can draw up a contract which says that so-and-so is an independent contractor. That isn't enough. No matter what the contract says, if any of the provisions of the independent contractor relationship are violated, the contractor will be considered an employee by the IRS. If that happens, the IRS may then levy back taxes, unpaid FICA taxes, and penalties and fines for failure to abide by tax laws. Loss of independent contractor status in this manner, then, can be a very expensive proposition, especially to the brokerage firm.

The advantage to the independent contractor relationship is that it saves the brokerage firm a lot of money that otherwise would be paid in taxes and bookkeeping costs. Independent contractors benefit by being able to act independently, and by the recognition that real estate sales is a very independent line of work, in which individual effort and responsibility and self-supervision must loom large. They also may like the idea that their independent situation allows them considerably more control over their own lives and destinies. The major disadvantage to independent contractors is greater personal responsibility for their own well-being, lack of fringe benefits, additional recordkeeping requirements, and greater personal expense.

Limited Control

The major problem to the brokerage firm is the obvious one of having limited control over the sales force. Some firms set up independent contractor relationships and then proceed to control the contractors as though they were employees. This works only so long as the IRS doesn't get wind of it. And it's poor business practice to use as a signif-icant foundation of the firm's organization the hope that the tax man doesn't find out something illegal is going on.

When highly skilled and talented salespeople are involved, there is little worry, since they can be relied upon to act properly. Some firms hire inexperienced sales per-sonnel as employees, and may reduce commission splits to account at least partially for the additional expense they incur. The employee status allows full control by the broker. The firm can require attendance at meetings and training sessions, floor duty, open house, etc. with no worries, since the people involved are classified as employees. Once they have proved themselves and earned independent contractor status, it can be given to them; by this time the broker has some assurance that they have the experience and ability to conduct themselves properly with little supervision.

Encouraging Desired Activity

In some areas, however, it would be nice to have control. Sales meetings are important for communication purposes, and most sales managers like all salespeople attend. It is essential that at least one licensee be in the office at all times to handle calls and walk-in business, so it is necessary to have some reliable means of scheduling floor time among the sales force to see to it that somebody is in the office.

The usual answer is to make it obvious to employees and independent contractors alike that there are real benefits to be had from attendance and floor duty, even though independent contractors cannot be specifically required to do either. Of course, a contrac-tor who does not seem to be doing his part can be simply let go when his contract expires, and if this happens a few times the others will get the message that their continued employment may depend on their willingness to engage in "voluntary" activity that meets with the approval and desires of management. However, such a solution cannot be the overt policy of the brokerage firm, because it will be interpreted as excessive control.

This kind of problem has no easy solution. Some brokerage firms try to make the floor duty and other "required" activity as attractive as possible, so that voluntary compliance is no problem. Floor agents usually have first priority on all walk-in and call-in business that occurs during their duty period. Many firms receive listing and sales leads through the officers and managers who are not active salespeople; referral of these calls and requests to active agents can be based upon floor duty time or other factors, so long as it is provided simply as incentive, with no specific promises. Firms that do have some salespeople in employee status may schedule them for such duties, while allowing independent contractors to request such activity if they want it. This leaves the matter entirely up to the contractor, which conforms with the proper requirements but is only successful where it is possible to fill all such duties with employees if no contractors wish to volunteer.

THE SALESPERSON'S CONTRACT

The contract of employment between the brokerage and the salesperson should be written. Depending upon the laws prevailing in the state where the firm is located, a verbal agreement may or may not be legal. Even if it is, the written instrument is far preferable because it provides a specific piece of evidence that each party can refer to whenever necessary. Furthermore, contracts employing independent contractors should be written if only because they may be the only foolproof evidence with which the independent status can be proved to the satisfaction of the IRS.

The contract (an example is presented in Figure 5-1) should be drawn up by the firm's attorney to reflect exactly what the firm and the contracting salesperson agree upon and to assure that all legal requirements are properly met. A standard form can be drafted by the attorney which the firm can use for a number of its salespeople. However, it must be remembered that not all salespeople will be doing the same types of things, so different types of agreements may be needed for different members of the sales force.

Salesperson's Status and Responsibility

The contract should mention a number of specific things. The status (independent contractor or employee) should be detailed, as the contractual requirements of each will differ considerably. If the salesperson is an employee, there should be a reasonable summary of the specific duties required and the manner in which the employee is to be controlled by the firm. The independent contractor's agreement has to be more general on this point. The contract should specify the manner in which the salesperson is to be paid by the firm, as well as how and when. Since his income will be shares of commissions that he brings into the firm, the manner in which those commissions are split with him should be detailed. If there are any bonus or incentive payments agreed upon, they should be included. Reference to the policy manual (described in Chapter 7) can be made in the contract. The employee can be required to abide by the rules and provisions set down in the manual, but for the independent contractor the manual must remain a guide and not a direct order.

Renegotiation

Contracts employing salespeople can be designed to be renegotiated from time to time. This can be accomplished by making the contract for a relatively short period of time, such as a year. The periodic renegotiation of the contract will give both salesperson and manager the opportunity for frank discussion of the salesperson's performance and also will provide management with an incentive tool. The salesperson can be told during a contract period that if his work achieves a certain level he may expect a new contract which reflects, perhaps, a better commission split or a more generous incentive program. Also, if a salesperson is performing poorly, he will know that the contract may not be renewed if improvement does not occur.

Termination

It is particularly important that the contract spell out the manner in which it may be terminated. For example, if the salesperson does not achieve a certain minimum level of activity, the firm may terminate the agreement before it expires. If the salesperson resigns, the contract should spell out what responsibilities he/she has to the firm by so doing. Severance pay (for employees) should be mentioned. There may also be language guaranteeing the salesperson renewal of the contract if certain performance goals are met. It is poor policy to keep people guessing until the last minute about their continued employment, and they feel much more secure if they know their contract guarantees their job if they do it well enough.

Support and Benefits

The contract should point out what supportive services the brokerage firm will provide for the salesperson, especially if they are better or worse than those normally provided by other firms in its area. The employee salesperson's contract should list the fringe benefits, if any, that the employee will receive. If it is a contract for a new employee, it may specify required training sessions, the specifics of draws against commissions, and other special provisions, including the eventual change of status to independent contractor when experience and competence permit. It is important to note and to agree in the independent contractor's contract that he/she will be responsible for paying self-employment taxes and making the quarterly payments of estimated taxes required by the IRS of self-employed people. Finally, signed copies of the agreement should be in the possession of both the firm and the salesperson.

DOVER REALTY COMPANY

1776 Twelfth Street, Waltham, Xxxxx 12345   (908) 555-4321

BROKER - SALES ASSOCIATE CONTRACT

INDEPENDENT CONTRACTOR

THIS AGREEMENT made this _____day of _____, 19____, by and between DOVER REALTY COMPANY, hereinafter referred to as Broker, and _____, hereinafter referred to as Sales Associate, for and in consideration of their mutual premises and agreements and for their mutual benefits.

W I T N E S S E T H:

WHEREAS, said broker is engaged in business as a general real estate broker in the City of Waltham and County of Roman, State of XXXXXXXXXXXX, and is duly qualified to and does operate a general real estate brokerage business and is duly qualified to and does procure the listings of real estate for sale, and prospective purchasers, and has and does enjoy the good will of, and a reputation for fair dealing with the public, and

WHEREAS, said broker maintains an office in said City, properly equipped with furnishings and other equipment necessary and incidental to the proper operation of said business, and staffed with employess, suitable to serving the public as a real estate broker, and

WHEREAS, said Sales Associate is a duly licensed real estate salesman and enjoys a good reputation for fair and honest dealing with the public as such, and

WHEREAS, it is deemed to be to the mutual advantage of said Broker and Sales Associate to form the association hereinafter agreed to under the terms and conditions hereinafter set out,

Figure 5-1. Independent Contractor Broker-Salesperson Agreement.

DOVER REALTY COMPANY INDEPENDENT CONTRACTOR AGREEMENT page 2

THEREFORE, for and in consideration of the premises and of the mutual convenants hereinafter contained, it is mutually agreed as follows:

1. Broker agrees to make available to the Sales Associate all current listings of the office, and agrees, upon request, to assist the Sales Associate in his work by giving advice and providing full cooperation in every way possible.

2. Broker agrees that the Sales Associate may share with other Sales Associates all the facilities of the office now operated by said Broker in connection with the subject matter of this contract, which office is now located at 1776 12th Street, Waltham, XXXXX.

3. Sales Associate agrees to work diligently and with his best efforts to sell all real estate listed with the Broker, to always solicit additional listings and customers, and otherwise promote the business of serving the public in real estate transactions to the end that each of the parties hereto may derive the greatest profits possible; it being understood that Sales Associate's only renumeration shall be by way of sharing in commissions collected as a result, in whole or in part, of his activities as hereinafter provided.

4. Sales Associate agrees to conduct his business and regulate his habits, so as to maintain and to increase the good will and reputation of the Broker and the Sales Associate, and the parties hereto agree to conform to and abide by all laws, rules and regulations, and codes of ethics that are binding upon or applicable to real estate brokers and real estate salesmen.

Figure 5-1. (*Continued*)

DOVER REALTY COMPANY INDEPENDENT CONTRACTOR AGREEMENT page 3

5. The commissions to be charged for any services performed hereunder shall be those determined by the Broker, and the Broker shall advise the Sales Associate of any special contract relating to any particular transaction which he undertakes to handle. When the Sales Associate shall perform any service hereunder, whereby a commission is earned, said commission shall, when collected, be divided between the Broker and Sales Associate, in which division the Sales Associate shall receive a proportionate share as set out in the Policy Manual of Dover Realty Company and the Broker shall receive the balance. In the event of special arrangements with any client of the Broker or the Sales Associate on property listed with the Broker or controlled by the Sales Associate, a special division of commission may apply, such rate of division to be agreed upon in advance by the Broker and the Sales Associate. In the event that two or more Sales Associates participate in such a service, or claim to have done so, they shall agree as to how the amount of the commission over that accruing to the Broker shall be divided. In no case shall either party be personally liable to the other for uncollected commissions, but when the commission shall have been collected from the party or parties for whom the service was performed, said Broker shall hold the same in trust for said Sales Associate and himself to be divided according to the terms of this agreement.

6. The division and distribution of the earned commission as set out in Paragraph 5 hereto, which may be paid to or collected by either party hereto, shall take place as soon as practicable after the collection of such commission from the party or parties for whom the services may have been performed.

7. The Broker shall not be liable to the Sales Associate for any expenses incurred by him, or for any of his acts, nor shall the Sales

Figure 5-1. *(Continued)*

DOVER REALTY COMPANY INDEPENDENT CONTRACTOR AGREEMENT page 4

Associate be liable to the Broker for office help or expense, and the Sales Associate shall have no authority to bind the Broker by any promise or representation, unless specifically authorized in writing in advance in a particular transaction. Sales Associate shall pay all of the cost of his own real estate license and bond, and of his dues for membership in the National Association of Real Estate Boards, and State Real Estate Association, the local Board of Realtors and any other dues, any applicable occupation tax, and notary bond, if any. It is specifically agreed that Sales Associate shall furnish his own automobile and pay all expenses thereof and that Broker shall have no responsibility therefor. Sales Associate agrees to carry public liability insurance upon his automobile with minimum limits of $100,000.00 for each person and $300,000.00 for each accident and with property damage limit of $25,000.00. Sales Associate agrees to furnish Broker a certificate prepared by the insurance company certifying that such insurance is in force and obligating the insurer to give Broker notice before cancellation.

8. This agreement does not constitute a hiring by either party. The parties hereto are and shall remain independent contractors bound by the provisions hereof. Sales Associate is under the control of Broker as to the result of Sales Associate's work only and not as to the methods or means by which such result is accomplished. This agreement shall not be construed as a partnership, and neither party hereto shall be liable for any obligation incurred by the other except as provided elsewhere herein. Broker shall not withold from Sales Associate's commissions any amounts for taxes or any other items. Broker shall not make any premium payments or contributions for any workman's compensation or unemployment compensation for Sales Associate.

Figure 5-1. *(Continued)*

DOVER REALTY COMPANY INDEPENDENT CONTRACTOR AGREEMENT page 5

9. (a) This contract and the association created hereby, may be terminated by either party hereto, at anytime upon notice given to the other; but the rights of the parties to any commissions which were earned and collected prior to said notice, shall not be divested by the termination of this contract. Upon termination of this agreement, Sales Associate shall not be compensated in respect to any commission resulting from the exercise of a sale after the termination of said agreement.

(b) Upon termination of this agreement, Sales Associate further agrees not to furnish to any person, firm, company or corporation engaged in the real estate business any information as to Broker's clients, customers, properties, prices, terms of negotiations nor Broker's policies or relationships with clients and customers nor any other information concerning Broker and/or his business. Sales Associate shall not, after termination of this agreement, remove from the files or from the office of the Broker any maps, books and publications, files or data, and it is expressly agreed that the aforementioned records and information are the property of the Broker. Sales Associate shall be entitled to photostats of certain instruments pertaining to transactions in which Sales Associate has a bona fide interest and Broker shall not unreasonably withhold the same from Sales Associate.

10. (a) Heirs, Successors and Assigns. This agreement shall be binding upon and the benefits shall insure to the heirs, successors and assigns of the parties hereto.

(b) Notices. All notices provided for under this agreement shall be in writing and shall be sufficient if sent by certified mail to the following listed addresses of the parties hereto or to such other address as shall be designated in writing to the other party:

Figure 5-1. (*Continued*)

DOVER REALTY COMPANY INDEPENDENT CONTRACTOR AGREEMENT page 6

BROKER: DOVER REALTY COMPANY
                 1776 Twelfth Street
                 WALTHAM, XXXXXXXX   12345

SALES ASSOCIATE: _____

(c) <u>Governing Law</u>. This agreement shall be governed by the laws of the State of XXXXXXXX.

(d) <u>Assignment</u>. This agreement is personal to the parties hereto and may not be assigned, sold or otherwise by either of them.

(e) <u>Waiver</u>. That the failure of any party hereto to enforce at any time any of the provisions or terms of this agreement shall not be construed to be a waiver of such provisions or terms, nor the right of any party thereafter to enforce such terms or provisions.

(f) <u>Entire Agreement</u>. That this agreement constitutes the entire agreement between the Broker and Sales Associate, and that there are no agreements or understandings concerning such agreement which are not fully set forth herein.

(g) <u>Severability</u>. That if any provision of this agreement is invalid or unenforceable in any jurisdiction, the other provisions herein shall remain in full force and effect in such jurisdiction and shall be liberally construed in order to effectuate the purpose and intent of this agreement, and the invalidity or unenforceability of any provision of this agreement in any jurisdication shall not affect the durability or enforceability of any such provision in any other jurisdication.

WITNESS the signatures of the parties hereto the day and year first above written to duplicate.

BROKER: SALES ASSOCIATE:

DOVER REALTY COMPANY   by_____   _____

Figure 5-1. (*Continued*)

SUPPORT PERSONNEL

Nearly all full-time and part-time support personnel will be classified as employees, but most when-needed service providers can be treated as independent contractors. This means that in addition to salaries for support personnel, the firm must withhold income taxes and social security payments from employees' salaries, and must pay the employer's share of FICA, workers' compensation, unemployment insurance and the like. Employees may be offered participation in pension, health insurance, life insurance, and other fringe benefit plans the firm may have, and the firm may choose to pay part of the cost for these on behalf of employees. Employees also may be eligible for profit sharing plans if the firm has them and wishes to include these personnel in them.

DISCUSSION QUESTIONS AND PROJECTS

1. Get samples of employment agreements used by one or two of the major brokerage firms in your area. If they use the independent contractor system, examine the agreements to see if they include any provisions that might violate independent contractor status.

2. Why do brokerage systems prefer the independent contractor status for their salespeople?

3. What would be the advantages and disadvantages of treating the sales force as employees instead of independent contractors?

4. What are the major problems associated with independent contractor status from the brokerage firm's point of view?

5. From the salesperson's point of view, what are the advantages and disadvantages of being an independent contractor?

6. Can you find any brokerage firms in your area that do not use written consent between the firm and the salesperson? Do they encounter any problems? If so, what problems are the most significant?

7. What means of compensation would be inconsistent with the independent contractor's status? Why?

A Case Study

INDEPENDENT CONTRACTOR .

This story has been making the rounds of the real estate brokerage business for years and years. It probably isn't precisely true, but there is more truth than fiction. And it's an instructive tale.

A large midwestern real estate brokerage firm was investigated by the IRS to determine whether or not its sales force fit the legal definition of the independent contractor. The investigators poked around for several days, and finally informed management that they wanted to meet with the entire sales force to report the results of the investigation. "How about the day after tomorrow at 10 AM?" asked the manager. "Fine," replied the investigators.

At the appointed time, the investigators entered a crowded conference room. "Is everyone here?" they asked, "Yes," replied the manager. "I called each one and told them to come, and they're all present."

"Well," said the chief investigator, "If all of them came here because you told them to, then by definition they are employees. If they were really independent contractors, you could not have required them to attend this meeting. So, according to our calculations, your firm owes several hundred thousand dollars in back taxes and penalties."

The story ends with the manager's response which, unfortunately, cannot be repeated here. Can you guess what it might have been?

REFERENCES

FISHER, FREDERICK J., *Broker Beware: Selling Real Estate Within the Law*, Reston, VA: Reston Publishing Company, Inc., 1981.

PHILLIPS, BARBARA, "Office Management for Brokers," in *The McGraw-Hill Real Estate Handbook*, ed. Robert Irwin, Ch. 33, New York, NY: McGraw-Hill Book Company, 1984.

SIX

PERSONNEL SELECTION

Recruitment Sources

The Selection Process

Support Personnel Selection

Termination

Finding and choosing the people who will work in the brokerage firm is of prime importance to its continued success. In this chapter we will consider the selection process and the means available to the firm of assuring the selection of the best qualified people. Because of their importance and the specialty of their skills, we will devote most of our discussion to the selection of salespeople. We will also give some consideration to the unpleasant business of terminating unsatisfactory personnel.

RECRUITMENT SOURCES

From time to time a real estate brokerage firm will be looking to hire more personnel. They may be salespeople or support people. Recalling our discussion in Chapter 4, adding to the firm's employees usually results from replacement, growth or expansion. Replacement occurs when someone resigns or is promoted, and their old job must be filled with someone new. *Growth* occurs when the business grows and the sales or support staff is enlarged. *Expansion* refers to entering new lines of business.

Most members of the public at large will not be qualified to assume a particular position that a firm has available; most people will lack the necessary skills, the interest in the work, or both. Therefore, the firm should try to concentrate its recruitment efforts in places where the desired person is most likely to be found.

The Firm Itself

The current staff of the firm should never be ignored as a source of people to fill new positions, particularly if they are replacement or growth positions. The advantage here is that promotion from within involves people who are already familiar with the firm and its methods, and who are known to the management. They are most easily evaluated because management has experience working with them directly and closely. They also may require less training since they already are familiar with the firm. The cost, both in money and time, of finding someone within the firm is very low, since no advertising has to be done and relatively little formal interviewing or getting acquainted is needed.

Promotion within the firm means that the person involved probably will be leaving an old job vacant. Therefore, in-house promotion within the firm usually means that while a certain job has been filled, another will open up, and eventually the firm will have to look outside itself to fill its staff completely. However, it may be that the vacated job will be easier to fill, and so the firm will benefit overall. As an example, if a member of the sales staff is promoted to sales manager, another salesperson will have to be found. However, salespeople are easier to find than good sales managers.

A big advantage of in-house promotion is that if it is known well in advance that a certain individual will be promoted, a lot of time is available to "groom" him/her for that position. It also can be a morale booster, especially for the individual affected. Handled properly, the promotion may make other staff members feel better because the firm has demonstrated that its first loyalty is to its own people.

On the other hand, in-house promotion can impair morale if several people think they are capable of handling the job and only one can be chosen. Those who are passed over will have to be handled with care for some time, since they may well feel that they have lost esteem or the appreciation of management. Furthermore, promotion from within can be carried too far. If the best person for the job is not someone who is in the firm already, then choosing someone from inside is detrimental because the firm will be overlooking better people simply because they are outsiders. Finally, jobs created by expansion are less likely to be filled adequately from within because they will call for skills, knowledge, and abilities that are new to the company and so might not be found in the staff members already present.

Other Firms in the Business

Newcomers to the real estate brokerage business will be surprised at the amount of job-hopping that goes on, especially among salespeople. As a result it usually isn't considered in bad taste for a company to try to entice into its fold superior producers at other companies. The firm is not going to improve its relationships with other firms by doing this, but at the same time it should be evident that most other companies are doing the same thing.

The reason is that while countless people may have real estate sales licenses, only a very few mature in the business to become good producers. Those few effective people are in high demand, and they are well known in the local business. Therefore, this kind of recruiting is not very expensive or time-consuming. The natural association that real estate brokerage people have with one another in their daily work usually is enough to get the word around as to who is satisfied where he is, and who might be available if the right offer were to come along.

Frequently, when a firm develops a vacant position, new or existing, and a candidate from within the firm is not available, management can easily come up with a list of potentially desirable people who are presently with other firms. This is particularly the case when the position is due to expansion, and the firm is necessarily looking for a person with experience in the new area. Such a person can best be found in another firm that already has developed the same area.

Other Related Businesses

People who are successful at selling something other than real estate may be good prospects for a real estate sales position; they have shown the ability to sell and to survive on a commission pay scheme. Successful sales experience in any field is a good predictor of successful real estate selling.

Other businesses may also be good sources of certain management personnel, since management is to some extent a universal skill. Particularly good sources in different businesses are large companies with very limited promotion opportunities. A highly motivated person eventually gets frustrated in such surroundings; the company is so large that he is never able to move to a position high enough for him to feel he is controlling or operating something significant. Also, in large companies many executives who are capable and eager eventually find themselves bogged down at some relatively high level of management above which they know they have little chance of advancing. People in these situations may find the smaller size of the typical real estate firm attractive. They can be in control of a significant part of a smaller firm, can have an important voice in the firm's policy and goals, and can see the results of their efforts much more clearly.

Schools, Colleges, and Other Training Centers

This source is not always available to a firm. To make most effective use of schools and other educational institutions that produce graduates with the skills desired, the company is best located near them. Then it takes little effort to call once or twice a year to find out whether or not there are promising graduates available, and to make known the firm's needs.

But even if such an institution is not nearby, it may be advantageous to contact the closer ones and to make the firm's needs known to them. This applies especially to colleges and universities, as more and more are introducing real estate subjects into their programs of study. Graduates will have acquired a lot of formal knowledge but relatively little actual experience in the business, so they will need additional training once they are on staff. However, they will have had a good introduction to the field and are likely to be interested in, and eager for, the real estate jobs they take.

People recruited from these sources do not need an intimate knowledge of the local business. Whether they graduate from a local institution or one some distance away, any decent training provided them by the firm will include a rigorous introduction to the market they will be dealing in. Their lack of local knowledge is a disadvantage in that they will require more training than someone already experienced, but they make up for it with the general knowledge of the business and its nature that they acquired in the classroom. Also, they are likely to be aware of the latest developments in the field and so may well bring knowledge and skills that will prove valuable. However, they may be too eager to put all they know to work, and it may be necessary to include in their training by the firm some suggestions concerning the knowledge they have that ought to be put aside, at least temporarily.

The General Public

It is usually expensive and rather unrewarding to solicit applications from the general public. Most people recruited from this source will have no experience in real estate and no demonstrated talent. They must be trained from the very beginning, and most will have to become licensed before the training can begin.

Even so, some firms are quite successful recruiting in such a general manner. One useful device is for the brokerage firm to have an associated real estate school (in states that allow them to do so). They require interested people to pay their own way through the preliminary and pre-licensing training. The firm then selects the most promising students as potential associates, thus using the school as both a recruiting and screening device. Other firms use advertising and other recruitment of the general public to attract people who may have an interest in real estate. Once they contact them, the nature of the business is explained and discussed and promising applicants are urged to take licensing preparation courses as a requisite for further consideration, at the firm's own school, if it has one.

The source of applicants is feasible only for the firm that is structured so that it can handle a fairly large training program and is willing to invest the necessary time and money in promising unskilled applicants. A smaller firm rarely can handle this type of recruitment. However, since good salespeople are so scarce, a firm may find that this method of recruiting is worthwhile if only a small percentage of people processed through the program turn out to be good real estate salespeople.

THE SELECTION PROCESS

Whatever sources the firm uses, applicants for an available position ought to appear once information about the position circulates. If they don't, the firm needs to rethink its recruitment process. Does the information being sent out describe the position attractively? Is the position itself unattractive? Are competitive pay and benefits offered? Sometimes there is no response because no one wants the job badly enough to apply for it. This problem usually crops up only when the job is very unusual and difficult to qualify for. But it also may mean that there is a general labor shortage in the firm's locality, or that the local population is so small that a limited labor force exists. On the other hand, if an unusually large group of applicants appears, then the position may be described too attractively, the pay and benefits may be too high, or the local area is experiencing relatively high unemployment and a lot of people are just looking for any job.

It's important to describe the position, salary and benefits honestly. This saves time and energy. If the description is overly positive, time will be wasted interviewing people who will lose interest when they discover the position is not as good as it sounds. There is also a risk of hiring someone who may not find this out until after he has taken the job, and who may resign quickly, leaving the firm to go through the whole process all over again.

If the firm offers too attractive a pay and benefits package, it may end up spending more money than it should to fill the position. Of course, sometimes a firm will deliberately offer better than average pay because it is seeking better than average performance in the job. If this is the case, it should be made known at the outset, when information about the position is first made available.

Generally, if superior performance is being sought, it should be rewarded with performance bonuses, productivity bonuses, or some other kind of payment that does not have to be made unless the person hired actually does perform to the unusually high standards desired. This provides the new hire an incentive to perform well, and the firm is not obligated to pay for exceptional performance unless it gets it. A careful effort should be made to define, at the very beginning, just what constitutes the superior performance desired and exactly how it will be rewarded.

When unemployment increases in an area, people become less selective in seeking jobs. When this happens, the real estate business may experience an influx of people desiring to become salespeople, as well as more activity from licensees whose activity had been minimal. This will mean more work for the brokerage management as it tries to sift the potential producers from a larger supply of applicants, but there is no easy way to avoid this except by insisting on a record of sales or real estate experience. Sometimes, of course, the slack in the local economy involves the real estate business itself. If it is bad enough, applicants may be discouraged simply because they do not see any genuine opportunity in the work.

The Application

A brokerage firm should have an application form which should be filled out by prospective employees when first contact with them is made. An example is shown in Figure 6-1. The application provides the firm with a lot of essential information which is needed from the very beginning in any dealings with applicants. The form should ask for the applicant's name and address, social security number, and home telephone. It should list the names and relationships of the applicant's immediate family. The applicant's current employment should be requested, as well as his previous employers, going back at least five years. These are necessary for background checking and for indications of stability in job performance. The application should ask if the applicant holds or, if not, has ever held a real estate license; if so, when was it received, and with which brokerage firm(s) has the applicant ever been associated? Education background should be included, especially any courses or other studies that are related to the real estate business. Finally, some information about the applicant's financial status is needed. Salaries and other pay at previous jobs will give some indication of financial objectives; other information, such as assets on hand and debts, can demonstrate financial responsibility.

Whenever an application is taken, some information about the firm and the job should be given to the applicant. Real estate sales positions require certain kinds of people with certain abilities and tolerances. It is only fair to an applicant to make sure that he/she knows the type of work required by the position, and at least some general information about the firm. A good practice is to have a one- or two-page letter that briefly describes the real estate sales field and the company's particular situation. Since it is relatively inexpensive to print up and send out this material, it should be handed out freely to anyone expressing an interest. An example of such a form letter is shown in Figure 6-2.

For purposes of completeness, our discussion here concentrates on processing of applicants who have relatively little experience. Obviously, dealing with experienced applicants may not have to be so involved. First, they are much more aware of the nature of the job they are applying for; thus, much of the explaining and description can be

D DOVER REALTY COMPANY

1776 Twelfth Street, Waltham, Xxxxx 12345   (908) 555-4321

APPLICATION FORM

ACTION_____ _____

POSITION_____   _____

DATE RECEIVED_____   _____

Thank you for considering Dover Realty Company. Please provide the information requested below. All information that you give will be held in the strictest confidence. However, in order to enable us to evaluate your application fully, we also will ask you to give us permission to contact references and previous employers and to secure a credit report on you.

FULL NAME_____SOCIAL SECURITY #_____

ADDRESS_____

TELEPHONE: Home_____ Work_____ DATE OF BIRTH_____

If you have a real estate license,   PLACE OF BIRTH_____

list type, state, number, expiration date:_____

DEPENDENTS (Give name, age and relationship):

_____

_____

_____

_____

List former residences for the last 10 years (address, city, how long there)

_____

_____

_____

_____

List all employment for the last 10 years, including your present job(s). Give name, address and telephone of employer; your job there; approximate monthly earnings; dates of employment and your reasons for leaving:

_____

_____

_____

_____

_____

Please note any that you would prefer that we do not contact. Explain why.

_____

Figure 6-1. Sample Application Form

EDUCATION: List schools, when attended, degrees (if any), grades or years attended, major (for college): _____

_____

_____

List all course work that you have completed in the REAL ESTATE area:

_____

MILITARY RECORD (dates, branch, type of discharge, present status):

_____

Do you have any health problems? If so, list them here, along with treatment taken: _____

_____

List make, model and year of your automobile: _____

_____

List any business, social, or community service organizations that you belong to, including how long, and any offices or other positions you have held and now hold: _____

_____

_____

List at least three people we can contact as references, giving name, address, telephone and relationship to you: _____

_____

_____

In a short paragraph, tell us why you want to join Dover Realty, why you want to be in the real estate business, how much you know about the business, and what you expect to get out of it: _____

_____

_____

I certify that to the best of my knowledge, the information that I have given in this application is true and accurate.

SIGNATURE: _____

Figure 6-1. (*Continued*)

D DOVER REALTY COMPANY

1776 Twelfth Street, Waltham, Xxxxx 12345   (908) 555-4321

We are pleased that you have expressed an interest in becoming an associate with Dover Realty Company. The purpose of this letter is to describe our firm to you more fully and to give an idea of what to expect in a career as a real estate associate, and what we at Dover Realty expect of our own associates.

Before you can become associated with our or any other company in a sales position,you must hold the proper license. If you are not licensed,you should make arrangements to take the licensing examination as soon as possible. There are many schools specializing in providing the necessary instruction to applicants for licenses, and we have one here at Dover; our tuition fee is $150.00 for the full six-week course that meets twice weekly for three-hour sessions. An advantage of taking your course from us is that you will meet some of our people and can get to know us better; however you may take your course, if you need it, wherever you like.

All Dover Realty associates are required to own and use a late-model, air-conditioned automobile which is clean and undamaged. While most associates use four-door sedans, some use luxury vans or station wagons. You should expect at least a three to six month period of no income as you undergo training and begin to do your first sales work. For new associates we can arrange a small draw on future commissions, not to exceed $750 per month; as your commissions begin to come in, 50% of your commission earnings will be retained by the company until your accrued draw has been paid off. If you leave the Company while still owing on the draw, our draw arrangement will make you legally liable to pay off the balance within one year, and an interest rate of 18% of the unpaid balance will be charged, beginning with the date of your resignation. In no case will draws continue for more than six months after initial association with the firm. At present it is our policy not to renew contracts of associates who do not earn at least $10,000.00 per year in commission to themselves.

Our commission arrangement is that the associate receives 50% of all commission income that he brings into the firm. We pay an additional override of 5% of commissions brought in in excess of a total of $40,000 per year, and a 10% override (a total of 60%) on any commissions in excess of $75,000.00 that an associate brings into the firm in one year. These overrides are payable on June 30 of the following year, providing that the associate is still under contract to our firm.

You should expect to spend at least four to six weeks in training after associating with us. We expect our associates to be knowledgeable professionals, and to undergo serious training and learning that will make them so. A new associate spends an initial probationary period as an employee of the firm,

Figure 6-2. Sample Informative Letter to Applicants

during which he undergoes our training program and begins his early sales experience. Upon satisfactory completion of this phase (usually four to six months) he becomes a full associate. All our associates are independent contractors: that is an arrangement which allows great professional flexability. For tax purposes, an independent contractor is self-employed and, so, must pay estimated taxes to both Federal and State Government during the year, must pay self-employed tax (instead of Social Security withholding), must arrange his own personal health, life and automobile insurance, and, generally, must handle his finances himself. None of these will be withheld from commission checks paid by the Company. However, during the probationary period the new associate is classified as an employee, and income and Social Security taxes will be withheld.

Because you will be responsible for your own finances, and because of the nature of commission income, you should be prepared to provide from your own savings or other sources available to you the income you will need to maintain the living standard you desire during the time you are on draw, and until your commission income reaches suitable levels. You should always keep a fairly large reserve of savings on hand to tide you over slack periods; proper management of your personal finances is absolutely essential to a successful career in real estate.

Real estate sales requires hard work. We do not normally hire associates who will be unable to devote their full time to their work with us because we do not believe it is the kind of job that you can take up only when it is convenient. Associates may find themselves working at all hours of the day or night and there is an abundance of work on weekends. All of our associates are expected to list properties as well as to sell them, and they are expected to spend a considerable amount of their time soliciting business from both buyers and sellers. Many aspects of this job are not glamorous, but they must be done, and done well, if success is to follow. Many people new to the business experience initial success by involving friends, relatives and acquaintances in deals, but this source soon dries up. The successful associate is the one who is able to deal with the public at large.

At Dover Realty we insist on the highest standards of ethical conduct and honest dealing. Our reputation is our most treasured possession, and we want our associates to value their own reputations just as highly. We do not engage in high-pressure tactics, nor do we try to sell people property that they may not really want or need. Our business is not just selling--it is service. We insist on friendly service, conscientious assistance and advice, and careful attention to all details by our Associates.

Again, we thank you for your interest in the real estate business and in Dover Realty. Now that you know more about both, you are better able to judge if this is for you. If it is, we will be happy to discuss it further with you.

Figure 6-2. *(Continued)*

passed over. Second, their abilities and reputations already may be known by the firm's managers, since successful salespeople are noticeable in the local business environment.

The Introductory Interview

Once the completed application has been examined, an initial personal interview can take place. If possible, it is advisable that the applicant have time to read over any available materials describing the position, the company, and the nature of the business. The application and initial interview can be handled during the same visit.

The introductory interview occurs between strangers who may not have known of one another's existence a few minutes before. Therefore, it cannot be expected to be a circumstance in which detailed personal matters are discussed. Its main purpose is to give both parties the opportunity to get some important impressions. This should be the interviewer's objective, and to make certain that the application is complete and ask any questions that are immediately brought to mind by the information it provides. The interviewer also should expect, and encourage, questions from the applicant.

Necessary Qualifications

Throughout the application procedure, both applicant and firm are free to say "No." That is, either may terminate the process. After the initial interview, the firm should proceed only if the following conditions are met:

1. *The applicant should have the personality and desire necessary for success in the business.* Clues to this lie in what the applicant says and the manner in which he/she acts. Overly forceful or negative personalities should be avoided. People do not like to be bullied by salespeople. Prospective salespeople ought to show some self-confidence, since they will be acting alone much of the time, and have to be trusted to do so. Also, a confident personality is more likely to be trusted by the people he/she deals with, and this is a very important quality for success in real estate brokerage. The applicant's demeanor and appearance should be pleasing.

Actual physical appearance is not so important, since even people who might be thought quite ugly can dress to cover whatever flaws they may seem to have, and a good personality can hide it completely. However, mode of dress is important. Peculiar clothing styles are to be avoided, as are general uncleanliness and slovenliness.

2. *The applicant should show a strong interest in the real estate business.* This is not an easy line of work in which to become established, and a person who does not have a strong interest is likely to lose heart and quit early on. The desire to make a lot of money is not enough: everybody wants to make a lot of money, but not everyone has the desire to make the sacrifices and do the necessary work. An applicant who chooses the real estate field because of a strong interest is preferable to one who just needs a job.

3. *The applicant should know what he/she will be getting into in the real estate business.* A lot of people think real estate looks attractive because they imagine themselves showing attractive homes to attractive people, and generally earning lots of money by taking pleasant afternoon outings. They are horrified to learn that they will be expected to solicit listings from total strangers; to conduct open houses; to spend boring floor time at the office; to conduct business at all hours of the day and night, especially evenings and weekends, to show ten or twenty homes to a prospective buyer, possibly without making a sale; and to find prospective buyers by themselves.

They must understand that they will have to study a lot of unfamiliar material so as to pass a licensing examination and become licensed before they can participate in the business at all. Even after the weeks of study needed to pass the licensing examination they will know only the rudiments of skills they will need. The period of training and learning they will need for success will barely have begun when they obtain their licenses.

If this doesn't frighten them away, they will discover that while the commission form of payment in real estate sales offers the opportunity of unlimited income, it also carries with it unlimited personal responsibility for one's financial well-being. If they do not list and sell, they do not earn any income. People starting out in the real estate sales field ought to have savings enough to sustain them for several months. Even if they are successful right away, the time delay between the signing of deals and their eventual closing (when the salespeople's commissions are paid) can be several weeks or months. Also, they must be prepared to deal with the feast-and-famine character of real estate sales, and to withstand the slow periods that affect even the most successful salespeople.

4. *The applicant should be a stable individual with the motivation and desire to succeed in the real estate business.* Success requires that in all but emergency cases the salesperson's job has first call on his /her time at all hours of the day, seven days a week, all year long.   Salespeople must be prepared to drop whatever they're doing to meet with a prospect, show property, iron out a problem. Most licensees work very peculiar hours. During the week, prospects often require that they meet with the salesperson early in the morning or sometime in the evening, for they are at work during the day. A considerable amount of business is done on weekends, when prospects are free to look at property.

A salesperson's family life and home life are subject to constant interruptions. This would suggest that people who are relatively footloose, and not bound by family ties would make better salespeople, but in practice the reverse usually is true. Salespeople with family responsibilities know that their loved ones are dependent upon them, and so they are motivated to work hard to provide for them. This reasoning holds both for men and women. While a woman with a family may appear to be a housewife first and a worker second, the money she earns is just as important to the family as that brought in by others, no matter how "traditional" the family may consider itself.

Some younger people may have difficulty in the real estate business. Most success-ful sales personnel are family people, in their late twenties or older, who have held one or two other jobs previously and are looking for something more independent and inter-esting. Unattached younger people, who have only themselves to look out for, may be satisfied with relatively low productivity. When they have families to support they begin to thick of increasing their earnings every year.

5. *Finally, the applicant must meet the basic requirements.* Applicants must be licensed, or be able to become licensed within a reasonable period of time. They must have the resources necessary to sustain themselves before commission income begins to come in. They must have the necessary tools of the trade, including a comfortable automobile to use when showing property.

Testing

Real estate selling is somewhat of an art; it can be difficult to measure a certain person's potential for success at it. Some firms prefer to measure the applicant's potential by using various kinds of tests. Many are available, although few are designed to measure potential success in the real estate business itself. Many kinds of tests are popular and using them may seem sophisticated and up-to-date. However, it is best that the users of these tests be very familiar with just what is (and is not!) being measured:

Interest inventories are extremely useful in a career counseling setting and might well be employed at a career night or as a prescreen, but they do not predict volume. Psychological tests are for use between therapist and client and are not appropriate for use by the real estate broker. He or she is not qualified to make use of the information and [Equal Employment Opportunity Commission] guidelines indicate that a test should be related to performance on the job. Behavioral style profiling is also popular and indicates if one is a high-dominant, high-analytic and so on. It may also label them bulls, lambs, tigers, and owls. This type of profiling is very useful in building sales skills and team communication, but again it does not predict sales volume.

Instead, the broker is best served by using a *personality profile* (not test – there is no passing or failing) validated in real estate sales. Such products do work and address first year attrition which is often a terrible drain on profit. Some profiles will also provide information on how to best manage, train and retain the individual.

An understanding of . . . the difference between types of products [is helpful] . . . Two university studies indicate personality profiling is two to three times more effective than the broker's "hiring" decision following an interview. The research indicates that profiling, in fact, works very well and most brokers would profit from using a well-chosen [personality profiling] product.[1]

Testing is not perfect, but neither are any other methods for choosing promising entrants to the real estate business. Many managers rely upon intuitive, "seat of the pants" evaluations. Others look for specific personality traits or other characteristics which they feel are good indicators. A good manager will use every method available and about which he/she has confidence.

---

[1] Emphases mine. The quote is from a letter from Mary Coveny, President of Career Match Consultants, Napierville, Illinois, dated May 26, 1989 and forwarded to me by Robert Kern, the editor of the second edition of this book. Ms. Coveny's letter offered these very helpful and useful comments about testing and its use in the real estate brokerage business. I could not improve upon what Ms. Coveny wrote, so I have quoted her remarks directly. Without altering what she had to say, I have rearranged them slightly so as to fit the context of my discussion. Note also that the references at the end of this chapter cite two longer works by Ms. Coveny in which the subject of testing is discussed much more thoroughly. I recommend them both highly.

Discrimination

Experience tells in the long run; whatever forms of evaluation management is comfortable with are the ones that end up being used. We must point out, however, that some intuitive measures can be illegal. For example, overlooking women or blacks specifically because they are female or black is discrimination and violates a host of federal, state and local laws.

Discrimination also violates good business practice. There is no valid reason why persons of certain racial, sex, or ethnic characteristics should perform any better or worse than anyone else. Discrimination leads to exclusion of many capable people who could contribute profit and professionalism to the business.

Investigation

If the application has remained in the running so far, some background investigation should be made. The thrust of this phase is to get a better picture of the applicant's reliability, honesty, experience, and general ability. Previous employers are good sources of this information. Applicants usually are asked to supply references, but one wouldn't expect them to list people who may give a poor rating. Indeed, they usually give references whom they know will be very positive, so information from such a source should be given less weight.

The firm should get the applicant's permission to run a credit check. Credit bureaus can lay bare someone's intimate financial secrets, and the manner in which a person handles personal finances often gives good clues to personality and some abilities. If the applicant is organized and relatively conservative in this area, one might expect equal care in other aspects of his/her life. Similarly, a poor credit record can reflect disorganization and poor judgement and management ability. In the real estate business, it also reflects something else: a potential lack of ability to understand personal finance and the management of borrowing. Since borrowing usually is an essential part of most real estate transactions, it might be expected that one who cannot control or manage his own borrowing satisfactorily would not be particularly suitable to advise others.

A concern of the investigation should be the applicant's stability; satisfactory explanations of all job changes should be found, and the ratings given by previous employers should be sought out. An applicant who has had a lot of jobs, especially in a variety of lines of work demonstrates a potentially unsatisfactory record. Some applicants will show numerous job changes which, upon investigation, prove to have been better and better jobs every time. This demonstrates ambition and self-confidence, since the person was willing to take some risks to improve his/her situation. If negative reports are received from previous employers, they should be weighed carefully. Everyone makes mistakes, and even the best performers may at one time have found themselves in untenable situations.

A checklist should be used when a background investigation is done. A fairly general list of questions to be asked can be provided. Usually the contact is by telephone, since it is fast and convenient. Some contacts may refuse to divulge information to a strange voice on the telephone, in which case a letter on company letterhead may be sufficient. The letter can outline the information needed, or a form can be made up and enclosed. The applicant can be asked to sign several forms or letters requesting that information on him be given to the brokerage firm to which he is applying. These could be sent to the contacts ahead of time, with a cover letter noting that the interviewer will call within a few days to ask for the information. A disadvantage of this advance notice is the possibility that the contact and the applicant may get together and rehearse the proper answers.

Less convenient is personal contact; it takes a lot of time by the interviewer and can be quite impractical if travel to other cities is required. However, a face-to-face interview with a contact can yield very good information, since people are more willing to talk in person.

The investigation also should assemble proof of claims by the applicant as to educational background, licenses held, and other earned designations and professional recognitions. It should include some information about the applicant's general health, although satisfactory information of this nature can be included on the application form and the initial interview.

Final Interview

By this point, relatively few of the original group of applicants will still be in the running. These should be interviewed once more, this time in considerable depth. This interview can be much less formal than the first; applicant and interviewer have met and they both know that the interview is serious.

While this interview can be conducted in the office, it is best if it is done at the applicant's home, especially if he or she has a family. Real estate sales is not a "nine-to-five" job with a weekly paycheck, so it will have a considerable effect on the applicant's family. An interview at home allows the interviewer to experience an applicant's home situation and to gauge whether or not there may be unusual stresses because of the nature of the job. A supportive family, especially a spouse, is a valuable asset to anyone in real estate sales, and their existence is a strong plus factor.

The interviewer should make sure that the applicant's family knows the nature of the job and the particular ways in which it will affect them. If they are unaware of it, there may be a reason for concern, since it is to be expected that a conscientious person would want those closest to him/her to know the full impact that such a job would have on their lives.

The final interview should be designed to get a better idea of the applicant's motivations and personality. The first interview was too short and too formal for this, and the other investigation and testing generated only second-hand information in this area. Specific questions and problem areas that appeared to the interviewer during the investigation process should be discussed, but only in general terms so as not to divulge information contacts thought they were giving in confidence. The attitude of the interviewer should be that of a listener and not a talker. The applicant will have taken pains to present himself in the best light possible; once the interview has become relaxed, his guard will begin to slip. The more he talks, the more he will say about himself and the more the interviewer will learn.

The Choice

When all applicants have been through the interviewing process, the choice will be made as to which will be hired. This should be done as quickly as possible, and all applicants still under consideration should be notified of the decision, although it is not necessary to tell unsuccessful applicants the identity of the person hired. The information is best given by telephone, with a follow-up letter. It must be stressed that the entire interviewing and selection process should be conducted as rapidly as possible. Not only is this fair to applicants, who ought not to be kept waiting for overly long periods of time, but it also assures that prime prospects will not take other positions in the intervening time.

In the earlier interviewing stages other applicants will have been dropped from consideration. Once they have been, they should be informed immediately. While giving such a message is not a pleasant task, it has to be done, and with practice it can be done with a minimum of stress. It is best to be relatively honest, although sometimes the reasons may be sensitive and best kept understated. A follow-up letter should be sent to each applicant turned down. It is particularly important that if it is necessary to turn down an applicant who is a minority or a female, the letter should point out the reasons very specifically so there is no question of discrimination.

SUPPORT PERSONNEL SELECTION

Selection of support personnel should be given the same care as that of salespeople. Generally, the first contact will come as a result of advertisement or other information intended to solicit potential employees. The applicant should be required to fill out an application form that assembles important information that can be used to make the hiring decision. Minimum information should include name, address, social security number, and names and relationships of immediate family members. Previous employment going back several years should be given, along with education and special training that is relevant to the job being applied for. The applicant should be asked to give two or three references, particularly previous employers who can be contacted.

A particular firm may choose to augment these questions with several others that may be considered important. Application forms in a standardized format are available at stationery or office supply stores, or the firm can prepare its own. In a pinch, the salesperson's application can be used; the inapplicable portions can be crossed out or ignored.

Some information about the job should be given to the applicant. A copy of the job description is usually enough. It should describe the duties, the salary range (if this is not flexible or negotiable), and the necessary qualifications for the job. If the job is one that will offer opportunities for promotion to more responsible positions, this should be mentioned.

Checking the applicant's qualifications should follow the same pattern as that shown earlier for salespeople, although a less intensive background search may be adequate, depending upon the job being filled. A final interview of the best candidates should be conducted. If possible, all personnel who will be working with the applicant should be introduced, but this is not always practical.

For some jobs, such as typing and stenography, it is possible to give simple and straightforward tests that measure aptitude and skills. Some employers also like to give more subtle tests, such as psychological ones, but these are much harder to grade and sometimes require the use of specially skilled personnel for evaluation and even for administration. Use of these kinds of tests should be kept in context; it should be remembered that the only sensible objective is to measure suitability for a particular job, and many psychological factors will have no bearing.

Once the application materials have been reviewed, the decision is made whether or not to continue the application procedure. Application review should be done quickly, in fairness to the applicants, and also because an applicant is not likely to retain a favorable impression of a firm that dallies in its initial relationship. If it is decided at this point to terminate discussion with an applicant, he should be notified immediately, preferably by telephone with a form letter to follow. The tone should be polite; the applicant should be thanked for responding and for considering employment with the firm and the turn-down itself should be worded gently and politely.

Compensation of Support Personnel

Many firms regard their support personnel as necessary evils and are determined to spend as little as possible of their resources on them. This attitude is highly inefficient. Support personnel are useful; they should be employed when it is profitable to do so, and their worth to the firm should be recognized. This is not to suggest that fabulous wages should be paid, but it is not good business to try to get away with the lowest pay scale and the cheapest labor. A quick glance at the "Help Wanted" section of the newspaper and a few calls to employment agencies and other sources of information will quickly establish the general range of salary that must be paid in the locality for the kind of personnel being sought. An offer to employ at the lower range of salary will bring forth relatively inefficient or inexperienced applicants who may well provide less useful work per dollar than someone capable who must be paid more. On the other hand, a high salary will attract capable people, but they may be able to do more than is really needed. In either case, money may be wasted.

Good performance should always be rewarded. Support personnel who do their jobs well are valuable, and keeping them happy will keep the level of their work high and, just as important, will keep them on the job. Any new employee, no matter how skilled or competent, must undergo some period of initial training to establish familiarity with the job, the firm, and the particular demands that the position will make; no two jobs are exactly alike in every respect. Once the employee is acclimated to the job, he/she can be trusted to do what is necessary with a minimum of assistance or supervision. If the employee leaves the job, a replacement must be found and trained, and this process cannot help but cost the company money and valuable time. This makes it worth money to keep capable and satisfactory employees, even though they may end up being paid more than a replacement would cost. A careful analysis of what they do and their value to the firm generally will show that they actually are doing quite a bit more for the company than a new person would be able to.

TERMINATION

Not all salespeople will be good enough for a firm to keep. Some will violate the law or will engage in practices the firm discourages. Others may work hard and proceed correctly but just won't be able to produce enough income to make it profitable for the firm to keep them. In these cases it becomes necessary to terminate their employment with the firm.

Firing people is a distasteful responsibility of management. From time to time it has to be done if the firm is to be operated properly. No matter how careful the process is carried out, there always exists an element of cold-bloodedness about it that makes most managers uncomfortable. Firing people ranks at or near the top of the manager's list of things he/she least likes to do.

Firing someone should always be done in person, and by the manager who works most closely with that person. The terminated employee or contractor is entitled the opportunity to talk over the situation and to learn firsthand what the reasons are. Some firings are automatic, especially when violations of law or ethical conduct or the firm's policies occurs. In fact, many firms write into their employment contracts language listing specific violations that will be cause for immediate termination by management. It is absolutely essential that all personnel be aware of actions that are forbidden and will result in their being fired.

The most difficult firing occurs when a sincere, hardworking person has to be let go because of poor productivity. This happens most often with salespeople who are fairly new to the business and who are discovering that the work simply is not what they are suited for. Often, arrangements can be made ahead of time to set some standards of performance so that individuals can monitor their progress as they go along. In many cases, those who are not measuring up will resign voluntarily, as they will know that their performance is not suitable.

Firings should be conducted in private and person to person. It is difficult to imagine any situation that would justify the public embarrassment, anger, and ill feeling that would occur if someone were to be fired in the company of others who are not direct superiors. The best technique is to explain the situation to the individual and to ask for a letter of resignation. In that manner, the records will not contain letters from management that spell out particular violations, and there is no risk that they will fall into unauthorized hands. If necessary, management can keep a separate set of private files, available only to select members of management, that provide more detail about the performance of the person who is fired. Records such as these should be kept under lock and key, or in a bank vault safety deposit box to which only authorized people have access.

Some people who are fired will seek employment elsewhere, and future employers may ask the brokerage firm for its information about the person. In such cases it is imperative to take great care, especially if the information to be given is derogatory. If a salesperson is fired for breaking the law, and there are public records of hearings or court activities in which he/she was found guilty, the firm can mention such public information and records with no fear of slander or libel. However, any other information given out that reflects poorly upon a person's ability or character must be fully documented. The firm should be prepared to prove, in a court of law, everything it says about someone.

DISCUSSION QUESTIONS AND PROJECTS

1. Interview one or two managers of large brokerage firms in your area. What do they think is their best source of new salespeople?

2. From the same source, find out what they think is the kind of person they look for when they hire sales people. What characteristics do they think are most important? What characteristics should be avoided?

3. If you are using this book in a classroom situation, divide the class into groups of two people each. One person "interviews" the other, taking down all pertinent information and making a decision as to whether or not the person being interviewed should be hired.

4. From the same source as in (1), find out the application procedure they use. Collect and evaluate all the materials used in the application process.

5. Why is a background investigation of a prospective salesperson important? What kind of information should be sought?

6. Assume you are the sales manager of a real estate brokerage firm. Draw up a list of the qualifications and characteristics you would look for in an applicant for a salesperson's position if that applicant has no previous real estate selling experience.

7. If the firm can afford to hire only one support person on its staff, what duties should that person be given?

REFERENCES

COVENY, MARY, *Improving the Odds: Effective Salesperson Selection Via Profiling*, ORER Paper Number 49. Urbana, Illinois: Office of Real Estate Research,

College of Commerce and Business Administration, University of Illinois, Urbana-Champaign.

Coveny, Mary, "Recruiting: A Manager's Toughest Job", *The Real Estate Professional*, November- December, 1988.

SEVEN

THE POLICY MANUAL

Purpose of the Policy Manual

Arrangement of the Manual

The Policy Manual and Independent Contractors

Revision

Example

In any organization the staff must be aware of management objectives and policy, and each staff member must know what his/her contribution to the attainment of management goals and objectives is supposed to be. In large firms, the individual employee's contribution is carefully described in the job description. In brokerage firms, the duties of support staff also can be. However, the sales force, which usually amounts to the majority of the firm's total staff, operates independently. Salespeople do much of their work outside the firm's offices, in unsupervised situations. It is essential that they have available a clear and precise statement of the firm's policies, goals and objectives. This statement must cover not only matters of doing business with the public, but also operation and cooperation within the firm.

PURPOSE OF THE POLICY MANUAL

A well-run brokerage firm accomplishes this objective by producing a written *policy manual*. The policy manual need not be very long; it is usually provided in a loose-leaf format so that amendments and changes can be made easily and the manual can be kept up to date. The function of the policy manual is to assure that each salesperson is given the best possible guidance concerning the firm's operating procedures and the performance standards which reflect the firm's desired image.

Many firms try to operate without a policy manual. This usually is a mistake. The advantage of a written manual is that it provides a clear statement of the firm's objectives and policies, as well as clear and written conduct standards for the sales force.

The manual should cover all significant aspects of doing business the company's way. It should cover any particular variations from the normal practice that the firm chooses to impose upon its own operation. It should provide a precise but thorough outline of the compensation policy within the firm, and of the manner in which the relationships among the sales staff and other branches of the firm should be conducted. The ideal policy manual provides sales staff members with a tool they can use so that they will be able to perform their duties according to the firm's criteria with very little or no supervision.

Since the sales force represents the company, the policy manual should properly present its business philosophy. It should describe all that the salesperson should do, as well as pointing out those activities the salesperson should not engage in. The manual should try to anticipate the normal problems the salesperson may encounter in his duties, so that he will be properly equipped to handle them in the manner in which the company wants them handled.

The policy manual also can be used as a recruiting tool. It can be shown to prospective salespeople as a convenient and concise way of explaining the firm's policies and the working surroundings and conditions that they might expect. A good policy manual can also be a training device.

ARRANGEMENT OF THE MANUAL

The policy manual should be divided into several parts. One should describe the company itself, including perhaps a brief history, a description of the company's current status, and a short description of the current goals and objectives. Another section addresses the manner in which the sales force should approach the public, both in the solicitation of listings and the handling of sales. One section will cover everything the salesperson should know about dealings within the company, and especially with others on the sales force. A section must describe the company's compensation practices, and its methods of handling various problems that might arise within the firm.

Many firms use the manual for more than just a statement of company policy. Changes in law and the company's business environment can be described. Trade articles, news items, newsletters and other information materials of general interest can be distributed from time to time, to be included in the manual. The manual can contain operating and use instructions for company equipment (computers, fax, copy machines, etc.), and for the use of services such as multilist, referral, etc. that the company uses. Including all this in the manual makes it a useful tool for the salesperson, and means that it will be referred to often.

Following are a number of topics and questions that should be covered in a policy manual:

1. Company history, objectives
2. Listing procedure
   a. Use of company contract
   b. Protection of listing prospects
   c. Listing presentation kit
   d. Solicitation procedure
3. Selling procedure
   a. Use of company contract
   b. Protection of prospects
   c. Solicitation of prospects, screening
   d. Advertising
   e. Offer procedure
4. Office procedures
   a. Open houses
   b. Floor time
   c. Intra-office handling of client- and prospect-sharing
   d. Sales meetings
   e. Signs

5. Compensation procedure

    a. Commission sharing arrangements

    b. Bonuses

    c. Incentives

6. Brokerage industry practice

    a. Multiple listing procedures

    b. Joint listing policy

    c. Cooperation with other firms

    d. New homes, subdivisions

7. Other

    a. State license law

    b. REALTOR® Code of Ethics (for REALTOR® member firms)

    c. Use instructions for multilist, referral services, etc.

    d. Operating instructions for company equipment

    e. News updates of interest

    f. Other useful and necessary information

THE POLICY MANUAL AND INDEPENDENT CONTRACTORS

Since independent contractors cannot be held to the kinds of rules and regulations a firm may use for its employees, the policy manual should be worded accordingly. Only matters of law and recognized ethical considerations should be worded imperatively (e.g., "Sales associates *must not* . . ."). Wording on other matters of policy should be given in less restrictive form: "Associates should try to . . .", "Salespeople probably will find it useful to . . ." These, and similar approaches, are better because they are *not* in the form of *commands*. Rather, they appear to be *suggestions*. This sort of wording is much less severe; framed as suggestions, the company's policies protect the independent contractor status of the sales force. Suggestions, rather than commands, also lead salespeople to feel that the manual is designed as a useful guide and aid to successful business practice rather than a set of rules of conduct.

Explanations of the company's policies also are useful. First, a clear and sensible explanation is more powerful, and appeals to reason. Secondly, explanations reinforce the "suggesting" nature of the manual. A well-explained "recommendation" will be convincing, and will be more likely than commands to lead to the behavior desired from independent contractor salespeople. It also will help to reinforce the independent contractor status of the salesperson.

REVISION

The manual should be kept up-to-date. A loose-leaf format is very helpful here, because it makes revision of the manual easy. Of course, a well-managed firm probably won't change its policies and objectives very often. However, changes in law, the business environment and other external matters can happen frequently, and ought to be distributed for inclusion in the manual.

Revision of policy should be undertaken whenever necessary, but not until there has been proper discussion and consideration of the changes to be made. Some may be needed just to make things clearer than the original statement. Some revisions, however, may bring about significant changes in the company's policies, goals and objectives. Proper management technique dictates that these changes be well advertised in the firm and, whenever possible, thoroughly discussed by all who will be affected by them.

Changes should not be made for their own sake, but in response to genuine need. A poor policy or one that isn't working ought to be changed. Good policy should be left alone. The growth and development of a business often leads to situations where changes in policy are necessary. So can changes in law, business conditions and other external factors. But any change, no matter how big or small, should be looked at carefully and thoroughly. It is better to stick with a policy that is not perfect than to try something that has not been thoroughly analyzed. Consistency is an important feature of comfort in any environment, and change usually starts out as disruptive, to some extent, even if everyone agrees that it is needed and favors it. These stresses, therefore, should be avoided except when they are absolutely necessary. When they are necessary, they should be handled carefully and with an eye toward making implementation of change as smooth as possible.

EXAMPLE

An example of a policy manual is shown in Figure 7-1. To keep it brief enough to present here, this example doesn't cover all the things that should be mentioned in most manuals. (Refer to the list of topics presented earlier in this chapter.) A real-life manual would include many topics missing in the example, and its treatment of each topic probably would be more elaborate and detailed. Also, it will contain copies of other material of interest (news items, trade publication articles, etc.) and use to the brokerage firm and its sales force.

To make revision easy, each major topic should be covered on a separate page or set of pages, and the manual should be loose-leaf. It doesn't have to be a work of art; copies of a neatly typed manuscript are perfectly adequate.

D DOVER REALTY COMPANY

1776 Twelfth Street, Waltham, Xxxxx 12345   (908) 555-4321

POLICY MANUAL

INTRODUCTION

This manual is to be used by authorized personnel of Dover Realty, Inc. It contains confidential information which should be treated as such. All sales personnel should be completely familiar with the contents of this manual and should regulate their daily practice by it whenever possible. This manual is a general guide and does not cover all possible situations. It is designed to keep friction and misunderstanding to a minimum. Whenever questions arise that cannot be resolved by policy presented in this manual, they should be referred to the appropriate officers of Dover Realty, Inc. for action.

HISTORY

Dover Realty, Inc. was organized on March 2, 1980 to provide the finest and highest caliber of professional service to the homeowning community of our city. Dover Realty prides itself on its ethical approach to the real estate business and its concern for the satisfaction of all its customers, whether buyers or sellers. Our policy and the hard work we have done have had excellent results; from a beginning when we employed five full-time salespersons, we have grown to have a staff of over 25 sales associates. Our listings and sales total over $15 million per year and we are growing rapidly. We expect all who are associated with our firm to reflect our ideals and ambitions, to our mutual benefits.

GENERAL

Our firm subscribes to the code of ethics of the National Association of REALTORS® and the rules and bylaws of the local Real Estate Board. All associates are expected to be familiar with these and to apply them rigorously in all aspects of their professional lives.

Figure 7-1. Sample Policy Manual

All associates should have an attractive, comfortable and clean automobile large enough to use for showing property comfortably. The costs of buying and maintaining the automobile are the responsibility of the associate. The associate also will be responsible for the cost of meals, entertainment, travel, business cards, sign stickers and MLS books.

Dover Realty will provide desk space, secretarial services, contract forms, telephone service at the office, advertising and literature, within reasonable limits. Dover Realty will handle paperwork concerning license renewals and REALTOR® memberships, though each individual salesperson will be responsible for the costs associated with the fees involved.

The office will be open from 8:30 am to 6:00 pm Monday through Saturday. Keys are issued to sales associates to enable them to use the office facilities at all other times when needed. When sales associates are away from the office they should check in every hour or two for messages; whenever possible instructions should be left with the receptionist for contacting sales associates who are out of the office.

SALES MEETINGS

Sales meetings are held every Monday morning at 9:30 am; they usually will last an hour or longer if need be. Attendance at these meetings is strongly advised since they are the forum in which much useful information will be made available. Associates who have information or questions that may be of interest to other associates are encouraged to make them known at the sales meetings. Special training sessions or other special-purpose meetings may be called at other times, and associates are urged to attend them.

LISTING POLICY

Listings are the bread-and-butter of the real estate brokerage business and sales associates are encouraged to make considerable effort to secure them. Listings must be taken on the company's listing contract form, and the listing description sheet must be completely filled out; these, along with at least two photographs of the listed property, should be submitted to the sales manager for copying and distribution to the other sales associates.

Figure 7-1. (*Continued*)

Normally, NO OFFER MAY BE SUBMITTED TO A SELLER UNTIL THE LISTING HAS BEEN SUBMITTED TO THE SALES MANAGER AND NOTIFICATION DISTRIBUTED TO THE SALES FORCE. Listing commissions will not be paid unless this procedure is followed. In unusual circumstances a sales associate may obtain a signed listing at the time the offer is presented, but only if it is patently necessary to do so in order to safeguard the company's right to a commission.

All original contracts must be kept by the sales manager, although copies can be run off and distributed when necessary, according to his judgment.

The associate securing the listing is entitled to advertise it in his name, and has the responsibility of servicing it properly. Improper servicing of listings will result in the listing being assigned to another sales associate.

Lock boxes are in the custody of the sales manager's secretary and should be signed out whenever they are taken and signed in when they are returned. DO NOT LOSE THEM. They are company property.

All listings are the property of Dover Realty, Inc. An associate who does not service his listings properly may find them reassigned to others. Associates who resign must leave all unsold listings with Dover Realty, Inc.

LISTING PROCUREMENT PROCEDURE

When a prospect for listing appears, company policy is to provide for an informal appraisal of the property and a presentation of the company's services to be made by the listing agent. An associate may "protect" a potential listing once the procurement process has gone so far as to have an appraisal presented to the owner; the associate has 15 days from that time to secure the listing. After that time, any of the company's associates may try to secure that listing.

Listing associates should endeavor to get complete information on all property they list, keep sellers informed of what the company is doing for them, and advise the seller on things he can do to facilitate the sale. The associate should be sure that the seller understands all terms of the listing and the manner in which the property will be sold. The listing associate must present ALL offers received on property he has listed, and must do so personally.

Figure 7-1. (*Continued*)

Associates should strive to secure listings on an exclusive-right-to-sell basis for a 90-day period. Any listing of less than 60 days, or nonexclusive, must be cleared with the sales manager.

All sellers should be notified of the progress of their listings every ten days or so. The listing associate is responsible for proper care of vacant property.

Dover Realty, Inc. does NOT accept "net" listings. Negotiations for other than our standard commission must be with the sales manager.

COMMISSION SCHEDULE

Single family, duplex, other small rental units - resales 7%

    "   "   "   "   "   "   " - new   5%

Building lots in developed subdivisions - 8%

Undeveloped land regardless of acreage - 10%

Commercial or office property - negotiated with sales manager

OFFER POLICY

All offers submitted on Dover Realty listings must be presented to the seller as soon as possible and in no case more than overnight. If the listing associate is unavailable to present the offer, the associate who has solicited the offer may do so if approved by the sales manager. Offers received from other firms may be assigned to sales associates by the sales manager, if the listing associate is unavailable.

Offers submitted by prospects recruited by Dover Realty sales associates should be written up on the Dover Realty sales agreement form.

No offer will be taken unless it is properly executed and is accompanied by an earnest money check or some other statement of earnest money to follow. The check should be made out to Dover Realty and must be deposited in the Dover Realty trust account at Second City Bank within 24 hours of receipt.

Acceptance of offers by owners is indicated by their signature on the sales agreement. Out-of-town owners must acknowledge acceptance by telegram. An offer must be accepted in full for it to become a contract; if any changes are made before the offer is accepted, it constitutes only a counter-offer and must be submitted to the original offeror as soon as possible for perusal.

Figure 7-1. (*Continued*)

ALL OFFERS SHOULD BE SUBMITTED AS SOON AS POSSIBLE, even if it means waking people up in the middle of the night. It is unlikely that something so important to a client will be an unwelcome interruption.

ALL OFFERS MUST BE PRESENTED AS SOON AS THEY ARE RECEIVED. Until a seller has accepted an offer he is entitled to see all offers. Prospective buyers must never be given the details of other offers, although the fact of their existence may be used as an enticement to quick action and good terms. It is illegal to hold back an offer for any reason except explicit instructions from the seller himself. Under no circumstances should a sales associate try to act in place of the seller or make his decisions for him.

As brokers, we represent the seller. No attempt should be made to influence prospective buyers that we are on their side or will negotiate on their behalf against the seller. Once a contract is signed it is our duty to see to it that both sides live up to it.

The sales agreement should be complete and proper. EVERYTHING agreed upon MUST BE IN WRITING. Sales associates should make every effort to seek out potential problem areas and solve them in the negotiation process. A sale which does not close is no better than no sale at all and may be worse: instead of perhaps being able to make a better agreement with someone else, we are unable to do much of anything until an agreement that was bad in the first place has fallen through.

PROSPECTS

Within the company a sales associate may "protect" a prospect once that prospect has been shown property by him or her. Telephone contact or other contact without showing property will not provide protection except under circumstances approved by the sales manager. Prospects who visit an open house are not considered to have been shown property except when negotiations get underway concerning the open house property itself. A prospect who has not been shown property by an associate for over eight consecutive days is no longer protected. The sales manager may reassign prospects if they are being handled improperly by the associate responsible for them.

Figure 7-1. (*Continued*)

The sales manager, officers of the company, receptionists and secretaries do not actively sell property. Any calls received by them from prospects will result in the prospect being assigned to an active sales force member. Calls coming in to a specific associate will be referred to him or her; if the associate cannot be found and the prospect is unprotected, the prospect will be assigned.

First priority in assignment always goes to the associate on floor duty at the time the call comes in. In some circumstances the sales manager will decide to assign the prospect to another associate, but this will only be done for good reason.

PROSPECT SHARING

Associates may agree to share prospects, but should avoid doing so unless it is necessary. A necessary situation might arise when an associate will have to be out of town, is ill, or is otherwise occupied. The sharing associates must agree on potential commission splits, and this information should be relayed by BOTH to the sales manager before such sharing begins.

FLOOR TIME

Each sales associate will be asked to spend one four-hour period per week of floor time in rotation with all other sales associates. Associates agreeing to floor time who do not take advantage of assigned floor time may switch assignments with another associate, if one day's notice is given to the sales manager and he approves. The associate on duty receives all cold calls for which an associate's assistance is necessary. Calls to another associate who is not present will be referred to the associate on duty and he is free to work with all unprotected prospects he finds in this manner. Protected prospects should be given the assistance necessary if an attempt to contact the protecting associate is unsuccessful. If a prospect must be shown property during an associate's floor time, the associate must find a replacement floor agent to fill in for him while he is gone.

If an associate on duty is required to show property to another associate's protected prospect, he should do so only after attempting to contact the protecting agent and after trying to get the prospect to wait until the protecting associate is available. If a sale results

Figure 7-1. (Continued)

from such a showing, the associate on duty will be entitled to one-third of the sales commission and the protecting associate the other two-thirds.

A complete log of all incoming calls should be kept by the duty associate. Additionally, a full log of all calls made trying to locate other associates asked for by callers should be kept, including a record of everyone spoken to in the search and the instructions that may have been received from such calls for finding the associate called for.

OPEN HOUSES

Each sales associate is encouraged to hold an open house at least once every other weekend. Choice of listings to be held open is left to the associate, except that new listings should be given preference. Normally a new listing should be held open on one of the first three weekends after the listing is obtained, if it has not yet been sold. If an associate is unable to hold a new listing open within this time, open house on that listing may be assigned to another associate by the sales manager.

Prospects recruited at open houses should be screened to assure that they are not protected by another associate. This screening process must not make the prospect aware of our prospect protection system, and it is up to the sales associate doing the screening to find out the necessary information given this restriction.

TELEPHONE

Telephones are provided for the use of all sales associates. Unlimited local calling is permitted. Long distance calling is permitted without restriction to relay offers. Other long distance calling is generally permitted without restriction so long as the sales associate is prepared to defend his long distance calling whenever asked. All long distance calls must be entered on the telephone log, including the agent making the call, the city and number called, the name of the person(s) called and the purpose of the call. Efforts should be made to use cheaper station-to-station and off-time rates when practical. Calls to submit offers should be made person-to-person at the soonest possible time after the offer is received, regardless of the time of day or rate structure in effect.

Figure 7-1. (Continued)

COMMISSION SPLITS TO ASSOCIATES - BASE COMMISSIONS

(1) Sales of Dover Realty listings by Dover Realty sales associates. In these we retain the full commission.

Listing associate's commission is 25% of total commission if an offer is accepted within 30 days of listings. 22½% of total commission after 30 days. On listings referred to a sales associate by a non-selling member of the firm, a 10% share of the total commission is paid. Selling associate's share of the commission is 25%.

(2) Sales of Dover Realty listings by other firms. In these the firm receives 55% of the total commission. Dover Realty listing associate's share of the total commission is the same as in (1) above.

(3) Sales of other firm's listings by Dover Realty sales associates. In these the firm receives 45% of the total commission. The selling associate for Dover Realty will receive 20% of the total commission.

COMMISSION INCENTIVE PLAN

Productive associates are rewarded with a commission bonus plan as described below. The bonus is calculated as a percentage of the base commissions earned each quarter in accordance with the commission schedule above. Bonuses are calculated according to the schedule below. Bonuses earned are payable 90 days after the end of the month when they are earned, provided that the associate is still associated with Dover Realty Company.

If the Base Commissions earned are

at least	but less than	the bonus will be
$4000.00	$4500.00	3% of the base commission earned
4500.00	5000.00	4% " " " " "
5000.00	5500.00	5% " " " " "
5500.00	6000.00	6% " " " " "
6000.00	7000.00	8% " " " " "
7000.00	8000.00	12% " " " " "
8000.00	10,000.00	18% " " " " "
over 10,000.00		25% " " " " "

Figure 7-1. (*Continued*)

DISCUSSION QUESTIONS AND PROJECTS

1. From brokerage firms in your area, assemble as much information as you can about their policy manuals. Which areas of business seem to receive the most attention? Why is this so?

2. Obtain a copy of one of the brokerage firms' policy manuals. Go over it carefully, prepare an analysis of its strengths and weaknesses, and make suggestions for improvement.

3. Are there major firms in your area that do not use policy manuals? If so, how do they handle the communication of the things that a policy manual usually contains?

REFERENCES

DOOLEY, THOMAS W., "The Real Estate Office of Tomorrow," in *The McGraw-Hill Real Estate Handbook,* Robert Irwin, ed., Ch. 36. New York, NY: McGraw-Hill Book Company, 1984.

EIGHT

LISTING MANAGEMENT

Listing Contract Form

Listing Contracts

Establishing the Right to the Commission

Listing Policy

Listing Information

Setting Commission Rates

Dissolving Listing Contracts

Listings are the mainstay of the brokerage business. They determine the success of the business and are the source of its income. All firms should have specific policy concerning the obtaining of listings, the kinds of listings solicited, commission rates and policy, and listing information exchange with other firms.

LISTING CONTRACT FORM

The real estate brokerage makes intensive use of two types of contracts: listing contracts and sales contracts. The first is the contract between the potential seller of the property and the broker hired to solicit buyers. The second is the contract between the buyer of property and the seller; this contract usually is negotiated with the help and assistance of the broker and or brokers involved. Normal practice requires salespeople to fill out sales contract forms and explain them to the people involved. Sometimes the they may engage in active negotiations involving the company's contracts (more often with listing contracts). Therefore it is essential that a brokerage firm's sales force be perfectly familiar with the contract forms used by the firm, and with the situations in which they are authorized to deal with them on their own.

Contract forms should be printed, with the appropriate blanks available to be filled in to suit them to each situation. They should be clear and concise, because the people who will be affected by them have to be able to understand them. Fine print is no longer an essential to a well-written contract. Indeed, it is looked upon with some disfavor by today's courts, especially when it appears that such "legalese" was put there to confuse some parties to the contract.

A brokerage firm's contract forms should be designed with the assistance of a competent attorney who is well versed in the purposes they are to serve. They must *never* be designed without such professional help! In some states, professional organizations within the brokerage industry (notably REALTORS® organizations) may produce such forms, with the assistance of attorneys, for the use of their members. Stationery stores often sell "generic" contract forms of many kinds, including those used in real estate. They can be used if they are suitable. However, if an already prepared form doesn't suit a given firm's purposes or policies, it shouldn't be used.

We must emphasize that a real estate license *does not confer upon the holder the right to practice law*. Drawing up contracts usually is considered legal practice Most states allow licensees to assist in the preparation of contracts when approved, preprinted forms are used. If any contract complications arise, an attorney should be consulted and his/her advice followed. The professional brokerage firm always will have consultation arrangements with a competent attorney for such instances.

Under the license laws of most states, the firm's principle broker is held *legally and personally responsible* for the contracts which, in the course of the firm's business, its agents and licensees provide, enter into, and assist in arranging. Obviously it is in the broker's own best interest to see to it that errors are avoided. Contracts and their uses are not fun and games. They are serious matters. While attorneys' fees and retainers may seem expensive, they are a pittance compared to the potential losses that can be suffered from mistakes made in contract dealings by unqualified people.

LISTING CONTRACTS

The listing contract is the contract between the brokerage and the client whose property the firm is being hired to *rent* or *sell*. Listings are the bread-and-butter contract for the real estate brokerage business. They provide the business's stock in trade: real estate for which buyers or other users are to be found. Figure 8-1 illustrates an example of a listing contract form. While details will vary from one state or firm to another, the illustration is a good representation of a simple, clear form that can be used in the residential brokerage business. All listing contacts should include the following information:

1. *A legal description of the real estate to be sold or leased.*

2. *The legal name(s) of the owner(s).* If there is more than one owner, all should be a party to the contract either by direct assent (signature) or by power of attorney granted to someone else. When a power of attorney is used, a copy of it should be attached to the contract.

3. *The objective of the contract.* In a listing for sale, this would be a statement that the broker is being hired to solicit buyers for the listed property.

4. *The terms under which the broker may offer the property.* This is an all-inclusive category, including the selling price being asked, and all special terms of the sale. These might include whether or not the seller will permit a loan assumption, will take back any financing on the property, will require payment in cash. Will the seller pay points on a buyer's new financing? Are there any other special circumstances, such as a date before which the seller does not want to leave, or certain fixtures that the seller does not intend to sell along with the property? All these should be spelled out in the listing contract.

5. *An expiration date.* Licensing law in many states requires an expiration date in all listings, and it is always advisable to put one in.

6. *The manner in which the commission is to be calculated and when and how it is to be paid.*

The sample contract form in Figure 8-1 has another useful feature, the "information card" that is printed on it. This section, in the top half of the form, provides space for the listing salesperson to insert relevant marketing information about the property. It is a simple matter for the brokerage firm to copy that part of the form and distribute it to all other salespeople for insertion in their listing books. A copy of this information can be relayed to cooperating brokerages and multilist services.

D DOVER REALTY COMPANY

1776 Twelfth Street, Waltham, Xxxxx 12345   (908) 555-4321

SPECIAL SERVICE—SALES MANAGEMENT AGREEMENT

In **Consideration** of the services of DOVER REALTY CO., hereinafter called the Agent, and efforts on his part and at his expense to obtain a purchaser for me for the property described herein, undersigned seller does hereby grant to said agent a term of _____ months from date, the **exclusive right to sell** the following described property situated in the City of _____,
County of _____, Xxxx to-wit:

Encumbrance		Term		Size of Lot		F	R	S	S
Original Date		How Payable		Addition				Lot	Blk.
To Whom		% Int.		Faces		Contour			
Style		School		Carpets		Color			
Material		Transportation		Drapes		Fireplace			
Age	Condition	Stores		Oven		Range			
Approx. Sq. Ft.		Taxes		Washer Conn.		220			
Bedrooms	Baths	Ins.		Disposal		Dishwasher			
Dining Room	Break. Room	Remarks:							
Living Room	Den								
Heat	Air								
Attic Fan	Hot Water								
Garage or C.P.									
Storage									
Foundation									
Termite									
Fence									
Vegetation		Occupant				Phone			
Street		Owner				Phone			
Curb		Address							
Sewer		Salesman		Phone		Keys			
Alley		Date Listed		Expires		Possession			
File No.	Address		E	O	Location		Price		

Interest, rents, taxes and insurance, if policies are acceptable to purchaser, are to be pro-rated from date of transfer. In the event a sale is obtained by said Agent, seller hereby agrees to convey said property by a good and sufficient grant deed to the purchaser thereof at the time required by the contract of sale.

When the agent has produced a purchaser on the terms set forth in this agreement, or on other items acceptable to Seller, or if Seller directly or through any other agent should during the term hereof sell or exchange said property, or if the Seller, after the expiration of this agreement should deal with, sell or exchange said property to any person to whose attention said property was brought through the efforts or services of Agent or on information secured directly or indirectly from or through Agent during the term of this agreement, then Agent shall be conclusively presumed to be the procuring cause of such sale or exchange, in any of which cases Seller agrees to pay Agent a commission of _____% of the selling price of said property. In all of said cases payment shall be made to Agent at his office in Waltham, Xxxxx
Seller hereby acknowledges the receipt of a copy of this agreement.

Seller _____
Seller _____

Waltham, Xxxxx

Address _____

_____ 19 _____   Telephone _____

As the duly appointed Agent for seller and in consideration of the appointment thereof by the Seller I do hereby agree during the term hereof, to make efforts to sell said property, including the following:

1. To advertise in a newspaper this or other property for prospective purchasers. Agent does not promise to advertise any specific individual property but to advertise such properties as will aid in securing prospects for seller's property.
2. To immediately prepare and process a complete sales management file.
3. To advise within the first 30 days_____brokers and salesmen of other real estate firms dealing in similar priced properties of the existence of this listing.
4. To discuss at my regular property sales management meetings the selling price and progress being made toward the sale.
5. To advise seller of the opinions of the salesmen who inspected the property as to the advisable selling price.
6. To cooperate on an agreed upon commission basis with any Realtor that generally cooperates with other Realtors on the same basis.

DOVER REALTY COMPANY

By _____

Figure 8-1. Listing Agreement Example

Agency Limitations

In a listing contract, the broker is hired to solicit offers to rent or buy the listed real estate. In residential listing practice, the broker makes few other decisions on behalf of the owner. The decision to accept or reject an offer, and whether or not to make an offer in return, is not the licensee's to make. This responsibility remains with the owner. Therefore, a licensee must transmit *all* offers to the owner, as soon as they are received. This is proper business practice. It also is required by license law.

A listing contract may be very specific as to the terms and conditions it specifies, but such language does *not* mean that the licensee should take the responsibility of rejecting or trying to improve offers that don't meet the listing's terms. Look over the listing contract in Figure 8-1. It says that the broker is hired to solicit offers, and describes the offer the owner wants. But describing the owner's desired offer this way does not restrict the owner to being shown, or to accepting *only* such an offer. The owner is free to negotiate with any potential buyer the broker brings, and very often will end up settling for terms that do not exactly match those outlined in the contract.

Expiration

A listing will expire on the date mentioned in the contract. However, the brokerage firm may *retain interest* in all potential buyers to whom its licensees have given information about the listed property. This means that for a certain length of time after the listing has expired, the firm still has a right to be paid its commission if the property is bought by anyone whom the firm "introduced" to the property before the listing expired. Just how long this "certain length of time" will be is not a specific matter of law. Usually the law allows a "reasonable" time. This isn't very specific. By being vague, the law recognizes that specific circumstances of each situation have an important effect upon the judgment of what is "reasonable."

In typical listing contracts, if the listing expires and the property remains unsold (or unrented), the broker receives no payment.

Types of Listings

Listing contracts are of various types, categorized in the manner in which the commission is paid, to whom it is paid, and the extent to which the broker's employer is responsible for paying a commission.

Open listing: A listing in which the principal agrees to compensate the agent only if the agent actually finds the buyer with whom the principal finally deals. Open listings are not exclusive. That is, an owner of real estate may have open listings with many brokers, since the obligation is to pay *only upon performance*. Brokers make their efforts at their own risk with open listings, since only the one who finds the buyer will be paid Generally there is no cooperation with open listings. In other words, the broker who finds the buyer usually has no obligation to share the commission with any other broker(s).

Exclusive agency listing: A listing in which the principal agrees to employ no other broker. Since only one broker is employed, the listing is *exclusive* to that broker. If the property is sold by any licensed agent, a commission will be paid to the listing broker. State license laws usually require that any agent with a buying prospect for property under exclusive listing to another agent must work *through* the broker having the exclusive listing. In this situation, the participating brokers will have to agree on how they will share in the commission. However, the commission always will be paid to the listing broker, who then may pay a share to the other brokers(s) cooperating in the deal.

The exclusive agency listing obliges the owner to pay the listing broker the agreed commission only if the eventual buyer is found by the listing brokerage, or by some other licensee. If the owner finds a buyer without the assistance of any licensee, then no commission is due.

Exclusive right-to-sell listing: A listing which guarantees that the principal will pay the broker a commission no matter who (including the owner) finds a buyer for the listed property. In effect, then, this listing says that if the property is sold, the listing broker will have earned the agreed-upon commission. Note that even if the owner finds the buyer with no assistance from any licensees, the commission still is payable.

Usage of the term *"exclusive listing"* varies from one place to another. In some localities the term refers to an exclusive agency; in others it refers to the exclusive right-to-sell. In still others it refers to both types interchangeably.

Net Listings

A *net listing* is one in which the principal agrees to limit his/her share of the selling price to a specific net sum. If the selling price exceeds that net sum, the listing broker receives the entire amount over the net sum as the sales commission. In many states net listings are illegal. In others they are not illegal, but are "frowned upon" or otherwise disapproved of and discouraged by license law officials. The big problem with net listings is that the agent can be strongly tempted to act in *his own* interest rather than that of his employer. Two particular situations illustrate this conflict.

To illustrate the first, suppose a net listing contract with a proposed net to the seller of $70,000 is agreed upon. By law, any time the broker receives an offer, no matter what the amount, it must *immediately* be transmitted to the owner of the listed property. Suppose an offer of $70,000 is made. If the broker transmits it, the owner probably will accept, because $70,000 is the net amount the owner wanted. Under the net listing the owner can't get any more than that, either, so he/she would have no incentive to hold out for a better price. But when the owner accepts this offer, there will be nothing left over to compensate the broker. In fact, even if the offer is for a bit less than the net price of $70,000, the owner might well accept as being "close enough." The owner most certainly will accept any offer which exceeds the $70,000 net price. However, if the excess is small, the broker may feel that the resulting payment will be inadequate for the effort expended.

Situations like these offer the broker a strong temptation to act in his *own* interest, rather than that of the principal. He may try to conceal such an unsatisfactory offer, hoping that a more suitable one will come along. He may, on his own, turn down such an offer, hoping to get the prospect to offer more. Obviously, these actions blatantly violate the agent's legal responsibilities to the principal.

A second source of trouble with net listings can arise when an unscrupulous agent deals with an owner who is not knowledgeable about the real estate market. The agent might be able to convince the naive property owner to sign a net listing at a price well below the property's true market value. Doing so would mean that the broker could get a very large payment by finding a buyer who will pay close to actual market value. As an example, suppose an unscrupulous broker knows that Widow Brown's house is worth $80,000, and that Widow Brown doesn't know much about what is going on in the market. The broker convinces her to agree to a net listing at, say, $60,000. The broker then finds someone who will pay $80,000, and thereby obtains a payment of $20,000 for selling Widow Brown's house for her. This is three to four times the payment due for a sale price of $80,000 for which the typical selling commission would be 6 to 8 per cent

Termination of Listing Contracts

Listing contracts are agency contracts, and as such can be terminated by a variety of events. These are divided into two categories. The first, *termination by action of the parties*, includes the following:

1. The contract is *terminated by performance* when both parties perform their duties as prescribed, and the event for which the agency is created ends. In the real estate busi- ness, a listing contract would be terminated by performance when there is a "meeting of the minds" between the principal and a buyer found by the agent. Sometimes, however, the contract will specify some other event (usually title closing, in the event of a listing sale) as the actual termination of the contractual relationship.

2. The parties may *mutually agree to terminate* the relationship before it would have been terminated by performance.

3. The agent may *resign*. If there is no valid reason for the resignation, the agent may be liable to the principal for damages due to breach of the contract, but he/she cannot be held to perform under the contract.

4. The principal may *discharge the agent*. If the principal has no valid reason for doing so, the principal too can be liable for damages due to breach of the contract, but he/she cannot be forced to continue the employment of the agent.

The agent may resign or the principal may discharge the agent without penalty if it can be proved that the other party was not properly discharging his/her duties under the contract. An agent would be justified in resigning if, for example, the principal did not provide him/her with enough information to do the job well; required that the agent perform an illegal act; did not provide the agent adequate opportunity to show the listed property, etc. The principal would be justified in discharging the agent if it could be shown that the agent did not carry out his/her duties faithfully, acted contrary to the interests of the principal; etc.

Automatic termination of an agency contract will occur, by law, under certain circumstances.

1. *Death* of either party terminates an agency relationship.

2. If either party becomes *legally incompetent*, the agency relationship ceases.

3. *Bankruptcy* of either party, so as to make continuation of the relationship impossible, terminates the relationship.

4. *Destruction of the subject matter* terminates an agency contract. In real estate this would include such events as a listed house burning down, or the discovery that the listing owner of the property does not have good and marketable title.

ESTABLISHING THE RIGHT TO THE COMMISSION

Under the law, if the listing contract doesn't say something different, the brokerage firm earns its commission in one of two ways: (1) when it produces a buyer with whom the owner reaches agreement concerning a sale or lease, or (2) when it produces a potential buyer who makes a *bona fide* (good faith) offer which meets or exceeds *all* the owner's desired terms and conditions as spelled out in the listing contract. From then on, the risk that the buyer may not end up going through with the deal rests with the owner. In effect, then, the law says that unless you state it differently, a listing means that the principal promises to the broker: "I will pay you the agreed commission if you find a buyer with whom I enter into a contract of sale, *or* if you find a buyer who will make *this particular offer* [the terms and conditions of sale agreed to in the listing]."

This says that the broker has earned the commission when the owner agrees to a sale contract, or when the broker produces an offer which meets the terms and conditions in the listing. This would be long before the actual sale takes place; many things can happen which would prevent the eventual consummation of the deal. Even so, the broker already has earned the commission and must be paid. Many brokers use listing contracts which state that payment to the broker will be made *at settlement*; that is, when the deal is closed. This effectively gives back to the broker the risk that the buyer won't go through with the deal. This seems fair: if there is no closing because the buyer defaults, the broker who found this "defective" buyer probably does not deserve to get paid.

Note that our listing contract example in Figure 8-1 *doesn't* state that the commission is due at closing. As a practical matter, however, most commissions end up getting paid at that time simply because sellers probably don't have enough money to pay them until they have access to the proceeds of the sale. Also, state courts are beginning to lean toward the view, anyway, that the broker should take the responsibility that the buyer whom he/she found will go through with the deal.

Suppose, however, that the sale does not reach closing and the blame rests not with the buyer, but with the seller, who also is the broker's employer. Here the broker has acted in good faith and has produced a buyer who is ready, willing and able to deal. In this situation, the broker usually has a good case that the full commission is due.

Now we must make a very important point: under most of the widely-used forms of listing contracts, and assuming that there is no discrimination which would violate civil rights laws, *the principal has no obligation to accept any offer brought by the broker*. This is because by signing a listing, the principal does *not* make any offers to anyone; he/she is hiring someone (the broker) to *solicit* offers to be made to the principal.

This means that the negotiations between the principal and a prospective buyer don't begin until the prospect makes an offer to the principal. Anyone who receives an offer has a perfect right to reject it, no matter how "good" the offer is. A buying prospect who makes an offer on a listed property has no legal right to expect that the offer will be accepted. Is this the case even if a buying prospect offers *everything* that the principal, in the listing contract, said that he/she wanted? *Yes*, in the sense that the principal does not have to accept the offer. However, the principal *will* have to pay the broker's commission: his contract with the broker says that if the broker produces a buyer who will make such an offer, then the broker has *done the job* and has *earned* the commission. In our sample listing in Figure 8-1, this is effected by the opening words of the second paragraph: "When the agent has produced a purchaser on the terms set forth in this agreement . . ."

Conditions for Right to Commission

If the broker's principal refuses to pay a commission the broker feels has been earned, the broker may sue in court to receive it. In order to be successful, the broker must prove three things:

1. That the broker and all other licensees involved in the transaction were *licensed* throughout the time beginning with the solicitation of the listing until the closing of the deal and the passing of the title (or notification by the principal that he/she would not accept an offer which met the terms of the listing agreement).

2. That the broker had a *contract* of employment (a listing) with the principal.

3. That the broker was the *"effective and procuring cause" of the sale*.

Being licensed isn't difficult to prove; the state's own records will confirm it. With respect to having a contract, the best evidence, of course, is a written contract. Indeed, some (but not all!) state licensing laws *require* that listings be written to be enforceable. Being "efficient and procuring cause of the sale," means that the broker actually brought about the sale *within the terms of the listing contract*. An open listing would require that the broker prove that he/she was the agent who found the eventual buyer. An exclusive agency listing would require the broker to show that the buyer was produced by a licensed agent. An exclusive right-to-sell listing effectively *defines* the broker as having produced the buyer and earned the commission when and if the property is sold.

If no sale occurs, the broker still may be due a commission, if he/she can prove one of two things: (a) The broker was the "effective and procuring cause" by bringing the seller a *bona fide* (genuine, good faith) buyer who made the seller an offer which met all the seller's terms as specified in the listing contract, although the principal *refused* the offer; or (b) The principal accepted an offer for which the broker was the "effective and procuring cause," but due to some fault of the principal, the sale never went through.

Disputed Trust Money

If a seller refuses to pay a commission, the broker may not withhold the commission from the buyer's earnest money deposit, or from the seller's settlement proceeds. Remember, earnest money and settlement monies are *trust monies*. They do *not* belong to the broker; the broker is holding them in trust for *someone else*. All the broker may do with such money is to disburse it as instructed by whomever it actually belongs to. If this means that the broker doesn't get paid what ought to be due, then that's too bad. The broker's only recourse is to take legal action to recover the disputed amount.

License Status

The requirement that an agent be licensed in order to collect a commission can be very far-reaching. Generally, the licensee must have been licensed from the very beginning of his/her involvement in the transaction until his/her duties were effectively terminated. Therefore, to be entitled to collect or share in a commission from a transaction, real estate agents must be licensed *throughout* the time of their own involvement, as agents, in the transaction. The agent who listed the property must have been licensed from the time when he/she first began to solicit the listing until settlement. The agent who found the buyer must have been licensed from the time he/she first began to associate with the buyer as a client, until the time of closing.

Consider an illustrative example: Joe S. takes the salesperson's license examination and is notified that he has passed it. However, it takes a few days for his license to be issued to his broker. During those few days he discovers that a couple he knows want to sell their house. "Hey, guys!" Joe says to them. "I just passed the real estate exam, and I'll have my license in a day or two. Would you like to wait a couple of days and then list with me?" Joe knows that he isn't licensed yet, and won't be until his broker receives Joe's license, displays it, and gives Joe his pocket license card. Joe, therefore, wants to wait until all this happens, and he is legally licensed, before having his friends sign a listing agreement. In such a case, Joe's friends could go along and, later, might be able to get out of paying the sales commission. Why? Because Joe solicited the listing *before* he was licensed. Never mind that nothing was signed until after Joe was properly licensed. Joe's involvement began when he first started to solicit the listing, and that happened *before* he was licensed.

Yes, this seems picky, and like splitting hairs. That's because it *is* picky. But real estate license law officials tend to be very hard-nosed when it comes to interpreting real estate license laws. Very often they themselves are real estate professionals, and serve in their official capacity out of a desire to protect and enhance the professionalism of their chosen field. Professionalism requires skill and knowledge. Certainly a part of that knowledge ought to be familiarity with the rules, regulations and laws under which the profession operates. Instead of complaining about "excessive" adherence to rules, laws, etc., a true professional should know what they arc and abide by them faithfully. For one thing, doing so keeps one out of trouble with the officials. For another, it also makes one contribute to the professionalism of the business.

Determining Existence of a Listing

Determining whether or not a listing existed can be easy or difficult. Many states require listings to be in writing to be enforceable. In those states, if there is no written agreement, there is no listing. If there is a written agreement, the court usually can decide very quickly if it qualifies as a listing or not. This leaves us with two major problem areas where a dispute over the existence of a listing may occur. (1) In all states there can be such a thing as an *implied* listing. (2) Several states allow verbal listings. In these states, if a listing is verbal, then the usual problems (A's word against B's: whom do you believe?) with verbal contracts can occur, and there's not much more to be said about that here.

So let's consider implied listings. Even when there has been no formal agreement, verbal or written, a contract can exist by *implication* when it is clear from the *actions* of the parties that there is a contract. Basically, then, if you *act* as if a contract exists, and do so *long enough*, the law will assume that there is a contract, even though there is no formal agreement. Consider this case: an owner posted a sign on her lot stating "For Sale by Owner, Call 555-5555, Brokers Protected." No contract was signed with any broker. However, the words "brokers protected" on the sign were construed by the court to be an offer for an open listing to all interested brokers who, if successful in finding a buyer, would be paid the normal commission for such sales in that area. By seeking buyers for this property, brokers were *effectively* accepting the open listing offer. Even though no actual person-to-person agreement ever was arranged between owner and selling broker, the court said that both their actions *implied* that a contract existed.

In another case, Green was chatting over the back fence with her neighbor Jones, who knew that Green made her living as a licensed real estate broker. In the course of the conversation Jones said: "If I could get $90,000 for this place I'd sell it!" No other mention of that subject was made. A few days later Green brought Jones a buyer who offered $90,000 for the home, and Jones sold. The court ruled that Jones was *not* liable for a commission because no contract existed. Green and Jones had never *expressly* agreed that Green was being employed to sell Jones's property. Merely expressing interest in selling does not create a contract. On the other hand, if Jones had said, "I'd pay a 6 percent commission to anyone who brought me a buyer who'd pay $90,000 for this place," *that* statement, spoken to a licensee, probably *would* have created a listing contract.

In the final analysis, it is always best to have a written listing contract that spells out all conditions. These will carry the greatest possible weight in court and are very difficult to argue against.

Cause of Sale

Showing that the broker brought about the sale also may be easy or difficult. In an exclusive-right-to-sell listing, the fact that the property was sold usually is enough to satisfy the requirement. Disputes more often arise with other kinds of listings and usually concern whether or not the broker, or someone else, caused the sale. If the listing agreement allows the owner to find his/her own buyer without having to pay a commission (exclusive agency or open listing), dispute can arise. Suppose a buyer saw the broker's sign in someone's yard, or saw the broker's advertisement in the newspaper, and then went directly to the owner to negotiate. Usually this situation is *not* enough to establish that the broker had enough professional involvement in the transaction to be entitled to a commission. The courts say that anyone can put a FOR SALE sign in the yard, or run an ad; such action is not specialized professional service. However, if the eventual buyer contacted the broker and was directed by him/her to the property, the broker usually has established the "claim" on that buyer.

It is wise for brokers to keep careful list of all prospects they have come in contact with for any property they have listed. When a prospective buyer has been shown a property, many brokers send the owner a letter naming the prospect and telling when the showing occurred; the broker keeps a copy of each of these letters in the appropriate files. This has the double effect of providing evidence that the prospect had dealt with the broker and also letting the owners know that the broker is conscientious about keeping them up to date on the progress of the selling effort.

LISTING POLICY

Real estate brokerage firms prefer to use the exclusive-right-to-sell listing contract whenever possible. Many insist on it and will not enter into any other kind of agreement. While it may appear that the best feature of this arrangement is that the broker gets paid even when the seller finds his own buyer, this really isn't the reason. Brokers and salespeople are professionals who want to do their job, and not lazy sluggards who hope that others will do it for them. In fact, owners rarely find the buyer anyway. Homeowners usually don't have the skills and knowledge needed to arrange an advantageous sale of their property. Even so, they might think it unfair that if, somehow, they are successful, they still should pay the broker. A much more important advantage of using the exclusive-right-to-sell listing is to get the owner *out* of the selling process. It makes it easy to convince the seller to refer all inquires to the broker, which is just what the broker wants, because he/she is much more capable of making the sale than is the owner.

An exclusive agency listing still encourages the seller to try to sell himself, and therefore encourages him to keep to himself all leads he obtains. While it is true that he may not make much of these leads, they will be lost to the broker, who is much more capable of turning one of them into a genuine or satisfactory buyer. Owners can be a valuable source of leads; they and their households spend much more time in and around the listed property than the broker can, so they may end up fielding the initial inquiries from some potential buyers who see the FOR SALE sign. With an exclusive-right-to-sell listing, the broker can tell the owner, "Refer all leads to me. Make me do my job; there's no sense in your doing it for me." In this manner he will get leads the owner accumulates, and so will have the best opportunity to do the most effective job. The owner should be instructed to give little information: tell the prospect to contact the broker and try to get the prospect's name and telephone number and relay those to the broker. The owner should not offer to show prospects around on his own and should politely refuse requests for showings.

Use of the Open Listing

The basic nature of the open listing appears very unattractive to the brokerage firm, since it receives no payment at all unless it is the one firm that finds the buyer. However, there are circumstances under which the open listing can be useful. It is handy when an owner really does not want to list, but the broker thinks he has, or easily can find, a good buying prospect. In such a case, the broker might be willing to risk an open listing. Getting an open listing may not be very difficult, either. The seller can be told: "What have you got to lose? You don't pay me unless I bring you a deal you are willing to take." A typical procedure is to open-list the property at a price higher than that which the owner is asking on a for-sale-by-owner basis. This allows the broker's commission to be included at no perceived loss to the seller.

The open listing also gives the broker a "foot in the door" with the owner. The broker now has the opportunity to demonstrate his/her qualifications first-hand to the owner. While an offer the broker brings in might not be as high as the open-listed price, the owner still will be confronted with a genuine offer: somebody wants to buy. The offer may not be as much as the asking price, but then, does the owner have any other reliable prospects of his own? Of course the owner might refuse the offer, but few brokers would be uncomfortable in the position of one who has a reasonable offer on a property that an owner wants to sell.

One particular use of the open listing is the listing of new homes from builders. Many builders are willing to pay a commission to a selling broker, but they are reluctant to give a single brokerage firm exclusive agency. (They usually won't give an exclusive-right-to-sell because they often have their own marketing efforts, they are in a good position to garner curious prospects by themselves, and they usually have some experience in selling.) Often an open listing is the only way to get a written agreement that a builder will pay a commission. The brokerage firm usually does not work an open listing as vigorously as it would an exclusive one, and the firm's sign rarely will be allowed on the property. Still, by getting builders' open listings, the firm increases the inventory of homes available for its salespeople to show.

Restrictions on Sales Force Listing Practice

The sales force is encouraged to list property, and usually is provided with listing contract forms for that purpose. However, no one should be given such a role without the experience necessary to handle it properly. It is good practice to limit the degree to which salespeople can negotiate listings based upon their experience and capabilities. Many firms require that all listings be approved by the sales manager before they become binding; this gives the manager the opportunity to look them over and to arrange for alterations where necessary.

By law, real estate sales commissions are negotiable. However, this doesn't prevent the firm from quoting a fixed listing commission when asked. Most important, negotiation of a commission rate other than the one usually quoted should be done by management or by trusted and competent salespeople who can be counted on to make the same decisions management would. There are times when departure from a fixed commission schedule may be advisable, but this discretion does not belong with the sales force.

"FOR SALE" Signs

The FOR SALE sign is one of the best means of advertising the brokerage firm and should be used in most circumstances. The exact use and design of this valuable tool is discussed in the next chapter, but some mention of its use is necessary here. First, some localities prohibit them and in others their use may be legal but not traditional. This occurs particularly in prestigious neighborhoods where residents may feel that the signs, no matter how handsome or unobtrusive, detract from the appearance of the community. A FOR SALE sign cannot be erected on an owner's property without his permission, and if the use of one is intended, permission to use it should be a part of the listing contract.

Recent practice has evolved the use, by some firms, of very large and impressive signs that actually have to be erected in the true sense of the word: a post-hole digger has to dig a real hole, and a large signpost is inserted. The brokerage firm has to assume responsibility for the damage done to the lawn or grounds by the sign. Smaller signs on wire stakes or narrow wooden posts do much less damage, but if any is done the broker will be responsible for necessary repairs. On the rare occasions when a listing expires and the property is not sold, the broker should remove the sign immediately.

When the property is sold, it is general practice to put a SOLD label on the sign; once again, this is very effective advertising on the part of the broker. It is advisable to stipulate in the listing contract that the SOLD sign can remain on the property until the deal is closed, or even until the new owner takes possession. Brokers differ in their practice as to when to put the SOLD label on. Some do as soon as the seller has accepted a deal; others wait until financing has been approved.

LISTING INFORMATION

Information is basic to the selling effort; giving information is the heart of the real estate agent's job. When a listing is obtained, it is necessary get as much information as possible concerning the property, its features, and terms and conditions under which the seller is willing to transact. The listing contract form shown in Figure 8-1 has a large part devoted to this kind of descriptive material. The information section can be copied and given to all the firm's salespeople. This information also can be passed to other brokerage firms, a practice that is frequent especially in areas where no multilist exists. If the firm does belong to a multilist program, then it is expected that extensive information will be obtained and put on the network. An example of a filled-out information form is provided in Figure 8-2.

SETTING COMMISSION RATES

Until the late 1960s, it was fairly common practice for local organizations of brokerages to establish uniform schedules of commission rates that were to be observed by all member firms. Since these groups tended to include all of the major firms in the area, the rate schedules they set also tended to dictate the norm. However, this practice also attracted the interested attention of the Anti-Trust Division of the United States Justice Department, which established that such policies were in restraint of trade and therefore illegal. From that time on, commission rates have had to be genuinely negotiable between the broker and employer. This, of course, does not mean that the individual firm cannot set up its own schedule of commissions for various kinds of deals. Doing so simply constitutes the same sort of thing as publishing a firm's "price list." Customers are free to try to negotiate different rates from the firm's schedule and to attempt the same with other firms.

Nevertheless, commission rates tend to be relatively standardized in a given area, although it is much more likely that these rates are set competitively than by collusion or agreement. Generally speaking, firms that charge higher than "going" rates will lose business to those firms whose rates are lower. Firms charging less than the going rate may get more business, but may also find that their commission fees are not enough to sustain the firm in the long run. Either they go out of business or they eventually raise their rates closer to the prevailing level.

The "Right" Commission Rate

What, then, is the reasonable rate that should be charged? This is a question that cannot be answered definitely because local and other considerations will have a significant effect. However, surveying the various real estate markets in the nation can lead to some generalized conclusions. The prevailing commission rate in most markets appears to be 6 to 7 percent on resale homes (that is, homes being sold by people other than build-

Encumbrance $66,787.09	Term 28 years ($663.45 PITI)	Size of Lot 48	F 48	R 113	S 113	S
Original Date 8/30/88	How Payable $663.45 P+1	Addition Marlowe Field		Lot 17	Blk. R	

To Whom Waltham Federal	% Int. 9.5	Faces east	Contour flat	
Style Patio Ranch	School Tennyson, Main High	Carpets yes	Color rust / white	
Material Stucco and cedar	Transportation walk	Drapes yes	Fireplace yes	
Age 2 years Condition excellent	Stores all, Waltham Mall 1 mi.	Oven double wall	Range built-in	
Approx. Sq. Ft. 1383	Taxes $1182.44	Washer Conn. yes	Range 220 yes	
Bedrooms 2 Baths 2	Ins. $348	Disposal yes	Dishwasher yes	

Dining Room no	Break. Room yes
Living Room yes	Den yes
Heat nat.gas	Air elect.
Attic Fan no	Hot Water elect.
Garage or C.P. 2-car carport	
Storage yes, in carport	
Foundation slab	
Termite Curry Pest Control	
Fence Cedar privacy 9'	
Vegetation see remarks	
Street cul-de-sac	
Curb yes	
Sewer yes	
Alley no	

Remarks: Lovely Marlowe Field patio townhome, lush landscaping, premium carpeting, living and master bedroom papered, deluxe appliances and appointments. Custom drapes stay with house as does all custom lighting. Covered flagstone patio off den and kitchen. Assumable loan; seller will consider 2nd mortgage for part of equity. Owner moving overseas, will consider selling some of furniture.

Occupant Jackson and Vera Marshall	Phone 555-0001
Owner same	Phone same
Address 12108 Cedar Road	
Salesman Chatham Phone 555-9991	Keys lockbox
Date Listed 9/30/88 Expires 9/30/88	Possession negotiable

File No.	Address	E	O	Location	Price
DR - 8199	12108 Cedar Road			Southwood	$96,500

Figure 8-2. Listing Information Sheet

ders). However, in markets where home prices are notoriously high, the commission rate tends to be lower: 5 to 6 percent. Still, these lower commission rates may result in higher *dollar* commissions paid since they are based on much higher than average prices. As an example, a home selling for $80,000 in Little Rock, Charleston, or Abilene will yield a commission of $5,600 at a 7 percent rate, while a similar home in a major California city may fetch $200,000 and yield a commission of $12,000 at a lower 6 percent rate.

Market forces will tend to force commission rates to a reasonable level. If commission rates are too low to allow reasonable profit, there will be pressure on brokerages to charge more. Eventually, one or more will begin to charge a higher rate and the others will follow because they think they will be better off with the higher rate than with the extra business they may obtain by continuing at a lower rate. Similarly, if rates are too high, some firms will switch to lower rates as a means of getting more business. They will find that even at the lower rate they are making enough to stay in business profitably and so will stay at the lower rate, and their competition will force other firms to reduce their rates as well.

Of course, other considerations will apply in addition to long-run market forces. In the short run, the local real estate market may be active or very slow. When there is a lot of business available, there is less pressure to reduce commissions since firms are operating about as intensively as they can and do not see any point in reducing rates to capture business that they do not have a reserve capacity to handle. In slow markets, commission cutting may occur as firms try all available means to capture what little business there is. Even if it means temporary losses, this may be preferable to closing down if it is expected that a recovery in the market will occur in a reasonable period of time.

Typically, about half of the total commission volume brought into the firm is paid out to the sales force as their share. If a firm considers cutting its commission rate below those charged by others, it will have to be prepared to absorb nearly all the drop in revenue per sale by itself, since a reduction in the share that is paid to salespeople will encourage them to leave for another firm that is continuing to pay better commissions. As we will see in Chapter 13, a firm operating in a normally competitive market will find it has a relatively small amount of its total revenue that it can consider to be *profit*: typically no more than 10 or 15 percent. Consequently, there is relatively little extra money to work with if commission cutting is to be considered.

Varying Commissions

To some extent, commissions can be adjusted to reflect the difficulty of obtaining the listing and, subsequently, the sale. Commission rates on very high-priced homes may be negotiated to considerably lower than the normal rate, since the dollar value of the commission still will be quiet high. (see Table 8-1).

For example, a home sold for $400,000 at a 4 percent commission will yield a total commission of $16,000; to earn an equivalent amount of commission selling $80,000 houses, the firm would have to make three sales at a 7 percent commission rate. If the expensive house is no more than three times as difficult to sell than an $80,000 house,

Table 8-1 Commission Amounts, Commission Rates, and Property Sale Prices

Sale Price of Property	COMMISSION RATE NECESSARY TO YIELD COMMISSION OF:	
	$5,000	$100,000
25,000	25%	—%
50,000	10	—
75,000	6.67	—
100,000	5	100
250,000	2	40
500,000	1	20
1,000,000	0.5	10
5,000,000	0.1	2
10,000,000	0.05	1

then the 4 percent commission is reasonable. In a similar vein, commission rates on very expensive commercial property may be as low as 1 or 2 percent; nonetheless, a 1 percent commission on a sale of a $10 million shopping center is $100,000, which is a handsome reward and a considerable incentive.

Commission rates on land, farms, and very inexpensive properties also may be higher than normal because these properties can be difficult to sell. Land and farms may require considerably more sophisticated and complicated negotiations and deals than sales of single family homes.

7-5-3 Commission

Some firms may adopt a sliding commission scale even with listings of homes. An example is the *7-5-3 commission* scale used by some firms in areas where the typical selling commission is 7 percent. This is an exclusive-right-to-sell listing; however, the commission varies, depending on who sells the house. If it is sold by *another* brokerage firm through a cooperative deal, the commission is the regular 7 percent rate. If it is sold by the *listing* firm, the commission is 5 percent. If the *owner* sells it himself, the commission is 3 percent. This plan sometimes will appeal to owners, especially if they have some reluctance to list to begin with: they might end up paying a lower than usual commission. However, the 7-5-3 commission is a two-edged sword to the listing brokerage firm. It may get the firm listings that it otherwise wouldn't. It gives the listing firm a slight advantage over competing firms, since it can bring in slightly lower offers that may be accepted because the lower commission rate still will mean a satisfactory realization for the seller. On the other hand, the seller is allowed to retain some incentive to do his own selling, since doing so means a still-lower commission. Therefore, the listing firm may lose the prospects that the seller himself obtains.

Flat-Fee Commissions

A fairly recent innovation has been the establishment of *flat-fee* brokerage services. Generally, these firms offer limited services such as placing a sign in the yard, advertising the property, and giving limited advice to the seller when in the process of negotiation and closing. All calls received by the firm are referred to the property owners, who are responsible for the actual property showing and selling effort. In effect, the flat-fee firm provides a centralized listing source for buyers and relatively little more. The buyers are attracted by the firm's advertising, which features the low commission and the suggestion that a lower commission means the seller will be willing to accept a lower price. Traditional brokerage firms contend that the limited service of flat-fee firms hardly qualifies them to be considered genuine real estate brokerage firms, even though flat-fee firms *are* required to be licensed.

It is true that such a firm is little more than a referral service, and it is likely that the market eventually will recognize them as such. They will serve a purpose for those who do not want full brokerage service, and for bargain hunters who would not have dealt with a full service brokerage anyway. Typical flat-fee charges vary quite a lot from place to place, but generally range between about $500 and $2,000 or so, depending upon the area and the amount of actual service offered.

Special Commission Payment Arrangements

Normally commissions are paid in cash at the time of closing. However, there is no reason other than sensible business practice to prevent different arrangements. In cases where sellers may be in a cash pinch, brokers might arrange to have the commission paid to them over time and, in effect, end up lending the commission to the seller for a period of time. Commission payments can be made in forms other than cash. Almost anything of value has been taken at one time or another by a broker somewhere. An occasional arrangement is for the broker to receive a partial ownership of the sold property instead of a cash commission.

In some cases there are advantages (such as income tax reasons) for the buyer to pay the commission, and a deal can be negotiated wherein it is recognized that the buyer pays the brokerage fee and the seller, in return, accepts a lower price that reflects the lack of a commission. When a broker or salesperson buys real estate for himself, he may find it advantageous from an income tax standpoint to forego his share of the commission in return for a lower price.

Whenever there is to be a deviation from the manner and amount of commission stated in a listing contract, the new arrangement should be written and signed by all parties involved. Frequently, this can be done on the sale contract; if not, then a separate amendment to the listing contract should be formally drawn up. Brokerage firms should study carefully any proposal that involves a delayed payment of a commission or a noncash payment. A business needs cash to keep going, and the overuse of special commission arrangements may result in a poor cash flow. A firm may find itself with a lot of commission owed to it and holding a lot of noncash assets that it took instead of cash commissions, with no ready money with which to pay current bills, obligations, taxes, and payrolls.

Expenses and Unsold Listings

In normal practice, the brokerage firm pays, out of its commission earnings, all the fees and expenses it incurs in making the sale. However, if the listing expires unsold there is no commission. Usually, the broker will have to absorb the expenses incurred in advertising and other services; the firm has not been able to provide a service to the seller, and so receives no compensation.

Sometimes, however, the property is unsold because the owner dismisses the broker before the listing contract expires, or the owner makes the broker's job so difficult that the broker resigns. Listing contracts should contain language to clarify what is to be done in these cases. Clearly, it is of little advantage to a brokerage firm to insist on keeping a listing when the owner of the listed property is dissatisfied with the firm and its services, even though a strict reading of most listing contracts would show that the owner is obliged to remain in the contract until the listed property is sold or the listing expires. Most firms will allow a dissatisfied property owner to cancel a listing contract provided that the broker is reimbursed for the out-of-pocket expenses incurred. Some require the payment of part (or, rarely, all) of the commission (based on the listing price) as a condition for termination of the contract.

The exact manner in which such problems are handled is a delicate matter. Too forceful an insistence on its rights by the brokerage might create further dissatisfaction and possible adverse publicity. If some way to dissolve the contract can be found without causing more trouble, it should be undertaken. If the seller is left with the feeling that he has been fairly treated, he may use the broker's services again at a later time, and he may say favorable things about the firm to others.

DISSOLVING LISTING CONTRACTS

The broker's principal may decide to dissolve a listing contract for a variety of reasons, and each should be handled differently. Some owners simply get cold feet and decide for one reason or another that they no longer want to sell. It is best practice for the broker to go along, and make little effort to convince them otherwise. To do so is a direct attack on the principal's judgement; a gracious withdrawal is in order. The broker should mention that there will be no charge for the expenses incurred, and express hope that the owner will list with the firm if and when he/she later decides to sell. Because of the brokerage's earlier efforts, the owner probably will feel obligated to the firm and may even steer other business toward it.

If the owner wants to dissolve the listing so as to list with another firm, a little more resistance may be employed. The broker should describe how much the firm has already done and how well the sales activity on the property compares to that of similar properties in the market. If there is evidence that another firm has been actively soliciting the seller during the listing period, it could be pointed out that such activity is illegal, implying that the owner might want to think twice about dealing with a firm that breaks the law.

Suppose the owner simply is dissatisfied with the brokerage's efforts. If the owner's objections are valid, then perhaps the firm needs to do some self-examination. Or it may be that the firm is doing a good job, but the owner is just one of those people who will complain about everything anyway. In either case, there is little point in continuing the relationship, and it should be terminated as painlessly as possible. However, a third possibility is that the owner simply is unaware of what is involved in selling real estate. The firm knows it is doing the job properly, and its actions should lead to a buyer in a reasonable time. But, still, what the firm is doing may not seem adequate to the owner. In this case, the firm should provide a clear and simple explanation of its actions. There is no need to go into a long lecture about the brokerage business. Evidence desciribing how long it took and what had to be done in other successful sales probably will be enough.

On rare occasions, the firm will decide that a contract should be dissolved. The reasons are varied, but usually will have to do with an owner who is difficult to deal with or a property that turns out to be very difficult to sell. In either case, the firm determines that the listing simply is not worth the effort. A common solution in such cases is to stop making any effort and to let the listing expire unsold. However, this is unprofessional, and it certainly is not fair to the owner. Although it may be more awkward to do, ethical business practice demands that the firm discuss such problems with the owner and, as diplomatically as possible, resign from the listing contract.

DISCUSSION QUESTIONS AND PROJECTS

1. Obtain copies of the listing contracts and information cards used by several firms in your area. Are there any improvements you think should be made in any of them? Compare them to find what you think are the best and worst ones. Why do you think so?

2. What sort of policy should a brokerage firm have with respect to suing sellers of property who refuse to pay commissions the firm is legally entitled to?

3. What are the prevailing commission rates in your area? Are there any firms that regularly charge higher or lower commissions? Are they more or less successful than the others in getting listing business? If there is a difference in their success, is it primarily due to the difference in commission rates? Why or why not?

4. Interview one or two sales managers to find out the reasons they would give for refusing to cooperate on a transaction with another brokerage firm.

5. Are there any brokerage firms in your area that use the flat fee commission? Are they successful? Compare the services they offer to those of full commission firms.

6. Examine real estate practice in your area to determine whether or not there is much use of the open listing. Is it confined to one or a few kinds of property? Why or why not?

7. What is the common practice in your area for allocating expenses of the brokerage if the listing expires unsold or is dissolved before sale? Are there any of these expenses charged to the owner of the listed property?

8. Are net listings in common use in your area? If so, is there any evidence that brokers use them to gain larger profits?

9. Under what conditions do you think it would be advisable for a brokerage firm to reduce its overall commission rate?

10. Under what conditions do you think it would be advisable for a brokerage firm to negotiate a smaller than usual commission rate on a particular listing?

A Case Study

COMMISSION RATES

Morris J., the sales manager of a medium-sized residential brokerage firm in Atlanta, Georgia, is speaking:

"Our basic commission rate is 7% of the sales price. We've considered being flexible, or going to a 7-5-3 schedule, but we don't think it will have much of an effect on our business. Most sellers in this market are used to the 7% rate. It's the rate that most firms charge. We certainly aren't making what I consider to be outrageous profits, and I'm convinced that we couldn't make it as a business for much less. We don't waste much money around here, and we pay our people well, which means that they bring in good business for us. If we reduced our rate, most of it would have to come out of the salesperson's share, and we'd probably lose our best people to other firms because of it.

"There are a few outfits here that have a 7-5-3 schedule, or which negotiate lower commissions frequently. I don't think they have very skilled sales forces. We picked up a very productive person from a firm that had gone to a generally lower commission rate, because we could offer her more money for each sale she made. We don't cooperate on sales with commission lower than 7%, unless the other brokerage will pay us the same amount our share would have been with the standard rate. A few have done so, but I don't see how they can stay in business long. The 7-5-3, in my opinion, is just a gimmick. I would guess that 4 out of 5 sales in this area are cooperated, so most listings would carry 7% anyway. However, the seller will be harder to convince when a cooperated contract comes in, because he'll be thinking of that extra 2 or 4 percent he could save if his broker sells or he sells himself. I'd rather have a 7% exclusive-right-to-sell, and keep the seller out of the process. When we're left alone to do our best we do very well!"

A Case Study

TERMINATING A LISTING

Sales manager Morris J. is speaking again:

"In our experience we've found that the best way to deal with a seller who has listed with us and wants out is to let him go with a friendly handshake. They have all kinds of reasons. Sometimes they just don't like what we're doing. Often they get cold feet; selling a house is a big event in lots of peoples' lives, and you have to treat them well and care about them and their feelings.

"I always tell our people to try to put themselves in the other guy's shoes when they're handling a listing. If they do, they can understand how one seller may think that his deal is the only one in the world, and he ought to get the best care and consideration possible. Of course, we handle a lot of them at once and sometimes the seller just doesn't think he's getting enough attention. We try to explain what we're doing and how much we are prepared to do, and it often works. But if the guy decides he wants out, we usually let him go without a fight.

"Our philosophy is that if we keep things friendly and understanding, at least we've got someone out there who has good experience with us. We've found that a pretty good number of people who' fire' us come back later. Sometime they've tried to list with someone else, and found that we were doing a better job for them. If they just got too nervous, they usually come back when they've thought it over. Occasionally one will get rid of us because he's got a private deal cooking, and he doesn't want to pay us a commission. But that really doesn't happen very often, and we just chalk it up to business experience.

"We've found that a good strategy with people who are nervous or are getting cold feet is to agree to put the listing on 'hold' for a couple of weeks. We don't actually terminate, but we just let things lie long enough for the seller to do whatever thinking he has to do. We promise him that if at the end of two weeks he still wants out, we'll let him out of the listing. Some do decide to go ahead with ending the listing, but they never forget that we were willing to go along with them."

REFERENCES

GOLDSTEIN, PAUL, *Real Estate Transactions.*   St. Paul, MN: Foundation Press, 1985.

HANSOTTE, LOUIS B., "Real Estate Contracts," in *The McGraw-Hill Real Estate Handbook,* ed. Robert Irwin, Ch. 22. New York, NY: McGraw-Hill Book Company, 1984.

NINE

MARKET OPERATIONS

Sale Contracts

Offers

Cooperating With Other Brokerage Firms

Franchising

Buyers' Brokers

Information Services

Settlement

Defaults

Qualifying the Buyer

When property has been listed for sale, the marketing procedure begins. In this chapter we will consider some of the policy matters brokerages must deal with in their marketing operations. A sale contract form must be developed, and policy on handling negotiations must be made. Since these are governed to a considerable extent by contract law and the law governing the making and acceptance of offers, these legal requirements will be discussed.

A specific procedure often handled by brokerage firms is conducting settlement of real estate transactions. Discussion of the basics of this procedure will be included. Finally, brokerage policy must be considered for one of the more unpleasant risks of the business: default on contracts by buyers and sellers.

SALE CONTRACTS

When real estate is sold, seller and buyer will enter into a contractual arrangement governing the terms of the sale. Almost never is the deed passed to the buyer and the transaction closed as soon as it is negotiated, because both parties usually have a lot of legal and other work to do before title can be properly passed. At the time that they agree on a sale, buyer and seller execute a *contract of sale* which states the manner and the time in which title eventually will be passed. This contract determines all the terms and conditions that will surround the passing of title. It also may include various kinds of *contingent* arrangements. These allow one or both of the parties to back out of the contract if unexpected events occur, or if one or the other isn't able to make certain arrangements that are necessary for the completion of the sale.

The actual sale contract is referred to by a variety of names, depending upon the locality in which it is being used. *Contract of sale, sale agreement, offer and acceptance,* and *binder* are some of the names used. No matter what it is called, however, it must contain certain essential information:

1. The identities and interests (buyer or seller) of the parties.
2. The description of the property.
3. The sale price and manner of payment.
4. The terms of the sale (all conditions, contingencies, etc.).
5. A date by which closing is expected to be effected.

When a sale is handled by a brokerage firm, it usually isn't a direct party to this contract. However, a broker or salesperson often is instrumental in drawing it up. This is because their experience with such matters is often much greater than that of the parties involved, especially in residential sales. When they aid in drawing up contracts of sale, licensees should take special care to be sure that the contract says what the parties want it to, and that they understand what it says.

Most brokers use a preprinted form for contracts of sale; it should be one which has been prepared by an attorney. This is both convenient and a precautionary measure, since spaces are provided for all the information and conditions usually required. However, the law does not require that a preprinted form be used, and sales contracts sometimes are written "from scratch" to suit a particular deal. In such a situation, an attorney should write the contract, even though some states' license laws allow licensees (sometimes only brokers) to prepare them. A person who doesn't have legal training (and most licensees don't) is asking for trouble by trying to prepare a contract on his own.

This is particularly important in sales involving nonresidential property. The terms of such sales can be very complicated, and preprinted contracts aren't very useful. These contracts most definitely should be drawn up by attorneys who have experience with real estate investment deals. This is especially important in investment oriented transactions because even the terms of the sale can have an effect on the income tax situation of both buyer and seller. An improperly drawn contract can cost thousands or even millions of dollars to the unfortunate parties, and it is not likely to earn much respect for the brokerage firms involved.

Contract Form

The residential brokerage firm can use a properly prepared preprinted form for most of its transactions. The form should be simple and direct, and should contain space for including all necessary information. Salespeople can be trained to anticipate the kinds of contingencies and terms that frequently will be encountered, and the forms designed to make it simple and problem-free to include them. Figure 9-1 displays such a form; Section 1 of the form provides a simple way to enter the most common financial contingencies that appear in these contractual arrangements.

Land Contracts

A *land contract* (also called *agreement for purchase and sale, land sales contract, installment land contract,* and *contract for deed*) is a form of purchase contract for real estate that is often confused with deeds. This arrangement allows the purchaser to pay for the property in installment payments made to the seller; however *no deed is given at the time of sale.* This means that the seller continues to hold title to the property after the "sale." Generally, the contract will allow the seller to remove the buyer from the property, and cancel the sale, if the buyer defaults upon the payments. Since no title has been transferred, no foreclosure proceedings are necessary.

A land contract specifies that the seller will pass title in a deed to the buyer at some agreed upon future time. Sometimes it is not until all payments have been made in full, but it can also commit the seller to provide a deed at any agreed upon time during the payment period. Land contracts (which can apply to all real estate, and not just to land) are not as widely used as they once were, but they can also be useful in the consummation of some transactions, so brokers should be aware of them. They are particularly useful in cases where buyers cannot secure mortgage financing and sellers are willing to be paid in installments but are reluctant to pass title without having already received at least a substantial amount in payment. They also are used frequently in land sales arrangements where land is subdivided and sold, but actual development and building are not expected to occur for some period of time.

OFFERS

A particular feature of the contract of sale is that as it is being prepared it often is used as an instrument by which *offers* are made during negotiations. For example, if a buyer wishes to make an offer on a listed property, he/she and the broker will draw up a sale contract that the buyer will sign. This offer will include all the provisions and conditions the buyer is willing to agree to, and it is presented to the owner for consideration. If the owner is willing to accept the offer *as it stands*, he/she signs it. Once the prospective buyer is notified that the seller has agreed to the offer, it becomes a binding *contract* between them.

But suppose the owner does not agree to the buyer's complete offer. For example, the offered price may be too low. The owner will reject the offer, but may want to make the prospective buyer another offer in return; this *counter-offer* rewrites the contract of sale to reflect the owner's desires. The owner signs the redrawn document, and it is presented, as an offer, to the prospective buyer.

Legally, the following has happened: The prospect made an offer to the owner. The owner rejected the prospect's offer. The owner, then, made *another* offer back to the prospect. This process of offer and counteroffer may go on for quite some time until the parties reach agreement, in which case a binding sale contract will exist between them. If they do not reach agreement, then neither has any responsibility to the other.

Alterations

It is common practice that if the party receiving the offer requires only minor changes to be made, these changes are made on the submitted offer itself by scratching out the items to be changed or deleted, and then writing in the new or changed items. The document is then signed by the *offeree* (the party to whom the offer was made), who initials each of the changes. It then is submitted to the original *offeror*. That person may choose to accept this counter-offer, in which case he/she also initials all the changes, and the contract in its revised form becomes binding on the parties. If the offeree does not agree to the counter-offer made on the altered contract form, then more alterations may be made and initialed, and the additionally altered form goes back to the other party for consideration.

A serious problem with this practice is that the erasures, new items, and initials can become messy and even indecipherable, and confusion can result. It is much better practice to fill out a new form if an offeree wishes to counter-offer with any substantial changes. Whether or not that is done, once a final agreement has been reached it always is wise to rewrite it, as it was agreed upon, on a fresh form or sheet so that the final agreement is neat and legible. This is particularly important because other parties such as

D DOVER REALTY COMPANY

1776 Twelfth Street, Waltham, Xxxxx 12345 (908) 555-4321

CONTRACT OF SALE

You are authorized to submit the following offer to purchase the property known as:

_____ more completely described as:

_____ upon the following terms:

1. PURCHASE PRICE: The Buyer agrees to pay for the property the sum of . . . . $ _____
as follows:

A. ☐ NEW LOAN: Conventional ☐ FHA ☐ VA ☐ Other ☐ Payable for _____ years.

The down payment shall be . . . . $ _____

Subject to the Buyer's ability to obtain a loan on the property in an amount not less than .. . . $ _____
Unless otherwise specified, all loan cost and prepaid items shall be paid by Buyer. If said loan is not
available or is not closed, Buyer agrees to pay for loan costs incurred including appraisal and credit
report unless failure to close is caused by Seller.

B. ☐ LOAN ASSUMPTION:

Equity in cash in the amount of . . . . $ _____

Subject to the Buyer's ability to assume existing loan in the approximate amount of . . . . $ _____

currently payable at approximately $ _____ per month, including _____ principal,

_____ interest, _____ existing taxes and _____ existing insurance. Payments on
existing loan to be current at closing.

C. SPECIAL CONDITIONS REGARDING FINANCING:

2. LOAN APPLICATION: Buyer agrees to make application for new loan or for loan assumption, if applicable, within _____ business days from
date of acceptance. Buyer hereby authorizes Dover Realty, Inc. to obtain any necessary information to assist Buyer in securing financing.

3. EARNEST MONEY: Buyer herewith tenders $ _____ as earnest money, which shall apply on purchase price/or closing costs if
this offer is accepted. This sum shall be deposited by Agent and if offer is not accepted or if title requirements are not fulfilled, it shall be promptly re-
funded to Buyer. If, after acceptance, Buyer fails to fulfill his obligations, the earnest money shall become liquidated damages, WHICH FACT SHALL
NOT PRECLUDE SELLER OR AGENT FROM ASSERTING OTHER LEGAL RIGHTS WHICH THEY MAY HAVE BECAUSE OF SUCH BREACH.

4. CONVEYANCE: Conveyance shall be made to Buyer, or as directed by Buyer by general warranty deed except it shall be subject to recorded restrictions
and easements, if any, which do not materially affect the value of the property.

5. ABSTRACT OF TITLE INSURANCE: The owner(s) of the above property, hereinafter called Seller, shall furnish, at Seller's cost, a complete abstract reflecting merchantable title satisfactory to Buyer's attorney; however, Seller shall have an option to furnish Buyer, in place of abstract, a policy of title
insurance in the amount of the purchase price, and submission of an abstract shall not constitute a waiver of this option. If objections are made to title,
Seller shall have a reasonable time to meet the objections or to furnish title insurance.

Buyer _____

Seller _____

Dated _____

Figure 9-1. Sale Contract - Offer and Acceptance Form

6. PRORATIONS: Taxes and special assessments, due on or before the closing date, shall be paid by the Seller. Current general taxes and special assessments shall be prorated as of closing date, based upon most current information available from County Assessor's office or upon the last tax statement, whichever may be applicable. Insurance, interest and rental payments shall be prorated as of closing date.

7. CLOSING: Closing date to be approximately _____ days after the closing date. Seller agrees

8. POSSESSION: Seller shall vacate the property and deliver possession to Buyer on or before _____ to pay rent to Buyer at the rate of $ _____ per day until possession is given after closing date. The enforcement or collection of any rental payments contained herein must be handled directly between Buyer and Seller.

9. WARRANTIES: Buyer certifies that he has inspected the property and is not relying upon any warranties, representations or statements of Agent or Seller as to age or condition of improvements, other than those specified herein. Seller certifies that to his best knowledge and belief all plumbing, heating, air conditioning, built-in appliances, and hot water tank are in working condition except as specified herein. Buyer shall have the right prior to closing to have any of the above mentioned items inspected at his own expense if he deems it necessary. If Buyer fails to have such inspections made within 5 days prior to closing, then he shall be deemed to have waived such right of inspections and agrees to accept the property in its present condition. The risk of loss or damage to the property by fire or other casualty occurring up to the time of transfer of title on the closing date is assumed by the Seller.

10. TERMITE CLEARANCE: Seller, at his expense, will furnish Buyer with termite clearance by a licensed termite control company.

11. OTHER SPECIAL CONDITIONS:

DOVER REALTY COMPANY will not be responsible for any agreements by the Buyer, Seller, or Agent except those written herein. Neither will the company be responsible for any guarantee (written or verbal) covering roofs, plumbing, heating, air conditioning, appliances or any other equipment or portion of the property.

12. This Offer is binding upon Buyer if accepted within _____ days from date.

13. Permission is hereby given to send a letter of introduction on my behalf to our new neighbors.

Selling Broker _____ Buyer _____

Selling Associate _____ Buyer _____

The above offer is accepted on _____ , 19_____ . I/We agree to pay the below named agent a fee of _____ for professional services rendered in securing said offer. If for any reason the earnest money provided for herein is forfeited by Buyer under the provisions hereof, same shall be divided equally between Seller and Agent after payment of incurred expenses.

Listing Broker/Agent _____ Seller _____

Listing Associate _____ Seller _____

THIS IS A LEGALLY BINDING CONTRACT WHEN SIGNED BY BOTH BUYER AND SELLER

Figure 9-1. (Continued)

mortgage lenders, settlement agents, and perhaps even a court of law may have to view the document, and they may not be so familiar with the negotiations or the handwritten appendages to a messy contract form.

Nonbinding Nature of Offers

An offer is not binding upon anyone. Until it is accepted *without any changes* by the offeree, the offer does not bind the offeror to anything. An offeror may withdraw an offer at any time so long as it has not been accepted in full. If an offeree makes a counter-offer, doing so is legally a *two-part* event: it means that the offeror's original offer has been *rejected*, and a *new* offer is being made the other way. This is so even if the offeree has agreed to some of the provisions of the original offer. When people offer and counter-offer back and forth, there never can be more than *one* single offer in existence at any one time. All offers and counter-offers are governed by the same rules of law; they are not binding upon the parties who make them until they become contracts by being accepted *in full* by the parties to whom they are made.

When someone receives an offer, there are only two choices: *accept* it or *reject* it. If the offer is rejected, the offeree has the additional option of making another new offer to the original offeror. If an offer is accepted, it must be accepted *in full*, with no alterations or changes made by the offeree. One cannot accept part of an offer; it's all or nothing.

When an offer is made, one of three things can happen to it: (1) the offeree can accept it, and it becomes a contract; or, (2) the offeree can reject it or, (3) the offeror can *withdraw* it, because an offer may be withdrawn at any time by the offeror, so long as he/she has not been notified that the offeree has accepted it. Once an offer has been rejected or withdrawn, it *ceases to exist*. This means that later on in the negotiation process, neither party can accept (and thereby make a binding contract out of) an earlier offer which was rejected or withdrawn.

For example, A says to B: "I offer you $150,000 for your house." B replies, "No, but you can have it for $160,000." A says "Forget it." B says "Okay, I'll take your offer of $150,000."

Is there a contract? *No*. B's first reply did *two* things: it *turned down* A's offer of $150,000: "No —." And, it made a *new offer* back to A: "— but you can have it for $160,000." A's original offer has been rejected and *no longer exists*; B can't accept it later on and expect to have a contract. In fact, as the conversation progressed, A also turned down B's offer: "Forget it." At that point, no offer at all existed between A and B; each had rejected an offer made by the other.

The reason offers are not binding until accepted is that they are *not* contracts. They are, instead, the critical elements of *negotiations* which may *lead* to contracts. Many offers state that they will remain open for a certain length of time after they are made. In fact, it is good practice to put make such an expiration time a part of an offer. (Our sample contract of sale form, in Figure 9-1, contains such a provision in paragraph 12.) However, inclusion of this language *should not* be interpreted to mean that the offeror is *obliged* to leave the offer open for any length of time! Since an offer is not a contract, nothing in it is binding upon anyone. So long as the offeror has not been notified of acceptance by the offeree, the offer can be withdrawn at any time.

A great many real estate licensees find the laws concerning real estate laws confusing, but it shouldn't be. Simply stated, offers are not contracts and carry no obligation upon the offeror until they are accepted in full. At that point they are no longer offers; they have become *contracts*. Offers that have not been accepted can be withdrawn at any time. Once an offer has been turned down, it ceases to exist; the making of a counter-offer by an offeree automatically is a rejection of the offer made to him/her.

Notification of Acceptance of Offer

A final point concerns the exact moment in time when an offer becomes a contract. This occurs at the time the offeror is *notified* that the offer has been accepted in full by the offeree. It is not enough for the offeree to sign an offer and then put it in his desk drawer without telling anyone; the offeror is entitled to notification that he has created a binding contract upon himself. Any form of notification is suitable, so long as it can be shown that the offeror received it and understood it to mean that the offer was accepted.

Consider the following example: Jones lists his house with broker Smith at an asking price of $80,000. Brown makes an offer for $72,000 for the house. Jones is satisfied with all the provisions of the offer except that he thinks the price is too low, so he counter-offers the same offer Brown made to him, except that the price is $76,000. In the counter-offer, Jones states that his new offer will remain open for three days. The next day a different prospect, Green, offers $80,000 for the house. Jones and broker Smith have heard nothing from Brown with regard to Jones's counter-offer of $76,000.

Since Jones and his broker have heard nothing from Brown, they can notify Brown that Jones's counter-offer of $76,000 is withdrawn. Then Jones can accept Green's offer of $80,000. Note that even though Jones's counter-offer stated that it would be open for three days, Jones is not bound to give Brown any particular length of time to consider the it. *There is no contract between them at this point!* Without a contract, they have no obligation to one another. The most that the "three-day" phrase can mean is that if Jones doesn't hear from Brown within three days, Jones's counter-offer will *automatically* be withdrawn.

Notification occurs whenever the person to be notified, *or his/her agent*, is told. Notification can be in person, by telephone, telegram, mail, etc. Since telling a person's agent is the same as notifying the person himself, a buying prospect can turn an offer from an owner into a contract by notifying the owner's broker. The broker is the owner's agent; notifying the owner's broker/agent is legally the same as notifying the owner. However, in most residential real estate transactions, buyers do *not* have agents representing them. Therefore, notification of a buyer that an owner has accepted his offer must be made to the buyer himself.

It is good practice, once an offer is accepted, for the broker to telephone the offeror and notify him, thereby establishing that the contract exists. Later, a signed copy of the contract can be given to him at a convenient time. It has been the practice of courts to rule that if the offeror is notified by mail, notification is considered to have been legally received the moment the document enters the mails. The reliability (?) of the mails being what it is these days, some courts are beginning to insist that proof of receipt of the notification letter is necessary. Such letters should be sent by registered mail, with a return receipt requested. Offers also can be accepted by telegram or any other means of communication. Finally, an offeror can specify particular forms of notice that he must receive if the offer is to be made into a contract by the offeree. For example, an offer may require that the offeree's written acceptance be in the hands of the offeror before it is considered to have become a contract.

COOPERATING WITH OTHER BROKERAGE FIRMS

It is common practice in the brokerage business for brokers to sell one another's listings cooperatively. That is, a broker may find a buyer for another broker's listing. When the listing brokerage is paid the commission on the sale, an agreed-upon portion of it will be sent to the brokerage whose agent found the buyer. Exclusive agency and exclusive right-to-sell listings give the listing broker all agency access to the property and require that other brokers desiring to find buyers for the listed property work through the listing broker. State licensing law also require that brokers respect one another's listings.

Requirements of Cooperation

When brokers cooperate on the sale of a property listed by one of them, certain arrangements must be worked out in advance, particularly the manner in which the commission will be split. The seller will pay the contracted commission to the firm which had the listing (the *listing broker*). The listing broker then will pay the *selling broker* (the firm whose agent found the buyer) the agreed-upon share. The seller of the property has no direct obligation to the selling broker; cooperation is an arrangement worked out entirely among brokers, and they must look to one another to respect these agreements. License law prohibits the listing broker from paying a commission share directly to the *salesperson* from another firm. The listing broker pays the other firm's broker its share of the commission. Each broker, in turn, pays shares of the commissions they receive to their own salespeople who were involved in the transaction.

Here is an example: Mr. Hotte is a licensed real estate salesperson with brokerage firm ABC Realty. He lists a house with his firm. Ms. Colde, a licensed salesperson with XYZ Realty submits an offer on this house. Eventually Ms. Colde's buyer buys the house listed by Mr. Hotte. The seller's listing contract is with ABC Realty, so he/she pays the commission to that firm. ABC Realty's principal broker then pays XYZ Realty its share of the commission for finding the buyer. (This share was agreed upon earlier between ABC and XYZ as part of their arrangement for cooperating with each other.) ABC's broker then pays salesperson Hotte the share of the selling commission which, according to Hotte's contract with ABC, is due for securing the listing. XYZ's broker pays to salesperson Colde her share of XYZ's share of the commission which her arrangement with XYZ entitles her to for finding a buyer.

A brokerage firm is not legally obliged to cooperate on its listings unless it chooses to do so. At least, there is no law *specifically* requiring cooperation, although provisions of some licence laws can be interpreted to suggest that cooperation should be required. However, there is some concern that in areas where cooperation is routinely practiced (and it is in most areas of the United States), it could be a violation of agency law *not* to cooperate. For example, suppose a competing broker appears with an offer that the seller probably would accept. Is it appropriate to the listing broker's agency responsibility to refuse to allow that offer to be presented, simply because it comes from another broker? Questions such as these have not been satisfactorily answered by the courts.

These problems do not affect firms whose policy is not to refuse cooperation. Even so, some of these firms may not care to cooperate with *certain* other brokerages whose practices they do not approve of, or with whom they have had unhappy experiences. This can be done entirely in good faith; the firm is convinced that its clients will be better off to avoid dealing with firms that it does not care to cooperate with. It is best that the listing contract contain language allowing the listing broker to cooperate with other brokerages of its choice, since this will eliminate the conflict with agency law. Sometimes the seller himself will desire that only the listing broker be allowed to handle the sale, in which case refusal to cooperate becomes part of the listing contract itself.

Multiple Listing

Many communities have *multiple listing service* (*MLS*) arrangements among brokers. These are private contractual arrangements among groups of brokers who agree among themselves to establish a system of listing cooperation. Member brokers may or may not be required to put all of their listings into the multiple listing program. Listings which are put into the system are automatically made available for cooperative sale by all other member brokerage firms and their salespeople. The information required for submitted listings usually is exhaustive, so that salespersons using the information can be as well informed as possible about each property. This information should include the name of the listing salesperson, so that others may contact him/her to arrange for showings. The arrangement specifies the manner in which the commission will be split and sets certain requirements which must be met by all listings submitted. In large metropolitan areas, several multiple listings arrangements may exist simultaneously, each covering a specific geographic area and having members who specialize or sell in that area.

Common requirements are that the listings be exclusive right-to-sell, and that certain information about the listed property be submitted. The multiple listing service then assembles all active listings into books that are distributed among member firms. Nowadays multiple listing groups also keep their listing files on computers; these files can be accessed, sorted, arranged, etc. by agents using terminals in the offices of member brokerage firms. This way each firm has up-to-date information about all multiple listed property. A particular advantage of computerized multilist files is that they can be used for much more than merely containing a file of existing listings: modern multiple listing groups supply lots of other information. Examples are information about available financing; about recent sales and closings, giving sale price, financing arrangements, sale date, and closing date. This information is extremely valuable not only in keeping the listing book up to date between editions, but also as a barometer of market activity.

The power of the computer also is used to make available easy sorting of listings in many ways. A salesperson can enter a prospect's desires, price range, location preferences, etc., and the computer searches the listing files and prints out all those which match the prospect's needs. By "flagging" listings as to status, the files can also carry closing and sale information, thereby building up a useful file of recent sales. This kind of information is handy for appraisers as well as brokerage firms.

Even though computers provide access to all the multiple listing service's files, MLS services still use the familiar MLS books that real estate salespeople always carry. This is because salespeople spend little time in the brokerage firm's offices, and can't easily access the central computer when they are away. Brokerage firms see to it that all active salespeople have up-to-date books. The multiple listing book is the salesperson's inventory. These books are updated frequently, often weekly in larger, active markets.

Because of its widespread use, multiple listing is a powerful tool and often can be used as impressive persuasion to property owners to list the properties they wish to sell. The image of an entire population of salespeople being provided with the information needed to effect the sale of a property is a powerful inducement.

Multiple listing arrangements are not free. Frequently they are sustained by reserving a small percentage of each commission on a multilisted transaction to be paid by the listing broker to the multiple listing service. Others are paid for by direct membership fees charged to brokers. The books are sometimes provided as part of the total package and sometimes are sold, as requested, to firms or to individual salespeople.

Cooperation Process

Although a brokerage may allow access to its listings to other firms, it still remains the contractor with the seller and is responsible for all selling activity that takes place. When another firm desires to show a listed property, it will contact the firm or the listing salesperson in that firm to arrange for an appointment. It is unethical (and in most states illegal) for one firm to contact the owner of a property under exclusive listing with another firm without first clearing the contact with the listing firm. When an inquiry about a showing by another firm is made, the usual practice is for the listing salesperson or someone else in his firm to contact the owner, arrange for the appointment, and say who will be arriving to show the property. Then the salesperson from the other firm is contacted and told of the arrangements.

Some brokerages will give others permission to make direct contact, but it is better not to. For one thing, by insisting that all dealings with a seller be made through the listing broker, the brokerage is able to keep track of all activity. Once the other brokerage's prospect has been shown the property, it is considered good and ethical practice to let the listing brokerage know how the visit went and what the prospect's reaction was.

When an offer is made by a prospect from a cooperating brokerage, it is mandatory that the offer be transmitted through the listing firm unless unequivocal permission to do otherwise has been granted. The listing salesperson almost certainly will want to be present when the offer is presented and very often will present it without any representative of the offering brokerage present. Furthermore, if the offer is rejected and a counter-offer made, this will usually be taken by the listing brokerage's salesperson to the counterpart at the cooperating brokerage, who then will submit it to the prospect. In this manner, all dealings between prospect and seller will pass through all involved salespeople.

FRANCHISING

A significant development in the real estate brokerage industry in the past decade or so has been the rapid establishment and growth of *franchised* networks of brokerage firms. Franchise firms are established in many parts of the country and are actively expanding their markets to include new areas. It is a continuous matter of concern to many brokerage firms to consider the advantages and disadvantages of affiliation with franchises.

The franchise is not free. The brokerage firm pays an initiation fee that may range from a few hundred to several thousand dollars, depending upon the particular franchise firm chosen, the services contracted for, and the size and nature of the brokerage firm. After that, a regular fee of some kind is paid to the franchising company. Usually it is a percentage of the firm's gross commission income, although the formula can be varied to consider only the firm's gross profits, the "company dollar" (see Chapter 13), or some other measure. The fee also can be a regular, flat, unchanging periodic fee or a combination of a flat fee and a percentage of income.

In return, the brokerage firm receives a number of benefits. Most significant is a nationally or regionally oriented identification, since the brokerage will use the franchise's signs and identify itself with the franchise network. The franchise system makes possible general advertising that is well beyond the means of a single brokerage firm. One example is television. Many franchise networks advertise on national television and cable, with the cost of the spots spread over the fees received from hundreds of affiliated firms. Similar national advertising campaigns are conducted in other media as well, and they are designed to promote a professional and successful image that will rub off on each franchise brokerage.

Franchise networks also operate sales training programs and management training programs that benefit members, and they supply a variety of other useful services. Most national franchise organizations have nationwide referral services (described in the next section). They may also provide their members with ancillary selling tools such as homeowner's warranty programs.

There are disadvantages to the franchising program as well. Many brokerage firms find the cost too high. Either they do not have the profit margin to allow for the additional costs or they feel that the benefits received do not justify the price they have to pay. In many areas, franchise networks have found greater success in signing up medium or small firms. The larger firms already have established name identification in their market areas and they do not feel a need to trade it, at a price, for the different identification the franchise offers.

Identification itself is a problem in some franchise situations. While the member brokerages remain independent in virtually all areas, the franchise advertising creates the impression in the public mind that they all are somehow branches of the same firm. The individuality of the brokerage may therefore be submerged, since the advertising features the franchise name, with the name of the individual brokerage firm either missing (in regional or national advertising) or added in smaller, less noticeable type (in the brokerage firm's own advertising).

Prospects who see the franchise-affiliated firm's sign on a property for sale will notice the franchise name on the sign more often than the smaller presentation of the firm's name. If they later decide to call about the listing, they may look up the franchise in the telephone book, and not the individual affiliated brokerage firm which actually has the listing. In the yellow pages, for example, they will see a block ad featuring the names of several firms; they may call one at random. As a result, a prospect who should have been generated for the brokerage firm through the visibility of its FOR SALE sign may end up with another firm. Since in these situations people tend to call the top number on the list, there is a slight advantage for brokerages with names such as *AAA Realty*. This may be quite an advantage if the franchise's own advertising creates a lot of interest, since people will look in the telephone directory to find out how to make contact.

Therefore, it remains for each firm to decide whether or not affiliation with a franchise is to its advantage. The costs and the benefits should be weighed very carefully. If possible, interviews with current and former members of the franchise should be made before a decision is finalized.

INFORMATION SERVICES

Several kinds of referral and advertising services are available to brokerage firms, if they are willing to pay the price for them. These can assist brokerage firms in their search for potential sellers and buyers. A number of nationwide referral agencies have been set up to provide a network of referral arrangements. Some simply monitor moves made by homeowners, collecting information on their destinations and sending it to the agencies' subscribers in destination cities. The subscribing brokerage then contacts the prospect arrival and offers to help him in the search for a new home. More sophisticated arrangements (including those provided by franchising operations) connect various brokerage firms in a loose nationwide network. When a member firm lists a home being sold by an owner who is moving to another city, the arrangement provides for notification of the member firm or firms in the destination city. Often the listing brokerage will refer the seller directly to the other firm, with a strong suggestion that he select that firm to help find the new home. In this manner, information is exchanged along the network, and member brokerages, especially in areas where a lot of people are moving in, receive a good source of buying prospects.

Some of these network agencies also publish "home magazines" for the market areas in which they operate. These describe properties currently listed by member firms and give a lot of standard information about the area that the reader moving there may find useful. These are sent to the prospect and often also are given away free at locations around the towns they describe. Typical distribution locations are airports, bus stations, hotels, motels, and restaurants. Free distribution of these materials is also a potentially valuable outlet for locally oriented advertising, since the brochures also will be picked up by local residents.

A firm can generate referrals locally by contacting local firms and employers that are expanding and are recruiting new employees from outside the brokerage's market area. Some of these companies will be more reluctant then others to divulge the names of newly arriving employees, but others may be quite cooperative. A particularly good source is a company that is moving its entire operation to the brokerage's town or opening a new facility that will require the transfer of people from other areas. Instead of getting references one by one, the brokerage can try for an arrangement whereby the incoming company will give it the names of transferees as they are reassigned.

BUYERS' BROKERS

We have pointed out many times that in the typical residential real estate transaction, the buyer has no agent; no broker represents the buyer. Some enterprising brokers have noticed that this suggests a need, by buyers, for their own agency representation. As a result, recent years have seen the beginnings of the establishment of *buyers' brokers*. These firms assist buyers, but *do not* take listings. The idea here is that the buyer needs someone to look out for his/her interests, and that is what these buyers' brokerage firms do. When a buyer's broker is involved, then, the listing broker and the owner must be informed that the brokerage firm dealing with the buyer is acting as agent for the buyer and not, as usually expected, as an agent of the owner.

Buyers' brokerage is new, and in many places has yet to gain wide acceptance. Some of the problems include informing the public of the need for buyers' brokerage, determining how the buyers' broker is paid, and cooperation with traditional brokerage firms. The first major problem for buyers' brokers, then, is the classical marketing problem: convince the market that your product or service is necessary, and then get them to buy it from you.

Public Awareness of the Need for Buyers' Brokers

Most people simply aren't aware that real estate brokers are all agents of the listing property owner. One may argue that it's the buyer's responsibility to know that he/she has no agent, but it also is true that most homebuyers are not legal experts and can't reasonably be expected to consider such a point on their own. Although few agents do so, the proper and ethical thing to do is to make sure that buying prospects know that they have no agency representation. Indeed, some licensees may lead buying prospects to believe that the licensee represents *them*; this is plainly illegal, deliberate misrepresentation. Other buying prospects may assume that the licensee is their representative, and the licensee does nothing to inform them of the truth. In both cases, the licensee is either contributing to or at least encouraging misinformation.

At any rate, many homebuyers are unaware that no one is looking out for their interests. They probably also are unaware that they might benefit from having an agent. Their uninformed nature is a big obstacle to buyers' brokers, who have a hard time marketing their service to a public which doesn't understand the need for it. Furthermore, while ethical licensees may explain the situation to prospects, they certainly aren't eager to refer them to buyers' brokers and lose the opportunity to work with the prospect themselves. Because of this, many states in recent years have enacted legislation requiring licensees to notify buying prospects of the agency relationship between licensees and the seller (see Chapter 3).

Payment to Buyers' Brokers

A second problem concerns the payment to the buyers' broker. Homebuyers *are* aware that they aren't expected to pay the broker: the seller does. This is a point which is made very emphatically by traditional brokerage firms in their advertising for, and dealings with, buying prospects. "Our services cost you nothing!" Therefore, even though a prospect may be convinced that having his/her own agent is useful, it is another thing altogether to convince the prospect to pay a significant sum of money for the service. Most buyers' brokers get around this problem by splitting the seller's commission with the listing broker in the usual way. However, to do so, both seller and listing broker must be informed that the buyers' broker is representing the buyer, and that part of the seller's commission will be used to pay the buyer's agent.

Legally, there is nothing wrong with this, so long as everyone involved in the transaction knows the situation and agrees to it. The way it usually is done is for the buyers' broker's preprinted contract to include language similar to the following: "Seller and seller's broker are aware, and acknowledge and agree that Homebuyer's Agency, Inc. is the buyer's agent in this transaction, that Homebuyer's Agency, Inc. represents the interests of the buyer, that Homebuyer's Agency, Inc. is not agent for the seller and does not represent the seller's interests, and that Homebuyer's Agency, Inc. will share in the commission paid by seller to seller's broker." To make sure that seller and listing broker understand the situation, many buyers' brokers insert this kind of provision into their preprinted sales contract forms, in capital letters. This runs the risk that the seller will object to paying for the buyer's representation, but it is much easier than trying to work out an arrangement where the buyer pays directly.

Buyer's Broker Cooperation With Other Brokers

Buyers' brokers normally do not take listings. To do so would put them in an awkward position: how can they represent both buyer *and* seller in the same transaction? However, since they deal only with buyers they may have trouble getting traditional brokerage firms to cooperate with them. One of the important advantages of cooperation is that the cooperating brokers share listings with one another, thereby increasing the inventories of all. A firm which has no listings to share may be viewed as little more than a parasite: its business is to sell the listings of other firms, without providing any in return. In order to have any chance for success, however, buyers' brokers must have access to most, if not all, of the listings of the traditional firms. This means that they must be members of local multilist organizations; if there is no multilist, they must have cooperation agreements with most of the other brokerages that deal in their area of interest. A key element of success, then, is to convince the traditional firms that dealing with a buyers' broker is good for them, in spite of the buyers' broker's lack of listings.

SETTLEMENT

A real estate sale is concluded when the seller executes a deed to the sold property, and conveys that deed to the buyer. But it isn't that simple, because there will be lots of other things that have to be done before this can happen, and at the same time that title is transferred. This whole process is called *settlement*, or *closing*.

It used to be traditional for settlement arrangements to be made by the brokerage company that handled the transaction; if more than one was involved, it generally was handled by the listing firm. However, in current practice in most areas, settlements are handled either by the financial institution making the mortgage loan to the buyer, or by specialized firms set up for the express purpose of settling real estate transactions. These firms are known by a variety of names, such as *title company*, *escrow agent*, or *abstract company*.

Even when a specialized agent is used to handle the settlement, license law still makes the listing broker responsible for a proper settlement. So, whether the brokerage firm settles its own brokered transactions or uses the facilities of another firm, brokerage management should be familiar with the settlement process. So should all members of the sales force. It is a cumbersome, complicated and confusing process. Frequently the firm's customers will not understand very well, and they will turn to the brokerage and its licensees for explanations. Also, the brokerage is involved in negotiating the transaction and "nursemaiding" it through to settlement. If it understands the process, it can help to expedite matters and make useful suggestions when changes in the original transaction have to be made before it is settled.

Reporting a Transaction to the IRS

The Federal Tax Reform Act of 1986 requires that the terms of many real estate transactions be reported to the U.S. Internal Revenue Service. The objective is to assure that both buyer and seller correctly report the tax implications of the transaction on their returns. The responsibility for reporting this information lies with the closing agent for the transaction. If a brokerage firm handles the closing, it must make this report. As noted above, however, in many instances settlements are handled by other closings agents. When they are, it is those agents and not the broker who must make the report.

Even though the broker does not handle the closing, the law provides for some situations in which the broker *still* may be required to report details of the transaction to the Internal Revenue Service. The law actually provides a "ranking" of the parties responsible for the report: (1) the closing agent, (2) the lender who provides new financing, (3) *the seller's broker*, (4) *the buyer's broker*, and (5) the seller. Thus, if there is no nonbroker closing agent for the transaction, and if no new financing is involved, a broker may have to make the report. (Remember, if a broker handles the closing, the broker becomes the "closing agent" for that transaction and *must* make the report.)

The Uniform Settlement Statement (HUD-1 Form)

At settlement, both buyer and seller are provided with statements describing all monies received and paid by each of the parties. The Real Estate Settlement Procedures Act (RESPA) requires all Federally-related residential settlements to use the *Uniform Settlement Statement*, also called the *HUD-1 form*. This form was prepared by the U.S. Department of Housing and Urban Development and is illustrated in Figure 9-2.

Like so many of the forms provided by your Federal government, it looks like a ghastly nightmare: two legal-size pages of relatively small print. Actually, it isn't all that bad. It is so long because it is designed to be universally applicable ("Uniform"). Therefore, it includes spaces for virtually any information that could possibly be relevant to any residential real estate settlement. Much of this space won't be relevant to a particular transaction, so for most transactions a lot of the form will be left blank because it does not apply.

The form is divided into several sections. The top third of the first page identifies the buyer, seller, property, lender, settlement agent, and dates used. Part J (items 100-303 in the left-hand column) summarizes the buyer's ("borrower's," if the buyer gets new financing) transaction. Part K (items 400-603 in the right-hand column) is for the seller's summary.

In Part J, Section 100 (lines 101-120) show how the gross amount due from the borrower (buyer) is calculated. Lines 101 and 102 describe the price(s) of the purchased property(ies). Line 103 lists settlement charges, from line 1400 on the opposite side of the form. Lines 106-112 cover payments due to the seller, such as prorated taxes, insurance, and other escrows. Line 120 totals all the payments the buyer must make. Section 200 (lines 201- 220) shows how the total amount paid by or for the buyer (borrower) is calculated. Lines 201-209 are for items paid by or for the buyer (earnest money, new loans,, assumed loans, etc.). Lines 210-219 are for items owed to the buyer by seller: prorated property taxes, assessments, etc. Line 220 shows the total for Section 200. This sum is subtracted from line 120 to get line 303: the amount still due from the buyer or due to him and payable at settlement.

Part K describes the seller's side of the transaction. Section 400 (lines 401-420) calculates the gross amount due to the seller. Lines 401-404 describe the payment(s) due to the seller for the property(ies) sold. Lines 405-411 cover payments due to the seller from the buyer; these items correspond to the charges against the buyer on lines 106-112. Line 420 adds these items to get the total gross amount due to the seller. Section 500 describes charges and fees paid by the seller. Line 502 is for the seller's settlement charges (from line 1400 on the other side of the form). Line 503 is for assumed loans, corresponding to line 203. Lines 504 and 505 are for seller's loan payoffs. Lines 510-519 correspond to lines 210-219 of the buyer's side, showing the items which the seller owes to the buyer. Line 603 is the result of subtracting line 520 from line 420, and shows the proceeds due to or from the seller, payable at settlement.

Prorated Items

Charges such as property taxes, interest on assumed loans, insurance, and rents are paid periodically. Usually settlement will occur in the middle of one of those periods, so it is necessary to split the charge for the item between the buyer and the seller. These items are *prorated*, which means that the charges to buyer and seller are split between them depending upon how much of the period covered by the charge will accrue to each. For example, suppose taxes are assessed for the calendar year and must be paid by June 1 of the year they are assessed. If the property sale is settled on July 31, the seller will have paid the entire year's tax bill, but the buyer will own the property for the last five months of the year. In this case, the buyer will be charged for 5/12 (five of the twelve months of the year) of the tax bill, and this sum will be entered on line 106 or 107, and on line 406 or 407. This will show that the buyer must be charged for the tax paid in advance for the full year by the seller, and that the seller will be credited with a similar amount. What really is happening here is that the buyer is reimbursing the seller for the buyer's "share" of the full year's property taxes already paid by the seller.

Suppose, however, that the property changes hands on March 31. This means that on June 1 the buyer will be presented with a tax bill covering the entire year, but the seller will have owned the property for three months of that year. In this case, the seller will owe the buyer 3/12 (or 1/4) of the annual tax bill at settlement. This amount will be entered on line 210 or 211, showing that the item had been unpaid by the seller; on the seller's side it will appear on line 510 or 511. The rule for prorated items is: If the *seller owes the buyer* for the prorated sum, it will be entered in Sections 200 and 500 of the HUD-1 Form. If the *buyer owes the seller* the prorated amount, it will be entered in Sections 100 and 400.

A. **Settlement Statement**

U.S. Department of Housing
and Urban Development

OMB No. 2502-0265

B. Type of Loan

1. ☐ FHA 2. ☐ FmHA 3.☐ Conv. Unins.	6. File Number	7. Loan Number	8. Mortgage Insurance Case Number
4. ☐ VA 5. ☐ Conv. Ins.			

C. Note: This form is furnished to give you a statement of actual settlement costs. Amounts paid to and by the settlement agent are shown. Items marked "(p.o.c.)" were paid outside the closing; they are shown here for informational purposes and are not included in the totals.

D. Name and Address of Borrower	E. Name and Address of Seller	F. Name and Address of Lender

G. Property Location	H. Settlement Agent	
	Place of Settlement	I. Settlement Date

J. Summary of Borrower's Transaction		K. Summary of Seller's Transaction	
100. Gross Amount Due From Borrower		**400. Gross Amount Due To Seller**	
101. Contract sales price		401. Contract sales price	
102. Personal property		402. Personal property	
103. Settlement charges to borrower (line 1400)		403.	
104.		404.	
105.		405.	
Adjustments for items paid by seller in advance		**Adjustments for items paid by seller in advance**	
106. City/town taxes to		406. City/town taxes to	
107. County taxes to		407. County taxes to	
108. Assessments to		408. Assessments to	
109.		409.	
110.		410.	
111.		411.	
112.		412.	
120. Gross Amount Due From Borrower		**420. Gross Amount Due To Seller**	
200. Amounts Paid By Or In Behalf Of Borrower		**500. Reductions In Amount Due To Seller**	
201. Deposit or earnest money		501. Excess deposit (see instructions)	
202. Principal amount of new loan(s)		502. Settlement charges to seller (line 1400)	
203. Existing loan(s) taken subject to		503. Existing loan(s) taken subject to	
204.		504. Payoff of first mortgage loan	
205.		505. Payoff of second mortgage loan	
206.		506.	
207.		507.	
208.		508.	
209.		509.	
Adjustments for items unpaid by seller		**Adjustments for items unpaid by seller**	
210. City/town taxes to		510. City/town taxes to	
211. County taxes to		511. County taxes to	
212. Assessments to		512. Assessments to	
213.		513.	
214.		514.	
215.		515.	
216.		516.	
217.		517.	
218.		518.	
219.		519.	
220. Total Paid By/For Borrower		**520. Total Reduction Amount Due Seller**	
300. Cash At Settlement From/To Borrower		**600. Cash At Settlement To/From Seller**	
301. Gross Amount due from borrower (line 120)		601. Gross amount due to seller (line 420)	
302. Less amounts paid by/for borrower (line 220)	( )	602. Less reductions in amt. due seller (line 520)	( )
303. Cash ☐ From ☐ To Borrower		**603. Cash** ☐ To ☐ From Seller	

Figure 9-2. Uniform Settlement Statement

L. Settlement Charges

700. Total Sales/Broker's Commission based on price $ @ % =	Paid From Borrower's Funds at Settlement	Paid From Seller's Funds at Settlement
Division of Commission (line 700) as follows:		
701. $ to		
702. $ to		
703. Commission paid at Settlement		
704.		
800. Items Payable In Connection With Loan		
801. Loan Origination Fee %		
802. Loan Discount %		
803. Appraisal Fee to		
804. Credit Report to		
805. Lender's Inspection Fee		
806. Mortgage Insurance Application Fee to		
807. Assumption Fee		
808.		
809.		
810.		
811.		
900. Items Required By Lender To Be Paid In Advance		
901. Interest from to @ $ /day		
902. Mortgage Insurance Premium for months to		
903. Hazard Insurance Premium for years to		
904. years to		
905.		
1000. Reserves Deposited With Lender		
1001. Hazard Insurance months @ $ per month		
1002. Mortgage Insurance months @ $ per month		
1003. City property taxes months @ $ per month		
1004. County property taxes months @ $ per month		
1005. Annual assessments months @ $ per month		
1006. months @ $ per month		
1007. months @ $ per month		
1008. months @ $ per month		
1100. Title Charges		
1101. Settlement or closing fee to		
1102. Abstract or title search to		
1103. Title examination to		
1104. Title insurance binder to		
1105. Document preparation to		
1106. Notary fees to		
1107. Attorney's fees to		
(includes above items numbers:)		
1108. Title insurance to		
(includes above items numbers:)		
1109. Lender's coverage $		
1110. Owner's coverage $		
1111.		
1112.		
1113.		
1200. Government Recording and Transfer Charges		
1201. Recording fees: Deed $; Mortgage $; Releases $		
1202. City/county tax/stamps: Deed $; Mortgage $		
1203. State tax/stamps: Deed $; Mortgage $		
1204.		
1205.		
1300. Additional Settlement Charges		
1301. Survey to		
1302. Pest inspection to		
1303.		
1304.		
1305.		
1400. Total Settlement Charges (enter on lines 103, Section J and 502, Section K)		

Figure 9-2. (*Continued*)

There are four items which typically can be prorated. We have discussed *property taxes*. The others are *rents, interest on assumed loans*, and *insurance premiums*. While most transactions will require property taxes to be prorated (where is there property that isn't taxed?), the other three may or may not come up in a particular transaction.

Rents are prorated only if the sold property is leased. Rent usually is paid in advance. Suppose an owner collected the monthly rents at the beginning of the month, and the settlement occurred later in the month. The seller will have collected the entire month's rent, but some of that rent money ought to go to the buyer for the portion of the month during which the buyer became the owner. If, for example, the settlement occurred on the 20th of April (a 30-day month), then the buyer will own the property for the last third of the month (10 out of 30 days). The seller should then pay the buyer 1/3 of the April rents, which the seller had collected in full before the settlement.

Interest on assumed loans is prorated only if the buyer assumes one or more of the seller's existing loans on the property. When the buyer makes the upcoming periodic payment to the loan, it will include interest for the entire *previous* period. During some of that time the seller was the owner. At settlement, then, the seller should pay the buyer a proper share of the current period's loan interest.

In some settlements the buyer takes over the seller's existing property insurance policy. At some previous time the seller paid a premium to the insurance company; the buyer will own the property for some of this time for which the seller already has bought insurance. Therefore, at settlement, the buyer should pay the seller for the share of the paid-up insurance which the buyer will get to "use."

One last important thing about prorated items: none of the commonly prorated items *must* be prorated at settlement. It simply is standard practice to do so. Actually, proration only occurs if the agreement between seller and buyer says so. However, proration language is a standard feature of preprinted contracts of sale. In our example in Figure 9-1 this language appears in section 6.

Listing of Settlement Charges

The second page of the form lists settlement charges made to both buyer and seller. It doesn't have separate sections for buyer and seller (borrower), but instead has separate columns for them in each section. Section 700 shows the calculation of the broker's commission and provides for splitting it between listing and selling broker, if required. Section 800 describes the charges associated with the creation of the buyer's new loan. Section 900 shows the advance payment items the lender requires; these are interest on the new loan between the settlement date and the beginning of the first regular loan period, mortgage insurance, and other insurance premiums payable at settlement.

Section 1000 is concerned with escrow or reserve accounts required by the lender. Most lenders require that borrowers pay, in addition to the loan payment itself, a monthly sum that will mount up to enough to pay property taxes and hazard insurance premiums as they come due. Sometimes these are scheduled to come due relatively soon, and the lender requires an initial deposit so that when the payments have to be made there will be enough money to make them. Section 1100 lists charges made for these, along with title charges such as abstract, title search, title insurance, document preparation, etc. Section 1200 includes recording fees and taxes, and Section 1300 includes any additional settlement charges that may be made.

The columns down the right hand side of the page provide space for listing the charge for each item to be assessed either to the buyer or seller. Line 1400 shows the totals for each party; these totals are transferred to the front page of the form, to line 103 for the buyer and to line 502 for the seller.

DEFAULTS

Default is one of the nightmares of the real estate brokerage business; it happens when a party to a contract *refuses to perform*. The professional brokerage firm, of course, ought never to default on a contractual obligation, but it has no way of guaranteeing the same high standards in all the buyers and sellers it will deal with. The major sources of default are default by the seller in a listing contract and default by either buyer or seller in a sale contract.

Listing Default by Seller

A seller can default in his obligations to a brokerage firm by trying to terminate the contract before the property is sold; this was discussed in Chapter 8 and is not a serious problem to have to deal with, although it is annoying to the firm. Much more serious is the seller's default on the payment of the commission after the sale has been concluded. If the seller refuses to pay the commission, there is little that can be done at that time. Whoever is in charge of settlement is an escrow or trust agent disposing of monies belonging to either seller or buyer, and must dispose of those monies only as instructed by them. This means that if the brokerage firm is handling the settlement itself, and the seller refuses to pay the commission, he must be given *all* his proceeds, and the firm must take legal action to collect the commission.

Suing for the Commission

Taking a dispute to court is inconvenient, costly, and time consuming. Even so, there are times when just that is necessary. Doing so can generate bad publicity and ill will, so a decision to sue for a commission should be very carefully weighed. Certainly, no decision should be made until an attorney has been consulted.

Most firms sue only in cases where blatant violation of the listing contract has occurred. Recalling the discussion in Chapter 8, it is technically true that the broker earns the commission as soon as a seller contracts with a buyer for the sale of the listed property. If the buyer should later illegally default on the contract, the seller still is supposed to be liable for the commission. However, few brokerage firms would seriously consider suing a seller for a commission under such circumstances. Regardless of the specific legal situation, few sellers would consider such a claim valid or moral, especially since it was the brokerage itself that brought the bad buyer. In these cases, most brokerage firms will join with the seller in an attempt to work things out for both of them.

Default by Buyer

Buyer default is probably the single most dreaded event in the brokerage business; it is the refusal of the buyer to perform under a sales contract. Worst of all is the absolute refusal to buy. This can happen because the buyer decides he does not want the property or because something happens to keep him from going through with the transaction. This is not to be confused with a buyer's withdrawing from a contract *for reasons that the contract allows*. Thus, failure to perform under a contract contingent upon financing when no loan can be found is not default.

Buyer default is usually unexpected. It most often occurs at, or very close to, the scheduled time for closing of the transaction. This only makes matters worse; the seller is financially and emotionally prepared to close the sale, and the broker is ready as well. To have a buyer refuse to deal at this time is very stressfu, to both broker and seller. Some brokerages try to prepare their sellers for such an eventuality, but even this kindness is dangerous. It could cause unwarranted worry during the many transactions in which there is no default or serious problem of any kind.

Little can be done immediately when a buyer defaults. The first thing to do is for both broker and seller to consult an attorney and make sure that a genuine default has occurred. The attorney can contact the buyer, explain the seller's position and the buyer's obligations to him, and try to convince him to go through with the deal and avoid the possibility of litigation. If this does not work, a lawsuit must be considered. Standard sale contracts provide that the buyer's earnest money deposit must be forfeited to the seller at the time of default. Most listing arrangements provide that the seller split the forfeited deposit with the broker in some manner.

When it is obvious that the default is genuine, a decision must be made as to whether or not the property should be put back on the market. Frequently, arrangements may have to be made to enable the seller to go ahead with other real estate transactions he had been planning as a result of the sale that defaulted. For example, he may have agreed to buy another property with the proceeds of his sale, and if he is to go ahead with it, some kind of temporary financing will have to be arranged.

The seller probably will blame the broker for the default, since he will reason that the buyer was found by the broker. Legally, the brokerage may be blameless, but this is not usually the time to insist on legal niceties. A professional brokerage will make every effort to ease the seller through the situation as painlessly as possible, including finding interim financing and, if necessary, legal assistance.

If a lawsuit is filed, it can be for *specific performance* or for *damages*. Specific performance would require the buyer to go through with the contract; damages would allow the buyer to default but require him to pay the seller the cost he imposed upon him by defaulting. In neither case would a lawsuit be an immediate solution to the problem unless the act of filing suit is sufficient to encourage the buyer to go ahead with the deal as contracted. Otherwise, it will be months or perhaps years before a court settlement can be reached. This is far too long to resolve the immediate problems caused by default. In a home sale transaction, specific performance may be futile anyway, since many defaults by home buyers are caused by financial inability, and the buyer would be unable to comply with a court order to transact. It may also be that the buyer has no, or few, assets to claim against, rendering even a damage suit a wasted effort. In such cases there is little to do except bear the costs and chalk the event up to experience.

A buyer who does not have the financial resources to transact may be helpless to go ahead with the deal even if he wants to. However, some buyers choose not to transact even though they are capable. Damage judgments against them may eventually pay off, and furthermore, the threat of a damage suit may be enough to goad them into completing the transaction.

Planning Against Buyer Default

In many cases buyer default can be at least in part the responsibility of the brokerage, particularly if a risky buyer is found. The seller relies on the brokerage to find a suitable buyer; it is up to the firm to make sure that the buyer really does want to buy and is able to do so. For these reasons, it is best to avoid high-pressure selling tactics, since these frequently will lead to offers from people who later will want to reconsider their decisions. In fact, buyers occasionally have sued brokers or complained about them to officials because they had been pressured into buying property they really did not want. It is much better, although perhaps more difficult, to obtain a buyer who wants the property. He will be much more likely to make every effort to go through with the transaction.

Other means of preventing default include requiring relatively high earnest money payments and careful qualification of the potential buyer by the broker. If the buyer has a large deposit at stake he will be more careful not to default, because he has a lot to lose. By qualifying the buyer, the broker makes sure that the property is suitable and that the buyer has the financial capacity to buy. This is done before the property is shown to a prospective buyer.

QUALIFYING THE BUYER

The most effective way to avoid buyer default is to *qualify the buyer*. This is a procedure done by the salesperson or broker at the time the buying prospect first is found. The salesperson tries to find out as much as possible about the prospect – not only the prospect's needs and desires with respect to real estate, but also the financial capability and limitations the prospect has. This includes inquiring about income and its sources, existing obligations, savings, other assets, etc. The objective is to build a financial profile of the prospect in order to determine borrowing needs (and ability), and the ability to meet the necessary initial cash expenses of a purchase.

Buyer qualification informs the professional real estate salesperson about the prospect. This information can be used to steer the prospect toward those listings which best suit his needs and ability to pay. It also helps the salesperson to inform the owner of the listed property when the prospect makes an offer. It can help avoid futile contracts, in which the buyer has little hope of qualifying for needed financing or coming up with necessary cash.

Buyer qualification is an essential duty of the real estate salesperson or broker. The function of brokerage is to bring buyer and seller together; the broker, in effect, brings potential buyers to the seller. Usually the seller does not even meet those who make offers; he sees only a written offer signed by a total stranger. Anyone can write anything on a piece of paper and then have it delivered to someone else. How is the broker's principal to know that the stranger making him an offer can go through with what is written? The principal must rely upon the broker to find out the necessary information and provide it to him.

A properly qualified buyer is much less likely to default. A major reason for buyer default is inability to handle the financial aspects of promises made. Properly qualified buyers encounter such problems infrequently.

If a buyer of questionable capacity makes an offer on a property, the broker should relay that information to the seller. Furthermore, the contract of sale should always be written to allow for all possible contingencies that may arise due to a particular buyer's circumstances. If the buyer has to borrow a small fortune from Aunt Minnie, the contract should say so and allow a reasonable time for him to arrange the loan; if he doesn't, the seller can call off the deal. The same should be done if the buyer has to sell a property before he will have the cash to pay for the one he is making the offer on, or if he will need to secure a mortgage loan. This gives the seller ample warning that the sale is conditional upon certain things happening, and it will avoid default if the conditions cannot be met within the specified time. Also, the seller will have the knowledge to turn down a deal when the conditions are unsatisfactory to him, instead of finding out much later what the true situation is.

DISCUSSION QUESTIONS AND PROJECTS

1. Examine the sale contract forms in common use in your area, analyzing their strengths and weaknesses. Are there any changes you would suggest making? Why or why not?

2. Prepare some examples of improper procedure by a licensee in the process of negotiating offers and counter-offers in a real estate transaction. What would be proper procedure in these situations?

3. Investigate the popularity of franchised realty firms in your area. Which ones are represented? What is the cost of joining? What benefits do members receive?

4. Look into use of referral services for out-of-town sources of prospects in your area. Do local brokerage firms find them useful?

5. What are the advantages and disadvantages of realty firm franchises?

6. Determine the current charges for usual settlement costs in your area. With this information, fill in the form in Figure 9-2 with simulated information for settlement of a hypothetical transaction devised by you.

7. Determine how taxes are assessed and prorated in your area.

8. Does your area use a multiple listing system? If so, examine it and analyze the charges, fees, regulations, and usefulness of the system.

9. Describe how an offer becomes a contract.

10. Develop a policy for dealing with buyer defaults that could be adopted by a medium-sized residential brokerage firm.

11. If a seller won't pay a legally earned commission, under what circumstances should the broker sue for the commission? Are there any situations in which it would be better for a brokerage firm just to forget about the commission? Why or why not?

12. Under what circumstances would it be advisable for a real estate sales transaction to involve a land contract?

13. Why is it advantageous for brokerage firms to cooperate with other firms in the sales of their listings?

14. Describe how a competent broker can take steps in the negotiation of a real estate sale transaction to provide assurance that neither buyer nor seller will default.

15. From a closing agent find out exactly what types of transactions have to be reported to the IRS, and how it is done.

16. Interview two or three salespeople and a sales manager. Find out what they do to qualify buyers. Find out also how they get people to reveal the information they need. Are there any suggestions you could make?

17. If there is a multiple listing system in your area, does it have its information on computer? Do member firms have terminals at their offices which can access the multiple listing computer for information? What kinds of information, sorting and searching capacities are available to member firms? Do you have any suggestions for improvement?

A Case Study

BUYER DEFAULT

Eleanor E. has been in the real estate business for twenty years and has been the principal broker for her own firm for ten years. When asked about buyer default, she said:

I know it sounds bad, but I would guess that in nine out of ten cases of buyer default in a brokered deal, it's the agent's fault. Usually, it's because the agent didn't pay enough attention to qualifying the buyer.

"When an agent high-pressures a person into buying something he can't afford, or doesn't really want, he's asking for trouble. The buyer has several weeks to realize that he's done something unwise and I've seen many cases where they just walk away from the transaction and refuse to close. If they get really mad, they can sue the agent. In a lot of cases like that, I would have to side with the buyer. A good agent has no business forcing people into deals that are not good for them.

"Qualifying is hardly any trouble at all, but even so I spend a lot of time in sales meetings on that point. People usually will tell you practically anything you want to know about their financial affairs. A few minutes' discussion can determine how much they can afford and what their needs are. At this time, the prospect gains the confidence that the agent is sincerely interested in helping him meet his needs in the best possible way. When the prospect sees something he likes, we try to discuss it thoroughly with him and work out a little form that shows what he'll pay, what cash he'll need, what his payments will be – even the moving costs. We don't try to speed him along or rush him into making an offer before he's ready.

"In peculiar deals we try to dig really deep. We had a real stinker last year that shows just what I mean. We had a lovely old seven-bedroom home listed in a downtown area that was well on its way to "coming back" into vogue. We listed it for $75,000. One day an agent with another company brought us an *all-cash* offer for $72,000. It was the cleanest offer I had ever seen: closing in 90 days, no loan, no points, no ifs, ands, or buts at all. The buyers were representing a charity that wanted to use the house for temporary housing for retarded adults who were being trained in vocational programs. When we discovered this, we pointed out to the agent that the house wasn't zoned to permit that. He responded that this wouldn't make any difference; they were willing to buy anyway and then go through the rezoning process. My seller was in heaven! Naturally he grabbed the offer; he had expected three to six months' hard work selling and then maybe taking a pretty low offer and paying all sorts of buyer's closing costs and loan fees.

"The day of closing the buyers defaulted. It seems that the charity's board of directors knew nothing at all about the deal! The people we had been dealing with were the executive director and one of the board members. Apparently, the board had discussed the possibility of getting federal funding to buy themselves a new place; when these two talked to the local HEW office they were told that if they qualified they could get the money. So they went right out and signed an offer to buy my seller's place with cash that they did not have and with no authority from their own board to do so. The day before closing they had a board meeting where all this came out, and the board repudiated the whole thing.

"I thought I was mad then, but that was nothing compared to how I felt after I talked to the other agent. He had never asked them where they were going to get the money. When we had mentioned the zoning to him, he answered without ever consulting them. If he'd just asked a couple of simple questions he would have known that they had no idea what they were doing. Instead he brought us this foolish offer from these foolish people, and ended up putting us all through torture. At least the board member who was involved in this paid for his experience: He wrote a personal check for the earnest money, which we kept, of course.

"My seller almost went crazy. After we got this contract on his house, we found him a new place, and he was expecting to use his equity to provide the money he needed to buy it. It took us three days of begging and wheedling all over town before we were able to get a bank to lend him the money he needed to close on his new house. It took him six more months before we finally got rid of his old place. While we had been waiting to close on the deal that defaulted, the interest rates had risen and the market practically died. He finally sold for $63,500 and paid four points on a VA loan. With the extra six months of loan payments he had to make, he ended up with almost $15,000 less than he would have gotten from the offer the charity people made.

"His lawyer discovered that the charity didn't have two dimes to rub together. So now he's suing the two people who made the offer to him. Also, they're about to sue the other agent's brokerage firm as well, for incompetence, malpractice — you name it. And frankly, if they call me to testify, I'm going to have to agree that the other agent did not do his duty properly. And you can bet that the next time he brings me an offer on one of my listings, I'm going to go over it with a microscope!"

REFERENCES

FISHER, FREDERICK J., *Broker Beware: Selling Real Estate Within The Law*. Reston, VA: Reston Publishing Company, Inc., 1981.

HULL, DONALD A., "A Complete Guide to Qualifying," *Real Estate Today*, August, 1979, pp. 43-52.

LEVINE, ARTHUR M., "Dual Agency Trap," *Real Estate Review*, Spring, 1985, pp. 109-112.

LIPPMAN, BARBARA J., AND LORRAINE CATUBIG, "Closing Costs: Closing the Door on Home-ownership?" *The Home Financing Transaction*, Fall, 1991.

U.S. DEPARTMENT OF HOUSING AND URBAN DEVELOPMENT, *Settlement Costs and You — A Guide for Homebuyers*. Washington, DC: U.S. Government Printing Office, 1989.

TEN

REAL ESTATE FINANCE AND APPRAISAL

The Language of Mortgage Lending

Interest Rates and "Points"

The Mortgage Lending Business

Financing and the Brokerage Business

Appraisal

This chapter provides a brief discussion of mortgages and appraisal. Financing and valuation usually aren't part of a real estate licensee's regular duties. However, licensees do have to be able to explaining financing and even deal with lenders. When a licensee is soliciting a listing, the first question a potential seller will ask is "how much can I get for my real estate?" Thus they have to be able to at least estimate the probable selling prices of real estate they wish to list. Sometimes, in the course of closing a sale, they have to be able to deal with appraisals and professional appraisers.

In the residential real estate market it is very rare for a sale to be made without some kind of mortgage financing involved. Homebuyers, whether they realize it or not, actually shop for *two* commodities at the same time: the *home* and the *borrowed money* they need in order to buy it. Most brokerage firms aren't directly involved in arranging new mortgage financing for their buyers. Even so, real estate licensees should have a good understanding of real estate finance. Probably the most important reason is that, for both buyers and sellers, real estate licensees are the ones they turn to for explanations and advice about mortgage financing.

Borrowed money is the lifeblood of the real estate business. Real estate is so expensive that very few buyers will have enough cash available to make real estate purchases without borrowing. Fortunately, real estate can be excellent collateral for loans. It lasts a long time, retains its value well, and usually is fairly easy to convert into cash within a reasonable time. As a result, mortgage lending (lending secured by real estate) in the United States is a business measured in the trillions of dollars.

One important thing must always be kept in mind. Remember, real estate salespeople are *not* lawyers. Therefore, any question which requires an answer of legal advice must be referred to a qualified attorney. Also, while licensees should be able to give general advice about mortgage financing, complex questions and detailed responses should be referred to the proper experts. In many cases the licensee knows whom to call, and is in a much better position to obtain the required information. Doing so, when necessary, is part of professional real estate brokerage service.

THE LANGUAGE OF MORTGAGE LENDING

The mortgage lending business has its own specialized language. Licensees need to know this terminology, not only to be able to "speak the language" with people in the lending business, but also because they often are called upon to explain it to buyers and sellers. Much of this lending "language" consists of acronyms and abbreviations.

Mortgages

A mortgage is *not* a loan of money; rather, it is the *security* for a loan. A mortgage is a collection of rights which an owner of real estate gives to a lender in order to provide the lender with *collateral* for the loan. Most important of these is to give the lender the right to require that the mortgaged real estate be sold to pay a *defaulted debt*. These mortgage rights cannot be exercised by the lender, so long as the borrower complies with the terms of the loan (essentially, makes the payments on time).

Title theory, lien theory: There are different kinds of mortgages. In *lien-theory* states, the document is called a *mortgage* and is treated as a *lien* against the mortgaged property. A lien is a legal claim. The claim of a mortgage lien, however, cannot be exercised against the property unless the loan is defaulted. In *title-theory* states, the lender actually receives *title* (a deed) to the property, while the borrower-owner retains *equitable title*, which includes all rights to use and occupy the real estate so long as the loan is not in default. In these states the "mortgage" contract goes by different names. For example, in California and Virginia it is a *deed of trust*; in Georgia it is a *deed to secure debt*. Some states allow both lien theory and title theory mortgages. In those states, the form used is the one which is easiest to foreclose. Note, however, that for most purposes it makes little difference to borrowers exactly what kind of mortgage, lien, title or whatever is used. Basically, so long as the borrower pays as contracted, the lender can do nothing but accept payments. And, if the borrower defaults, in all cases the lender may foreclose in some way or another.

Foreclosure: If the borrower defaults, the lender's mortgage rights are "activated." These rights can be exercised and the mortgaged property can be sold to pay the debt. This procedure is called *foreclosure*, and the sale is called a *foreclosure sale*. Many states require *judicial foreclosure*. This procedure requires that the lender go to court to obtain a court order for the sale of the foreclosed real estate. Some states also permit *non-judicial foreclosure* which allows the lender to take possession of and sell the mortgaged property without court supervision. In order to exercise non-judicial foreclosure, it must be allowed to the lender in the mortgage contract (and, of course, permitted by the state where the property is located).

Mortgagor and mortgagee: Since the mortgage rights are given by the property owner (borrower) to the lender, the borrower is called the *mortgagor*, and the lender is called the *mortgagee*. This terminology is backwards from what most people would expect, because they think a mortgage is a loan. Licensees must know who mortgagor and mortgagee are, though, because in the mortgage lending business, these terms are usually preferred to "borrower" and "lender." However, just to confuse things further, it is common in that same business to refer to mortgage loans as just plain *mortgages*, even though, strictly speaking, mortgages aren't loans at all.

Equity: The borrower's *equity* in the property is calculated by subtracting from the market value of the property all mortgages and other claims against the property. Essentially, then, the owner's equity is the dollar value of his/her "share" of the property value. Suppose Jones's home is worth $115,000. Jones has a first mortgage for $76,000 and a second mortgage for $11,000. Jones's equity, then, is $28,000. (The two mortgages add up to $87,000. Subtracting that amount from the property value of $115,000 yields an equity of $28,000.)

First mortgage, second mortgage, junior mortgage: When a foreclosure occurs, the property is sold and those who have claims on the foreclosed property are paid from the proceeds of the sale *in order of priority*. The claimant with highest priority is paid *in* *full* before any payment is made to the claimant next in line. A claim for unpaid property taxes always has first priority. Other claimants have priority based upon when their claim first was entered. The oldest claim has highest priority, and the most recent has lowest.

If there is more than one mortgage on a property, the oldest one has highest priority and is called the *first mortgage*. The next ones are called the *second mortgage*, the *third mortgage*, etc. Also, all mortgages except the first are called *junior mortgages*. Priority is important to mortgage lenders. If foreclosure occurs, funds from the sale must pay off the first mortgage in full before any others are paid anything. A second mortgage, then, is secured only by whatever amount the property value exceeds the first mortgage.

Mortgage Lending Terminology

Loan to Value Ratio (LTV): The *loan-to-value ratio (LTV)* is the ratio of the amount of the loan to the market value of the mortgaged property. It usually is expressed as a percentage. So, a loan of $80,000 secured by a mortgage on a house worth $100,000 has a LTV of 80%. Often, in the mortgage business, it would be referred to as an "80% loan."

Assuming Loans: The buyer can *assume* the seller's existing loan under certain circumstances. Loan assumption is an agreement between the buyer and the original borrower (the seller), that the buyer will retain, and make the payments to, the seller's existing loan. When a loan is assumed, it is not paid off at closing, but instead remains in existence to benefit the buyer. Loan assumption may be attractive to buyers for several reasons. It usually costs much less than the fees and costs associated with originating a new loan. Also, an existing loan may have a lower interest rate than in the current market and, so, can save the buyer money in monthly payment costs.

An important point to remember is that loan assumption *does not necessarily relieve the original borrower of responsibility to the lender*. The liability for the loan can be transferred to the new owner of the property only if the lender is willing to agree to a *substitution of mortgagor*. Normally, this only can happen if the new mortgagor (the buyer who assumes the loan) can *qualify* for the loan with the lender. Qualification entails some expense for credit reports, verification of income and debts, etc., and the loan also may require a transfer fee if it is assumed. Not all conventional loans can be assumed; a loan which contains a *due on sale clause* can be *accelerated* by the lender if the borrower sells the underlying property. (A loan is accelerated when the lender declares the entire remaining balance due and payable immediately.) FHA loans are fully assumable, but require substitution of mortgagor. VA loans are assumable, even without substitution of mortgagor. Licensees should be sure to advise sellers with assumable loans that if the buyer does not qualify for the loan, and is not substituted for the seller as mortgagor, then the seller will *remain liable* for the loan. Once they understand this, most sellers will insist that the buyer qualify for an assumed loan.

Closing costs: Closing costs are the fees, charges, and other costs associated with settlement of a real estate transaction. Both buyer and seller will have closing costs; these are described in Chapter 9. A large portion of typical settlement (closing) cost is the cost of originating a new loan. Typically, these costs will run from about 3% to as much as 6% or more of the amount of the new loan. These costs include origination fees and points (discussed later in this chapter), as well as application fees and costs of title insurance, appraisal, survey, credit check, income verification, document preparation and recording, etc. FHA loans will require payments to the FHA insurance; high LTV conventional loans will require payments for *private mortgage insurance (PMI)*. These are described later in this chapter.

Amortization: *Amortization* of a loan refers to paying it down. Any loan which is paid down by any amount during its term is called an *amortizing loan*. Most home mortgage loans (as well as most other consumer loans) are *self-amortizing*. This means that the payment schedule of the loan is structured so that over the term of the loan, the balance is paid down to zero. That is, the monthly payments pay both interest and principal so that when the last payment is made, the loan is fully amortized (paid off).

Some loans are structured to amortize only partially over the loan term; at the end of the term, the remaining balance has to be paid at once. These loans are called *balloon loans*, because the final payment "balloons" to much more than the payments were during the loan term.

PITI (Principal, Interest, Taxes and Insurance): Monthly payments to self-amortizing loans include payment of interest and a payment to principal. Most mortgage lenders also require their borrowers to pay an additional monthly amount which is used to pay toward the borrower's property taxes and property insurance. This kind of payment to a loan is referred to as a *PITI* payment: *P*rincipal, *I*nterest, *T*axes and *I*nsurance.

The additional monthly payment (the "*TI*" amount) is 1/12 of the lender's estimate of the borrower's annual property tax and property insurance cost. The lender requires these payments so as to be sure that the property is insured against loss, and that the property taxes are paid. These extra payments are kept by the lender in an *escrow fund*. Funds held by a lender in escrow are, legally, not the lender's money at all; these funds are held on behalf of someone else (the borrower, in this case). So this escrow fund actually belongs to the borrower, but it is earmarked for taxes and insurance. Property tax and insurance bills, then, are sent to the lender, and the lender pays them out of the borrower's escrow fund.

Origination fee: Most lenders charge an *origination fee* when a new loan is created. This fee usually is about 1% of the loan amount, but can vary. The fee doesn't pay for anything in particular; rather it helps to defray some of the lender's paperwork and busywork costs of setting up a new loan.

Loan Description

There is a great variety of mortgage loans available in today's "sophisticated" market. There are conventional, FHA, and VA loans. Each of these can be had in many forms: *adjustable rate mortgage (ARM)*, *fixed-rate mortgage (FRM)*, *level payment*, *graduated payment*, *fully amortizing*, *balloon*. Also, almost any term of years up to 30 is available, though the most common terms are 15 and 30 years. New borrowers can be quite bewildered when they look over the "menu" of offerings from a mortgage lender. To whom do they turn for advice? Most likely the licensee(s) handling their transaction, so licensees must be able to give this assistance. Note that assisting the buyer with financing does not violate the licensee's agency relationship with the seller; after all, helping the buyer to buy is most definitely in the seller's interest. However, licensees must remember that they ought not to give bad advice or steer a buyer into a damaging mortgage transaction just to make the sale. And, if the buyer has complicated questions, the licensee should offer a reference to an expert. Mortgage lenders can provide prospective borrowers with literature (written, supposedly, in "simple" English) explaining the various offerings; licensees often will be called upon to "translate" it.

ARM, FRM (Adjustable Rate Mortgage, Fixed Rate Mortgage): These terms refer to the interest rate on the loan. A FRM has a *fixed rate*: the interest rate never changes over the life of the loan. An ARM has an *adjustable rate*: the interest rate changes periodically to reflect changes in interest rates in the overall economy.

ARM's can be structured in many ways, but only a few patterns dominate. The most common is the *annual ARM with 2% and 6% caps*. "Annual" means that the interest rate is adjusted once a year. The "caps" refer to the amount by which the rate can be adjusted. The first figure is the *periodic cap*: it is the maximum amount by which the interest rate can be changed at any single adjustment. The second figure is the *lifetime cap*: it is the maximum adjustment from the original rate which is allowed over the life of the loan. Thus, 2% and 6% caps mean that the loan's interest rate can be adjusted by no more than 2% at any one time, and by no more than 6% over the life of the loan. So, if such a loan started out with an interest rate of 7%, then the 6% cap would mean that the interest rate never could exceed 13% (7% + the 6% lifetime cap). Also, at each adjustment the interest rate could not be changed by more than 2%; when the loan is a year old, it can be adjusted to no less than 5% and no more than 9%.

Adjustments to ARM interest rates aren't arbitrary. Usually they are tied to some "index" of interest rates. These indices are beyond the control of both borrower and lender. A commonly used one is based on the interest rates on US Treasury 1-year notes. Most indices result in low rates (the US Treasury is a better lending risk than a family making mortgage payments); when they are used, the loan contract applies a *margin* when calculating the interest rate adjustment. When it is time to adjust the interest rate on a loan, this margin is added to the rate shown by the index to arrive at the new rate on the adjustable rate mortgage loan. For example, if the margin is 3%, and the index shows a rate of 5%, then the loan's interest rate will be adjusted to 8% (5% index rate + 3% margin).

ARM's are less popular than FRM's. Borrowers are uncomfortable with the uncertainty of the ARM, because adjustments in the loan's interest rate will mean adjustments in the monthly payment. This is nice if interest rates fall, because the payment will fall too. But if interest rates rise, the payment will go up, and many borrowers don't want to be subject to the risk of that happening.

However, lenders do try to make ARM's more attractive. One way is to make them *convertible* into a fixed-rate loan. Usually this means that at certain of the adjustment times during the life of the loan (usually the 3rd, 4th and 5th "anniversaries"), the borrower will have the option of "locking in" the new rate for the remainder of the loan term. This effectively converts the ARM into a FRM at that time; usually there is a fee charged for doing so (typically about 1% of the remaining loan balance).

Also, ARM lenders frequently offer unusually low interest rates for the first year of the loan. These *teaser rates* may be as much as 3 or more percentage points below the interest rate for new fixed-rate loans. For example, if fixed-rate loans are being offered at 9%, ARM's may be offered with first-year rates of 6% or less. This represents real savings to the borrower, but virtually assures that the loan's interest rate will rise by the full periodic cap after one year, and may rise the next year too. However, the teaser rate offers one other advantage: the lifetime cap is based on the *original* interest rate for the loan, so a teaser rate for the first year also means that the lifetime cap on the loan is lower. For example, if the ARM first-year rate is 6%, then a 6% lifetime cap would mean that the loan's interest rate could never go above 12%.

FHA, VA and conventional loans: *FHA loans* are *insured* by the Federal Housing Administration. *VA loans* are *guaranteed* by the Veteran's Administration. Both kinds of loans are made by private lenders – *not* the Government. *Conventional loans* are mortgage loans which are neither insured by FHA nor guaranteed by VA. Well over half of the home mortgage loans originated these days are conventional loans. Typically, conventional loans are limited by most lenders to 80% of the purchase price or appraised value of the home. Conventional loans may be made for more than 80% LTV if they have private mortgage insurance (see below).

FHA and VA loans are made by private lenders, just as conventional loans are. FHA insurance is paid for by the borrower. The insurance benefits the *lender*. If a FHA loan is defaulted, FHA pays off the lender and then takes over, itself, the problems associated with working the loan out, foreclosure, etc. The FHA insurance fee, beginning in 1993, is about 3% of the loan amount. It can be paid in full when the loan is originated. Also, part of it can be financed over 8 or 10 years, by adding an additional amount to the borrower's monthly payment.

The VA guarantee is paid for by the US Government; VA guaranteed home mortgages are one of the benefits provided to members of the US armed forces. When a VA loan goes into default, the lender goes through the foreclosure procedure. Once it is over, VA will reimburse the lender for any money lost on the loan. This reimbursement is limited to the amount of the veteran's *entitlement*. Currently (early 1993) this entitlement is $46,000, but it changes over time as home prices change.

FHA and VA loans are popular because they require relatively low down payments from buyers. VA loans require no down payment at all. Indeed, they may be for as much as 101% of the purchase price of the home; the extra 1% is to cover some of the closing costs. FHA loans may be for as much as 97% of the purchase price of a home bought for $50,000 or less; this means that for such low-priced homes, the minimum down payment is only 3%.

If the home costs more than $50,000, the required FHA down payment is $750 plus 5% of the portion of the price over $25,000. (Example: The allowable down payment for a house priced at $80,000 would be $3,500. This is $750, plus 5% of the amount of the price over $25,000. [$750 + (.05 X $55,000) = $750 + $2,750 = $3,500] There is a maximum limit to the amount of a FHA loan. Currently (early 1993) it is about $150,000; in some notoriously expensive areas it is higher. All of these limits change over time as median home prices vary. Everyone is eligible for FHA insurance. Only members of the US armed forced may originate VA loans. However, *anyone* can *assume* FHA or VA loans.

Level payment, graduated payment loans: Most loans are *level-payment* loans. That is, the payment to fixed-rate loans remains the same throughout the loan term; for ARM's, the payment may change at each adjustment, but between adjustments it remains the same. Some loans, however, are structured so that the payments start out low, and then rise during each of the first few years of the loan term. These are *graduated payment mortgages (GPM's)*. GPM's are relatively uncommon these days; they are used to improve "affordability" of housing by "easing" borrowers into the payment stream in a gradual manner.

GPM's are more risky to both borrower and lender because, in their early years, they exhibit *negative amortization*. (Since "amortization" means paying a loan *down*, "negative amortization" goes the other way: the loan amount goes *up*.) This happens because in the early years of a GPM, the payments are not even enough to cover the interest due. This "unpaid" interest is *added to the loan amount* each month, so the loan balance *rises*. Each year the payment to the GPM also rises, so this unpaid interest amount gets smaller. Eventually the payment rises high enough (usually after 4 or 5 years) so that it is enough to fully amortize the higher loan balance over the remainder of the loan term.

PMI (Private Mortgage Insurance): Legal restrictions, and the dictates of prudent investing, usually limit a lender's "exposure" on conventional loans to 80% LTV. This does not mean that no conventional loans may be made at greater than 80% LTV; however, it does mean that someone *besides* the lender has to take the default risk on the part of the loan that exceeds 80% LTV. Enter the *private mortgage insuror*, who provides *private mortgage insurance (PMI)* for high LTV conventional loans. PMI insures, to the lender, that part of the loan which exceeds 80% LTV. If the borrower defaults, PMI will pay any loss of principal on the amount that exceeds original 80% LTV. The cost of PMI is paid by the borrower, usually with a part payment at origination and a small monthly payment added to the regular loan payment. The exact cost of the PMI depends upon the dollar amount being insured and how much over 80% LTV the loan is. (For example, the PMI fee on a 95% LTV loan is much higher than on a 90% LTV loan on the same property.)

Suppose someone buys a house worth $100,000, and secures a new mortgage loan on it. If the loan is $80,000 or less, there will be no PMI at all, since it is at or below most lenders' 80% LTV risk threshold. If the loan is for more than $80,000, LTV will exceed 80%. The lender will require the borrower to pay for PMI on the amount by which the loan exceeds 80% LTV. For example, if the loan is for $90,000, it will have 90% LTV; the borrower will be required to buy PMI on the amount over $80,000 ($10,000). PMI payments will continue until the loan is paid down to an amount equal to 80% LTV *as of origination*. In the example of the $90,000 loan, PMI payments, then, will continue until the loan is paid down to less than $80,000.

Seller Financing: *Seller financing* (sometimes called *creative financing*) occurs whenever the seller provides the buyer a loan for part of the purchase price. It can be a first or junior mortgage, depending upon whether the buyer has any other mortgages on the property. For example, Robert sells his house to Carol for $150,000. Carol gets a new mortgage loan for $100,000, and pays Robert $30,000 in cash. She and Robert arrange for Carol to owe him the remaining $20,000 of the price. The $20,000 is seller financing: the seller agrees that the buyer will owe him/her some of the purchase price to be paid after closing.

Seller financing always should be set up as a written debt (note) contract. It is advisable for the seller-lender to require the buyer-borrower to secure the debt with a mortgage on the property. If this is done, the mortgage is called a *purchase-money mortgage*. This is a term which usually is used incorrectly. It does not refer to *any* loan used for proceeds with which to purchase. It refers *only* to a loan from seller to buyer of the property secured by the loan. What "purchase-money" really means here is that the buyer's IOU to the seller *substitutes* for part of the cash due to the seller at closing; the seller agrees to receive that part of the "purchase money" at some later time(s).

Seller financing sometimes can be used to facilitate the sale of real estate, by reducing the amount of cash that a seller requires from a buyer at closing. Licensees should not be afraid of seller-financing deals, or of recommending seller financing as a selling tool. However, they should be sure to advise the seller to require credit checks and other necessary assurances that the prospective buyer will be able to pay as contracted.

INTEREST RATES AND "POINTS"

Interest is the "price" of borrowed money. In effect, we could look at interest as the cost of "renting" somebody else's money. The *interest rate* is the amount of interest, expressed as a percentage of the loan amount. Interest rates usually are expressed as *annual* rates. In fact, truth-in-lending law requires that most loan contracts prominently display the *Annual Percentage Rate (APR)* of interest applied to the loan.

Since interest is the cost of borrowing money, it follows that the real estate market, which depends upon borrowed money, will be very sensitive to interest rates. This is especially easy to see when we remember that most buyers will pay a lot of attention to the monthly payment required on the loan they need for the property they want to buy. When interest rates are high, loan payments will be high. When rates are low, payments will be low. This is demonstrated effectively in Table 10-1.

Interest rates from 7% to 14% are shown in the left-hand column of the table. Column set (1) shows the monthly payment required for a $75,000 loan at each of the interest rates. Payments for 30-year and 15-year terms are shown, since these are by far the most common terms chosen for home mortgage loans. Note the significant differences in monthly payment resulting from a seemingly "small" change in the interest rate. For

Table 10-1 Relationship of Interest Rates and Loan Payments

Interest Rate	(1) Monthly Payment for $75,000 Loan		(2) Loan Amount for $750 Monthly Payment	
	30-year	15-year	30-year	15-year
7	$498.98	$674.12	112,731	83,442
8	550.32	716.74	102,213	78,480
9	603.47	760.70	93,211	73,945
10	658.18	805.95	85,463	69,793
11	714.24	852.45	78,755	65,986
12	771.46	900.13	72,914	62,491
13	829.65	948.93	67,800	59,277
14	888.65	998.81	63,298	56,317

example, if the interest rate rises from 9% to 10%, the payment on a 30-year $75,000 loan increases by almost $55: from $603.47 to $658.18. An extra $55 a month out of the budget can mean the difference between "affordable" and "too expensive" for many families. Thus, as interest rates rise, we see more and more households being "priced out" of the housing market. Along with rising interest rates, we usually see shrinking real estate brokerage (sales) business.

When interest rates fall, however, payments are lower and real estate becomes more affordable. This is being written in early 1993, and the recent past has seen this happier situation. Since 1990, interest rates have fallen from over 10% to as less than 8%. As the table shows us, this means that in 1992 the monthly payment to a newly originated $75,000, 30-year loan was over $100 less than it was for loans of the same size originated in 1990.

Column set (2) in the table is even more interesting, since it reflects the way homebuyers look at how much house they can afford. These columns show how much can be borrowed, at various interest rates and terms, by a household which can budget the sum of $750 a month for the principal and interest payment to a mortgage loan. The table demonstrates that a given monthly payment "buys" more and more borrowed money as interest rates fall.

Suppose our hypothetical household has $30,000 to use as a down payment, and can afford to pay $750 a month to the loan. Assuming a 30-year loan is used, we see that in 1990, when the interest rate was 10%, the household could afford to buy a house costing about $115,000. This is because their $750 a month would pay off a 10% interest, 30-year loan of $85,463; adding that amount (the amount they can afford to borrow) to their $30,000 yielded a little over $115,000. However, if they had waited until 1993, the home mortgage interest rate would have fallen to about 8%. At that rate, they could have borrowed over $102,000 for the *same* $750 a month. This means that for $30,000 down and $750 a month, in 1993 they could have bought a $132,000 house, whereas the same $30,000 down and $750 a month would have bought only a $115,000 home three years earlier, when interest rates were higher.

Points

A fee called *points* (sometimes called *discount points* or *discounts*) sometimes is required at origination of some mortgage loans. Points are charged when the interest rate in the loan contract is *below* the "market" rate of interest at the time the loan is originated. Points can be viewed as "interest" paid in advance, in return for a lower rate of interest on the loan in the future. One point is equal to one percent of the loan amount. (1 point = 1% of loan.)

Points often are charged on VA and FHA loans. Until late 1992, this was because the Veteran's Administration used to set an allowable maximum interest rate on new VA mortgage loans, and would not guarantee loans made at higher rates. If the "pegged" rate was below the market rate that lenders wanted, they would charge points on new VA loans. In effect, then, they were asking that a payment (the "points") which "made up" the difference between the pegged rate and the market rate be made at origination. The payment was expressed as a certain number of points. For example, suppose the pegged VA rate was 8.5% interest. If a lender quoted new VA loans at 8.5% + 1.5 points, it meant that the lender required a payment, at origination, of 1.5% of the loan amount before a new VA loan at 8.5% interest would be finalized. Obviously, from the lender's point of view, an interest rate higher than the pegged 8.5% rate was desired.

Until the mid-1980's, FHA loan interest rates also were pegged, and points sometimes were charged on them, too. Today both the FHA and VA rates "float" with the market. However, the tendency in the lending business still is to offer FHA and VA loans at slightly low rates, along with whatever points are being charged for loans at that rate. Basically, this is a result of inertia in the market. Sellers in low-cost markets (where FHA and VA loans dominate) have typically paid loan points and, often, most other closing costs for their buyers. Current financing practice in these markets has been to continue charging sellers some loan points, and thus providing buyers with lower interest rates than they otherwise would get.

Note also that conventional borrowers also might pay points, though they usually pay their own. They are doing it for the same reason: to secure interest rates below the market rate, in return for paying points at origination.

Calculating Points

The exact manner in which points are calculated is very complicated. A passable rule of thumb for 30-year loans is that 1 point pays for a reduction in the loan interest rate of approximately 1/6 of a percentage point. For example, if the market interest rate for home mortgage loans is 8.5%, then a payment of about 3 points would "buy down" the interest rate on a loan to 8%. (Apply the rule of thumb: 8% is 0.5% less than 8.5%; 0.5% is the same as 3/6%; charging 1 point for each 1/6% difference between the loan rate and the market rate means that approximately 3 points will be charged.)

Try the following numerical example: For a 30-year $75,000 loan at 8.5% interest, the monthly payment is $576.69. The lender offers to reduce the interest rate on the loan to 8%, if 3 points are paid at origination. The 3-point fee will be $2,250 (3% of $75,000). The payments on the 8% loan of $75,000 will be $550.32. Thus, in return for paying $2,250 at origination, the borrower saves $26.37 per month with the lower payment due to the lower rate of interest. Now look at the lender's point of view. The lender may give the borrower $75,000, but at the same time the lender also is paid $2,250. Actually, this $75,000 loan at 8% interest only "costs" the lender $72,750 ($75,000 less the 3-point fee of $2,250). If monthly payments of $550.32 will pay off $75,000 at 8%, then if the lender actually gives up only $72,750 to "buy" this stream of payments from the borrower, the lender must then be getting more than 8% interest on the $72,750.

If you know how to use a financial calculator (and all licensees should), then you can figure out that if this loan lasts the full 30 years of the term, the lender will get about 8.32% interest on the loan. But, like we said, the actual calculation is more complicated. This is because lenders assume that new loans will "live" a much shorter time than the 30-year term in the loan contract. In fact, research has shown that the "typical" home mortgage loan is paid off in about 8 years. This doesn't mean that "typical" homeowners somehow come into lots of money after 8 years and, so, pay off their mortgages. But they do move, and buy other homes much more often than every 30 years. Usually, when they move, they sell their old home. The mortgage loan on the sold home often is paid off at settlement, and the buyer gets a new loan.

Why Pay Points?

The whole idea behind points is "Pay me now, or pay me later – but you gotta pay me!" It's reasonable to ask why a borrower would want to lay out a lot of money now, rather than pay slightly more per month in the future, particularly since most buyer-borrowers wouldn't be expected to have that kind of extra money lying around. The reason is simple: get *somebody else* to pay the points. Who? That somebody else is the *seller*. Sellers often *do* have lots of money at closing, since they receive cash for the equity in the property they are selling. Since VA and FHA financing predominates in lower cost markets, sellers often pay some points on buyers' new FHA loans. In fact, in many low-cost markets sellers find that it is normal procedure for them to pay *all* of the borrower's closing costs (except for required down payments) in order to make the sale. This is because buyers in these low-cost markets are the least likely to have much cash available for fees and costs; also, the lower the interest rate on their mortgages, the lower the payments and the easier it is for them to qualify for the loan.

Even in sales involving conventional loans, some sellers, as a selling ploy, offer to pay some or all of the buyer's closing costs, and/or to pay a certain number of points on the borrower's new loan. By doing so, they offer *their* buyer cash savings at closing and/or a slightly lower interest rate on the new loan.

THE MORTGAGE LENDING BUSINESS

Most buyers have to borrow money in order to be able to make real estate purchases. As a result, the mortgage industry is, in dollar volume, one of the largest business segments in our economy. New mortgage commitments amount to hundreds of billions of dollars annually. Home mortgage lending is a national business.

Primary and Secondary Mortgage Markets

The market in which loans are originated is called the *primary mortgage market*. The *secondary mortgage market* is the market in which originators and investors buy and sell existing mortgage loans as investments.

Most mortgage loans are *brokered*. This means that the firms that borrowers think are lending to them actually only *originate* and *service* the loans. This is the *primary mortgage market*. The originators of the loans sell them to *investors*, in the *secondary mortgage market*. These investors usually are large financial institutions such as pension funds, insurance companies, investment companies, FNMA (see below), etc. They seek relatively safe investments which offer good returns, and home mortgages often fit the bill. The investors seek only to invest funds and earn returns; they don't want to become involved in the paperwork and other busywork of actually qualifying borrowers and making the loans (origination) or collecting payments and supervising the loans once they are made (servicing). In return for fees, *mortgage brokers* and *mortgage companies* originate loans, and service them for the investors to whom they are sold.

Mortgage investors do not buy loans one at a time; rather, they buy *packages* of mortgages, up to several million dollars worth at a time. In order to safeguard their investment, they insist that certain universal standards be applied to the loans they buy. The standards they usually want are those set by the Federal National Mortgage Association (FNMA, or "Fannie Mae"), which is the largest single secondary market investor in home mortgages in the USA.

FNMA

FNMA is a private corporation, created by Federal law. Simply, FNMA issues bonds and notes and uses the proceeds to buy home mortgages. The returns from the mortgages are expected to pay FNMA's expenses and pay off the bonds and notes. FNMA's debt (the bonds and notes) is guaranteed by the Federal Government; this makes it quite safe and, thus, means that FNMA pays a fairly low interest rate on this borrowed money. This in turn means that FNMA can be satisfied with fairly low returns on the mortgages it buys and, as a result, allows FNMA to provide copious amounts of funds for mortgage lending at reasonable interest rates. Another large investor in mortgages is the Federal Home Loan Mortgage Corporation (FHLMC or "Freddie Mac"); it is wholly-owned by the Federal Government. It too buys mortgages, financed by issuing Government-guaranteed debt. Although it doesn't have to, FHLMC usually uses FNMA standards for its loans as well.

FNMA has developed a detailed set of guidelines which must be met by any loans which it buys. These standards assure FNMA that all the loans it holds ($100's of billions worth) meet at least certain minimum standards relating to the borrower's credit quality and ability to pay, and the value and marketability of the properties securing the mortgages.

Although they don't have to, most other large mortgage investors use FNMA standards as the ones they require. This leads to a large national market in "*FNMA conforming*" loans which are easily bought and sold since dealers in them know that they all fit a certain acceptable standard.

FNMA Standards

FNMA Standards are not uniform throughout the US. In certain high-cost areas (notably the West Coast and the Northeast) they are more lenient than elsewhere. Furthermore, they are changed from time to time. Only a general discussion of some significant points can be given here, and readers should check local up-to-date sources for detailed descriptions of the standards which apply in their areas.

Income qualification: In most of the country, FNMA's income qualification standards for borrowers are based upon the borrower's *gross monthly income*. This is monthly pay and other verifiable, regular income of all household members who will be obligated for the mortgage loan, *before* any deductions for taxes, Social Security, etc. are taken out. For loans of 90% LTV or less, the *28-36 rule* applies. What this rule means is that the PITI payment to the mortgage loan cannot exceed 28% of borrower's gross monthly income, and the mortgage loan payment plus *all other monthly obligations* cannot add up to more than 36% of borrower's gross monthly income. Other monthly obligations could be car payments, credit card payments, etc. FNMA counts only those monthly obligations which have more than 11 months remaining. For loans which exceed 90% LTV, the *25-33 rule* applies: of borrower's gross monthly income, no more than 25% may go to the PITI mortgage payments, and no more than 33% to all monthly obligations combined.

Consider an example: A household has an annual income of $40,000, which is $3,333 per month. Under the 28-36 rule, the household's PITI mortgage payment on the loan cannot exceed $933 per month (28% of $3,333) and the loan payment and all other monthly obligations cannot exceed $1,200 per month (36% of $3,333).

Both parts of the rule will be applied: the household must meet *both* the 28% *and* the 36% criteria. This means that if the household's other monthly obligations are more than $267 per month ($1,200 less $933), then the allowable PITI loan payment must be less than the $933 maximum. Suppose the household has $430 of other monthly expense:

a car payment of $350 per month and another loan payment of $80 per month. Their maximum PITI payment will be the 36% maximum total, less the $430 of monthly obligations, or $770 per month ($1,200 - $430 = $770). Conversely, even if the household has *no* other monthly obligations, their PITI payment will be limited to the 28% maximum of $933.

If the household seeks a loan with LTV above 90%, then the 25-33 rule applies. For the household in the example above, if their loan exceeds 90% LTV, the maximum PITI payment will be $833 (25% of $3,333) and the maximum total for all monthly obligations will be $1,100 (33% of $3,333).

FNMA appraisal requirements: FNMA requires all mortgaged properties to be appraised; the loan (and its LTV) will be based upon the *lower* of the purchase price or the appraisal. Appraisals must be done by state-certified appraisers, and must meet FNMA appraisal standards. These standards include rules with respect to the type of information included in the appraisal, and are discussed later in this chapter's section on appraisal.

Other FNMA requirements and standards: There is a *maximum* allowable amount for FNMA-conforming loans. This upper limit is changed yearly, and is based on median home prices for the previous year. For 1993 the FNMA maximum is expected to be between $205,000 and $210,000. All loans require *title insurance*, a *survey* of the property, *income verification* (acknowledgement of borrower's pay by employers; self-employment income must be verified by tax returns), and *credit verification*. PMI is required on all loans with LTV above 80%.

Non-FNMA Standards

FHA and VA have standards of their own for loans which they will insure (FHA) or guarantee (VA). Their standards are more liberal than FNMA; their lower down payments are one example. However, even though these loans do not conform to FNMA standards, investors are happy to buy them because they are insured or guaranteed by the US Government.

Non-Conforming Loans

Conventional loans which do not meet FNMA standards are called *non-conforming loans*. There are two kinds: the first consists of loans which meet all FNMA standards *except* that they exceed the FNMA maximum loan amount. These loans are called *jumbo* loans. Many investors will buy them, since it is only the size of the loan which doesn't conform to FNMA standards. Therefore there is a market for such loans, though they typically carry somewhat higher interest rates than conforming loans.

The second group consists of loans which fall short of FNMA standards by criteria other than a too-large amount. These are much more difficult to market, since most investors do not want to spend the time and effort to select their mortgage invest- ments on a case-by-case basis. Typically, then, these loans will be made by lenders who do *not* intend to sell them in the secondary market.

FINANCING AND THE BROKERAGE BUSINESS

Now that we have had a brief discussion of mortgage lending, we will take a look at how real estate licensees deal with financing. Some things already have been noted. If loan assumption or seller financing are likely to be involved with a particular listing, the licensee should make sure that the seller is aware of the risks involved. Loan assumption without substitution of mortgagor will leave the seller liable for the loan; if seller financing is used, the seller should make it subject to obtaining credit and income verification on the buyer.

Many home sales will require the seller to pay some costs and fees for the buyer's mortgage arrangements. Sellers must pay "points" on any buyers' new VA financing. As part of the terms of a particular sale, a seller may agree to pay other loan origination fees on the buyer's loan, including applicable points on new FHA or conventional loans. In some markets, particularly for low-cost homes, this sort of thing is quite prevalent. The salesperson must be able explain the advantages and disadvantages to the seller.

Buyer-Borrower Qualification

For most mortgage loans there are standardized borrower qualification requirements which must be met: FNMA, FHA, or VA. All have guidelines related to the applicant's income, other debt, etc. The salesperson's initial qualification procedure for each buying prospect should include information about income, obligations and available ready cash (for down payments and closing costs). This information can be used by the licensee to make up "dummy" loan qualification and settlement summaries for the prospect. Doing this will establish a price range of homes which are affordable, and will demonstrate to the prospects their eventual financial situations after the purchase. This infor- mation also helps to determine which type(s) of loan, and how large a loan, will be possible for the prospect. This means, of course, that the salesperson must be up-to-date on mortgage lenders' requirements. Also, the licensee must be ready to explain these sometimes confusing qualifications and procedures to prospective buyers.

Assisting Buyer Financing

Brokers, because they are familiar with the real estate market, often are in a position to assist buyers with their financing arrangements. Loan availability and terms often are the key element in whether or not a potential sale can occur. While the price of the home is very important, nearly every buyer will want to know how much initial cash is needed, and what the monthly payments will be.

Knowing what is happening in the mortgage market is an essential component of a competent real estate professional's knowledge. Usually there is no such thing as *the* interest rate; rates and terms will vary somewhat among lenders. The salesperson or the firm's sales manager ought to know at any given time which mortgage lenders have the best terms, and should try to steer buyers toward them. This saves the buyers money and increases their satisfaction with the firm's performance. Satisfied customers provide good references and good word-of-mouth advertising for the firm.

Professional brokerage firms make it a point to keep up-to-date information about financing rates and terms available in their areas. Mortgage lending officers are frequent visitors to their sales meetings, to keep the sales force current with the latest information. Many multilist systems also survey local lenders and put their rates and terms into the computer files and books where they can be accessed by member firms and their salespeople.

Sometimes real estate brokerage firms will be paid by mortgage lenders for referring borrowers to them. Such "finder's fees" are accepted practice in many areas, and collecting them usually will not violate the broker's agency responsibility to the seller. Certainly, helping the buyer to find financing is no violation, since it facilitates the sale. This is, after all, the whole objective of the agency relationship. This is one area in which the broker's actions on behalf of the buyer definitely benefit the seller.

Financing Arrangements as Sales Incentive

At times, special financing arrangements offered by the seller can be used to promote the sale of listed property. Sellers may make advance arrangements with lenders, or may agree in the listing contract to offer to pay certain transaction costs for buyers. Sellers even can arrange, for payment of a fee (i.e.: a certain number of points), for "below market" interest rates on loans to be made available to the buyers of their listed properties. In some markets such arrangements are necessary in order to make the listed property saleable. In other markets they may provide a competitive edge which will result in a quicker sale, possibly at a better price. But for such buyer incentives to work they must be arranged ahead of time and used in the selling effort. The listing agent usually must understand them in order to be able to use them effectively and to explain their advantages to buying prospects.

Most sellers are not sophisticated about the subtleties and more arcane features of mortgage lending. Thus, it usually is the listing agent who suggests and explains financing arrangements, and their use as possible buyer incentives. Clearly, the licensee must make sure that the seller understands the situation fully, and is aware of any risks or costs involved.

FIRREA

The *Financial Institutions Reform, Recovery, and Enforcement Act of 1989*, known more commonly by its acronym *FIRREA*, is the "savings and loan bailout" law which saddled several future generations of American taxpayers with hundreds of billions of dollars of debt stemming from the self-destruction of the savings and loan industry that occurred in the 1980's. FIRREA also reorganized much of the mortgage industry, and impacted several other areas of the real estate business.

The appraisal business, in particular, was significantly affected by this legislation. FIRREA encouraged FNMA to implement very strict standards for appraisals on conforming loans. Also, it required *state-certification* of appraisers. Until 1989, few states had any licensing or other certifying requirements for real estate appraisers. Now, however, FIRREA requires that appraisals accompanying any *Federally related* mortgage loans be done by "certified" appraisers. "Federally related" effectively means any FHA or VA loan, and any loan which is to be saleable to FNMA or FHLMC. These include nearly all home mortgage loans. (Remember, most secondary-market investors require FNMA-conforming loans.) Therefore, the effect of the legislation has been to require certification of all appraisers who do appraisals for home mortgages. (There is some discussion going on about exempting appraisals on lower-cost homes – $50,000 or less – from the requirement.)

Certification is very similar to licensing, in that appraisers must pass examinations showing that they have a certain level of knowledge about the procedures of real estate appraisal. Certification is required of *all* home mortgage appraisers, including those who were in the business before FIRREA was passed in 1989. The law originally required that state-certification be in place by the beginning of 1991. However, the states dragged their feet and Congress delayed the implementation requirement to January, 1993.

APPRAISAL

Real estate appraisal is the process of *estimating* the value of real estate. Many kinds of value can be estimated (replacement cost, estate value, etc.) but so far as real estate brokers are concerned, the value estimate which is most important (and most often asked from appraisers) is *market value*. Market value is defined as the price a property will bring in today's market, under today's circumstances, when sold by a ready, willing and able seller to a ready, willing and able buyer.

Note in the paragraph above that appraisal is described as *estimating* value. It is important to understand that appraisers do not *determine* value; that can be done only by the market itself. To find out *for certain* what a property is worth, you have to *sell it* and see how much you get. However, an experienced and professional appraiser, familiar with the appraised property and the market it is in, can come up with an estimate that will be very close to market value.

Figure 10-1 displays the *Uniform Real Estate Appraisal Report* (*URAR*) which commonly is used by appraisers for house appraisals. The property being appraised is called the *subject property*. It is described on the first page of the form. On the second page is the appraisal analysis. Appraisers always use three separate "approaches" (*cost, income and market*) when they estimate a subject property's value. Spaces for each of the three are on this page of the form. The traditional idea is that each approach, done separately, should come to the same approximate result as the others, thus strengthening and verifying the overall estimate of value. However, as we will see, some properties are more amenable to one of the approaches than to the others.

UNIFORM RESIDENTIAL APPRAISAL REPORT File No.

SUBJECT

Property Address	Census Tract
City	County	State	Zip Code
Legal Description	
Owner/Occupant	Map Reference
Sale Price $	Date of Sale
Loan charges/concessions to be paid by seller $	
R.E. Taxes $	Tax Year	HOA $/Mo.
Lender/Client	

LENDER DISCRETIONARY USE

Sale Price $
Date
Mortgage Amount $
Mortgage Type
Discount Points and Other Concessions
Paid by Seller $
Source

PROPERTY RIGHTS APPRAISED
- Fee Simple
- Leasehold
- Condominium (HUD/VA)
- De Minimis PUD

NEIGHBORHOOD

LOCATION	Urban	Suburban	Rural
BUILT UP	Over 75%	25-75%	Under 25%
GROWTH RATE	Rapid	Stable	Slow
PROPERTY VALUES	Increasing	Stable	Declining
DEMAND/SUPPLY	Shortage	In Balance	Over Supply
MARKETING TIME	Under 3 Mos.	3-6 Mos.	Over 6 Mos.

PRESENT LAND USE	%	LAND USE CHANGE	PREDOMINANT	SINGLE FAMILY HOUSING
Single Family		Not Likely	OCCUPANCY	PRICE $(000) / AGE (yrs)
2-4 Family		Likely	Owner	
Multi-family		In process	Tenant	Low
Commercial		To:	Vacant (0-5%)	High
Industrial			Vacant (over 5%)	Predominant
Vacant				–

NEIGHBORHOOD ANALYSIS	Good	Avg.	Fair	Poor
Employment Stability				
Convenience to Employment				
Convenience to Shopping				
Convenience to Schools				
Adequacy of Public Transportation				
Recreation Facilities				
Adequacy of Utilities				
Property Compatibility				
Protection from Detrimental Cond.				
Police & Fire Protection				
General Appearance of Properties				
Appeal to Market				

Note: Race or the racial composition of the neighborhood are not considered reliable appraisal factors.

COMMENTS:

SITE

Dimensions		Topography
Site Area	Corner Lot	Size
Zoning Classification	Zoning Compliance	Shape
HIGHEST & BEST USE: Present Use	Other Use	Drainage

UTILITIES	Public	Other	SITE IMPROVEMENTS	Type	Public	Private	View
Electricity			Street				Landscaping
Gas			Curb/Gutter				Driveway
Water			Sidewalk				Apparent Easements
Sanitary Sewer			Street Lights				FEMA Flood Hazard Yes* No
Storm Sewer			Alley				FEMA* Map/Zone

COMMENTS (Apparent adverse easements, encroachments, special assessments, slide areas, etc.):

IMPROVEMENTS

GENERAL DESCRIPTION	EXTERIOR DESCRIPTION	FOUNDATION	BASEMENT	INSULATION
Units	Foundation	Slab	Area Sq. Ft.	Roof
Stories	Exterior Walls	Crawl Space	% Finished	Ceiling
Type (Det./Att.)	Roof Surface	Basement	Ceiling	Walls
Design (Style)	Gutters & Dwnspts.	Sump Pump	Walls	Floor
Existing	Window Type	Dampness	Floor	None
Proposed	Storm Sash	Settlement	Outside Entry	Adequacy
Under Construction	Screens	Infestation		Energy Efficient Items:
Age (Yrs.)	Manufactured House			
Effective Age (Yrs.)				

ROOM LIST

ROOMS	Foyer	Living	Dining	Kitchen	Den	Family Rm.	Rec. Rm.	Bedrooms	# Baths	Laundry	Other	Area Sq. Ft.
Basement												
Level 1												
Level 2												

Finished area **above** grade contains: Rooms;   Bedroom(s);   Bath(s);   Square Feet of Gross Living Area

INTERIOR

SURFACES	Materials/Condition
Floors	
Walls	
Trim/Finish	
Bath Floor	
Bath Wainscot	
Doors	
Fireplace(s)	#

HEATING	
Type	
Fuel	
Condition	
Adequacy	
COOLING	
Central	
Other	
Condition	
Adequacy	

KITCHEN EQUIP.	
Refrigerator	
Range/Oven	
Disposal	
Dishwasher	
Fan/Hood	
Compactor	
Washer/Dryer	
Microwave	
Intercom	

ATTIC	
None	
Stairs	
Drop Stair	
Scuttle	
Floor	
Heated	
Finished	

IMPROVEMENT ANALYSIS	Good	Avg.	Fair	Poor
Quality of Construction				
Condition of Improvements				
Room Sizes/Layout				
Closets and Storage				
Energy Efficiency				
Plumbing-Adequacy & Condition				
Electrical-Adequacy & Condition				
Kitchen Cabinets-Adequacy & Cond.				
Compatibility to Neighborhood				
Appeal & Marketability				

AUTOS

CAR STORAGE:			
No. Cars	Garage	Attached	House Entry
Condition	Carport	Detached	Outside Entry
	None	Built-In	Basement Entry
		Adequate	
		Inadequate	
		Electric Door	

Estimated Remaining Economic Life   Yrs.
Estimated Remaining Physical Life   Yrs.

Additional features:

COMMENTS

Depreciation (Physical, functional and external inadequacies, repairs needed, modernization, etc.):

General market conditions and prevalence and impact in subject/market area regarding loan discounts, interest buydowns and concessions:

Figure 10-1. Uniform Residential Appraisal Report

UNIFORM RESIDENTIAL APPRAISAL REPORT   File No.

Purpose of Appraisal is to estimate Market Value as defined in the Certification & Statement of Limiting Conditions.

COST APPROACH

BUILDING SKETCH (SHOW GROSS LIVING AREA ABOVE GRADE)

If for Freddie Mac or Fannie Mae, show only square foot calculations and cost approach comments in this space.

ESTIMATED REPRODUCTION COST – NEW – OF IMPROVEMENTS:

Dwelling _____	Sq. Ft. @ $ _____	= $ _____
	Sq. Ft. @ $ _____	= _____
Extras _____		= _____
		= _____
Special Energy Efficient Items _____		= _____
Porches, Patios, etc. _____		= _____
Garage/Carport _____	Sq. Ft. @ $ _____	= _____
Total Estimated Cost New		= $ _____

	Physical	Functional	External
Less			
Depreciation _____			= $ _____

Depreciated Value of Improvements .... = $ _____
Site Imp. "as is" (driveway, landscaping, etc.) = $ _____
ESTIMATED SITE VALUE .... = $ _____
(If leasehold, show only leasehold value.)
INDICATED VALUE BY COST APPROACH .... = $ _____

(Not Required by Freddie Mac and Fannie Mae)

Does property conform to applicable HUD/VA property standards? ☐ Yes ☐ No

If No, explain: _____

Construction Warranty ☐ Yes ☐ No
Name of Warranty Program _____
Warranty Coverage Expires _____

SALES COMPARISON ANALYSIS

The undersigned has recited three recent sales of properties most similar and proximate to subject and has considered these in the market analysis. The description includes a dollar adjustment, reflecting market reaction to those items of significant variation between the subject and comparable properties. If a significant item in the comparable property is superior to, or more favorable than, the subject property, a minus (−) adjustment is made, thus reducing the indicated value of subject; if a significant item in the comparable is inferior to, or less favorable than, the subject property, a plus (+) adjustment is made, thus increasing the indicated value of the subject.

ITEM	SUBJECT	COMPARABLE NO. 1		COMPARABLE NO. 2		COMPARABLE NO. 3	
Address							
Proximity to Subject							
Sales Price	$	$		$		$	
Price/Gross Liv. Area	$ ☑	$ ☑		$ ☑		$ ☑	
Data Source							
VALUE ADJUSTMENTS	DESCRIPTION	DESCRIPTION	+ (−) $ Adjustment	DESCRIPTION	+ (−) $ Adjustment	DESCRIPTION	+ (−) $ Adjustment
Sales or Financing Concessions							
Date of Sale/Time							
Location							
Site/View							
Design and Appeal							
Quality of Construction							
Age							
Condition							
Above Grade Room Count	Total ¦ Bdrms ¦ Baths	Total ¦ Bdrms ¦ Baths		Total ¦ Bdrms ¦ Baths		Total ¦ Bdrms ¦ Baths	
Gross Living Area	Sq. Ft.	Sq. Ft.		Sq. Ft.		Sq. Ft.	
Basement & Finished Rooms Below Grade							
Functional Utility							
Heating/Cooling							
Garage/Carport							
Porches, Patio, Pools, etc.							
Special Energy Efficient Items							
Fireplace(s)							
Other (e.g. kitchen equip., remodeling)							
Net Adj. (total)		☐ + ☐ − $		☐ + ☐ − $		☐ + ☐ − $	
Indicated Value of Subject		$		$		$	

Comments on Sales Comparison: _____

INDICATED VALUE BY SALES COMPARISON APPROACH .... $ _____

INDICATED VALUE BY INCOME APPROACH (If Applicable) Estimated Market Rent $ _____ /Mo. x Gross Rent Multiplier _____ = $ _____

This appraisal is made ☐ "as is" ☐ subject to the repairs, alterations, inspections or conditions listed below ☐ completion per plans and specifications.

Comments and Conditions of Appraisal: _____

Final Reconciliation: _____

RECONCILIATION

This appraisal is based upon the above requirements, the certification, contingent and limiting conditions, and Market Value definition that are stated in

☐ FmHA, HUD &/or VA instructions.

☐ Freddie Mac Form 439 (Rev. 7/86)/Fannie Mae Form 1004B (Rev. 7/86) filed with client _____ 19 ___ ☐ attached.

I (WE) ESTIMATE THE MARKET VALUE, AS DEFINED, OF THE SUBJECT PROPERTY AS OF _____ 19 ___ to be $ _____

I (We) certify: that to the best of my (our) knowledge and belief the facts and data used herein are true and correct; that I (we) personally inspected the subject property, both inside and out, and have made an exterior inspection of all comparable sales cited in this report; and that I (we) have no undisclosed interest, present or prospective therein.

APPRAISER(S)

Signature _____

Name _____

REVIEW APPRAISER
(if applicable) Signature _____

Name _____

☐ Did ☐ Did Not
Inspect Property

Freddie Mac Form 70 10/86 12 Ch. MC3/89 Forms and Worms Inc.® 315 Whitney Ave., New Haven, CT 06511 1(800) 243-4545 Item # 111710. Fannie Mae Form 1004 10/86

Figure 10-1. *(Continued)*

Cost (Replacement) Approach

The *cost approach* (also called *replacement*, or *replacement cost* approach) applies only to the subject property's improvements: building, landscaping, other constructed items, or everything but the land. The land has to be appraised using a different method. The idea here is to estimate what it would cost today to build new improvements *similar* to the existing ones. Note that we said similar, not *identical*. A replacement is *not* a reproduction; rather, it is *today's version* of the same kind of improvement that the subject property has. A figure for replacement cost isn't hard to get: builders can provide estimates, and appraisers have access to several kinds of building cost guides which they can use.

Depreciation: But this replacement cost of a new structure is only the starting point. Most subject properties are *not* new; therefore the replacement cost figure must be *depreciated* to take account of the age of the subject. The idea of depreciation associated with real estate seems strange; we are used to properties increasing in value over time. However, in an important sense, real estate improvements *do* depreciate.What happens is that the cost of replacing them increases *faster* than the increases in values of existing properties. The older they get, the larger the gap between their market value and their replacement cost. You can verify this for yourself: pick a house that is 10 or 15 years old and for which you know the market value (one which has recently sold would be a good example). Subtract the value of the land, so that you get a "value" for the house alone. Then get an estimate of what it would cost today to build the same house (to today's standards). Almost always you will find that the replacement cost is higher.

Types of Depreciation: Real estate appraisers recognize that real estate assets can depreciate. They observe three different kinds of depreciation. Note that these have nothing to do with "depreciation" for tax purposes. Rather, these are three ways in which real estate assets lose value overr time.

Physical deterioration refers to wear and tear. A leaky roof, a crack in the wallboard, a worn out furnace; all of these are physical deterioration. It is an inevitable result of the use of the improvements over time.

Functional obsolescence refers to things which become out-of-date, or which no longer match up well with the changing tastes of the market. A house with little or no insulation in the walls is functionally obsolete. When it was built it may not have been normal practice to insulate walls, but now that energy has become very expensive, it is common for new homes to be very well insulated.

Physical and functional depreciation are features of the subject property itself. *Economic, or external, depreciation* is a catch-all term for depreciating factors *outside* the property: the local economic situation, changes in the immediate neighborhood, etc. Economic depreciation considers *locational* attributes of the subject property.

Appraisers also classify each of the three kinds of depreciation as *curable* or *incurable*. This does not refer to whether or not it is *possible* to cure the depreciation, but rather to whether or not it *pays* to do so. Economic depreciation generally is considered incurable; since it has to do with factors outside the property, the only way of dealing with it would be to change the property's environment, or move the building to a better location. Physical and functional depreciation will be curable or incurable, depending upon whether it pays to fix the problem.

As an example of physical deterioration, suppose a home's furnace doesn't work properly, and it will cost $500 to repair it. If repairing the furnace will add at least $500 to the subject property's market value, then this physical deterioration is curable. If it won't add as much as $500 to property value, then it is incurable.

For functional obsolescence, we can consider insulation. A poorly insulated attic is functionally obsolete. However, it usually is fairly easy to add more insulation to an attic, since it is easily accessible. In most cases, improving the insulation will save considerably on utility bills, and therefore can pay for itself quickly. In this situation, it definitely "pays" to add the insulation, so the obsolescence is curable. However, if the *walls* of the house are poorly insulated, it may be another story. The interiors of walls are not easily accessed; the cost of adding insulation may have to include the cost of removing the wallboard or plaster to get to the uninsulated area; once the insulation is installed, new wall surfaces have to be installed. This would be very expensive to do. The savings in utility bills probably wouldn't come close to justifying the cost, so this obsolescence would be incurable.

Problems With Cost Approach: Depreciation is the bugaboo of the cost approach. Appraisers haven't been able to come up with any systematic method or rule of thumb to use to estimate depreciation. Therefore, any estimate of depreciation is difficult to arrive at and difficult to defend. As a result, home appraiasals don't put a lot of emphasis on the cost approach. In the form in Figure 10-1, its main usefulness is to provide a space to list the three elements of depreciation as they affect the property.

Income Approach

The income approach determines the *net income* that could be earned from the property, if it were rented. Net income is not *total rent*; the *costs of ownership* (property taxes, maintenance, etc.) have to be subtracted from rent to get income. Once the property's net income is determined, the appraiser's analysis essentially asks the question: "What would a reasonable investor pay to get the income this property provides, considering the risks involved?" This is a glib question, but it is difficult to answer, and involves procedures which are beyond the scope of this book. Suffice to say that many appraisers who are good at appraising houses aren't adept at the arcane methods needed to do a proper income approach analysis.

Income property, obviously, is best suited to this approach. However, when houses are being appraised, the usual approach taken is somewhat of a cop-out. The appraiser estimates the monthly rent which the property could earn. Then the appraiser applies a factor called the *Gross Rent Multiplier (GRM)*. The GRM is the value of the property, divided by the rent: GRM = Value / Monthly Rent. So, if a property is worth $90,000 and produces monthly rent of $750, then GRM = 90,000 / 750 = 120. The appraiser is supposed to determine GRM and rent by finding similar properties which *are* rented. Their rentals will give an indication of the likely rent for the subject property. Comparing their values to the rents they produce will give an indication of the GRM for the neighborhood. A problem here is that in many residential neighborhoods, very few properties are rented, and the appraiser may not be able to obtain enough reliable data with which to make these estimates.

Market Approach

The market approach (also called *comparable*, or *market comparison* approach) works like this: find several properties *similar* to the subject, and which *recently sold* in the same market as the subject is in. These recently sold similar properties are called *comparables*. Their recent sale prices ought to give a good indication of the estimated value of the subject. As the form in Figure 10-1 shows, it is typical practice for appraisers to use three comparables for a house appraisal.

Once again, this is more difficult than it seems. In fact, the market approach involves a lot of "judgment calls" by the appraiser. How similar must a comparable be to be "similar enough"? How recently must the comparable have sold to be "recent enough"? And, finally, the appraiser must cope with the fact that while similar comparable properties may not be too hard to find, it is usually impossible to come up with comparables *identical* to the subject. Therefore, the appraiser has to deal with some differences between the comparables and the subject. These differences are handled by making *adjustments*.

Adjustments: The appraiser starts with the comparable's sale price. The idea is to make adjustments to this sale price, up or down, to take account of differences between comparable and subject. The Form in Figure 10-1 lists several areas of possible difference. In the first (left-hand) column, the appraiser enters the description of the *subject*. For each comparable, there are two columns. In the first the appraiser enters the comparable's description (or "same," if it does not differ from the subject in this area). In the second the appraiser enters a *dollar adjustment*. This number will be positive or negative, depending upon whether the subject is better or worse than the comparable for the feature under consideration.

Adjustment Examples: Consider a couple of examples. First, let's assume that the subject property is 1600 square feet in size, while the comparable is 1660 square feet. Here the comparable is "better" (bigger) than the subject. The appraiser now must answer this question: "In this market, would the comparable have sold for less if it had been the same size as the subject (60 square feet smaller) and, if so, *how much less?*" Let's assume that the answer to the first part of the question is "yes"; now the appraiser must make an adjustment. This is a judgment call; there are few reliable references which an appraiser can use to come up with an exact answer. This doesn't mean that the answer is impossible, but rather that the appraiser must rely upon his/her experience and knowledge of the market to get the answer. Suppose it is the appraiser's opinion that, in this market, "raw" square feet are worth $20. Since there is a 60 square foot difference, the adjustment would be $1,200 (60 X $20). This adjustment would be *negative*, since the comparable is *better* than the subject. So, for this feature (size), the appraiser adjusts the comparable's sale price *downward* by $1,200, since the comparable would have sold for *less* if, like the subject, it had only 1600 square feet.

A second example: this same comparable has a two-car carport (a roofed parking area with no walls) while the subject has a two-car garage (an enclosed parking area). In most markets, buyers would prefer the garage to the carport: greater security, less exposure to weather, possible storage space, etc. Here, then, the subject is *better* than the comparable. In the appraiser's judgment, the garage has a market value $2,000 greater than the carport. So the appraiser adjusts the comparable's price by $2,000. This adjustment is *positive* (*upward*), since the comparable presumably would have sold for *more* if, like the subject, it had a garage instead of a carport.

Measuring and Describing Houses: This is a good place to mention some conventions used in the real estate business for describing buildings. Square footage is the *area* of the structure. Usually it refers only to the *heated and finished* interior space: the "livable" part. When calculating square footage, we *do not* include outdoor "finished" spaces such as porches, patios, balconies or garages (even if they are heated); also, we do not include *unfinished* interior spaces such as basements and attics.

The square footage area is measured along the *outside* of the space. This means that different thicknesses of siding will yield different areas for otherwise identical buildings. For example, two houses, side by side, were built from the same plans. Inside they are identical: corresponding rooms have the same dimensions in each one. But one has frame (wood) siding, the other has brick. Brick is about 4 inches thick, while frame usually is less than 2 inches thick. Therefore the brick house will measure several inches more in every direction and, so, will be calculated to have the larger square footage.

When counting rooms in a house, count only the *major spaces*. Do not count closets, storage areas or bathrooms. Counting "dual-purpose" rooms can be a problem. Many houses have a "living-dining room," or "great room" which serves as living room, dining room, and den all in one space; kitchens with space for a breakfast table also are popular. These are counted as single rooms, unless their shape or layout clearly defines different areas for different purposes.

Bathrooms are counted separately, and there is special convention for them also. A bathroom with a sink and toilet, but no bathing facilities (no tub, no shower) is a *half-bath*. A *three-quarter bath* has sink, toilet and shower stall, but no tub. One with sink, toilet and tub (whether or not the tub has a shower) is a *full bath*. So is one with double vanity sinks, a whirlpool tub, a separate shower room so high-tech that its manufacturer calls it a "cleansing system", a bidet, a sauna, a fireplace, bar, satellite dish, ski slope, etc. No matter how fancy it is, it still is counted only as one full bath.

Adjusted Sale Price: For each area of difference between the subject and the comparable, the appraiser calculates adjustments like the ones described previously. Then all the adjustments are added to arrive at a *total adjustment*. The total adjustment is applied to the comparable's sale price to arrive at the *adjusted sale price*. Since some adjustments are positive and others are negative, the total adjustment may not be all that large. For example, if the two adjustments in our example above are the only ones needed, then that comparable's total adjustment would be +$800 = (-$1,200) + (+$2,000). This means that this comparable's adjusted sale price would be $800 more than the price it actually sold for.

The whole idea behind these adjustments is to make each comparable, on paper, *more like the subject*, by adjusting their prices for their differences from the subject. In effect, the adjusted sale prices mean this: "This is the price that the comparable would have sold for *if it had been identical to the subject*."

Since the appraisal process is not perfect, appraisers don't expect the adjusted sale prices of all of the comparables to end up exactly the same. However, they should be fairly close; say within 5% or so of one another. The appraiser then averages them to get a value estimate from the market approach.

Reconciling the Approaches

As we mentioned above, an appraisal is supposed to use all three approaches. The three estimates thus obtained are *reconciled* into one single figure: the appraiser's estimate of the subject property's current market value. As a matter of fact, however, the market approach is the one which usually is most applicable to houses. This is because in all but the smallest or most sluggish markets, and for most "typical" houses, there usually will be lots of comparable sale information. The objective of the appraisal is to estimate the subject's market value. Since the market approach is the one which most closely uses direct market information, it provides the best "gut feeling" to appraisers. Therefore, when they can get good market information they are likely to give this approach much greater weight when arriving at their final estimate.

FIRREA and Appraisal Standards

Our previous discussion has pointed out that the FIRREA legislation of 1989 required that appraisers who provide valuations included in *Federally-related* mortgage loan applications must be "certified" by the state where the mortgaged property is located. The definition of "Federally-related" is very broad, so it includes practically all first mortgage home loans originated today. All home mortgages insured (FHA) or guaranteed (VA) by the U.S. Government are Federally-related, as are all conventional loans eligible for purchase by Federally-related agencies such as FNMA and FHLMC.

FIRREA also led to the development of a fairly strict set of appraisal "standards" by FNMA. The entire set of standards takes up a good-sized book; we will mention a few which caused significant changes in appraisal procedures.

Comparables now are required to be "near" to the subject property: this usually means within 1.5 miles or less. This standard means that appraisers no longer can use comparables from "similar," but distant neighborhoods.

The adjusted sale price of a comparable must be within 10% (above or below) its actual sale price. This means that appraisers must use comparables which, even before adjustment, are very similar to the subject. So, practices such as using sales of $75,000 homes to justify the estimated values of $100,000 properties are no longer allowed.

Also, *time adjustments* of comparable sale prices aren't permitted any more. In rapidly changing markets, appraisers used to adjust comparable prices for the *time of sale*. For example, if the appraiser believed that prices in a particular market were increasing by 8% per year, he/she would make a time adjustment to a six-month old comparable sale by adjusting its sale price upward by 4% (one-half a year's worth of 8% annual home price inflation).

The objective of these standards is to make appraisals more reliable and, incidentally, more *conservative*. All three of the practices described above could have been used to help increase estimated value; since they no longer are allowed, these (and other) opportunities for overoptimistic inaccuracy are minimized. It should be noted, however, that these standards are not absolute. FNMA recognizes that some properties can only be appraised properly if some of the rules are bent or broken. Appraisals may violate the standards, but only if the appraiser can provide good, written justification for doing so.

"Informal" Appraisals by Brokers

Most firms, as they solicit listings, will present the property owner with a brief estimate of the value of the property, for the purpose of supporting the agent's suggested listing price. While these estimates may be referred to as "appraisals," *they are not professional appraisals, and they should not be presented as such!* Generally, a few recent sales of similar properties in the neighborhood can be presented as a basis for determining a reasonable listing price for the property under consideration. Figure 10-2 shows an example of a letter describing this sort of estimate.

Note that the letter makes no mention that an "appraisal" has been done. The potential seller is presented with bare details about recent sales of similar properties in the immediate neighborhood. The summary, which suggests a listing price, is not represented as an estimate of value in the true appraisal sense, but only as a suggestion. When this approach is used, the licensee should be prepared to defend any information and conclusions presented. If it is difficult to gather the needed information, then another means of estimating a reasonable listing price should be used.

Disputing Appraisals

Real estate salespeople most often encounter appraisals when a buyer seeks new financing, because lenders require that the property be appraised. The buyer's loan will be based upon the *lower* of the purchase price or the appraisal. Normally, if the appraiser's estimate of value is equal to or above the sale price, the appraisal will show the sale price as the estimate of value. If the appraiser's estimate is lower than the sale price, then his/her lower estimate will be presented.

It is this situation of a too-low estimate which creates the real estate licensee's most obnoxious, deal-killing problem with appraisals. Buyers will want to back out of the sale

DOVER REALTY COMPANY

1776 Twelfth Street, Waltham, Xxxxx 12345   (908) 555-4321

September 28, 1988

Jackson Marshall

Vera Marshall

12108 Cedar Road

Waltham, XXXX 12345

Dear Mr. and Mrs. Marshall:

We have examined your home at 12108 Cedar Road and compared it to other similar homes in your area which have recently sold. From this information, we believe that a listing price of $96,500 for your home would be reasonable. This would give "bargaining room" to result in a selling price which we believe would be over $90,000. Please note that this is a survey of available information, and <u>not</u> a professional fee appraisal.

We examined the following recent sales:

(1) 12101 Allison Road. Two bedrooms, two baths, kitchen, great room, dining area. Average lot and landscaping, excellent interior decoration, upgraded carpeting and appliances. 1401 square feet. Contracted 9/16/88, will close within 3 weeks. Listed at $96,000, sold for $93,000, or $66.38/square foot.

(2) 12222 Mallow Lane. Two bedrooms, two baths, kitchen, living room, den. This is the same model as your home. However, landscaping is only average and there is no carpet or appliance upgrade and no special

Figure 10-2. Sample Appraisal Letter

decor. 1381 square feet. Contracted 9/2/88, closed 9/25/88. Listed at $93,500, sold for $89,900 or $65.00/square foot.

(3) 4335 Toronado Circle. Two bedrooms, kitchen, den, living area. Excellent landscaping, superior appliance upgrade, average decor and carpet, good lot. 1277 square feet. Contracted 8/17/88, closed 9/19/88. Listed at $88,900, sold for $85,500 or $66.95/square foot.

This information suggests to us a base price of about $66 per square foot, or about $91,000. However, the excellent landscaping, appliances and decor of your home could bring as much as $1.50/square foot additional, or up to $93,000 or so, based upon your home's area of 1381 square feet. We suggest listing at $96,500.

I hope that you find this information satisfactory, and I look forward to listing your home with us.

Sincerely,

Joe Chatham

Senior Sales Associate

Figure 10-2. *(Continued)*

because the lender won't provide all the money they need and because the appraiser has told them, in effect, that they're paying too much. Sellers may be offended with the low estimate and refuse to sell at such an "unrealistic" price.

The only solution is for the licensee, sales manager or principal broker to dispute the appraisal. However, before doing so, the licensee should make sure that he/she has an effective argument. This would mean being able to dispute adjustments made to comparables or, even, the particular comparables selected. A strong arguing point is that the buyer and seller arrived at the price in a reasonable manner, so their action ought to be taken as a reasonable market transaction. Probably they arrived at their price by considering other sales and offerings in the market, and these can be presented to the appraiser to support the licensee's argument. We are not saying that disputing an appraisal always will be successful, but it doesn't hurt to try. It may work, and the licensee shouldn't let a deal fall through without at least giving it a good shot. (In the author's own experience, he once argued an appraisal up from $75,000 to $90,000, so it *can* be done.)

DISCUSSION QUESTIONS AND PROJECTS

1. Has your state established Federally-mandated certification for Appraisers? When? How is certification administered?

2. Discuss with appraisers in your community the impact of certification standards upon their businesses and upon the profession in general.

3. From a local mortgage lender, obtain a copy of its current "offerings." How many different kinds of loans are offered? How many different interest rates are available for fixed-rate mortgages, and how many points must be paid for each? What are the terms on available ARM's (term, caps, margins, teaser rates)? What are the available rates for "jumbo" loans?

4. How have mortgage loan interest rates fluctuated in the past year? The past five years? The past ten years? Do you notice any relationship between interest rates and the volume of home sales?

5. Discuss with local brokers and salespeople the procedures their firms use to assist buying prospects to determine the amounts and kinds of financing they are eligible for. How much "explaining" do they have to do before a typical buying prospect understands the financing options available?

6. What kinds of assistance do local brokerage firms provide buyers in obtaining financing?

A Case Study

READING THE MORTGAGE LENDER'S "MENU"

A very confusing experience for homebuyers is the first time they look over the list of loan options provided to them by a mortgage lender. There are all kinds of loans: FHA,

VA, conventional, jumbo; Fixed-rate, adjustable rate; 30-year term, 15-year term. Often the licensee handling the transaction will be asked to explain what these are.

But before the different offerings can be explained, the buyer often needs to have explained the "shorthand" that's used to present the various options. Typically, the lender's "menu" will look something like this:

30-year fixed-rate: $8.5 + 0$ $8.25 + .75$ $8 + 1.5$ $7.75 + 2.5$ $7.5 + 3.5$

This line gives the lender's current quotes on 30-year fixed-rate loans. Each quote is an *interest rate* and the *points* required for that rate. For example, the entry "7.75 + 2.5" means that the lender offers a 30-year loan at 7.75% interest, and it requires payment of a 2.5-point discount at origination. In this example, the 8.5% rate requires no points to be paid; 8.5%, then, is the *market rate*. For offerings at lower rates, the point payment goes up as the offered rate falls. This is in keeping with the discussion of points in this chapter.

Offerings for ARM loans would look like this:

1-year ARM $4.75 + .25$ 2%, 6% caps,   index + 2.75%,   convertible

This line describes an adjustable rate mortgage which is adjusted once a year. The first year's interest rate is 4.75%; the loan requires a 0.25-point discount to be paid at origination. The loan has a 2% annual cap and a lifetime 6% cap. The annual rate adjustments are calculated as the index + 2.75%. (These listings usually don't say *which* index is used: you have to ask.) The loan can be converted to a fixed-rate loan at some time in the future. You'll have to ask exactly when this convertibility privilege is allowed, and what the fee will be.

REFERENCES

BRUEGGEMAN, WILLIAM B. AND JEFFREY D. FISHER, *Real Estate Finance and Investments*, 9th Edition. Homewood, IL: Richard D. Irwin, Inc., 1993.

FRIEDMAN, JACK P. AND NICHOLAS ORDWAY, *Income Property Appraisal and Analysis*. Englewood Cliffs, NJ: Prentice-Hall, Inc., 1986.

LIPPMAN, BARBARA J., AND LORRAINE CATUBIG, "Closing Costs: Closing the Door on Homeownership?" *The Home Financing Transaction*, Fall, 1991.

RUSHING, PHILIP J., "The Economics of Accelerated Principal Repayment," *ORER Letter*, University of Illinois at Urbana-Champaign, Winter, 1991.

The Appraisal of Real Estate, 10th edition. Chicago, IL: The Appraisal Institute, 1992.

ELEVEN

COMPENSATION OF SALESPEOPLE

Commission Sharing

Incentive Plans

Company Listings and Referrals

Nonmoney Compensation

Salespeople in real estate brokerage firms receive their compensation by being given portions of the commissions that they bring into the firm. The exact split depends upon the contracts they have with the firm, but generally they will run from about 40 percent of the total they bring in, up to nearly 100 percent. To some extent, the exact split is determined by competition in the market. If a firm offers a split worse than that offered by most others in its area, it will not retain people for long, especially good producers. If it offers a better split, it will be paying more than it should.

COMMISSION SHARING

It would be impossible to spell out rigid rules for commission split arrangements that could apply to all companies in all locations and in all situations. However, we can examine typical plans as a guide to the formulation of those to be used by specific companies and in particular situations.

Listing and Selling Commissions

It is normal practice for firms to pay commissions separately for listing property and for selling it. A firm may agree with its salespeople that they will receive 50% of the commissions they bring in. The firm then will determine that a certain portion of each *total* commission is received for listing the property and the remainder for selling it. For example, the firm may decide that half of the total commission is payment for listing and half for selling. If a property is listed by salesperson A and sold by salesperson B, each will receive 25% of the total commission with the company receiving 50%. A will have brought in half of the total commission by listing the property; her half of this is 25% of the total, and the other 25% goes to the company. B brings in the 50% of the total commission allocated to selling the listed property. His share is 25% of the total (half of what he brought in) and the company gets the other 25%.

In earlier times, and in some rural areas today, the practice was to pay most of the commission for selling and relatively little for listing. This practice may appear to be logical, since one can argue that without a sale there is no point to a listing. However, this encourages salespeople to sell but not to make much effort to list property, unless they are reasonably sure that they can sell it themselves and so get the much larger share of the commission. The modern brokerage firm realizes that unless a very strong buyers' market exists, listings are more valuable than sales because there is always a good chance that a decent listed property will sell, while there is little chance of selling to a good buying prospect if there are few listings to sell.

Adjustments

The exact commission sharing arrangement will be determined by a number of things. Is the commission for a listing, a sale, or both? Was the listing solicited by the salesperson or assigned by the firm's management? Was it a particularly difficult transaction or an easy one? Many firms have incentive programs that offer better commission splits to salespeople who produce well. While the commission split is the primary means of compensation, it is not the only one. Employee salespeople can receive all kinds of fringe benefits. While these cannot be given to independent contractors, other benefits can be. The firm may have particularly pleasant offices to work in or may provide very good support staff service. In the latter case, a salesperson may be satisfied with a smaller split because the support given by the firm makes it possible to spend more time on the primary activity of soliciting listings and making sales.

Depending upon market conditions, the firm may want to revise its commission payment arrangements. If it is a seller's market, there will be relatively few properties for sale and many people wanting to buy. In such markets it is easier to find buyers than it is to get good listings, so the firm may want to reduce the commissions paid on sales and increase them for listings, to encourage its salespeople to spend more time getting listings. In a buyer's market there are many properties for sale and relatively few buyers. Here a firm might reverse its policy and pay a higher commission split for sales than for listings.

Cooperated Sales

Cooperated sales occur whenever a salesperson at one brokerage firm sells property listed by another. Many firms have adopted policies that give different treatment to commission splits on properties listed by other brokerage firms. Naturally, the firm would prefer that its own salespeople sell its listings, since the firm receives a larger amount of the total commission by splitting with its own sales force on both listing and sale. To encourage this, a firm might pay its salespeople only 40% of commissions brought in by selling listings of other firms, instead of the 50% that it pays on sales of its own listings. This will encourage greater effort to sell the company's own listings, since the pay is better.

The attractiveness of these arrangements also is affected by the manner in which brokerages split commissions between themselves on cooperated sales. In some parts of the country, the total commission is split 50-50 between the listing broker and the selling broker. But in other areas the split is uneven, usually with the larger share going to the listing broker. This smaller cooperated selling commission provides an additional incentive for a firm's salespeople to concentrate on its own listings, since the firm can offer a better payment for doing so.

The 100% Commission Arrangement and Variations

In recent years a new manner of employment and compensation has emerged that usually is referred to as the *100% commission* arrangement. Salespeople pay the brokerage a flat fee, usually monthly, for the use of the firm's facilities. They then keep *all* of the commissions they bring in. Some firms vary the program slightly by charging an additional fee to the salesperson for each transaction, but the basic effect is to allow salespeople to keep amost all the commission income they produce. This kind of arrangement is particularly useful in independent contractor arrangements, since the contractor actually pays the firm the fee for its services, instead of the other way around.

There are advantages and disadvantages to this type of arrangement. The fees charged by the firm to the salesperson are designed to cover its costs (plus a reasonable profit) of having the salesperson on its sales force. Fees charged for transactions processed by the firm cover the firm's costs in that regard. The main advantage to the firm is that almost all of the risk with respect to doing business is borne by the salesperson, who must pay the fees to the brokerage firm whether or not he/she produces commission income. The firm has a regular source of income from its sales force that will not be affected by conditions in the real estate market. Financial planning is made much easier for the firm and a lot less risky or uncertain. At the same time, the firm will make relatively less money from a very good producer, since it does not share in the commissions generated, but collects only the agreed upon fees.

From the salesperson's point of view, the arrangement can be either good or bad. A good producer may profit quite handsomely. A mediocre one probably would be better off under a conventional splitting arrangement. Table 11-1 illustrates this point.

The 100% commission arrangement has been tried by many firms across the country. Some have found it highly desirable, while others have reverted to a more conventional system. Whether or not it is the right arrangement for a given firm will depend on many factors. It certainly is a way of weeding out poor producers; they will not be able to afford the fees and charges. It is also a way of rewarding very good producers, since they can earn significantly more under most 100% commission plans. As for the large majority of sales people who are neither very good nor very bad, the advantages and

Table 11-1   100% Commission or 50-50 Split ?

Total Commissions	SALESPERSON'S SHARE	
Generated per Year	50-50 Split	100% Commission
$ 20,000	$ 10,000	$ 4,000
30,000	15,000	13,200
40,000	20,000	21,600
60,000	30,000	38,400
100,000	50,000	72,000

Depending upon the amount of commissions generated, the 100% commission arrangement can be good or bad for the salesperson. The better he/she is, the better it will be for him/her. Here we assume a 100% commission arrangement that requires the salesperson to pay the form a fee of *$1,000 per month, plus $400 for each transaction.* We also assume an average commission brought in per transaction of $2,500 — either the listing or selling share of a total commission of $5,000.

disadvantages can be quite variable. The result is that most members of sales forces of 100% commission brokerages are good producers who profit from the arrangement. Also, as seasoned professionals, they work with relatively little supervision from the managing broker.

Many firms do not go to the 100% plan simply because they find their salespeople don't want to. Often there are other incentive programs that will greatly increase earnings of good producers, and many ways can be found to weed out the poor ones without resorting to a completely different way of calculating compensation. Many salespeople do not like the extra potential burden imposed by the 100% commission plan. It's enough, they feel, that they work on commission and have to live with the uncertainty and irregularity of that kind of income pattern. Adding a regular, fairly high fee does not appear to be adequately compensated by the opportunity to keep more of the commissions they generate.

Some 100% commission firms charge relatively small fees to their salespeople and then add in the costs of all the separate services used. An elaborate schedule of fees is set up, including charges for telephone usage, secretary time, message referral, handling of transaction, and the like. A salesperson then has some control over the total fees he/she incurs by controlling the amount of the firm's services that are used.

Other companies have gone to variations of the 100% commission, such as paying salespeople fairly large splits (75%, 85% or more) of commissions they generate and then leaving them to do their business as they choose. These companies concentrate upon good producers who might prefer to operate independently but do not want the bother of operating their own firms.

In summary, 100% commission plans and their variations require a complete rethinking of the relationship between the brokerage firm and the sales force. Instead of the sales force working "for" the firms, the firm exists as a sort of contractor to salespeople, providing the conveniences of an office and support personnel in return for fixed payment. Salespeople can be said to be "renting" the firm's facilities when they need them and operating virtually independently otherwise. So long as the sales force is composed of competent, experienced people, this independence shouldn't be a problem. Obviously a 100% commission firm is not the place for a newcomer to real estate sales.

Firms under 100% commission are more difficult to run tightly, since there is less genuine control over the sales force. Assigning open house duty or floor duty becomes more difficult, although it is possible to arrange it so that part of the salesperson's payment to the firm would be in assignable work time instead of cash. However, the effect of this arrangement on the independent contractor relationship is uncertain. Firms might instead have some of the employee support staff acquire sales licenses so that they can take messages, give out information, and otherwise engage in activities that might legally be restricted to licensees.

Practical Considerations

Whatever the commission payment plan chosen, it should accomplish certain objectives. Since it is the source of salespeople's incomes, it should be designed so that they believe they're getting a fair share of the total. The firm should demonstrate that its share is being spent on facilities, service, and work that is of benefit to the salesperson.

In areas where a large number of firms exist, competition among them and among salespeople will result in commission sharing arrangements that work well for both the firms and the salespeople. Inefficient firms will be driven out of business along with poorly producing salespeople, and the efficient and productive ones will remain.

INCENTIVE PLANS

While salespeople may see their compensation as a source of income and sustenance, to the firm it also can be a form of incentive for productive work. Naturally, each successful listing or sale will add to the salesperson's income, and that is indeed an incentive. It pays for the brokerage to have very productive salespeople, because no matter how good they may be, each still uses only one desk and one space in the office. Also, the productive salesperson sets an example for those who are less so, and often is able to provide hints and even outright instruction to the newer or less able salespeople in the firm.

The best incentive for greater productivity is to offer the salesperson a more generous share of the commission income generated for the firm, if he/she generates a lot of it. Several types of plans are in use in the industry today, but they all have the feature of paying the more productive sales force members larger shares of each dollar of commission income they create for the company.

Bonus Plans

The most common form of extra compensation is the bonus plan. These take a variety of forms. A popular one is to set a certain minimum of commission income a salesperson must earn during a particular period. Those who earn more than the minimum receive a bonus. Many of these plans *graduate* the bonus, so that the greater the excess over the minimum that the salesperson earns, the larger the proportion of the commission dollar is paid. The bonus plan outlined in the Policy Manual example (Figure 7-1 in Chapter 7) is a program of this nature. Here a minimum of $4,000 per quarter of *earned commissions* is set. (Note that by "earned commissions" we mean the total of commission income actually *paid to the salesperson*. This is not the total amount of commission income that was paid to the firm because of his/her efforts; since our example pays the salesperson 50% of total commissions brought in, $4,000 of earned commission results from $8,000 of commissions brought in.)

Table 11-2   Effect of Bonus Plan on Salesperson's Commission Income (Quarterly Plan)

Commission Receipts Brought In	Salesperson's Share				Salesperson's Share as a Percentage of Firm's Commission Receipts
	Earned	+ Bonus	=	Total	
$ 8,000	$ 4,000	+ 0	=	$ 4,000	50 %
10,000	5,000	+ 250	=	5,250	52.5
12,000	6,000	+ 480	=	6,480	54
14,000	7,000	+ 840	=	7,840	56
16,000	8,000	+ 1,440	=	9,440	59
18,000	9,000	+ 1,620	=	10,620	59
20,000	10,000	+ 2,500	=	12,500	62.5
22,000	11,000	+ 2,750	=	13,750	62.5
24,000	12,000	+ 3,000	=	15,000	62.5

This table assumes the following: (a) That the bonus plan is the one described in Figure 7-1, and (b) that the salesperson's base commission averages 50% of the total commissions he/she brings into the firm.

If the salesperson earns between $4,000 and $4,500, the bonus is 3% of total commission earnings for the quarter. One who earns $6,000 in one quarter will receive a bonus of 8% of earnings. And if a salesperson's earnings total $10,000 or more for the quarter, the bonus is 25%. As Table 11-2 shows, the higher the salesperson's earnings are, the larger the percentage bonus, and therefore the larger is his/her earned share of each commission dollar he/she is responsible for bringing into the company.

Variations in Commission Split

Instead of using a bonus plan, some firms pay salespeople different commission splits, depending on the company's evaluation of their performance. A good producer's contract may specify a split of 60% or more of the commissions generated for the firm, while new salespeople or poorer producers receive smaller shares. This method recognizes those who have proved themselves to be superior. Of course, this plan also assumes that good producers will continue to be good at their work and will justify the faith placed in them by the brokerage firm. At the same time, there should be provision to adjust commission splits for salespeople as their productivity changes. A good producer may lose interest or just burn out, and a newcomer to the business may learn quickly and grow into a valued professional. If differing commission splits are given to salespeople, the firm must be able to assure all of them that the variations are *fair*. The firm should have some sort of formula by which it measure performance, and that formula should be known to the sales force. This way, the more advantageous split becomes a kind of bonus, in that salesperople know they can earn it by performing to a certain standard.

Delayed Bonuses

Some brokerage firms' bonus plans are designed with a built-in *payment delay*. Our example in Figure 7-1 has one: the bonus is not actually paid until ninety days *after* the end of the period in which it was earned, and then only if the salesperson is *still in the service of the company*. The purpose of the delay is to encourage good salespeople to remain with the company. A salesperson who resigns will forfeit bonuses that have been earned but have not yet been paid, so good producers, who will earn large bonuses, have an incentive to remain. At the same time, relatively poor producers will be earning little or no bonus, so they will not have as much incentive to remain with the company; since they are poor producers, the company will not miss them all that much if they leave.

One drawback to delayed bonuses is that real estate salespeople are a notoriously independent breed. Many of them feel insulted by delayed bonus plans because they think a brokerage ought to do more to keep them than just holding back part of the money they already have earned. The variable commission split arrangement, although it may have other faults (such as creating poor morale among less able producers), is a solution to this problem, since the salesperson does not actually earn money, but rather the right to earn a higher commission split once she has proved herself. This way, instead of having part of the earned pay held back, which is a negative kind of encouragement, there is the positive goal of an objective which can be striven for.

Encouraging Specific Activity

The plans discussed thus far encourage greater productivity of all kinds. However, the commission arrangement can be designed to encourage *specific* activity by the sales force. As we have mentioned, commission shares for listing and selling can be adjusted from time to time depending upon conditions in the real estate market. If buyers are scarce, listing commissions can be reduced and selling commissions increased. The opposite can be done if sellers are hard to find. However, this kind of changing of the commission structure should be undertaken only if there are remarkable departures from the norm in the real estate markets in which the firm operates.

Some firms also institute changing listing commissions that are reduced if the property takes a particularly long time to sell. For example, if a firm normally pays 25% of the total commission to the listing salesperson, it might also stipulate that if the property does not have an offer accepted on it within ninety days, say, the listing salesperson's share of the commission falls to 22%. The effect of such a program will be to encourage salespeople to bring in *good* listings. These are the kinds that sell fairly quickly: the price is reasonable and the terms under which the seller is willing to transact are not unusually difficult. At the same time, once the listing is in, the listing salesperson has an incentive to "work" the listing vigorously to try to sell it before the high commission period has expired.

COMPANY LISTINGS AND REFERRALS

In a small firm, the managing broker and sales manager may be active members of the sales force as well. In that case, if they secure listings or sell property, they collect the commissions due them. In large firms, management often does not engage directly in selling. However, the management personnel are likely to have contacts or friends who may approach them to list or look for real estate. In these cases, the firm itself secures the listing or finds the prospect. However, for the actual sales work, the listing or prospect is referred to one of the active salespeople.

Buying prospects are referred to a salesperson. Listings are handled in one of two ways: as *company listings* or as *referred listings*. A referred listing is a listing prospect given to the salesperson, who then must negotiate the listing contract. A company listing is an actual contracted listing taken by a management member of the firm. Most often these involve multiple properties, such as a company listing with a construction firm that authorizes the company to sell its newly constructed, under construction, and planned properties.

Referred Listing

Probably the most prized business possession of a real estate salesperson is a good listing. His name is featured in the advertising of the property and appears on the FOR SALE sign. He will receive calls from people who may become prospects. Dozens of other agents will be working to sell the listing and, so, produce a commission for him.

Sometimes someone in management secures a listing prospect. If the firm's management people don't do sales work, then the listing prospect will be referred to one of the firm's salespeople. This *referred listing* is a bonus of sorts to a salesperson. For this reason, many firms pay smaller listing commissions on referred listings; sometimes they pay no commission at all. The idea is that the listing referral itself makes up for the lack of a regular commission, since the salesperson can work the listing and benefit from doing so. He/she will be able to use it as a source of prospects and, of course, will have the inside track among the firm's salespeople with respect to selling the listing and earning the selling commission.

The exact amount of commission to be paid, if any, on referred listings should depend on the amount of work that is involved in handling them. Some firms require that the listing salesperson be primarily responsible for "nursemaiding" the listing through to the final sales and settlement, even if another salesperson produces the buyer. If this is the case, then the listing salesperson is required to do considerable work, so a portion of the regular listing commission probably would be appropriate here. On the other hand, if the brokerage firm itself, through its support staff and management, handles most of the detail work once the property is under sale contract, the listing salesperson may be adequately compensated just by getting the listing referral. In either case, the listing salesperson handles the property until an offer is accepted, but the other advantages of having the listing may be viewed as sufficient compensation.

The handling of referred listings is a sensitive matter. The company should make them attractive by paying an adequate commission, depending on the work involved in handling them; otherwise the sales staff may think of them as a burden to be avoided. It is particularly important that there be no obvious favoritism or unfairness in the manner in which referred listings are distributed among the salespeople. When a manager of a firm gets a call from a friend or business acquaintance, and it appears that a referred listing will result, the immediate concern is that the salesperson assigned to the listing will do a good job and make a favorable impression. This could lead the manager to refer listings to the better, more accomplished salespeople. It is apparent that if this is done all the time, the less favored salespeople will feel slighted, and the firm will not be doing its part to help them out.

The manager must weight the goodwill of the friend against the overall benefit to the company and the morale of its salespeople. Management may establish certain ground rules for referred listings, such as a minimum level of performance required of salespeople before listings will be referred to them. If this is done, management must be scrupulously careful to assure that referrals are distributed fairly among the qualified people.

As an example, a list may be posted on the bulletin board, with the names of qualifying salespeople drawn at random. As referrals come in, management simply goes down the list in choosing the salesperson to whom it is referred. On occasion it may appear worthwhile to skip over someone on the list because of a special case. Perhaps a referral comes in for a listing in an area in which the next salesperson on the list does not frequently operate; it may be assigned to someone else who does work that area well, and the person skipped over will be assured of receiving the next referral. This sort of procedure should be kept in the open so that the sales force can be assured that management is committed to fairness. In any case, management should reserve the right to skip around in the list if need be, simply because it is management that is running the company, and it is management that knows what is best for the firm as a whole.

The temptation may exist to refer some listings secretly so as to give them to favored salespeople without the knowledge of the others. That does not work for long. In a brokerage firm where people work with one another every day, it is easy for anyone to find out practically anything. Properly handled referrals are prized commodities among highly competitive people, and management can count on the fact that some sort of "grapevine" will exist among its sales force.

Company Listings

Company listings are those secured and managed by the firm itself, rather than being assigned to a specific salesperson. Even in a firm where management ordinarily does not engage in listing and selling, there may be special cases in which management members will take the listing themselves. Often this occurs when the property involved is of a specialized type that no member of the sales force is capable of handling well. It may be located in an area which no one on the sales force regularly works, or it may belong to a particular friend or other contact of the management person, and the manager wants to be absolutely certain it is handled well.

A frequent source of company listings is new homes. Builders are reluctant to list their new homes for sale under exclusive contract, but they are willing to sign open listings. In such a case, the firm earns no commission at all unless one of its salespeople makes the sale. Therefore, there is no guarantee that a referred listing will generate any commission to the firm or to the salesperson. Also, the total commission paid on new home sales is traditionally quite a bit lower than that paid on resales. For example, in your author's town the normal commission on resales is 7%, while the commission on new home sales is 5% "of improvements." The improvements are the building itself and other construction; the cost of the lot is left out of the sales commission calculation. Thus, a new $80,000 house on a $20,000 lot would generate a total commission of $4,000 (5% of the $80,000 value of the building) on a sale totaling $100,000. If that $100,000 sale had been an existing resale, the commission would have been $7,000 (7% of $100,000).

Generally, open listings on new houses are taken as company listings, in the name of the company. No referral is made, the listing is not "worked," and no salesperson is required to handle the listing end of the transaction. If one of the company's salespeople finds the buyer, the company collects the commission from the builder, and the salesperson is paid an appropriate share. Generally, it will not be as high a percentage share as on other commissions, because the firm will have to handle some of the closing and settlement arrangements, just as it would on any other listing. However, in most communities, new homes are easier to sell than resales. The smaller commission would reflect the easier job.

NONMONEY COMPENSATION

While the bulk of compensation will take the form of money, it is possible for the firm to reward salespeople and employees in other ways. Contests can offer prizes to top producers: gifts and prizes can be awarded to all who achieve certain goals. Other types of incentive programs with rewards other than money can also be instituted. These will be discussed more fully in the next chapter.

Advertising

One form of high valued compensation is advertising of the salesperson himself by the firm. Since it is important to a successful salesperson to be as well known as possible, company-sponsored advertising that features his/her name is extremely valuable. These advertisements can publicize the firm itself, as well as the salesperson involved. Many firms have a policy of running such an ad in the local newspapers on a regular basis. Some determine the identity of the feature salesperson based upon certain performance criteria; in this manner, being featured in the ad can be a form of "prize." A slight disadvantage of this system is that a few of the firm's salespeople may appear in the ads again and again because they consistently outproduce all the others. Another method is to run a separate ad every so often for each salesperson who achieves a certain level of income, commissions, or other performance measure. Some firms routinely run down their entire list of active salespeople as such ads are prepared, and each salesperson knows that every so often he/she will be featured.

Because of their interest in their communities, a great many real estate salespeople will be involved in charitable, civic, and sometimes governmental organizations. Many firms have a policy of running a feature ad whenever one of their people achieves some civic honor or is elected to an office in a worthy organization. This rewards the salesperson for community effort and at the same time presents the firm as one that is interested in the welfare of its community.

Support Service

A very real form of compensation is extensive support service provided to the sales force by the firm. Here the compensation is in the form of *time* rather than money, although it costs the firm cash to supply these services. Examples are excellent secretarial service, reliable message taking, assistance in handling details of settlement and closing, etc. Also, management assistance in some of the areas of normal sales work sometimes can be of benefit. This usually is most valuable to the newer salesperson who is learning the essentials of the business or the methods of the firm.

When support service is good, the sales force can devote more time to actual listing and selling work and spend less on paperwork and administrative details. Consequently, they should be able to get more listings, show more property, and deal with more prospects, thus generating more commission income both for themselves and for the firm.

Training

Training methods will be discussed in the next chapter. However, training sessions of various kinds can be viewed as compensation, since they improve and sharpen skills and so make the salesperson more effective. Many firms regularly have specialists come in and present lectures and seminars on particular points of real estate selling. Also, the firm can encourage its salespeople to attend courses offered outside the firm. One source of these is the Graduate REALTORS® Institute, administered by the state REALTORS® associations. In many areas, colleges and universities provide specialized real estate courses. Some firms will go so far as to pay all or part of their salepeople's tuition fees to attend these sessions.

COMPENSATION DURING TRAINING OF NEW SALESPEOPLE

It can be several months before a new salesperson will generate enough commission income to cover even the bare necessities. Therefore, some firms put new salespeople on a *draw*. This is a minimal payment at regular intervals, large enough to prevent starvation and bankruptcy, but not enough to warrant continuing in the business on that basis alone. A draw is really an advance of unearned commissions; the draw payments will be deducted from earned commissions, once they begin coming in. The salesperson should be required to acknowledge legally that the draws are against future commissions, and that if he/she does not earn enough commission income to cover them within a certain length of time, his/her employment may be terminated and he/she may be liable to pay back the unearned balance. Draw status should be recognized as a temporary situation and one the employee should be able to do without as soon as possible. The draw should never be enough to encourage the employee to stay on for it alone. Note that *being on draw is inconsistent with the independent contractor relationship!* While it might be done by calling the draw payments "loans" that legally must be repaid, the U.S. Internal Revenue Service will look very closely at any situation that combines a draw with an independent contractor relationship.

However, it usually is unwise to treat new salespeople as independent contractors, since they're not likely to be able to perform adequately with the necessary degree of independence. Good practice is to make new salespeople employees; in this manner a draw can be paid, if desired, and the employee can be closely supervised and controlled. An effective training period, which can only be required of an employee, will enable the new salesperson to learn faster and more quickly become skilled enough to warrant the genuine independence of the independent contractor. This supervision and control is essential during the early stages of acclimatization to the job. If the employer is free to require the employee to perform certain functions at certain times, a much more effective training program can be carried out. The new salesperson must learn listing and selling procedures, how the office functions, and how to handle a variety of problems. Many firms have specific training sessions that these people ought to attend and may wish them to spend considerable time on floor duty or at other duties as part of their training. They also can be assigned to experienced salespeople willing to take them along on listing tours, showings, or open houses.

DISCUSSION QUESTIONS AND PROJECTS

1. Interview sales managers in your area to determine the typical commission split between brokerage firms and their salespeople.

2. From the same source, collect and evaluate information about any bonus plans these firm use. Could you improve any of them? How?

3. Are there any firms in your area using the 100% commission plan or a similar scheme that allows the salesperson to keep the bulk of the commissions he brings in? How do these plans work? How do the managers of the firms using these plans compare them to the methods they formerly used?

4. What is the typical manner in which buying and selling brokerages split the total commission between them on cooperated transactions? Does this have any effect upon

the incentive within a particular firm to encourage the firm's own sales force to sell its listings?

5. How do firms in your area handle company referrals and company listings? Can you make any suggestions for improvement to any of them?

6. How can a commission split plan be structured to give the greatest incentive to the sales force to do the kind of business that is most profitable to the brokerage firm?

7. What use can a firm make of its advertising to reward productive salespeople?

8. Contrast the commission splitting system of a firm with little support service to that of a firm with extensive support personnel.

A Case Study

SALESPERSONS' COMMISSIONS

Sarah M. is a successful real estate person. She was approached by officers of a competing brokerage, who suggested that she resign from her current firm and join theirs. In her current position, she earned a 50-50 split on all commissions she brought in. Bonuses and productivity overrides brought her average share to more than 55%. The competing firm offered her a straight 65% share of total commissions generated.

She thought very seriously about their offer. She knew that her own firm wasn't showing unusually high profits; obviously, they spent much of the commission income they retained on *something*. The sales manager was very well paid, but it was his practice to have himself and his staff work out the details of processing sales once the sales force brought them in. This meant that Sarah had a lot of time freed from "busy work." As she reflected, she realized that this extra time was put to use in generating more business. Over the years, her firm had established very close relationships with a number of lenders. Several times in recent months, it was the firm's management that had been able to work out the critical financing needs that meant the difference between a successfully closed deal (and a commission for Sarah) and one that floundered and died.

The competing firm was smaller, and everyone in management was actively involved in sales work as well. They expected their salespeople to "nursemaid" their own deals as much as possible. Management people naturally used their "connections" to get their *own* deals through first; only then did they try to work things out for other salespeople.

After analyzing the situation, Sarah decided to turn down the offer. Although they would have paid her a better commission split, she decided that she would have had to work much longer on each deal, and probably would not end up making any more money. Her own firm made good use of the larger share of the commission that it kept, and she herself benefited greatly from the extra services the firm provided to her. She appreciated the professional attitude that led her company to handle the work she herself did not do well, and that left her as much time as possible to do what she did best, and what she liked doing the most.

TWELVE

SALES MANAGEMENT

Sales Meetings

Training

Contests and Incentives

Marketing Procedure

Prospect Management

Property Advertising

Professionalism

Although real estate salespeople operate independently, the brokerage firm has to coordinate their actions, provide training and motivation, and supervise the listing and selling processes. In a large firm this is the duty of the sales manager. In a small firm the broker-owner may take on these duties or assign them on a part time basis to a salesperson. Whatever the system, it is essential that there be some organization of the sales force and regular, systematic communication with its members.

SALES MEETINGS

The most popular means of communication and management of the sales force is the *sales meeting*. Most firms hold them regularly and often. Sales meetings provide an excellent means for the firm to communicate with its sales force. Brokerage firms use them to keep the sales force up to date on the firm's listings and sales, and to keep abreast of all developments in the market. All matters of importance to the entire sales effort can be discussed in the meeting, and it can be used as a forum for any matters which might be important to the entire sales staff.

The sales manager usually conducts the meeting, and normally will have an agenda of matters to discuss. Even though the agenda may be very small, perhaps only a couple of brief announcements, the meeting still ought to be held at its regular time and place. This is because individual salespeople should be encouraged to bring up matters of particular concern to them. They may want to describe a new listing, or report on some matter of interest they may have heard about. They can use the meeting for problem solving as well, such as soliciting the advice of the other salespeople for suggestions about how to handle a particular problem. A regular meeting gets the sales force together frequently; they can keep abreast of each other's doings, and exchange ideas.

A lot of brokerage firms also use the sales meeting as a way of providing the sales force with useful presentations, sometimes by outside speakers. Every now and then someone from a mortgage lending firm ought to be invited to present the latest goings-on in that very important business. Someone from another brokerage firm can present that firm's latest, most interesting listings.

A particular kind of sales meeting is the *showing trip*. Instead of staying at the firm's offices, the salespeople travel with the sales manager to visit and look over newly listed properties. These trips familiarize the entire sales force with each of the firm's listings; these informative trips see to it that the sales force knows about all of the firm's listings and, of course, are then better able to sell them. Some trips also might include visits to particularly interesting listings of other brokerage firms.

TRAINING

There are all kinds of training methods the firm can use to sharpen and improve the skills of the sales force. Some, such as instructional videos or particular kinds of presentations, can be made a regular part of sales meetings. Some may be offered in specially scheduled presentations. Also, especially in larger cities, organizations such as the state or local REALTORS® association, will present their own real estate education sessions.

Seminars

A frequently used training method is a *seminar* conducted during or after the sales meeting, while everyone is present and has the time. These are relatively brief instructional sessions which concentrate on a single topic. Some may last only for one session, while others may continue over several meetings. Many topics can be covered. Examples are financing methods, listing techniques, selling procedures, fine points of licensing, agency or contract law. Recent or upcoming changes in areas such as these are perfect opportunities for useful seminars.

A popular type of seminar is the "inspirational" session, in which a motivation specialist will provide an uplifting and enthusiastic presentation designed to improve the self-confidence and self-esteem of the listener. The nature of selling means that salespeople must rely heavily upon themselves and their own ability for their own incomes. In their dealings with the people they work with, they always are trying to convince clients and prospects to act. To do this successfully requires a lot of self-confidence and self-esteem, so salespeople in general usually feel that they get a lot out of these "inspirational" presentations. These sessions can be variable in their effects. Many just inspire listeners for a few days, but in a short while the "inspiration" has worn off and they return to their regular pattern. Some, however, can have long-lasting effect, and can present salespeople with permanently useful methods and techniques. Sales managers considering such a presentation might want to consult with other firms that have done so, to be sure to select a presentation that will have good effect and will stay with the salespeople for some time.

Role-Playing Sessions

A frequently used form of training is *role-playing*. A salesperson is asked to get up in front of the others and play the role of a participant (listing or buying prospect, stubborn lender or appraiser, etc.) in some aspect of the business. Another salesperson then will try to get the first one to agree to buy a property or to overcome his objections as he tries to convince him to list, buy, accept a contract offer, and so on. The first "player" is the *foil*; the other's goal is to convince the foil to undertake some action, or agree with some proposition, in a framework designed to be as close as possible to genuine practice. The other salespeople present will observe the scene, and when it is done they will critique it and offer suggestions.

Role-playing sessions can be valuable training devices, but they must be conducted with great care. Each scene should last only a few minutes, and should be taken seriously by all parties concerned. The foil has to be particularly careful. By playing the role of, say, a property owner who is reluctant to list, the foil must be careful not to overdo it. He/she must remember that the average person does not know as much of the business as a salesperson does, and so must take care that his/her responses are appropriate to the role.

It is tempting to have the role of the foil played by the sales manager, the principal broker, or one of the senior salespeople, on the theory that they have had a lot of experience and are more aware of these kinds of situations. However, because they probably are successful salespeople they often are very forceful, dominant personalities with good powers of persuasion, and not the typical personality types salespeople will encounter in their work. If they get too involved in their roles, they will dominate the less experienced salespeople, and the value of the experience will be lost. Therefore, it is better to have less experienced salespeople play both roles, so that they can see the situation from both sides. Then the manager, broker, and senior salespeople can critique the session and offer their suggestions and advice.

Recorded Sessions

Many recorded training courses available. Those on audio cassettes can be played almost anywhere, and many salespeople play them in their cars as they travel among appointments. Video courses can be shown at sales meetings or played by salespeople at home. Some brokerages also use camcorders in-house. Salespeople's training sessions are taped and the tape played back immediately so they can see themselves in action and even join in the critique. Recorded visits to listed properties also can be shown at sales meetings; this can replace the longer, more cumbersome showing trip.

CONTESTS AND INCENTIVES

Many brokerage firms use contests of some kind as an incentive to the sales force. There are three basic kinds of contests:

1. *Each salesperson competes against the others*. Such a contest might offer a trip, a prize of money, extra referred listings, or some other incentive to the salesperson who gets the most listings, sells the most property, or does best in these combined. The disadvantage to this kind of contest is that there is only one winner, and all others are losers even though they may have expended a lot of effort to try to win.

2. *The sales force is divided into teams that compete against one another*. The number of teams depends upon the size of the sales force; the ideal team should have three to five members. The winning team receives a group prize; losing teams may receive consolation prizes. This kind of contest fosters cooperation among team members and among the sales force. The prizes don't have to be especially valuable, since the excitement of the contest itself often is good motivation. Some firms have very good success with a contest in which its sales force is divided into two teams. The winning team is treated to dinner at an elegant restaurant and the losers get a free meal at a fast food chain.

3. *The salesperson competes against himself.* In this kind of contest, everyone can win, since the prizes are awarded on the basis of how much business the individual does. A common contest of this nature is a "points" contest. For example, getting a listing that is subsequently sold is worth 5 points; selling a property is worth 5 points; holding an open house is worth 1 point; a salesperson selling his/her own listing receives 2 points; and so on. The salesperson's prize depends upon the number of points earned in a given period of time. It is possible for each person in the firm to receive the top prize if they earn the necessary points. A firm known to the author regularly holds a contest of this nature every quarter. The prizes range from a portable black and white television (for 20 points earned in the quarter) to a Cadillac automobile (for 300 points earned in one quarter). No one ever has earned the Cadillac, but the fact that the firm actually will award it lends excitement to the contest.

The objective of contests is to provide an incentive for more productivity. Since the prizes cost money, offering a lot of contests will reduce the ability of the firm to award cash bonuses. Generally, firms find that a contest or two every year will spark interest and, if they are properly scheduled, will liven up business during normally slack times. At the same time, they will not cost so much money that the firm's bonus program has to be cut back significantly.

MARKETING PROCEDURE

The marketing procedure of the sales force should be kept under constant supervision by the firm. Techniques and methods should be constantly updated. Following is a discussion of some of the common procedures used.

Open Houses

The *open house* is a favorite selling device. OPEN HOUSE signs can be found most Sunday afternoons in neighborhoods where there is frequent real estate activity. The objective of the open house is to attract prospects. It is rare in practice that a prospect who visits an open house will buy that particular home, but the salesperson doesn't mind; the objective of the open house is to lure prospects, and the salesperson doesn't expect to sell the house to one of them that day. But once the prospects appear, the salesperson can try to work with them and to arrange to show them other listings.

Three kinds of people come to open houses: nosy neighbors, curiosity seekers, and genuine prospects who may be interested in buying a home. The salesperson, of course, is interested in the last, but should treat all visitors courteously and make sure they have the salesperson's card when they leave. Today, perhaps, they only want to look through their neighbor's closets or get in out of the rain, but they may be buyers some other day, and it doesn't hurt to make oneself known to them.

The salesperson should get the name and telephone number of everyone who visits the open house. If at all possible he should accompany visitors as they look around. The owners and residents of the property should go somewhere else; the salesperson does not want them around, and they will make the lookers uncomfortable. A house is best held open when it is newly listed. If it is held open more than once, later open houses will usually attract fewer genuine prospects.

Showing Property

It is almost impossible to sell property to someone without showing it to them first, Property showing is probably the most significant activity of a salesperson in terms of the time spent on it.

A set of general rules for showing property is given in the boxes on the next two pages. They should be observed as closely as possible. Showing property means entering someone's home as a stranger, with other strangers in tow. The privacy and property of the owners must be protected. The salesperson must also protect the right of the listing agent to know that a showing occurs. This is not difficult in the case of a listing made by the salesperson himself or someone in his firm. However, if the listing is held by another firm, the salesperson should contact the other firm's agent to arrange for the showing.

Many firms leave keys to listed homes in *lockboxes* attached to the doorknob or fitted over the door itself. These are designed to be opened with a special key; each firm will have its own key pattern to its boxes. The box contains a key to the listed home; anyone who has a key to the lockbox will be able to get into the home.

While this is a convenient way to make access available to authorized agents, careful security must surround the use of the lockbox and the depositing of the keys to it. In some areas, firms that cooperate with one another regularly will exchange lockbox keys; otherwise an agent desiring to show property listed by another must stop by the other's office to get the lockbox key. Whoever in the brokerage office is in charge of the lockbox keys must keep careful track of them and must be able at any time to give an accurate rundown of who has them. When the property has been shown, the salesperson should return the lockbox key as soon as possible, especially if it was obtained at the office of another firm.

In some localities, the local Board of REALTORS® has instituted a lockbox system for member firms and licensees. The local Board supervises the system, and all lockboxes used by all members can be opened with a single key. Member firms apply, on behalf of each of their salespeople, to the Board for the keys and the Board keeps records of who has keys. Both the salesperson who has the key and the firm are responsible to the local Board for each key issued. A big advantage of this type of arrangement is that firms do not have to keep each others' keys on hand. Also, there is rigorous supervision of the use of the keys. Many firms do not use lockboxes at all, especially in relatively high crime areas or on houses that contain a lot of valuables. In theses cases, the keys to the home are kept in the firm's office and must be checked out by salespeople who wish to show the property.

Guidelines for Showing Property

1. **Make appointments at least twenty-four hours in advance.**

2. **Try to see to it that residents of the property are *out of the home* when it is shown.** If this is impossible, make sure that they are in another part of the home as you show it. Better yet, send them outside while you show the inside, and send them in while you show the outside.

3. **Call a few minutes before you arrive, if possible.** Also, call anytime it is necessary for you to change the schedule or if you are running more than a few minutes late.

4. **Don't take children along!** You want the prospect to pay attention to the property you're showing, not the kids. Children get bored on showing trips and must be watched constantly to make sure that they don't disturb anything in the homes being shown.

5. **Don't take along anyone who will *not* be making the decision to buy.** Grandparents like to go along sometimes. Leave them at home, babysitting the kids. You don't need their comments about how high prices are or how they don't like what they see. Don't allow someone else to intimidate your prospects.

6. **Listen a lot more than you talk.** You don't have to open the bathroom door and say, "This is the bathroom," or point to an appliance and say, "This is the dishwasher." People know what these things are, and they don't like being told the obvious. Answer all questions as best you can. When you talk, ask if they like what they see. Find out what they *like* and *don't like* and *WHY.* You should use a showing trip to get information about your prospects' needs, so you can find them the home they want.

7. **Research the property *before* you show it.** If at all possible, take a look

PROSPECT MANAGEMENT

A touchy point in many firms is the manner in which a given salesperson claims a particular prospect. Clearly, if a salesperson has spent a lot of time working with someone, that person should not be fair game for other salespeople in the firm. Most firms have a system that allows a salesperson to "protect" a prospect to whom he has provided a certain minimum of service. For example, listing prospects can be protected by preparing an informal appraisal for them. Some firms, allow salespeople to "register" any prospects they have found and protect them in that manner. In such a system, however, it is good polity to *require* that the salesperson achieve some results within a certain span of time or else lose the right to protect the prospect against other salespeople in the firm.

Sometimes one salesperson will have to serve another's protected prospect. The protecting salesperson may be out of town, showing property to another, ill, or otherwise on your own first. Nothing makes you look dumber than wandering around property without knowing where you are. If you've seen it, you can prepare your prospects for what they will see. If you're not able to see the property first, tell your prospects something like, "This one was listed so recently that I haven't had time to take a look at it myself." Even in these situations, you should get all the information you can from the listing agent.

8. **If the prospects really like what they see, begin talking about writing up an offer.** Do so even if it means eliminating other scheduled properties from the showing trip. When people have found what they want, they lose interest in looking, and *you* should encourage their interest in making an offer!

9. **Don't schedule a showing trip to last more than two or three hours.** You don't want to exhaust your prospects. If time is precious (they're in for the weekend from out of town), you can violate this rule.

10. **If you stop for refreshments, pick up the check.** It's only a few dollars, and it's a very nice gesture. Avoid alcohol, especially for yourself.

11. **When you arrive at a property, ring the doorbell two or three times before using the key to enter.** When you enter, go first and announce your presence to make sure nobody is at home. If someone answers the door, introduce yourself and the prospects and then try to get the residents to get out of the way. (See #2)

12. **When you leave property, *make sure* that you leave it locked and that you leave it the way you found it.** If weather is messy, make sure nobody tracks anything in even if it means removing shoes and walking around in stocking feet.

13. **Always clear showings through the listing agent.** *Never* show property without the listing agent's knowledge. If the residents are there when you show, give them your card. If they aren't, leave it in a conspicuous place.

unable to provide service. Some firms have elaborate formulas for allocating commissions earned in cases where more than one salesperson is involved. Others allow prospect sharing but insist that the salespeople themselves work out the allocation of the commission. In such cases it is best to get them to agree in a written statement that the sales manager can put in the file for that particular sale.

Protection of prospects among *firms* is different. Trying to work directly with prospects who have been dealing with another firm usually isn't illegal, except that license law forbids licensees to negotiate directly with property owners who have exclusive listings with other brokers. Even so, since real estate brokerage firms work with one another all the time, it is wise to avoid situations which could cause conflict. Therefore, some firms have rules which forbid salespeople to deal with other firms' prospects.

Prospects themselves can create this kind of problem. Buying prospects in particular may not think it necessary to deal with only one salesperson from one firm. And, indeed, there is no legal reason why they should. Often they will pick a salesperson at random to deal with, or will have met one at an open house. It may turn out that the prospect doesn't like working with that salesperson, or perhaps the prospect just wants to "comparison shop" among different salespeople. A salesperson can guard against this to some extent by assuring prospects that the salesperson can show virtually any listed property, so that consultation with another agent is not necessary.

The problem is different if a salesperson is approached by a prospect who has been dealing with another licensee. On the one hand, one doesn't want to offend one's colleagues in the business. On the other, who wants to send a perfectly good prospect away? Probably the best approach to this situation is not to actively solicit other licensees' prospects, but to go ahead and work with prospects who show up on their own. Mistakes will be made, but salespeople who appear to make a habit of trying to steal others' prospects soon will find that the others will be reluctant to deal with them or offer them cooperation when they need it. Prospects responding to advertisements or solicited from open houses might be prospects of other firms or of salespeople in one's own firm. The salesperson certainly should not steal the prospect from someone in his/her own firm. Continuing to work with a prospect who has been dealing with another firm should be decided on a case by case basis.

PROPERTY ADVERTISING

In most areas, advertising in the classified section of the newspaper is the mainstay of residential brokerage advertising. While ads appear every day of the week, a weekend edition of the newspaper usually will carry the bulkiest section of real estate advertising. Some newspapers have special weekend real estate classified sections which also feature syndicated articles concerning real estate matters. Classified advertising may seem very old fashioned and unimaginative, but it works. Many brokerage firms have tried advertising in other media, but almost inevitably they find that use of the classified section reaches the audience they need more efficiently and cheaply. The apparent function of classified advertising is to advertise particular properties the firm has for sale. And indeed it does do that, but it serves many more important purposes for the advertising and promotion of the brokerage itself and of the salespeople.

It is rare that someone who responds to an advertisement for a particular home or other property ends up buying the property advertised. However, his response makes him known to the brokerage and salesperson, and therefore makes him a prospect. If the advertised property is unsuitable, perhaps some other will be more attractive. The salesperson gets exposure in the advertising because his name usually is included in advertising for his listings and interested prospects will call him. The brokerage benefits because the advertising features its name as well.

The more homes a firm advertises, the more frequently its name appears. Frequent appearance of the name suggests to a reader of the ads that the firm has lots of listings and therefore can show a wide variety of properties. While the owners of properties advertised may think that they are the major beneficiary of the ads, the fact is that advertising largely benefits the firm and its salespeople. Indirectly, of course, it then will benefit the owners of listed property by helping the firm to accumulate a larger number of prospects.

Column Ads

There are two types of classified advertising: *column ads* and *multiple-column ad*s, which often are nicknamed *tombstones*. Column ads fit into a single classified column. They are categorized into two groups, the *single ad* and the *multiple ad*.

The single ad is the kind most people think of when they consider classified advertisement. It is a few lines long and advertises a single property. The multiple ad is longer; it may advertise several properties. Many firms design their advertisements to feature the name of the brokerage in much larger type than the rest of the ad; it may take up as much as half the space devoted to a single ad. A firm with several properties to advertise may choose to put all of them into a multiple ad, run each of them as a single ad, or do a combination. Some firms feel that the multiple ad is more impressive, since it gives the impression that the firm has a number of properties by listing several in one place. Also, since the firm's name appears only once, less advertising space will be used to advertise a given number of properties, compared to the space required for single ads for each of them. This will slightly reduce the advertising cost per property, and cost is an important consideration.

Other firms prefer several single ads, especially if they use a large, recognizable symbol or representation of the firm's name in each ad. While the cost per property will be a bit higher, the reasoning is that having the firm's name peppered all over the page, instead of in one place, is an advantage. It will be difficult for anyone looking at the page to miss seeing the name, and it also can give the impression that the firm is very active because the name crops up in several places.

Tombstone Ads

The tombstone ad stretches across two or more columns. These ads usually are reserved for the weekly real estate section. They feature the name of the brokerage in very large print. Very large ones can display the firm's name and logo more than once. These ads also are used to advertise, prominently, the firm's open houses for the weekend. Some firms also use pictures in their ads. It's expensive but, in some situations, the effect is worth the cost. A favorite technique is to "advertise" a home that has already been sold, and have the word SOLD superimposed on the ad. This shows that the firm gets results, and can give the impression that they sell homes so frequently that they don't always have time to get them out of their ads.

Size is important for a good tombstone ad; the larger the better, since the very size of the ad and its large concentration of listings impress the viewer. There is a limit to size, of course; some firms use ads as large as two full newspaper pages side by side, but much smaller, well-designed (and cheaper) ones can be quite effective, also. Some firms with lots of properties to advertise may opt for two or more smaller ads, scattered through the classified listings. Whatever the approach that is used, the primary objective of this kind of advertising is to get the firm's name, and those of its salespeople, into the minds of readers.

Composition of Advertisements

Advertising space costs money. Therefore, great care should be taken to assure that it is used effectively to gain for the firm and its salespeople the maximum exposure per dollar spent. Many firms require that all ads be written by the sales manager or some other person who knows how to write an ad properly. If this is not done, then at the very least the sales manager should review each salesperson's ads before they are submitted for publication.

Separate ads for individual properties can be large or small. It is possible, using accepted abbreviations, to compose a two-line ad that transmits the necessary information, but one so small won't attract the desired attention. On the other hand, it is not advisable to use long, wordy ads, which may discourage people from reading them fully. Generally, four or fine lines will be plenty. It isn't necessary to put in every item of interest about a particular property. Prospective buyers usually will know something about the areas in which they are interested and something about the kinds of property they may expect to find there. Furthermore, it is impossible to describe a property accurately in the relatively few words available in a proper ad.

Brevity and generality in the ad have an additional advantage. Brief descriptions attract potential buyers who may want something similar to the advertised property, but not exactly like it. The more detailed an ad is, the more limited the number of prospects it will draw. An ad that describes a home as a four-bedroom, ranch style colonial at $98,000 will draw more response than if it goes on to describe a lot of minor details; the details will cause a number of prospects to pass the property over (and therefore not call the firm or salesperson) because the extra information in the ad tells them that the property isn't suitable.

Even if relatively little detailed information is given, the ad can be made attractive enough and long enough to generate interest. This is done by pointing out features that generally are important to most people. These include such physical features as fireplaces, good landscaping, location on quiet streets, nearby facilities, and the like. Phrases such as "beautifully decorated," "custom deluxe kitchen," "zoned heat and air conditioning," "energy saving," usually don't turn people away. Other features such as advantageous financing terms may also be mentioned. Low down payments, low interest loans or loan assumptions, and the availability of second mortgage financing where large equities are required are sure-fire selling points, and should be featured whenever they are available. The main function of this type of advertising is to feature the firm and its salespeople, and to *bring in prospects*. Buyers will respond to advertisements which catch their interest. Potential sellers will also be impressed with a firm that has a large number of listings and appears to be active in the market and capable of selling.

Truth in Advertising

Many states and localities have laws and regulations governing advertising. Blatant misstatement of fact is always a legal violation. However, in some areas more subtle exaggeration and the like may be specifically prohibited.

Usually the legal system will allow advertising and sales effort to use a certain amount of *puffery*. Puffery is not easy to define. It can be ridiculous exaggeration which any reasonably intelligent person would recognize. ("Use our product and your love life will be perfect." "Buy this house and you will be happy forever.") It also includes *euphemism*, where flowery or cute language is used instead of blunt truth. A tiny, cramped house is called a "doll house." "Handyman special," or "needs a little tender loving care" are phrases which mean "this place is a dump, wreck, disaster area, etc." An ad suggesting that the buyer "use your imagination" may mean a peculiar floor plan, an interior that needs considerable rehabilitation, or who knows what.

Some other statements, however, may have to be verifiable and true if they are made. *Regulation Z* (see Chapter 3) requires that any advertisement for real estate which mentions financing terms must also state the *annual percentage rate* of interest (APR). Stating the size of the home or building (usually in square feet) may be inadvisable in some areas because court decisions have held that advertisers are liable to buyers for damages if there is any discrepancy. (Square footage traditionally is measured around the *outside* of the heated area of the building and does not include porches, garages, balconies, or unfinished attic or basement space. However, the courts may not necessarily agree with this method.)

Value judgments may have to be avoided in advertising. What is a beautiful and stylish home to one person may be gaudy and pretentious to someone else. One person's "unique" may be someone else's "weird," "frightening," "ridiculous." More importantly, advertising and selling technique should *never* make promises which may not be literally true. A "20-year roof" may leak in five years. "Low utility bills" may not seem so attractive to a buyer moving from an area where costs are even lower. Most important, *no selling technique should ever suggest that a purchase will produce future gain!* It is tempting to suggest to a buyer that a given purchase can be sold at a nice profit sometime in the future, but it is impossible for anyone to predict such a thing. Doing so also is a violation of license law in most states.

PROFESSIONALISM

Throughout this book we have stressed that the real estate brokerage firm operates within a very strict legal environment. License law and agency law are two examples, but there is much more. The industry has been trying for decades to convince the public that real estate brokerage is a profession. These efforts are now bearing fruit. While it is prestigious to be considered a professional person, it also carries its own additional responsibilities. A major aspect of professionalism is that it involves specialized knowledge and/or talent. Again and again the courts have held that the public may expect more from a person recognized as a professional. When professionals do not provide what is thought to be a professional service, they may be sued for *malpractice*. Physicians and lawyers have been sued for centuries; now real estate brokers often are too.

Broker Liability

A professional provides advice, guidance, or skills not normally found in ordinary people. People have a legal right to expect a high standard of performance from professionals, and are entitled to damages if they do not get it. In the past decade or so, real estate professionals have come under increasing scrutiny by the courts. As is often the case in other aspects of the real estate business, this trend originated in California.

In the early 1980s several brokerage firms in that state were successfully sued for their performance in arranging "creative financing" among buyers and sellers during the credit crunch of 1979-84. Buyers could not afford the high prevailing interest rates, and so sought purchases in which they could assume a low-interest loan. However, many such situations involved properties in which sellers had large equities (the difference between the value of the property and the amount of the assumable loan). Buyers usually did not have enough cash to buy out such large equities. With the broker's advice, the sellers took some cash and a junior purchase money mortgage from the buyer for the remainder of the equity. These mortgages usually had modest payments and were at a relatively low interest rate. However, they were written to come due fairly soon, sometimes in as little as two or three years. The idea was that during that time interest rates probably would fall and the buyer could refinance the entire property, paying off the assumed loan and the junior mortgage to the seller with the proceeds.

Unfortunately, interest rates did not fall as quickly as some of these arrangements anticipated, and some buyers were unable to refinance when the junior mortgage came due. Some sellers foreclosed; some of the buyers sued the brokers who had arranged the transaction. Other sellers reluctantly renegotiated the terms of the junior mortgages, allowing the buyer more time to pay. Some of these sellers sued their brokers. In many of these cases the courts ruled that the brokers involved had indeed given bad advice, and found against them.

This is a spectacular example of broker liability, but there are many other pitfalls. Improperly qualifying a buyer can lead to trouble. Assumption of older VA and older FHA loans can, too, since the original borrower *may still remain liable to the lender*. A broker who brings a seller a buyer who later defaults on such a loan assumption may find himself in court over it, especially if he did not advise the seller of this risk.

Sellers expect competent service from brokers, and they deserve it from someone whose service is going to cost 5%, 7%, or more of their sale proceeds. The broker is expected to give advice, especially to the seller. One advantage of hiring a broker is that a competent one is good at smoothing out potential trouble spots between buyer and seller, and aiding negotiations to a successful conclusion. All of these factors contribute to the broker's professionalism, both in fact and in the image the public has of him. But they all also represent areas of possible liability as well. Liability for one's actions is one of the prices of professionalism.

How, then, to deal with these problems? The best way, of course, is to handle things so that if anything goes wrong, no one will think it is the broker's fault. This is not easy to do, especially in tandem with the broker's goal of being thought of a providing good service. The best course of action is to make everyone involved aware of the entire situation, the potential trouble spots as well as the advantages. A good rule to follow, when possible, is this: *explain but do not advise*. What this means is that the broker provides others with the information they need to make decisions *themselves*. Of course, the broker should make sure that the information provided is accurate and reliable.

Disclosure

As was pointed out in Chapter 3, several states have passed *disclosure laws* which require sellers of homes to fill out a mandated disclosure form, in which they answer questions about possible detrimental features of their properties. During the life of this edition of this book, it is likely that disclosure laws will be passed in many more states. Licensees should keep up to date with the progress or existence of such legislation. And, of course, licensees who work in states which already require disclosure should be familiar with the relevant law and the disclosure forms which must be used. Normally, this form is filled out at the time the property is listed, and it, or a summary of its contents, must be shown to all buying prospects before they make offers.

While disclosure laws may seem to be just one more bit of obnoxious government paperwork, in fact these laws are very beneficial to the real estate brokerage business. This is because the brokerage firm, as the seller's agent, may be legally liable for the seller's misrepresentation or failure to impart important information. Certainly brokers have been sued many times over defects or other undesirable aspects of real estate which purchasers discovered after they took possession. By requiring disclosure by sellers, the law lets the broker off the hook. First, it makes it easy, indeed, necessary, for the licensee to question the seller about any and all possible problems which ought to be disclosed. Second, by requiring disclosure, these laws make it much less likely that buyers will encounter unpleasant "surprises" later on, and about which they may try to sue the broker. It is no accident that in states which have disclosure laws, the real estate brokerage industry was very active in the effort to get them passed.

In states where disclosure is not required, many brokerage firms now insist on it anyway; they have their own disclosure forms which they require for all their listings. This, again, is a form of self-protection for the firm. Disclosure questions concern the structural integrity of the building, repair history of the building and its equipment and major appliances, vulnerability to certain hazards (termites, basement leaks, settling ground, snow load, winds, etc.).

Whether or not the law or the firm's policy requires disclosure, a licensee who stumbles upon some major problem with a property should *never* keep it secret. If the property is listed for sale, the sales manager should be told about the problem; if prospects are looking at it, they should be told as well. If a salesperson can be proven in court to have known of a significant problem without informing anyone else, the salesperson and the brokerage firm will be helpless to prevent a serious damages judgment.

Recall, also, from the discussion in Chapter 3 that many states now require licensees to inform buying prospects of their agency relationship with sellers.

Proper Performance

In dealings with the general public, the broker must act within the law and the proper ethics of the profession. *Proper performance* is essential not only to avoid legal action, but also to maintain a reputation for honesty and reliability. The brokerage firm's management should insist that all salespeople conduct themselves in this manner.

Some people do not view the real estate brokerage business with great esteem. This is in spite of the fact that just as in any other business the large majority of brokerage professionals act with integrity and pride in their business dealings. In fact, poor practice is not significantly more frequent in the brokerage business than it is in most others, but for various reasons the unsavory or inept activities of a few loom larger in the public mind. One of the reasons is that it is a complicated and difficult business. Still, it is not difficult for people to get into the business. Many believe that once they have passed the licensing examination they have accumulated all the necessary knowledge and are perfectly prepared for all aspects of it. In fact, most full time brokerage professionals will tell you that one of the genuine plagues of the profession is the brand-new, ill-prepared, and ignorant licensee who sets out blithely into the business, often only part time, woefully unable to handle even the simplest transaction. Brokerage is a business in which having only a little knowledge can be harmful indeed.

Another factor is that real estate plays such an important role in the lives of most people. We all need a place to live; the businesses we deal with need offices, and we need parking lots, stores, warehouses, and factories. In addition to providing us with the space we need for living, working, and playing, real estate in recent years has become a popular investment vehicle. This interest in real estate often seems to have the effect of making everyone into a self-styled "expert." Having but a little knowledge is dangerous to a consumer, too; in spite of the broker's warnings, one may leap into a transaction, find it less attractive than expected, and then search around for someone to blame. At that point the broker becomes a handy outlet for frustrations the individual may have caused entirely by himself.

Buying a home is usually the largest single purchase a family may ever make. 25% to 40% of income may be devoted to making payments and maintenance on a purchase that can amount to three or four years' total income in price. Obviously, where such enormous amounts of a family's resources are involved, there will be a great sensitivity to difficulties that may arise, and once again the broker can be an attractive and convenient target for blame.

DISCUSSION QUESTIONS AND PROJECTS

1. What is the function of the sales meeting?

2. In the class (if this book is being used in a classroom situation), try some role-playing situations involving typical brokerage problems.

3. Write some sample advertisements for a property selected by you.

4. What is the purpose of property advertising?

5. How can contests be used to increase the sales force productivity? What problems should be guarded against?

6. How should property be shown? Why rules should be observed?

7. Why is it best not to have property owners or occupants present during open houses or when property is being shown?

8. Try to attend sales meetings of two or three brokerage firms that will let you observe. How are the meetings used? What sorts of things are discussed? Could you suggest any improvements?

9. Are there any limitations on real estate advertising in your area? If so, what are they, and how do they affect the effectiveness of such advertising?

10. Are there any unusual "puffery" terms or euphemisms that are used in real estate advertising in your area? Make a list of them, along with their "real" definitions.

11. Why should real estate salespeople be knowledgeable about terms and requirements in the mortgage market?

12. Investigate the issue of broker liability in your community. Have there been any unusual or ground-breaking cases in your locality or state?

Case Studies

PROPER PERFORMANCE

1. A prospective buyer asks the broker or salesperson whether or not the asking price of a property is reasonable. The broker must remember that he is employed by the seller and not the buyer (except when he is a buyer's broker, or is otherwise employed by a buyer, in which case this discussion would not apply). In situations such as this the broker should put himself in the seller's shoes: Would *the seller* admit that the asking price is unrealistic in a conversation with a potential buyer? No, he wouldn't.

Many prospective buyers assume that the broker works for *them* and is going to protect *their* every interest, so they have no compunction about asking questions they would never consider mentioning to the owner himself. It is best if the broker can let them know just what his legal responsibilities are, so long as he doesn't do it so crassly that he scares them away in the process. Of course, if the broker honestly feels that the asking price is reasonable, he should say so. If he thinks the property is a bargain, he should say so. In either case he is doing his best to convince the buyer he should buy, and that is what he is hired by the seller to do.

However, suppose the broker honestly believes that the property *is* overpriced. He can protect himself from this situation in the first place by not soliciting listings from sellers who wish to price their offerings unreasonably, but that is no help in the case where he is showing an overpriced property listed by another broker. It is a common misconception, even among real estate licensees, that in this case the broker who is showing the prospective buyer around is, somehow, that buyer's agent, and the listing broker is the seller's agent. This is not the case; *both* brokers are agents of the seller. Therefore, the broker cannot say the property is overpriced, at least not directly. The best technique is to get the prospective buyer to make up his own mind, by asking him what *he* thinks. He can consider the asking prices and characteristics of other properties he has looked at, and more properties can be shown to him to get his reaction. If a property is overpriced, he soon will get the idea, by comparing it with others.

2. The prospective buyer asks the broker, "How much should I offer for this property?" This case is similar to the first one; the broker should try to get the prospect to make up his own mind about the amount to be offered, while of course trying to get him to offer as much as possible.

3. The buyer asks the broker to try to talk the seller into accepting his offer. The broker should make it clear that the offer will be submitted promptly, and that the seller will make a decision quickly. The broker should not let the buyer assume that he will act on the buyer's behalf in negotiation with the seller. If he does so as a sales ploy, to give the buyer the false impression that he is on his side, he is being unethical at best and probably is breaking the law, depending upon the exact circumstances.

4. The broker refuses to allow another broker to show property listed. This is a very touchy problem. By far the best way of handling it is to make it perfectly clear and *agreeable* with the owner that the broker will not cooperate with other brokers. Some brokers only refuse to cooperate with certain other brokers, and for what they think are legitimate reasons. In such a case the broker should advise his principal that he will not deal with certain other firms because of his previous business experience with them; he need not divulge his reasons (it is not necessary to court a libel or slander suit), but he should make it clear to the owner, writing it into the listing agreement if possible, that the broker will cooperate only with other brokers of his own choosing. Otherwise, the owner might have a case supporting poor performance by the broker, especially in areas where cooperation among brokers is a common practice.

5. The seller tells the broker not to divulge to anyone that the house is infested with termites. If he agrees to this, the broker is becoming a party to fraud or misrepresentation. Legally, he has no choice under these circumstances: either he must convince the seller to allow him to divulge the information, or he must terminate the listing. Otherwise he risks his reputation, his license, and his business, as well as possible suits for damages and criminal prosecution. It is quite legal for him to cancel a contract if maintaining it would require him to act illegally.

6. The broker aids (and gets paid for) financing arrangements for a buyer. This is normally all right. Even though he is performing a service for a buyer, by doing so he facilitates a sale for his owner-employer and so serves him too. The broker may do anything he wishes for a client or other parties so long as it does not interfere with his ability to properly represent his employers. It is wise to include in listing agreements language that notifies owners that the broker may receive compensation from other sources in return for such things.

7. The broker shows a prospect several houses. This is reasonable because it enables him to arrange a sale with that buyer. While the sale will not benefit everyone with whom he has listings, it is presumed that the same sort of practice will eventually benefit them all, and showing property in order to determine the genuine wants and needs of the buyer is accepted as normal brokerage practice.

8. A broker refuses to show a house to a prospect he knows cannot afford it. This too is permissible. The broker owes it to his employers not to waste their time or use their homes and properties for unnecessary sightseeing. So long as the broker has every reasonable cause to believe that the prospect is not capable of buying the property, he has nothing to fear by refusing to show it to the client, and indeed, may be doing everyone involved a favor by keeping that prospect's attention elsewhere.

REFERENCES

SCHNEIDER, JULES, J.D., and BILL TUINE, DREI, *Who's My Boss? Seller, Buyer, Both, Neither.* Scottsdale, AZ: Gorsuch Scarisbrick, Publishers, 1989.

THIRTEEN

FINANCIAL CONTROL

No business can survive without control and management of its financial operations. No business can operate indefinitely without earning profits or at least breaking even. Proper financial control requires considerable skill and knowledge, including a grounding in the fundamentals of accounting. In the space we have available here we can only hit the high spots. However, some initial warnings and comments are necessary.

A real estate brokerage firm should have available the services of an accountant who will keep track of the firm's financial records and transactions. Accurate records should trace each transaction as it progresses; so long as the records are up to date, it is quick and easy to make up a statement of the operating and financial situation of the business. Good financial records serve many important purposes. They are absolutely necessary in order to file proper income tax and other tax statements and returns. Also, they provide continuous indications of performance of the business. This makes it possible to compare results among various periods of time and to keep track of the profitability of the firm's various operations. License law in every state requires real estate brokerage firms to keep accurate books for the brokerage's trust accounts and handling of trust monies. These include earnest money payments, escrow monies, undistributed rents, and the like. These records and funds should be handled in exact accordance with the laws and regulations set down by the state in which the firm operates.

SOME BASIC FINANCIAL CONCEPTS

Economists, financial analysts, and accountants identify many concepts important to the proper analysis of the financial well-being of a business.

Revenue is the total of all payments, commissions, fees, and other incoming cash and notes that the firm collects. It also is called *gross income*. It is a good measure of the *volume* of business done by the firm, but not of its *profitability*.

Costs are the sum total of the money that the firm pays out, except for income taxes and profits. These include all payments to employees and independent contractor salespeople, all commission payments to cooperating and multilist brokerages, all expenses of operating the business, depreciation on all owned real estate and equipment, all supplies, and all fees paid to others.

Income is what is left of revenue after all costs have been paid.

Profit, the "bottom line," is what remains of income after the firm has paid all income taxes due on the income it has earned. Profit is available for distribution to the firm's owners or stockholders, or to be "plowed back" into the firm for investment in expansion, new equipment, etc.

Fixed costs are those costs which a firm must pay no matter how much or how little business it does. These costs remain constant as the firm's business grows or shrinks. Examples are licensing fees, privilege taxes, rent on office and equipment, scheduled payment on debt, salaries of people who will be employed no matter how large or small the business is.

Variable costs are costs that rise and fall as the firm's business increases or decreases. A good example is commissions paid to salespeople. If no sales are made, no commissions are paid. As sales volume grows or shrinks, the amount of commissions paid to salespeople grows and shrinks. Other variable costs are property advertising, and fees paid to settlement agents.

Many cost items are partly fixed, partly variable. Consider a salesperson's automobile expenses. Auto loan and insurance payments are fixed, but much of the car's gas, oil, and maintenance expenses varies with the amount of business (and, therefore, driving) the salesperson does.

Cash flow is another important concept. It refers to the quantity of ready, spendable cash that the firm generates. Regardless of the ultimate profitability of an operation, it always must have enough cash available to pay current bills, costs, and fees. Many a business has failed, not because it was unprofitable, but because its cash flow structure put it in a cash bind.Here is an unusual but illustrative example. A firm gets a listing on a property with a sale price of $10 million and a 4% selling commission payable upon completion of the sale. The commission will be $400,000, and the firm anticipates that its share, after cooperating with other brokers and paying its salespeople their commissions, will be $100,000. It also figures that it will have to spend $50,000 on advertising and other costs associated with the sale before it can sell the property. In spite of the fact that there is a $50,000 profit due eventually, the firm cannot handle the listing unless it can come up with the $50,000 that it must spend in order to accomplish the sale. Therefore, there must be some sort of cash flow during the selling period to generate that part of the $50,000 cost that it does not already have available.

Company Dollar

The *company dollar* is that part of revenue that ends up belonging to the real estate brokerage before it deducts its own cost of business. To arrive at the firm's company dollar figure, all commissions and fees paid to other brokerage firms (cooperated and multilist transactions) and to its own salespeople are deducted from revenue. While the quantity of company dollars is an indication of the amount of business a firm does, it is not an indication of profitability. All the firm's costs must come out of the company dollar.

The Company Dollar and Profits

Profit is the amount of the company dollar that is left after the firm's costs have been paid. There is a lot of variation among real estate brokerage firms in the percentage of the company dollar that ends up as profit. A rule of thumb is that the "average" firm shows about 30% of the company dollar as profit and 70% as cost. The company dollar itself is about 50% to 60% of total revenues, which means that the average firm distributes about 50% to 60% of its revenues to other firms and to its salespeople. Therefore, profits usually are about 5% to 15% of total revenues.

Table 13-1. The Company Dollar

REVENUE	**100%**
less fees & commissions	<u>55%</u> of revenue
equals COMPANY DOLLAR	45% of revenue
COMPANY DOLLAR	**100%**
less:	
Advertising	20% of company dollar
Telephone	5% of company dollar
Salaries	15% of company dollar
Operation of firm	15% of company dollar
Space & equipment	15% of company dollar
Other	<u>0-20%</u> of company dollar
TOTAL PROFITS	**10-30% of company dollar**

Table 13-1 shows an example of the way in which fees and expenses relate to the company dollar. These figures are approximations, of course. You may expect to see a lot of variation among firms, and among differing geographic areas. Competition and business practice make a big difference. So does the size of a brokerage firm: larger ones often have higher expenditures as a percentage of the company dollar, but their higher revenues (more company dollars) can mean that their total profits are larger than for small firms. The "Other" category represents differences between smaller and larger firms, mostly in the area of sales management: special incentives, sales manager's salary, office expenses, etc. Once again, these figures are approximate, and are not meant to represent a set of guidelines for all brokerage concerns. Furthermore, they are representative of firms operating in normal markets. Where unusual conditions exist, such as buyers' markets or sellers' markets, a firm may vary considerably from its normal pattern.

Profit Analysis of the Average Sale

A useful measure the firm can employ is the average profitability of a sale. This can be done in many ways. For example, the company may take the total sum of its company costs divided by the number of sales in the period. This will give the *average cost per sale*. Clearly, a sale that does not produce enough company dollars to cover the average cost per sale will appear unprofitable. However, that may not always be the case. In each situation, the company should look at the variable costs associated with the sale to see if it contributes to profit.

A sales transaction only generates *variable costs*, since fixed costs have to be paid whether or not there are sales. Therefore, to be worthwhile a transaction only needs to cover those variable costs that it generates by itself. Suppose a firm has a total annual company costs of $100,000. Half, or $50,000, is fixed cost and the other $50,000 is variable cost. If 200 sales occurred during the period, the average cost per sale was $500. The fixed cost per sale was $250 and the variable cost per sale was $250.

Now a sale opportunity comes along which will generate a total of $400 in company dollars. If we look at the *average cost* per sale, we find that it is $500 and conclude that the sale will cost the firm $100. But that's not true, because sales don't generate fixed costs. They can't, because fixed costs *remain the same* no matter how many or how few sales occur. If the sale involves the firm's typical $250 of variable costs, that will leave an additional $150 of profit from it: the $400 of new company dollars, less the $250 of new variable costs leaves a profit of $150. What has happened is that company dollars have increased by the $400 generated by the sale. Total costs, however, have increased by only $250. Fixed costs don't increase at all, so they remain at $50,000. Variable costs increase by $250 to $50,250. Total costs, then, increase to $100,250 and not to a larger figure.

FINANCIAL CONTROL

One of the most difficult processes in the financial analysis and control of any business is the evaluation of the expenditures a firm makes. If the budget and the relationship among revenues, costs, and profits is not constantly watched, it is easy for cash-draining habits to instill themselves.

Many signs can suggest that review is necessary. Is the business flexible – can it adjust quickly to changes in its markets? Recent experience has shown that real estate is a volatile business. A firm that does not have the flexibility to adjust is at a serious disadvantage. Is the firm using the right amount of space and equipment? While luxurious offices and expensive equipment are nice, they should be *justifiable*. Each item should be analyzed for the contribution it makes to the profitable operation of the firm in comparison to its cost. Are all aspects and departments of the firm's business producing profits? It may be that some are bleeding profits from others. If a part of the business is not profitable, or if the business will be more profitable without it, that part should be eliminated. Are there employees and salespeople in the firm who are not paying their way? This is a very difficult area because if some people are not producing, they must be let go. Particular problems may crop up in the case of people who once were useful but who have been "coasting" for a long time. If there are such people in the firm, they should be let go or convinced to regain their former productivity.

Budgeting

Budgeting is a form of financial planning which is done on a periodic basis. Most firms prepare *annual budgets*, perhaps with quarterly *summaries* to use as guides as the year proceeds. The function of budgeting is to generate forecasts of income, revenue, and costs and to reconcile them so that the financial comfort of the business is assured.

If budgets and forecasts show that a firm's total costs for a certain period will exceed projected company dollars, this can be an important signal, especially if the period considered is pretty long. A business may survive a short period of accumulating losses, but not for long. Costs and revenue forecasts should be analyzed to see if any are excessive. If the shortfall doesn't appear to be temporary, then some changes will have to be made. Either costs have to be reduced, somehow, or revenues have to increase (make more sales!).

A profit is forecast when the budget shows that projected total company dollars will exceed projected costs. Even so, a well-run firm always should be analyzing revenues and costs to find ways of *increasing* profits either by increasing revenues, decreasing costs, or both. Many businesses fall into the trap of believing that if profits are anticipated, things must be operating well, but there is nothing wrong with making good profits better.

Budgeting is a preliminary exercise, and it usually isn't expected that a budget will be met exactly as projected. Budgets are *estimates* of what to expect. If results later turn out to be a lot different from the budget, then the firm needs to do an analysis to determine why. Perhaps the market took an unexpected turn, or some misfortunes (or good luck) in business happened. If the discrepancy between budget and results can't be explained, then there is something wrong with the budgeting process.

A good budget should be based upon previous experience with the firm's revenues and costs. However, there also are traps in budgeting. Many firms are satisfied with the performance of various sectors of the company so long as they do not exceed budgeted expenditures or fall short in revenues. This can lead to unwarranted loss of profit because it is not always true that doing something "the way we always have" is the *best* way.

Many organizations formulate budgets by starting with items that always have been spent, adding new programs, and then coming up with a final budget. This process does not require justification of expenditure patterns that have been established. A recent development in budgeting procedure is the *zero base budget*. Zero base budgeting requires that *all* budgeted expenditures for the period be justified anew every time a new budget is formulated. No spending patterns or programs are immune to scrutiny, and each time the budget is formulated everything has to be justified, so *all* items have to be given careful consideration.

Using Borrowed Money

"Neither a borrower nor a lender be!" This is a quaint, conservative old saying that is best forgotten. In today's world, properly managed and controlled borrowing is an integral part of good management and business success. A business may rent equipment or office space; borrowing money and paying interest on it simply is "renting" money. Many firms will borrow to purchase expensive equipment that they need but do not have the cash to buy; the income provided by the additional equipment is partly devoted to paying off the loan taken out to acquire it.

Borrowed money has several uses in an ongoing business. Its availability means that the firm need not have substantial cash on hand, since it can borrow when it runs into temporary cash flow problems. Often a firm will borrow to cover the expenses of starting up because the people involved do not have enough cash themselves; some of the business's early profits are used to pay off the loan.

Often, just as useful as borrowing money is having an arrangement that will allow for a certain level of borrowing on short notice. This is called a *line of credit*. A brokerage firm may arrange with a bank to be able to borrow up to a certain sum anytime it needs it. While it may go some time without using any of its borrowing power, it also knows that there exists a reserve amounting to the unused portion of the line of credit. Immediate availability of borrowed money can be very useful: deals that have to be made immediately can be undertaken and unexpected cash flow problems can be relieved. So long as management uses the line of credit as a resource for temporary and occasional use when needed, it can be very valuable.

COST EFFECTIVENESS OF PERSONNEL

All personnel in a business cost the business money and should be kept on only if they are worth their cost. For some jobs, it is easy to determine *cost effectiveness*; in others it is more difficult than it might appear. For salaried employees, one can establish the general range of salary that is necessary to hire and keep personnel with certain desired skills; the question then becomes whether or not these services are worth the cost to the firm. If no one is hired to do these things specifically, will they get done by others already employed? If not, are these activities necessary? If others will do them, is that an efficient use of *their* time and skills? As an example, if members of a brokerage's sales force are doing all their own typing and filing, and are handling all incoming phone calls and relaying messages on their own, could their time be better spent in sales activity if a secretary-receptionist were hired? These are not necessarily easy questions to answer, but a good manager will be able to get a reasonable idea of what the answer is. Some measure of the value to the firm of secretaries and other support personnel can be developed to determine how many are necessary.

Many firms, especially smaller ones, tend to underestimate the value of support personnel. A secretary's salary, fringe benefits and other costs will cost the firm $15,000 or more per year from the company for a full time position. Creating such a position will take a lot of the "busywork" load off the sales. Presumably, then, they will be able to concentrate more on listing and selling, and so increase the firm's business. The idea, of course, is for the additional business to more than justify the cost of the new support position. But it isn't easy to measure how much *more* listing and selling a particular sales staff may be able to do when a secretary-receptionist is hired. Perhaps the staff will just take more time off, or perhaps they will use the freed time for more of the productive work that they do best. It is up to the manager of the brokerage to be familiar enough with the sale staff's capabilities and desire for work that he can evaluate the profitability of creating a support position.

As a firm grows, it obviously will create more of the kind of work that support personnel should be doing. A staff that has too much work to do either has to start cutting corners or let backlogged work pile up. Both are inefficient and can be very costly. The function of the support staff is to handle the paperwork and other kinds of busywork that take valuable marketing time away from the sales staff. If they cannot perform this function adequately, they are not serving their purpose, and the firm will suffer.

Desk Cost

One of the least understood financial facts of the real estate brokerage business is that sales staff members cost the firm money as well. At first it may appear that, since they are paid on commission, salespeople pay their own way and no real concern need be given to what it may be costing the company to have them on the staff. Many brokers seem to reflect this view by being willing to hold licenses for as many salespeople as wish to join. They assume that if the salesperson earns no commissions he does not have to be paid, and therefore will not cost the firm anything.

This is not true, except possibly in the case of a salesperson who is so ineffective that he never appears at the office, never has any calls, never talks to any of his colleagues, and never asks the sales manager for advice. Brokers who understand the financial nature of their firms realize that for each active member of the sales force, there exists what the brokerage business calls a *desk cost*. Desk cost reflects the fact that salespeople make use of support staff, use the telephone, need desk space at which to work, and take up some of the time of colleagues and managers. The space and equipment they use cost money, as do the support staff services. The time they spend talking to colleagues and management is valuable as well. Looked at this way, it should be obvious that the presence of a salesperson on the staff is not free, and that each salesperson should be able to generate at least enough business to pay the cost to the firm of retaining him.

Opportunity Cost

A second factor associated with desk cost is something that economists call *opportunity cost*. In brief, when a given salesperson occupies a slot on the staff, no one else can occupy that particular position. The question to ask, then, is whether or not that person is the best (*most profitable*) one available to the firm to occupy that slot. The sales manager must be concerned with more than just whether or not a given staff member is covering his basic desk cost. Rather, the manager also should make sure that the salesperson is not taking up a space that someone *better* could be occupying instead. While things may seem OK if every salesperson covers the cost to the firm of keeping him on, the company is in business to make money, and not just to provide space for a collection of people who meet a minimum production standard. The truly successful firm fills its sales staff with people who do far more than merely cover their costs, making more money not only for themselves, but for the company as well.

INSURING THE BUSINESS

Insurance should be part of any financial control system. In return for fixed payments to an insurer, the firm transfers the risk that large losses or other unexpected costs will occur. Nearly all owned equipment should be insured against theft or loss, and buildings should be insured against fire, weather, and other casualty damage. Automobile liability insurance coverage should be very high, both on company-owned vehicles and those owned and used by salespeople and employees. Most real estate brokerage firms also carry insurance against professional liability.

Property Insurance

Whether the firm rents or owns its offices, insurance should cover its investment in equipment and furnishings. If the office space is owned, the building should be insured as well. Property insurance covers a variety of perils, and the firm can pick and choose among them. Insurance against theft, vandalism, fire and weather normally is carried. "All-risk" policies cover all forms of damage or loss, except for a very few which are specifically listed in the policies. Riders covering even these exceptions can be purchased to include them.

Some special coverages which are not included in standard policies may be worth considering. *Valuable papers and records coverage* reimburses cost of recreating such documents when they are lost or destroyed. Standard policies do not insure against *electrical damage* (except by fire). Data processing equipment is vulnerable to line surges, brownouts, and the like. If the firm owns a lot of such equipment, insurance against this peril should be considered. *Glass and sign coverage* extends insurance to large expanses of glass and signs which are not part of the building. *Floods and earthquakes* usually aren't covered by standard policies, and must be contracted for separately in areas where such a risk is real. Water damage coverage might not include sprinkler leakage without a special insurance rider.

If there is a fire or other damage, a firm will incur more costs than just those involved in repairs and rebuilding. Such additional costs would include the temporary use of other space and equipment until the lost or damaged property is replaced or repaired. These are called *consequential losses*, and *extra expense coverage* is required if they are to be covered as well. *Leasehold interest insurance* covers loss when, due to damage or destruction, rented property unexpectedly has to be replaced with other property having higher rent. If the firm owns a building so large that it rents part of it out to others, then *rental value coverage* will insure against loss of rental income if the building is damaged.

Liability Insurance

Liability is the potential responsibility for damages due to negligence of some kind. Liability insurance pays actual damages, damage judgments, and court costs, up to the policy limit, for the insured's covered liability.

One area of liability is personal injury: one's negligence causes bodily injury to someone. Someone can trip over a loose carpet, be injured by faulty machinery, etc. *General liability* policies protect individuals and businesses against personal injury on the insured's premises, or due to the insured's actions off the premises. *Owners' and contractors' protective liability* policies insure against injury caused by contractors or subcontractors working on the insured's property. *Comprehensive general liability* policies insure against these perils and several others in a single policy. *Workmen's compensation insurance*, mandated by state laws, insures against injury to employees while on the job. (But note that independent contractors are *not* covered!)

We all are familiar with *automobile liability insurance*, since practically anyone who owns a car is required by state law to carry it. It looms large in the brokerage business, too, since so much of the sales force's work requires auto travel. The real estate brokerage firm's policy should be that all salespeople provide frequent proof that they carry high auto liability coverage; usually much more than the minimum mandated by state law. It also should be the proper *type* of insurance. Most insurance companies rate business use of the car differently from normal household use. The firm also should try to get its own ancillary auto liability insurance to protect itself against claims made on the firm due to its salespeople's use of their autos.

Professional liability insurance covers against mistakes and negligence of a professional nature. In the real estate brokerage business, this usually is called *errors and omissions insurance*, and is basically the same sort of coverage that the general public thinks of as malpractice insurance. It covers claims against the insured due to negligence, error, failure to perform, or lack of knowledge by the broker or salesperson. The firm's insurance covers *the brokerage* against any such claims; individual salespersons ought to have *personal* professional liability insurance to protect themselves as well.

STARTING UP

Getting a business underway costs money. A real estate brokerage business in particular will need "seed money" even if it starts out vigorously and successfully, because commissions usually are not payable until transactions close. Therefore, even if transactions are made very early in the firm's existence, it will be some time before money from them flows in. A more likely situation, however, is one in which the amount of business grows slowly, and several very lean months may have to be weathered before the firm finds the solid financial footing to keep itself going on the income it generates.

Projecting Financial Needs

It is absolutely essential that reasonable financial planning be done before the business actually is set up. "Dry runs" can be played out on paper (or on a computer spreadsheet program) to examine what might happen if certain assumptions about the immediate success of the firm are made. These imaginary run-throughs cost no more than the time it takes to work them out, but they can prove valuable when the time comes to make serious decisions about starting a business and keeping it going. The two worst and most frequent mistakes made by people going into business are (1) that they are too optimistic about how their business will start out, and (2) they start out with too little available cash. Sensible planning can avoid both problems.

Over-optimism can be thwarted by making every effort to be *reasonable*; if errors enter into the estimates, they should be too conservative rather than too cheerful. In the first case, a broker might find himself with a larger business than expected, and a need for expansion sooner than had been anticipated. But if too much optimism entered the picture, he might instead be faced with mounting debt, rapidly depleting cash reserves, and heavy overhead expenses; this is the road to quick bankruptcy. Clearly, it is better to find more business than expected than less; a firm with too many paying customers usually is a lot better off than one with too few.

Conservative planning allows for the worst and realizes that any business venture entails risks that ought to be anticipated. A certain amount of money is absolutely necessary for the establishment of a business, if it is to have a reasonable chance of success.

Projecting Business Activity

There will be a period of time at the beginning during which a lot of work will have to be done, but not much income will be generated. This is because at the outset, the firm probably has no listings of its own. Usually, salespeople leaving one firm for another are not allowed to take their current listings or prospects with them. Therefore, the only income a new brokerage firm can begin to produce right away is from selling the listings of other firms. Even so, planning must allow for delays between the time properties are put under contract and the time, weeks later, when the deals close and the firm actually receives its commission shares. Income from the sale of its own listings will be delayed even more: before the firm can make money from its own listings, it has to get some.

Suppose the new firm's sales force, as a group, had been generating ten new listings a month at their old brokerages. Almost certainly it will take them some time to work up to that same level as the new firm gets underway. A conservative projection might allow for four new listings the first month of the new brokerage firm's operations. Activity would grow to six in the second month, eight in the third, and finally reaching the old average of ten in the fourth month. Projecting sales might be a little more difficult. If the sales staff had generated ten sales a month on the average, a scale of growth similar to that of listings might be anticipated, but some significant questions should still be answered. If a salesperson's record shows that he tends to sell largely his own listings, then it would be unwise to expect rapid sales results from him until he has had time to accumulate a listing portfolio of his own with the new firm. But a salesperson who sold lots of other peoples' listings could be expected to get his successful efforts under way sooner.

Deeper analysis of the outlook of the new firm would focus upon the details of the experience of the sales staff in their previous employment. Some may have been with firms that had provided considerable support service to their sales staff. How well will these people do in a new firm that may not initially afford to provide all this support? Salespeople who leave their previous firms on good terms may find that they will be able to sell those firms' listings easily, and so begin to generate income to the new firm quickly. Others may find it difficult to gain access to their old firm's listings. Some salespeople may have cultivated a considerable group of regular customers whose loyalty will lead them to deal with the new firm; some may not bring this asset with them.

Forecasting Costs and Expenses

Once a reasonable forecast of the business potential of the new firm has been made, it becomes possible to make significant financial analyses. The forecasts of activity will describe the income pattern that may be expected. This should be contrasted with the projected expenses to determine whether or not the new business is financially feasible. For no matter how nice and enjoyable it may be to run one's own business one's own way, if it doesn't make money it won't last very long. Expenses and income ought to be projected on a month-by-month basis for at least a full year; longer, if the business won't have reached its full potential by that time.

The first important objective in estimating expenses is to determine just what will be needed and will have to be paid for. Offices and equipment are obvious considerations here. Perhaps we should emphasize that an equally important consideration is the elimination of unnecessary expense items. Each anticipated need has to be carefully evaluated, and the costs involved must be estimated. Startup plans should try to avoid large initial cost items such as office machinery, etc. These can be hard to dispose of if the business does not succeed, and they drain away badly needed cash. Many such items can be rented at the outset and purchased when the firm is more financially stable.

STARTUP EXAMPLE

In Tables 13-2 through 13-6 we examine an example of the steps used to make financial forecasts and plans for a hypothetical new brokerage firm. Keep in mind that the figures shown are purely for demonstration purposes, and shouldn't be taken as representative examples for a real-life situation.

On the next page, Table 13-2 is a breakdown of startup costs, and Table 13-3 analyzes the firm's monthly fixed costs. This firm is large enough to require a secretary-receptionist and a manager, who will be either a sales manager or broker- manager. Their salaries, and the payroll taxes and fringe benefits based upon them, are fixed costs. $1,200 per month is budgeted for the secretary- receptionist; the manager's base salary is $1,000 per month. This amount may seem stingy, but in our example the manager also receives an *override* of 10% of the gross company dollar. The override is a *variable* cost, since it is based on company dollar volume, which rises or falls as business grows or decreases. It is shown in Table 13-4, on page 253, as part of the cost of sales.

Table 13-2. Projected Startup Costs

A. INITIAL ADVERTISING			
Newspaper Advertising	$1,770.00		
Radio Spots	800.00		
Local and Cable Television Ads	3,700.00		
Mailouts	1,445.00		
Open House	800.00		
Marathon Sponsorship	1,000.00		
TOTAL INITIAL ADVERTISING	8,115.00	8,115.00	
B. OTHER COSTS			
Privilege License	388.70		
Signs and Labels	1,222.50		
Answering Machine	132.25		
Furnishings	4,900.00		
Equipment	4,882.50		
Rental Deposits	1355.00		
Utility Deposits	155.00		
Miscellaneous	2,000.00		
TOTAL OTHER COSTS	15,035.95	15,035.95	
C. TOTAL STARTUP COSTS		$ 23,150.95	

Table 13-3. Projected Monthly Fixed Costs

Office Rental		1,335.00
Utilities		280.00
Telephone (business 4-line)		98.25
Salaries		2,648.20
Secretary-receptionist	1,200.00	
Manager's base pay	1,000.00	
FICA, fringes, taxes	448.20	
Advertising Contracts		335.00
Equipment rental		943.50
MLS computer/terminal		225.00
Computer equipment		620.00
Copier		98.50
Miscellaneous		750.00
TOTAL FIXED MONTHLY COSTS		$ 6,389.95

Table 13-4 is an analysis of revenues, fees, company dollars, and profits of sales. There are three kinds of sales: *In-house sales* occur when the company sells one of its own listings and so does not share the commission. The second kind is the sale of one of the firm's listings by another brokerage firm. The third occurs when the firm's sales force sells a listing of another firm. In these last two situations, we are assuming that the two firms split commissions on cooperated sales as follows: 55% of the total commission goes to the listing firm and 45% goes to the selling firm.

We are also making some other assumptions: (a) that the average value of property sold is $118,000, with an average commission rate of 7%; (b) that the firm's salespeople receive 50% of the commission revenue they bring into the firm; (c) that experience has shown that variable costs should be $550 per sale for listing and $220 per sale for selling; and (d) the sales manager receives a 10% share of the company dollar. A brokerage firm in preparing its own information of this nature will base its assumptions on experience.

A firm should make forecasts of the number of each of the kinds of sales it expects to make. In this example we are assuming that the firm is new. Its objective is to achieve

Table 13-4. Analysis of Company Revenues From Sales Figures

	In-house listing and sale	COOPERATED SALES	
		Company listings sold by other brokers **	Other brokers' listings sold by Company**
(1) Gross Revenue*	$ 8,260.00	$ 8,260.00	$ 3,717.00
(2) Payment to other firms	0.00	(3,717.00)	0.00
(3) Net revenue	8,260.00	4,543.00	3,717.00
(4) Salespersons' commissions***	(4,130.00)	(2,271.50)	(1,858.50)
(5) COMPANY DOLLAR	4,130.00	2,271.50	1,858.50
(6) Sales manager's 10%	(413.00)	(227.15)	(185.85)
(7) Variable costs****			
(7a) Listing	(550.00)	(550.00)	0.00
(7b) Selling	(220.00)	0.00	(220.00)
(8) NET COMPANY RECEIPTS PER SALE	2,947.00	1,494.35	1,452.65

Figures in parentheses are negative. They are cost items which must be subtracted from revenues.

* Based upon average sale of $118,000, commission rate of 7%.

** Assuming listing firm receives 55% of total commission, selling firm receives 45%.

*** Assuming the firm's salespeople receive 50% of the commissions they bring in to the firm.

**** Based upon experience.

Table 13-5. Sales Forecast for New Firm (First 7 Months)

	MONTHS:						
	1	2	3	4	5	6	7 and later
Company listings sold in-house	0	0	1	1	2	2	3
Company listings sold by other brokers	0	1	1	2	2	3	3
Company sales of other brokers' listings	2	2	3	3	3	4	4

a level of monthly business at which it sells three in-house listings, sells four listings of other brokers, and has three of its own listings sold by other firms. However, it expects to start slowly. It will be relatively easy to sell listings of other firms, since they already exist; listings acquired by the new firm will take longer to accumulate, so these kinds of sales will grow more slowly. Table 13-5 summarizes the listings and sales forecast. Note that in it we project it will take seven months for the new brokerage to achieve the goals it wants as an established firm.

The elaborate Table 13-6 combines all the information we have assembled in Tables 13-2 through 13-5 into one single financial forecast, spread over a period of nine months. We assume that each month the firm makes sales as shown in Table 13-5. But, since it takes some time between the time a sale is made and it is closed (and the firm gets paid), we will assume that the firm's income from sales doesn't come in until the month *after* the sales are made. Therefore, although Table 13-5 shows that the firm is expected to sell two of some other brokers' listings in its first month of operation, the income from those sales doesn't show up in Table 13-6 until the *second* month. In the same pattern, the income from sales made in Month 2 arrives in Month 3, and so on.

We begin with the startup costs. Month 1 shows no income and no variable costs. However, the firm does sustain one month's worth of fixed costs in that month. Also, we have to include all the initial startup costs shown in Table 13-2. For each of the remaining months we give several figures. Column (1) is *total revenue*, calculated from Line 1 in Table 13-4 applied to the appropriate kinds and numbers of sales shown for each month in Table 13-5. Column (2) is the *company dollar* remaining after commission payments to other firms and to salespeople have been paid: this corresponds to Line 5 in Table 13-4. Column (3) is monthly *fixed costs*, from Table 13-3. This figure is the same for all months, since fixed costs do not vary. Column (4) shows *variable costs*, once again taken from Table 13-4, this time using Lines 7a and/or 7b.

Column (5) is the 10% *manager's override* on the company dollar. Column (6) shows the *monthly profit* or loss (losses are shown in parentheses). We get these figures by starting with each month's company dollar figures in column (2), and then subtracting the month's fixed costs (3), variable costs (4), and the manger's override (5). The result is that month's profit or loss.

In the early months (1, 2 and 3) the monthly figures show *losses* because costs *exceed* company dollars. However, these losses get smaller each month, as sales volume grows. Beginning with Month 4, the company shows monthly profit. Profit increases each

Table 13-6. Firm's Business Forecast for First Nine Months (Based on data in Tables 13-2 through 13-5)

	(1)	(2)	(3)	(4)	(5)	(6)	(7)
	Total	Company	Fixed	Variable	Manager's	Profit	Cumulative
Month	Revenue	Dollars	Costs	Costs	Override	(Loss)	Profit (Loss)
			INITIAL STARTUP EXPENSES:			(23,150.95)	(23,150.95)
1	0.00	0.00	6,389.95	0.00	0.00	(6,389.95)	(29,540.90)
2	7,434.00	3,717.00	6,389.95	440.00	371.70	(3,484.65)	(33,025.55)
3	15,694.00	5,988.50	6,389.95	990.00	598.85	(1,990.30)	(35,015.85)
4	27,671.00	11,977.00	6,389.95	1,980.00	1,197.70	2,409.35	(32,606.50)
5	35,931.00	14,248.50	6,389.95	2,530.00	1,424.85	3,903.70	(28,702.80)
6	44,191.00	18,378.50	6,389.95	3,300.00	1,837.85	6,850.70	(21,852.10)
7	56,168.00	22,508.50	6,389.95	4,070.00	2,250.85	9,797.70	(12,054.40)
8	64,428.00	26,638.00	6,389.95	4,840.00	2,663.80	12,744.25	689.85
9	64,428.00	26,638.00	6,389.95	4,840.00	2,663.80	12,744.25	13,434.10

month until Month 8, at which time the firm's goals are achieved. We assume that business steadies at the Month 8 level. If it does, then figures for columns (1) through (6) will stabilize and remain the same in Month 9, as well as for later months.

Column (7) shows the firm's *cumulative* profit or loss. This is found by adding up the figures for column 6 for all the months up to and including the current month. Note that the firm starts out with a beginning loss of over $23,000 before it ever gets underway: this is the startup cost from Table 13-2. The accumulated loss will *rise* in any month that shows a loss, and will *fall* in any month that shows a profit.

In Table 13-6, the cumulative loss in our example rises in Months 1, 2, and 3, since losses are run in each of these months. At the end of Month 3, the accumulated loss reaches $35,000. Beginning with Month 4, the firm starts to show monthly profits. When a firm has profits, its cumulative profit will rise (or, as in our case, its cumulative loss will become smaller). By the end of Month 8, the profits earned in Months 4 through 8 have been enough to wipe out the firm's accumulated loss, so in Month 8 the firm shows a small accumulated profit. Now its recent monthly profits have been enough to offset its startup costs and early months of losses. From this point on, accumulated profit will increase each month (as it does in Month 9).

This kind of financial forecast is very useful. In our example, the information in Table 13-6 tells us that as the owners of the firm prepare to start up, they will need at least $35,000 on hand or readily available. This cash will be needed to see the business through the formative period, because it is forecast that at one point (Month 3) in its early months of operation, it will have a cumulative deficit of that amount. To be on the safe side, it wouldn't hurt to have even more than that, to provide a reserve for *contingency* (unplanned expenditures or deficits). If, for example, a fund of $45,000 is budgeted as *seed money*, an extra $10,000 will be available as a "cushion" to cover unforeseen problems and expenses. If business develops more slowly than expected, or surprise expenses are encountered, this extra money will come in handy. This sum need not be held in cash; the firm can arrange a line of credit for some or all of it, and borrow from it only when necessary.

DISCUSSION QUESTIONS AND PROJECTS

1. Analyze the concept of the *company dollar* and explain its usefulness.

2. Discuss the concept of *desk cost* and *opportunity cost* with respect to the retention of salespeople.

3. Survey two or three firms in your area to determine how much of revenue becomes company dollars.

4. From these firms determine what the average expenses (in terms of percentage of the company dollar) are in the categories defined in the text.

5. Based upon the information you gathered in 3 and 4, determine what percentage of the company dollar in your area is retained as gross company profit.

6. Interview a manager of a relatively new firm. Find out what kinds of costs were sustained to get the business under way and how long it took to recoup these costs. How long did it take before the business considered itself established? What kinds of problems were encountered?

7. Based upon information you can gather about the operations of the brokerage firms in your area, develop a profile of the "typical" firm, showing volume of sales activity, revenue, company dollars, costs, and profits.

8. Develop a budget for the next twelve months of the firm you profiled.

9. From a typical brokerage firm in your area, determine the variety and extent of insurance coverage that it carries. Explain anything unusual. Do you have suggestions for improvement?

A Case Study

TIME MANAGEMENT

In a recent interview, the principal broker of a respected residential firm had the following to say about the efficient use of time.

"I always try to tell my people to evaluate everything they do on the basis of the time it will take. I use the example of listings. Before they accept a listing, they should consider the time and effort that it will take to get the property sold. They should 'work' every listing they get: I don't want our firm to get the reputation of accepting listings and then just letting them sit until they sell themselves. This means that if a particular property is going to be hard to sell, they will have to invest a lot of time and effort into it.

"If the listing is going to be a dog, I tell them to consider if they might be better off turning it down, and spending the time it would have taken by getting other listings that will be easier sales. Naturally, they expect that they will have to work on all their listings, and that they don't earn their commissions by just sitting around doing nothing. But I've seen too many cases where a salesperson spent enormous amounts of time trying to sell a bad listing, when he could have handled two or three others at the same time.

"For some reason this example really hits home. Once it does, I go on to suggest other ways of budgeting their time. I suggest that they plan an afternoon of showings to a prospect so that they waste as little time as possible driving from one home to another. I suggest that they do their listing negotiations in the evenings when people are at home and when it's too late to do showings anyway. When they're on floor duty, doing open houses, or otherwise have some moments of free time, I suggest that they do some cold calling or check up on recent clients just to say hello.

"And finally, I tell them that if they organize their time they can accomplish an awful lot without wearing themselves out."

REFERENCES

CARTER, JERRY T., CRB, "The Company Dollar: A Vital Budgeting Tool," *Real Estate Today*, January, 1976.

"Staying Small", "Growing Large," *Real Estate Today*, May-June, 1976.

FOURTEEN

THE WORKING ENVIRONMENT

Locating the Office
Office Layout
Furnishings and Equipment
Computer Facilities
Outside the Office

At first glance, it may seem that a real estate brokerage firm's office isn't really all that important. After all, the sales force will be spending most of its time someplace else. However, it is an important home base, as well as a symbol to the general public of the firm's efficiency and professionalism. Much of the work done by a brokerage must take place in the office, including everything done by those who are not active salespeople. Even sales personnel will need a place to keep their records, meet people, and do much of their work that does not involve direct contact with the public. An office which is well located, well equipped, and properly designed and staffed, can contribute greatly to the overall efficiency and profitability of a real estate brokerage firm.

The office should have a convenient and visible location and a proper design and layout that makes the available space as useful as possible. It should be staffed with permanent support personnel whose services will be available to the salespeople. It also serves as a central place where much important information is kept available for the use of the firm's personnel.

LOCATING THE OFFICE

Newly licensed brokers, especially if they intend to work alone, are tempted to get by with as little office space as possible; usually a room or a corner in the home. This kind of location is very disadvantageous. It's hard for customers to find, and is awkward for receiving them when they do find this "office." It also doesn't do much for public confidence that the broker's business doesn't seem to be a full time and professional one. Furthermore, many localities have zoning ordinances that prohibit housing a business such as a real estate brokerage in residentially zoned districts. It would be embarrassing if a real estate broker, of all people, were to be found in violation of zoning ordinances.

Any broker intending to establish a permanent and successful business ought to have a genuine office. Particularly when he begins to take on salespeople, the office in the home becomes an unwise and inconvenient choice. Very small but comfortable offices can be found in even the most prestigious buildings. Shared facility offices have recently been developed, wherein the occupant rents a single office in a large, well-arranged suite, and shares a receptionist and other facilities provided by the building management. These arrangements are relatively inexpensive, while offering many useful office services whenever the tenant may need them. They also provide a serious, businesslike environment that enhances the credibility and appearance of even the smallest enterprise.

Site Selection

Given that a general district for location has been chosen, it still is necessary to pick a specific site for the business. The new firm has a lot of options. It could build a structure to house its offices; it could buy an existing building; or it could rent available space. Renting usually is the best option for a new firm, because it involves the lowest immediate cost. Also, as the business grows (and a new business, one always hopes, will grow) it will need more and more space. Expanding to larger spaces is easier when the space is rented than when it is owned. The firm can leave rented space at the expiration of the lease. If it owns its office space, it either has to sell it and buy a new one, or undergo the inconvenience of adding to the owned space, if that is even possible. Finally, most new firms have to conserve cash, and the expenses of buying space require lots of ready cash; much more than the deposits and initial lease payments of rented space.

Location in Small Towns

In a small town, location selection tends to be limited. There are few (maybe only one) business districts to choose from. A real estate brokerage firm usually chooses a location in the most important business district, since it probably will be most convenient to the entire area, and is likely to have in it most of the other businesses with which the firm deals. In many towns, however, the older "central" business district is being replaced with a newer, more modern district on the fringe of town, in the direction of most intensive growth. This is especially so if new highways, which bypass the central parts of town, have been built. If this is the case, the brokerage firm is faced with a choice: the older or the newer business location. Since there is more real estate activity in newer areas, the probable logical choice will be the new business district. However, other factors, such as cost and distance from the firm's areas of activity, will be considered too.

Location in Larger Towns

In a large town or a city, the general location of the brokerage firm is pretty much dictated by the area of town in which the firm specializes. The kind of property the firm deals in has an important influence. Residentially-oriented brokerages locate in the areas they serve, preferably along some well-known street that customers are familiar with and easily can find (see Figure 14-1). A firm specializing in commercial sales and leasing more often locates in the central business district, or, in large cities in satellite business districts close to areas it specializes in.

Attraction

In the real estate business, "walk-in" traffic is not a very important source of business. That is to say, people rarely walk through the door, announcing that they want to buy or sell property. For this reason (and because it is very expensive), residential real estate offices usually are not located, say, in the middle of large regional mall shopping centers. Businesses in such centers cater to browsing and depend on walk-in traffic, but it is rare that someone wandering through the mall will suddenly evolve on the spur of the moment into a customer willing to spend several years' income for a house.

This doesn't mean that location is unimportant, but rather that it is not essential to locate specifically with an eye toward walk-in traffic. Still, an attractive location should be chosen, and one with easily available parking. The main road location provides not only a recognizable address, but an opportunity to erect an eye-catching sign that a lot of

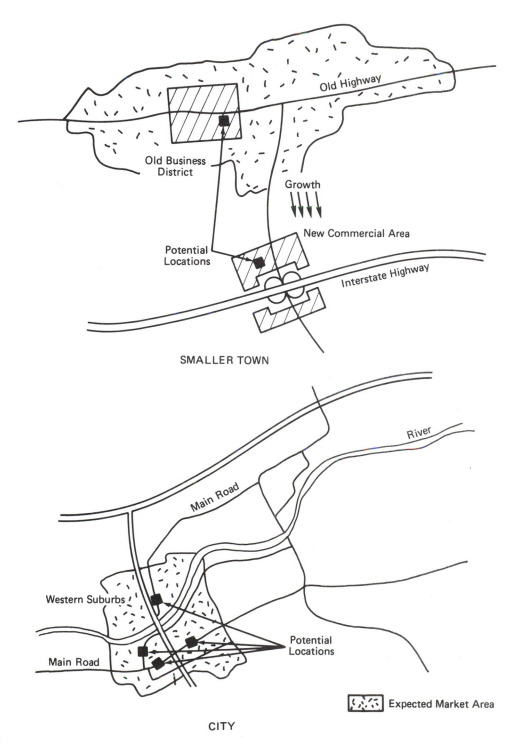

Figure 14.1 Location Choices

motorists will see. While they will not turn into the business on the spur of the moment as they drive along, they will know that the brokerage is there, and may remember it when it is time for them to buy or sell a home.

Site Features

The office itself should be on a site that does not detract from the image the company wishes to project. This means that rundown, unattractive locations should be avoided; but it is not necessary to rent the Taj Mahal, either. The office should be in a clean, well-run building with good parking facilities and an attractive, businesslike appearance. It should be easy to find and easy to get to. Addresses along limited access roads or roads with center dividers can pose access problems. (See Figure 14-2 for advantages and disadvantages of various locations.) If there are no local ordinances prohibiting signs, there should be some provision for identifying the location of the business in a way that will make a good and *memorable* impression upon passers-by.

Commercial and Investment Firms

A firm specializing in commercial or investment sales or property management has different locational needs. Usually it should locate in the central business district of the city, close to the financial institutions, investment firms, attorneys, and others with whom it will do business. Furthermore, in this area of brokerage there is little or no geographical discrimination; a firm would be expected to deal with properties in any part of the metropolitan area in which it is located, and it wouldn't be unusual to find it dealing on a statewide, regional, or even national basis. The location should be at a reasonably prestigious address. It doesn't necessarily have to be in the most expensive or impressive building in town, but should be in a location that would be comfortable and secure to clients used to dealing in very large sums of money.

OFFICE LAYOUT

A large, impressive (and very expensive) office doesn't have to be established at the outset; it is only important that there be enough room for the firm's work to be done comfortably and efficiently. When the business grows, adjacent space can be added; or it can move to a new, larger location. However, if it is at all possible, some forethought should be given to the likelihood that more space will be needed, and it should be planned for accordingly. A location that offers the opportunity to expand directly into connecting space at some time in the future would be ideal. Almost as good would be the opportunity for future expansion to larger quarters elsewhere in the same building or center. In either case, growth could be accomplished without having to educate the public about new addresses.

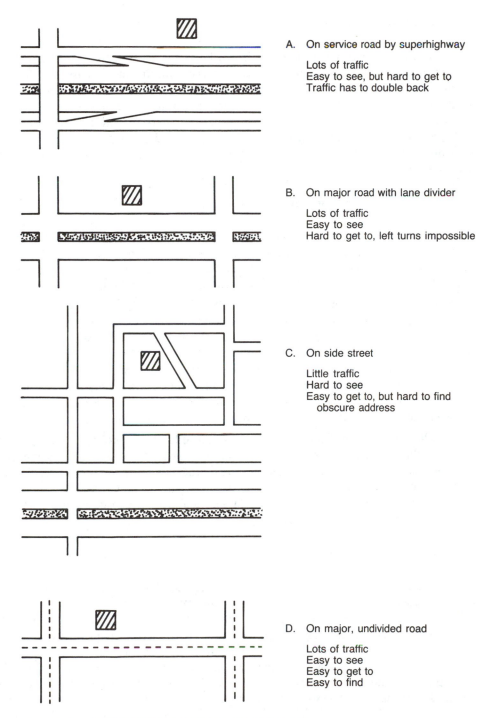

A. On service road by superhighway

Lots of traffic
Easy to see, but hard to get to
Traffic has to double back

B. On major road with lane divider

Lots of traffic
Easy to see
Hard to get to, left turns impossible

C. On side street

Little traffic
Hard to see
Easy to get to, but hard to find
    obscure address

D. On major, undivided road

Lots of traffic
Easy to see
Easy to get to
Easy to find

Figure 14-2.   Location Alternatives, Advantages and Disadvantages

Room Arrangement

The office space must meet certain needs. There must be some kind of reception area at the front through which all traffic – walk-in and invited – must pass. The area should be large enough to accommodate a receptionist's desk and equipment, and there should be enough seating space for people who are waiting to see brokerage staff. Usually the licenses of the sales force are required by state law to be displayed in this area. Other wall space can be devoted to displays featuring current listings, accomplishments of the staff members, and certainly any awards and certificates of a professional or community service nature.

Conference Room and Sales Work Areas

A fairly large conference room can be very useful. This space can be multipurpose: it can be used for sales meetings, closings, and gatherings of any other groups that are too large to be accommodated in the firm's other office spaces. Generally, there is an office for the broker-owner. The sales staff themselves can have individual offices, or there can be a large space (called a "bullpen") in which the salespeople's desks are arranged.

While individual offices give the salespeople a sense of importance and a certain degree of privacy that may occasionally be needed, they also offer the opportunity to be reclusive and to separate themselves from the rest of the staff. The bullpen arrangement sees to it that the sales staff are accessible to one another, and provides a convenient and comfortable arrangement for sales meetings and other large gatherings of the firm's members. However, it does eliminate most opportunities for privacy, and could be a problem when dealing with people who want their discussions to be in private..

The actual choice of office or bullpen has to be left to the broker-owner's particular vision of the firm's needs, but the prime objective should be to obtain the arrangement that contributes most to the firm's efficiency and productivity. A compromise could be the arrangement of cubicles: small office-like spaces separated by partial walls, sometimes glassed, which create the feeling of some privacy and personal space without closing the entire office into small, separated spaces.

Broker's and Manager's Offices

The broker and the sales manager, if there is one, should have separate offices near the salespeople's work area. In a bullpen arrangement, the sales manager's office can have glass walls, but there must be some way of assuring the broker's office of privacy (curtains across glass areas, for example), because he will need it frequently. Often he will discuss matters with individual staff members that are their business alone. Also, there will be occasions when he, as a manager, needs a disturbance-free environment in which to do planning and decision-making. Figure 14-3 shows two possible arrangements of a typical 1800 square foot (30 x 60 feet) office area.

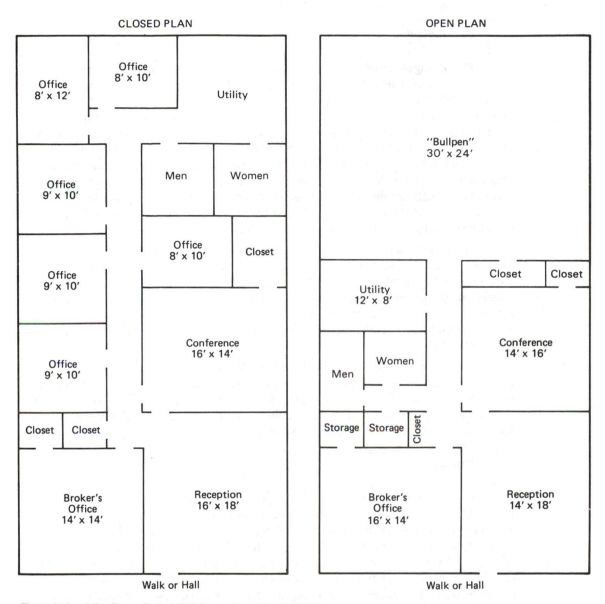

Figure 14-3. Office Plans - Typical 1800 Square Foot Office (60' X 30')

Sound control requires careful attention, especially in bullpen arrangements. Carpeting and acoustical ceiling absorb a lot of noise, but wall paneling and other flat surfaces reflect it. The use of draperies, tapestry-type wall decoration, and the like will cut down considerably on reflected noise. It should be noted that a quiet environment is an impressive one, and that the relatively small cost of sound control can pay big dividends with respect to earning the admiration of customers for the brokerage's surroundings.

The Reception Area

The arrangement of the reception area is of great importance, as it is the first part of the office space that potential and actual customers will see. It should be decorated conservatively and comfortably, and people should feel at ease when they enter it. Lavish surroundings are not necessary, but the appearance and comfort of the area ought not to detract from the firm's image objective. A typical reception area arrangement is shown in Figure 14-4. The receptionist's work area is arranged to allow for typing, answering telephones, and greeting customers. The desk space should be large, but not imposing, allowing for proper work space without crowding, and identifying the receptionist as the person that a customer should speak to upon entering. A small, comfortable seating area is located within easy view of the receptionist but far enough away that waiting customers can converse without feeling that they are disturbing anyone.

The arrangement provides a large wall area for display, if desired, and a clear path from the main door to the doorways leading to the offices. However, this path goes directly past the receptionist, thus providing control over entry into the office area. Usually the receptionist will call whomever the visitor wants to see; the desired party then will come to the reception area to escort the customer to his office or desk. The receptionist can escort them back into the office area, but this will mean leaving the reception area unattended.

The reception area should have separate doors leading into the office area and to the conference room, especially if that room is used for closings and other frequent meetings with customers. If the office area is of the bullpen type and the door from the reception room opens directly into it, it's advisable to provide another door, if possible, between the reception area and the broker's private office.

Storage

The brokerage firm will require a large amount of storage space. A lot of records have to be kept on file for a long time. Some of this recordkeeping is mandated by law; all of it is good business practice. This means that the real estate brokerage firm needs a lot of storage space, not only for these files but also for office supplies, unused signs, and some office equipment. Much of this space could be incorporated into a utility room, which could also contain coffee machines, a refrigerator, a hotplate, and other such things for the use of the staff. The conference room ought to have a storage closet, especially if it is used for staff meetings: items and exhibits used in these meetings could be kept there. A bullpen arrangement might include a handy supply closet for storing contract forms, stationery, and office supplies. A hall closet can be used in layouts with separate offices. And, of course, the office must have a bathroom. Larger offices need separate ladies' and men's rooms.

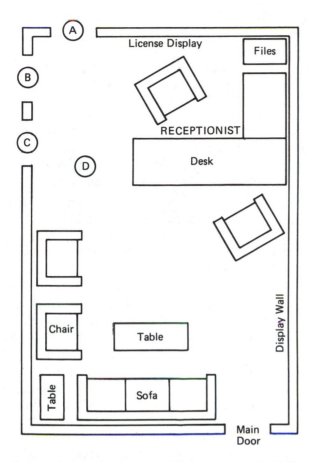

A, B, C: Doors should lead to conference room and to offices. If office area door leads directly into bullpen-type area, a third door should lead into broker's private office.

D: Location of doors gives receptionist control over passage to them.

Figure 14-4. Typical Reception Area - 14' X 18'

FURNISHINGS AND EQUIPMENT

Office equipment and furnishings should be chosen for comfort and efficiency. Luxury for its own sake should be avoided because it wastes a lot of money and because comfortable surroundings are more important to good business performance than expensive trappings. This doesn't mean that the office should be stark and bare, but rather that money spent on furnishing and equipping the office should return value in the form of better performance by the firm and its personnel.

The Salesperson's Station

Salespeople spend much of their time outside the offices of the firm itself, so they will usually equip their automobiles and homes with some of the things they need. Still, they will need places to work in the office as well. Ideally, each salesperson should have a desk (or "station") for his/her exclusive use. The desk can be any type, so long as it is comfortable to use. Most salespeople will appreciate one with two file drawers, instead of a row of smaller drawers, since they will have to keep many records, contracts, and papers in a place where they can be well organized for easy reference. If desks don't have space for files, then there must be access to filing cabinet space for each salesperson.

A salesperson's desk needs a telephone; preferably one with a very soft ring, since blaring telephones are disturbing, particularly in bullpen arrangements. While it may seem extravagant to put a telephone on each desk, real estate sales people make extensive use of the telephone, and assigning more than one to a telephone can create difficult conflicts and lots of unproductive inconvenience.

Access to typewriters and/or word processing equipment will depend upon the availability of secretarial service in the firm. If the sales staff does most of its own letter writing and other typing, then several machines should be provided, although it is not necessary for each salesperson's station to have one. An efficient system is to have two or three machines arranged along the wall of the bullpen for use by all salespeople.

Many brokerage firms keep typewriters on hand, even when they have sophisticated computer-based word processing equipment. The typewriters are for typing up contract forms. These forms are in multiple parts (i.e.: carbons), and most printers don't handle multi-part forms very well. Also, aligning pre-printed forms in a printer is almost impossible. Typewriters should be electric, preferably with carbon film ribbons. These make clean, crisp copy and strike hard enough to make several clear copies at once. Since contracts forms have multiple copies, the need for clarity and the ability to strike through several sheets at once is obvious.

Office Equipment

(Note that computer equipment is discussed in a separate section below.) Office equipment is required for word processing and information storage. A copying machine is a necessity, but only the largest firms will require sophisticated copiers capable of rapid copying and with extra features. The broker's office should be equipped with a fireproof safe in which essential documents and valuables may be kept. Brokerage firms must keep large numbers of records, so filing space and cabinetry are essential.

The telephone system is very important, since so much office business uses it. One of the worst false economies in a brokerage office is to "save" money by scrimping on the phone system. A real estate brokerage office needs several incoming lines, and a phone at every salesperson's desk or station. The receptionist should be able to connect any call with the appropriate person quickly, and should be kept up-to-date with regard to who is in and who isn't available. If the firm has no receptionist, then whoever does answer the phone should be able to do the same. Real estate brokerages get a lot of new business over the phone, so the firm's phone system will be the brokerage's initial introduction to a lot of people. It doesn't create a very favorable first impression to leave a potential customer on "hold" for a long time, listening to cute elevator-music versions of old disco favorites.

Reference Materials

Brokerage firms have to keep a lot of information on hand where it can be referred to easily. Up-to-date records of all sales and listing activity in the firm's areas of interest keep the brokerage abreast of its markets. So does current information on lending rates and the lending standards of local lending institutions. A small library of useful references should include a dictionary, a law dictionary, a real estate dictionary, current and back issues of trade publications, and books covering real estate principles, appraisal, finance, property law, and sales and listing techniques.

Certain specialized reference materials also are necessary. Highly detailed maps of the firm's areas of interest should be available, and kept up-to-date. Most firms keep *plat books*: these are large volumes of specialized maps showing the division of the area into separate plots, lots and parcels. These often give measurements and names of owners as well, and are provided by various service companies. They are expensive, but very valuable, and should be kept current. City directories are assembled by business groups or private firms. These attempt to list most of the local population of households, with as much information on them as they can get (address, phone, family characteristics, profession, income, etc.). Address-first telephone books are handy; they list telephone numbers by address rather than by user name.

COMPUTER FACILITIES

Certainly the most revolutionary office innovation in the 1980's was the introduction and rapid acceptance of the desktop computer. Before the past decade, computers were mysterious, alien objects which mystified most people. Now, in the 1990's they are everywhere. Businesses and offices without them seem like Stone-age relics. Computers have become (relatively) cheap. Before the 1980's they were, mostly, room-size installations costing hundreds of thousands of dollars. Today they fit on a desk and cost only a few thousand dollars for a "slam-bang" system, and well under $2,000 for very powerful "single-user" systems.

Along with them has come computer vocabulary. Computer equipment is called *hardware*. Hardware is the "box" and the workings of the computer itself, *printers* and other *peripheral equipment,* the *monitor* that displays the tasks being undertaken. The "programming" which enables the system to do useful things is *software*.

There are dangers in using computers. One is buying either too much equipment, or the wrong kind; another is getting stuck using the wrong software. A real problem for the business person who is not a computer expert is getting the information needed to make reasonable decisions about computer equipment and software use. There are computer stores almost everywhere, but few of their salespeople know much about using them in the real estate business. We can provide a brief review here.

Computer Equipment

Today's small computers come in several forms. Most common is the desktop unit, the kind most of us are used to seeing. Tower units are a bit larger, but stand on end so as to take up less room or to be put on the floor. Also there are portable units, from fairly large "luggables" to small, battery-operated "notebook" computers not much bigger than this book.

A typical desktop system includes the computer, a monitor, and an assortment of peripherals. The computer box contains the workings of the machine, and also *cards* (or *boards*) which are installed for special purposes. The monitor looks like a small TV, but good ones have much finer resolution than any television set, so that they can present clear, readable images. A *modem* (usually installed in the computer) lets the machine use telephone lines for sending and receiving data; some modem boards will send and receive faxes as well. Many computer systems also include a *mouse*, a hand-operated pointing device which makes a lot of newer software easier to use.

A computer system will have a printer. Inexpensive ones produce *dot-matrix* copy (the kind where the characters are made up of little dots); the quality of the printing can range from awful to surprisingly good. *Laser printers* are more expensive, but they produce very good copy. Some printers print in color; they are expensive, though, and there really is little need for them in a real estate brokerage office.

The important aspects of a computer are its speed and memory. Speed is determined by the *CPU*, or *processor* (the "computer on a chip" that runs the whole thing). It's usually best to get the *fastest* affordable type. The amount of memory in the machine affects its speed, to some extent, as well as its ability to handle some new and very useful, but very "memory hungry" software. Memory is measured in *bytes*. One byte is roughly the same as one character (letter, symbol) of written information. Memory used to be measured in *kilobytes*; one *K* is 1,024 bytes. Nowadays, though, software applications require lots of memory, and the cost of putting memory into a computer is quite low. Therefore, it is more common today to measure memory in *megabytes*. One *MB* is slightly over *one million* bytes, or 1,024 K. Even the most rudimentary new computer these days has at least a couple of MB of memory, but today's "standard" (1993) is more like 8 MB. Soon it will be even more, as more complex and sophisticated (and "memory-hungry") software becomes available.

A significant advantage of computers is that they can handle lots of information. The memory inside the computer is used to analyze and manipulate data, but computers also *store* information. This is done with *disks*. The *floppy diskette* is a piece of magnetic material in a stiff envelope of cardboard or plastic. When inserted into the *disk drive*, it can be "read" and "written to" by the computer. The disk becomes a permanent copy of the information on it, available for use on the computer at any time. High-density diskettes in common use today hold over a megabyte of information; soon diskettes holding 2 to 4 MB will be common. (This is a lot of information! The manuscript for this entire book fits on a single high-density 1.44 MB diskette with room left over.) A *hard disk* is a high-tech extension of the same principle, able to hold tens of millions of characters of information. Hard disks usually are installed within the computer itself. The computer can "access" the data on them much more rapidly than diskettes. Modern software requires enormous memory storage space; as a result, a typical "standard" desktop system will have a hard disk of 200 MB or greater capacity.

Choosing Computer Equipment

In the early 1990's intense cost-cutting competition among producers of office computers has considerably reduced the cost of computer power. A minimal desktop computer, monitor and rudimentary printer can cost less than $1,000. Less than $4,000 will buy a very powerful desktop system with a laser printer. Those who wish, still can spend many thousands more for the very latest "state of the art" equipment. The differences have largely to do with data storage capacity, computer memory (RAM), and speed of execution.

A basic unit should have the maximum available RAM memory, at least one floppy disk drive, and a hard disk. Color displays are almost universal. Monochrome displays cost much less and, for the real estate brokerage, show everything necessary. Some larger firms may wish to consider a *local area network (LAN)*. With this arrangement, a powerful central computer (the *server*) is connected to several smaller computers (*workstations*) located throughout the office. The central unit contains the data storage system, and may even do the "computing" for the remote units. Such systems are expensive, but they may end up costing less than the cost of putting a stand-alone computer on every desk. LANs may not offer much real advantages to smaller firms.

Two important features seem to be the norm of the computer world: things are changing all the time, and everything is getting cheaper. Today's state of the art is tomorrow's relic. In the computer business, two years or so is the lifespan of one "generation." Usually, whatever is (or is about to become) "previous generation" equipment is the best buy. It has been around a while, has had the bugs worked out, and has a lot of software applications. It usually is much less expensive than the very latest developments, and yet has very elegant and powerful sophistication. "Brand name" equipment costs the most, but there are many "clone" computer producers whose wares cost less, with no noticeable loss in quality or reliability. Most of these sell by mail-order, and some have begun to establish outlet stores of their own in larger cities. Many cities will have local computer firms which produce their own "brands" of machines, assembled from stock parts.

Access to service is important. If a service center for a particular brand is not conveniently nearby, that brand should be ignored, unless the purchaser is willing to run the risk of time-consuming and, possibly, damaging shipping of the unit back and forth when necessary. Many mail-order computer sellers include "on-site" service as part of their warranty policy.

Software

Computers are good at two things: high-speed calculation and storage and retrieval of information. From these capacities, a wide variety of software applications has been derived. For business use, the most popular groups of these are *word processing, spreadsheets, database analysis,* and *accounting.*

Word processing is the production of documents – anything from letters to novels, and more. Though word processors can be used simply as expensive typewriters, where such software shines is in its editing capacity. A document can be written and then changed, edited, and rearranged at will, quickly and easily. Most word processing software packages also have *mailing list* features that can be of great use to the real estate brokerage. These features allow the production of a "boilerplate" document, such as a letter. From a list of names and addresses, and possibly other information, the computer can generate printed letters based upon the boilerplate version, but with the recipient's address and possibly other "personalizing" features added in.

Spreadsheet analysis develops tables of data, usually financial in nature. This software features the ability to alter an entire set of numerical data if changes are made in parts of it. This would be of most use to the accounting arm of a brokerage firm. A firm which does a lot of commercial real estate dealing may find such software useful for making income and investment return projections on properties. Most spreadsheet software also can generate useful real estate information, such as mortgage amortization schedules, investment projection and analysis, etc.

Database analysis is generalized, systematic filing with the computer. The database can be anything of interest: invoices, salespeople's records, listings. Appraisers use it to keep track of comparable sales. The database program keeps and stores data, and can sort and rearrange the information to present all or part of it in a variety of useful ways.

Accounting software does what the name implies: it keeps the books for the firm. Most applications have a general module and then allow the user to purchase other modules as needed (general ledger, invoice, payroll, etc.). Many sophisticated software systems combine features of all of these into very powerful applications. In addition, a huge variety of specialized software performs certain limited functions.

A real estate brokerage firm might use accounting software for its own books and payroll. Database software could handle listings, salesperson data, comparable closed sales, etc. Word processing software could generate all written information for the firm, and could store it as well. For documents such as policy manuals, boilerplate letter, contract forms, and the like, information stored on disks can always be accessed and easily edited to allow for incorporation of changes as they become necessary.

Choosing Software

Two important questions must be asked when any software purchase is being considered: (1) is it useful to the business; and (2) how difficult is it to learn and use? Usefulness to the business can be a very deceptive thing. While it is nice to know that a given software package will perform this or that function, are those functions really needed? And if they are, is this particular package the best of its kind for the needs of the firm?

A very important consideration is the degree to which the firm itself will have to be discommoded in order to use the software. Some software is fairly rigid, and permits only limited flexibility of use. An accounting package, for example, may do a lot of useful things, but if its required format means that the firm will have to change its accounting records around and alter the ways in which it has been summarizing information, will it really be such a useful tool after all? A key factor will be the degree to which the business itself will have to adjust to fit the software it uses. Ideally, the software should be adjustable to suit the firm's way of doing things.

Some software is very sophisticated, and learning to use it takes a lot of time. If this is the case, then only a few people in the firm actually will use it. For some software, that may be all right, but it certainly will not do for that which is intended to be used by the entire sales force. Great strides are being made in this *user interface* problem with software, and as time passes we will see more and more very powerful applications that can be easily learned and used.

Note also that there is plenty of real estate-specific software available. Probably the most popular is property management software, because it involves so much record- and account-keeping, and so takes great advantage of the computer. You won't find much real estate software advertised in the popular computing magazines, but there are articles, information and advertising about it in many real estate trade publications (for example, *Real Estate Today*, published by the National Association of REALTORS®).

OUTSIDE THE OFFICE

Salespeople do much of their work outside the office. In fact, the average salesperson may spend more time in his automobile than he does in the firm's offices. Thus, it is important to give some consideration to the equipment and environment for these out-of-office times.

Work Space at Home

The salespeople and the managers of the firm should set aside some space in their homes for a work area. Even if it is only a desk in a corner of a room, it will be a valuable asset to the job. A lot of the desk work that does not need supervision can be done here, with the comfort of home nearby. If the salesperson's firm has its own network computer, the salesperson may be able to connect a home computer to the office using a modem and the telephone. It usually pays to have a telephone with a separate line because a real estate salesperson spends a lot of time on the telephone. Also, a separate line gives the salesperson an exclusive number for business calls. An answering machine is a must.

The Salesperson's Automobile

Salespeople spend a lot of time in their cars. It may seem odd to discuss the choice of an automobile in a book that concerns real estate brokerage, but for many of the firm's customers the salesperson and his/her car are the only evidence of the firm they see until they arrive at the offices for the signing of settlement documents. Some customers never see anything else. The automobile must double both as a temporary office of sorts for the salesperson and as a carrier of passengers. It should be chosen to do both well. Unfortunately, most cars are wretchedly designed for the first purpose. Since the salesperson does the driving, it would be nice to have space in the front seat to store listing books, contract forms and other materials used. Glove compartments and parcel shelves (if there are any) usually are quite inadequate. Usually there is nothing to do with these materials except to pile them in the front seat or on the floor. FOR SALE signs, stakes, and other less frequently needed things can go in the trunk. The salesperson often takes others along in the car, especially prospects who are being shown property. The car has to be comfortable for passengers.

Given all these requirements, the specific nature of the automobile can be stated with reasonable precision. It should be a four-door sedan. Passengers – especially married couples – will tend to ride together in the back, and will not appreciate having to crawl over, and past, the front seats to squirm in and out of the front doors of a two-door car. It should be a fairly large car; regardless of the number of doors, the back seats of many smaller cars are very uncomfortable. The car should be air-conditioned, except perhaps in the coldest climates. It should run quietly, because there is likely to be considerable conversation going on among the occupants.

What we have described is, essentially, a full-sized, four-door sedan. But these aren't being made much anymore, and few modern smaller cars, even with four doors, can be said to be particularly spacious. One alternative is a van. Large ones may be awkward to drive, but several manufacturers produce minivans. These are relatively small and fuel-efficient, but due to their design can be extremely roomy inside.

DISCUSSION QUESTIONS AND PROJECTS

1. How should the location of a real estate office be selected?

2. How should a real estate office be arranged?

3. Compare and contrast the advantages and disadvantages of the bullpen sales area and the plan of giving individual offices to salespeople.

4. Take a small survey of successful real estate salespeople in your area. What kinds of cars do they use? What equipment do they keep with them and at their homes?

5. Examine the reference area of a local successful brokerage firm. What kinds of materials does it keep on hand? What purposes do they serve?

6. Survey some of the computer retailers in your area to determine how helpful they could be to a real estate brokerage firm seeking computer equipment and software for the firm.

REFERENCES

DOOLEY, THOMAS W., "The Real Estate Office of Tomorrow", in *The McGraw-Hill Real Estate Handbook*, Robert Irwin, ed., Ch. 36. New York, NY: McGraw-Hill Book Company, 1984.

QUE's 1992 Computer Buyer's Guide. Carmel, IN: Que® Corporation, 1992. This is just one of several useful reference books of its kind; most are updated annually.

FIFTEEN

ESTABLISHING AND MARKETING THE SUCCESSFUL REAL ESTATE BROKERAGE

A real estate brokerage firm is in the business of selling. Not just selling real estate, but selling *itself*, and convincing the public to use its services. Much of this selling of the firm is done by the sales force. When they solicit business for themselves, they have to sell their firm as well. Even so, management of the firm also should have its own marketing policies and programs. In this chapter we discuss this effort as it applies both to the new brokerage firm, and the firm which has become established in business.

ESTABLISHING A NEW BROKERAGE FIRM

Once one has obtained a broker's license, he has the legal right to set up an independent real estate brokerage business. A great many potential broker-owners stop at that point; they set up shop in their own homes and languish from then on. They have invested time and money in the preparation and fees necessary to obtain the required licenses, but do not follow up with the even greater investment necessary to get their business off the ground and heading for possible career success. They set up offices in a spare room, in the corner of the recreation room, or even in the glove compartments of their cars. They may handle a listing here or there for friends or acquaintances, and may on occasion show a buyer around to listings held by other, better-established firms. But their chances for long-term success are very limited, since they don't really exert the effort to establish themselves as recognizable, credible businesses with genuine, working operations.

Broker Qualifications

License law requires a broker license applicant to have been a licensed salesperson for a certain length of time. This does not guarantee that new brokers are genuinely experienced, since they could have had their licenses held active for the required period of time without actually participating to any significant extent in the business. While such poorly prepared new broker licensees face a tremendous uphill battle, they can achieve success by diligence and hard work, although many of them will find they know so little of the true nature of the business that they will become disheartened and give up.

Many new brokers, however, have had extensive experience in the real estate sales field, and seek to establish their own businesses as a logical continuation of their career pattern. While they may have the talent and expertise to handle sales, they must become aware of the requirements and responsibilities of actually running a business for themselves. They know where and how to find the customers that they need, and are familiar with the real estate markets they will operate in. They may even have regular customers they cultivated previously, and who will continue to deal with them once they set out on their own. Even so, actually running a business entails much more than they have been used to doing. In any case the manner in which a business is established and the amount and suitability of the effort undertaken to get it underway are essential to future success.

Permanent Business

In order to establish a successful business, a real estate broker needs more than listings or potential buyers. These will only last a short time, and must continually be replaced with new listings and new buyers. A new broker may experience an initial flush of success as he makes deals involving his friends and family, but soon they will run out. They cannot be expected to be frequent repeat customers, because few people engage in real estate transactions more than once every few years. Occasionally, the new broker may find a buyer or two who is interested in accumulating properties, and so may be a frequent customer, but unless these people deal in large, expensive purchases, it is unlikely that they can sustain the broker with their commissions alone. Furthermore, investors and large-scale buyers rarely find the services of a new broker satisfactory when they just as easily can use the services of established and experienced firms. It is even less likely that a new broker will find a seller with many properties to sell, and so many listings for him. A large-scale owner seeking to sell holdings is almost certain to employ an experienced firm with a good track record.

Long-Range Plan for Success

If the new firm is to succeed, it must be planned for sensibly. A simple idea that it would be nice to run a business or organize with certain people is not enough. The firm must be viewed as a *business enterprise*. A vision of what the firm should be and will be is necessary, and it must include all aspects of the business. Even at the very beginning, the new firm's planning should anticipate *reasonably* what it can expect to encounter, how to cope with the problems that will arise, and what goals and objectives to strive for. Plans should be made for every step of the process of making a successful, permanent business out of a new one.

The following considerations all play an important part in the proper establishment of a new real estate brokerage business: (1) The firm must select the geographic market area and the types of properties it will specialize in initially. (2) An office must be set up, with proper consideration given to location and physical layout. (3) An initial publicity and advertising plan should be designed to familiarize the public with the firm and the services it offers, and to create a public view of the firm as a successful business offering reliable and desirable service. (4) From the very beginning, the firm should have a management plan that establishes the philosophy and goals of the business, and considers future growth and development. The new firm's managers should understand the proper management and organizational techniques required to assure success in achieving its goals.

Some aspects of (2) and (4) already have been discussed in previous chapters.

CHOOSING THE MARKET AREA AND SEGMENT

Quite often the type of geographic and property market the brokerage will concentrate on already is decided by the experience and knowledge of the participants in the new firm. Obviously, it makes sense for them to continue, at least initially, in the same market areas in which they have achieved their success. Nonetheless, it is necessary to point out some possible pitfalls.

First, it appears from experience that a great many brokers starting new firms pick that time to try to enter new markets as well. Thus the time and effort they should be spending getting their new businesses going is cut into by the equally demanding tasks of expansion of their business horizons. Each of these efforts is important and deserves the kind of attention that it can get only when there are no other serious considerations (including each other) to be handled. The new broker who has achieved success as a salesperson already has a certain degree of knowledge and expertise concerning his own specialized niche in the market. While he concentrates upon establishing his business, he should limit his market penetration to those areas he already knows. Once a new real estate brokerage firm is on a solid footing and running smoothly, it can begin to concentrate upon well-planned and conducted expansion.

Experience of the Sales Force

Not all participants in the new brokerage firm may have been specializing in exactly the same types of property and geographical areas. Indeed, a diversity of background among the sales force of the new firm can make for much more efficient development, in that the experienceand knowledge of each member becomes easily available to all the others. Still, it is not advisable for a new firm's sales force to be so widely divergent that the firm's *own* market penetration, which is essentially the sum of that of all its participants, is too widespread. The reason is that the firm itself will establish a market identity, and this identity ought to be be something that appears concrete and well thought out. A firm that covers the map in all types of real estate may appear to be spread too thin. It may seem to offer only the services of an *individual* who is associated with the firm, instead of the services of the total sales force of a *business*. Very large firms can offer a wide diversity of services because they have depth in all of them. The small firm just starting out is better off to give the impression that while its services are limited to particular areas, in those areas it can offer depth and considerable knowledge, talent, and expertise.

Geographical Areas

In a small city or town the geographical area of specialization may not be particularly important, since most brokerage firms in such places are expected to cover it entirely. However, in larger cities it may be important to consider only a part of the metropolitan area as the prime district in which the firm will specialize. Too large a geographical area can lead to a number of problems. First, there will be great distances between some of the properties being listed and shown, and the firm's offices; this will lead to a lot of time spent traveling to and from appointments, and consequent loss of valuable direct contact time.

More important, the market itself will be accustomed to firms that specialize geographically. This means that a firm located some distance from a particular neighborhood may be at a competitive disadvantage with those firms that more obviously specialize in that area. Furthermore, in larger cities there is much more significant diversity among large sections and neighborhoods. This can mean that a firm located in one area will be viewed as specializing in that area only, and in the types of properties predominating in that area. Firms with different locations will have to work harder to establish confidence in their ability to compete head to head with more local firms. Larger firms can overcome this problem by setting up branches in each district in which they do business; they can capitalize on the prestige and impressiveness of their overall size, as well as offering the specialization associated with each branch.

A multiple branch business usually is well beyond the capability of a new firm, and is not advisable for it in any case. There is little point in exposure to more problems than are absolutely necessary. Therefore, the new firm should make a very careful assessment of the location it will occupy. The knowledge and experience of the members of the firm should be taken into consideration. If it appears that the total area of possible coverage is too large for a single firm to handle properly, certain compromises have to be made. It is not necessary to prohibit sales force members from dealing in certain market areas, so long as it is within their capabilities, but the choice of location can create a public image suggesting certain areas of specialty, and the firm must consider just what this image will be. It will tend to force a certain amount of specialization upon the firm, and, therefore, a location should be chosen with an eye to promoting the forms of business the firm is most likely to perform well.

Market Segment

Only the largest firms are equipped to handle comfortably all kinds of real estate sales; the new firm generally must specialize in a particular *market segment*, and depend on growth and experience to allow it to expand its offerings. Usually the types of property that will be handled by a firm are determined by the experience of the sales force that is assembled. Most new firms specialize in houses, since this is where the experience of most salespeople lies. Of course, experienced commercial or land salespeople may decide to start their own firms, and, when they do, they are best advised to continue in the areas that they have experience in. Also, an occasional new broker may establish his own firm for the specific reason that it allows him to branch out into new types of properties that were forbidden to him during his employment with other firms. In these cases, the new broker will be taking some extra risk: not only is he setting up a new firm, but he also is trying to establish himself in a new market.

It generally is easiest for new brokerage firms to establish themselves at first as residential sales specialists. The market for homes is by far the largest and broadest real estate market, and one in which new firms are familiar sights. Homeowners and buyers are not likely to have built up loyalty or confidence in particular firms or salespeople, so they can be receptive to employing a new firm. Buyers and sellers of investment property are much more discriminating in their choices of real estate firms to use, and are more difficult to convince that a new firm can provide the services that they need – unless, of course, the new firm includes personnel with whom they are familiar and comfortable.

MARKETING THE NEW BROKERAGE

The main objective of a new brokerage firm is to get its business going as quickly as possible. Advance organizational planning prepares the new firm to operate efficiently as soon as it is established. However, in order for it to be successful and efficient, it must have some business to do. So, the new firm should undertake an initial advertising and publicity campaign, designed to make both the public and the rest of the local brokerage industry aware of the new firm, its personnel, and what it can do. This kind of advertising may initially be considerably wider in scope and more expensive than the ongoing advertising and publicity efforts that will be maintained once the firm is established.

The new firm should pay special attention to making cooperative arrangements with other firms, and to join the local multilist if at all possible. The new brokerage usually lacks listings, since it is generally impossible (and in most states illegal) for a salesperson or broker to take his listings with him when he transfers to a different firm. Therefore, it is important for the new firm to establish good relations with other firms, which then will allow the new firm to cooperate on the sales of their listings. In return, of course, the new firm agrees to allow the existing cooperative firms access to its own listings once they begin to accumulate. The reputations of the members of the firm can help to minimize any difficulties

Publicity

A brokerage firm which has been in business a long time can rely upon reputation, repeat business and referrals from satisfied customers, its continuous presence in the market in the form of advertising, and its signs on listed and sold properties. A new firm's success depends upon its ability to attract customers, so potential customers have to be made aware that the new business exists, that it offers service they will need, and how to find and contact the firm for service. Even before the business opens, planning should be under way to introduce the new firm to the public. Once the firm is established, it should have a continuing program of advertising and other publicity to keep its name before the public and to make the public aware of the quality of its services. Several means of introducing the firm and continuing publicity and advertising efforts can be employed.

Previous Customers of the Sales Force

The brokerage's experienced sales personnel will have built up their own reputations in their earlier activities, and these reputations should be traded on vigorously. Periodically, each salesperson should contact all customers for whom he has provided satisfactory service within the previous year or two, so as to maintain their acquaintance. This is usually accomplished by letter, although telephone and other more direct contact should not be ruled out.

If the salesperson has joined a new firm, the message should emphasize the salesperson's enthusiasm concerning his new association, and should point out the advantages to his customers of his new firm and the new people he will be working with. A brief but informative description of the new brokerage should be included, as well as special mention of any particular emphases the new firm plans to add to its services that would be of interest to potential customers. Particular qualifications of the salesperson's new associates should be mentioned, as well as indication of how his new association will enable the salesperson to improve his service.

The same kinds of communication should be directed at other people who might be a future source of business to the salesperson; this would include members of organizations he belongs to, friends, acquaintances, and others whom he has met in the course of business. Former customers and friends and associates are valuable sources of referral business; they should be cultivated continuously all during a salesperson's career. Informing them of his change of position and the new firm he has joined will have the double effect of bringing both himself and his new firm to their attention.

Other Brokerage Firms

A real estate salesperson quickly establishes relationships and connections among other agents and firms in his business, even though they are also his competitors. Since so much real estate selling involves more than one brokerage firm, these relationships are important. The new firm should communicate its existence to all the others with which it may do business in the future, and it should join multilist arrangements as soon as possible. If cooperative deals between brokerage firms are common, the new brokerage should communicate to other firms its cooperative services policy, including the terms under which it will engage in cooperative deals. It should also describe any other special services that it intends to offer. The new firm's sales force should inform the salespeople and firms with which they have dealt of their new situations. The objective of all of this is to introduce the new firm to the local real estate brokerage business, and to get it into the mainstream of that business.

An existing firm maintains contact with other firms through its day-to-day business activity, so the need for formal communications of a purely publicity nature is reduced. Other firms will be able to evaluate the brokerage by its performance and the ease (or difficulty) of dealing with it, and these are far more important and impressive than specific publicity efforts can be.

Personal Contacts

An experienced real estate salesperson knows a large number of people who ought to be kept informed about him. These include people with whom he regularly deals, friends, associates, members of organizations he belongs to, and others who are important contacts because of their influence or ability to useful useful leads and information. Whenever any important change occurs in a salesperson's business life, these people should be contacted individually, preferably by telephone or face-to-face meeting. At the very least they should be sent letters – not the same letter used in cold canvassing, but one that is more personal and less of a form letter.

Each of these contacts represents an opportunity to publicize the salesperson and his/her brokerage firm. Therefore, this kind of publicity shouldn't be reserved only for moves to a different firm. Rather, any plausible "news" about the salesperson or the firm is a good reason for spreading the word: listing or selling a high-profile property, receiving a public service award, a promotion, making the Million Dollar Club, a brokerage's new branch office.

Community Activity

Individual salespeople and brokers can generate considerable positive public response for themselves and their firms by becoming involved in community activity. Fraternal and charitable organizations always need volunteers for fund drives and other community work. Firms themselves sometimes may be able to act as corporate sponsors for civic and charitable events. The list of possibilities is long. However, certain ones should be avoided, especially if they are controversial or are intended to advocate certain policies. A high profile in these activities can alienate those who hold the opposite view. For example, visibly working to promote a popular charity drive will likely produce only desirable and beneficial responses from the public. On the other hand, demonstrating in favor of controversial proposals and positions can alienate people who disagree. For the same reasons, partisan political activity should be kept quiet, unless it is likely that most members of the public whom the salesperson or firm wants to impress hold the same views.

Advertising in the Media

While advertising through the media is not as effective an attention-getter as individual contact, it is very valuable because it reaches a lot of people at a relatively low cost per contact. *Newspaper* advertising should be done in series, rather than as a single explosion of one or two large ads, even though this may mean that smaller ads must be used. Traditionally, placement of such advertisements is in the classified section or homes section of the newspaper where real estate advertising predominates, or in the financial section. The former location aims at the market itself, while the latter usually impresses only those most economically important citizens who may have a reason to read the business section of the paper on a regular basis. Over time, the ads should tell quite a lot about the firm. One shouldn't try to squeeze too much information into a single ad, especially if it leads to a cluttered look. The actual layout and composition of these advertisements is very important, and they should be designed by professionals in the field, unless the new firm happens to have someone on hand who can produce good advertising copy.

Radio and television advertising can be effective, but it is expensive. While popular newspapers tend to get into the hands of practically everyone in a given area, radio and TV are much more selective. Therefore, it is essential that some information be gained before launching a radio or TV campaign to assure that the right people will be contacted by the advertising. Spot ads (ten seconds or less) are effective and relatively inexpensive, but they cannot relay much information, and are most useful in establishing name recognition. Longer ads require more elaborate production, particularly in television, where visual interest is so important and so expensive to obtain.

Different times of day are priced differently for ads, and the advertiser should make a careful analysis of the composition of the audience he will reach compared to the cost he will entail. One analytical technique used in the radio and television business is the *cost-per-thousand* measure, in which the cost of the commercial is compared to the number of thousands of people whom it reaches. But the composition of those "thousands" of people exposed to the ad is important as well; a cheap cost per thousand isn't much use if the ad reaches mostly children, or other groups who aren't likely to use the services of a real estate brokerage.

One drawback to most media advertising is that the ad reaches an audience considerably larger than the one the brokerage firm is aiming for. In some states, a given television station's signal may be sent via cable to an enormous geographical area. Most of its inhabitants will be outside the advertising brokerage's service area. It's not much consolation to a brokerage firm to discover that its television advertising has made it a well-recognized name in areas where it does no business, while competitors' more locally oriented advertising has given them the edge in the areas where the firm actually operates. Even in larger cities where radio and television audiences may be local, the individual brokerage will find that its message gets all over town, including into many areas in which it does not operate. Therefore, before a brokerage firm spends money on radio/television advertising, it should get as much information as possible about the medium's reach into its own market area, so that the effectiveness of the advertising can be accurately measured against its cost.

Brokerage Office Open Houses

An effective way to introduce a new business is the open house, at which members of the public are invited to the new office to see and learn about the operation first hand. A single event can be held, but it often is more effective to have a series of open houses. This will make it more convenient for people to come when they can, and will create a continuing hospitable atmosphere. Open houses should be informal gatherings. Most of the salespeople should be present, but little actual "selling" should occur. The objective of the open house is to introduce the business to the neighborhood, but it also is an excellent source of prospects for present and future business. Visitors should be encouraged to leave their names and addresses; since they were interested enough to show up it is likely that they may become customers in the future. Brochures can be distributed to visitors, and attractive displays emphasizing the firm's services can be set up. Salespeople should circulate among the guests and find out all they can about them; if any of them express interest in doing business they should be cultivated, but even curiosity seekers should be made to feel welcome. If visitors leave with a positive impression of the business, they may relay that feeling to others.

The established firm also can make good use of the open house. Instead of introducing itself as a new firm, it can reintroduce itself to the community from time to time. Open houses can be combined with other community functions the firm sponsors. Many firms prefer to sponsor some activity away from the office, just to avoid the disruption.

The open house should be well publicized in advance; newspaper advertising is effective, as is mention of the open house in any mailings that are made. If the brokerage has decided not to send out cold letters, then it ought to consider sending open house invitations to residents of the neighborhoods in which it will operate. Invitations and envelopes can be made up at relatively modest cost; sometimes in the form of postcards, which greatly reduces the cost and complexity of envelope stuffing and mailing.

Mailouts

Mailouts are letters, brochures, or other information mailed to individual members of the general public who are unknown to the person or firm doing the canvassing. A brokerage can send a mailing to every address in the geographical area in which it expects to concentrate. In this letter the new firm is described, its services promoted, and one or more of its agents profiled. The objective, of course, is to make the firm known to a large population in a manner somewhat more personal and direct than media advertising. The direct contact, it is hoped, will make a more significant impression, and so will help the firm and its services to be remembered. It is likely that such a mailing will reach people who actually are considering buying or selling real estate, so the enclosures should solicit them to contact the new firm for a future discussion of its services.

A key factor in a mail campaign is assuring that the letters will be opened and read by the addressees. The firm's own letterhead should be used, and the design and appearance of the letterhead, paper, and firm's logo (the identifying symbol that it uses on its signs, advertising, and forms) should encourage the proper degree of curiosity. Most people ignore mail that is obviously of an advertising nature, so it is important to assure that at least at first glance the letter appears interesting enough to open.

Address labels pasted to the envelope are obvious indicators of a commercial mailing, as is cheap paper or printing. An effective ploy is to use stamps, at the first-class rate, on the envelopes. Better the slight extra expense and effort of first-class stamps than the dead giveaway of "Bulk Rate" and other low-cost postage markings which may be nothing more than first-class tickets into the trash. People are more likely to open mail from an apparent stranger if it appears that he took the effort to affix a stamp. Stamped letters also appear to the recipient to have been important to the sender. The recipient does not know what the letter contains, and if he is given the impression that the sender made a special effort to send it to him, he is much more likely to open it.

The enclosure and its purpose cannot be disguised, but it can be made attractive. A salutation that begins "Dear Sir —" or "Dear Occupant —" makes a very poor impression. Best of all is a genuine typewritten name and address of the recipient, followed by "Dear Mr. [Mrs., Miss, Ms, Dr., etc.] _____." This looks like a personal letter, and as such, will rarely be ignored. Even if the recipient is not immediately interested in the brokerage's services, he cannot but be impressed by the obvious care and effort devoted to gaining his personal attention, and this favorable impression will remain with him. Once again, the letter should be on good-quality letterhead paper with the firm's name, address, and telephone number attractively and prominently displayed.

The letter should cover no more than one page, and should be brief and to the point, without crowding the page. Some firms consider mailing attractive brochures in which a great deal more can be said about the firm, but the brochure is much more impersonal and less likely to be read. It is not necessary to tell everything at first contact; a better strategy is to say enough to get the person interested in the firm, but not so much that he becomes bored with the details, or chooses not to read anything at all because it looks too imposing or time consuming. Therefore, for mail canvassing, the letter is preferable.

Figure 15-1 shows such a letter. It is attractive and not wordy. Still, a lot of information is contained: (a) the fact that the firm is new; (b) that the firm was organized to improve the opportunities for its founders to give good service; (c) that the salesperson writing the letter is experienced and professional; (d) that by implication his associates are, too; and (e) that the new firm intends to offer a high standard of service. The letter leads off with an invitation to the new firm's open house; this is an effective opening because the hospitable offer creates a positive mood in the reader.

Costs

Sending individual letters isn't cheap, but the expense usually is worth it for such an important objective as introducing a new business to the public. On occasion the established firm may want to do a mailout, especially if it has a carefully weeded mailing list made up of people who are apt to respond: former satisfied customers, certain friends and business associates of the firm's principals, etc. Individually typed letters for a mailout are very costly. However, most word processing computer software packages include "mail merge" features. These insert names and addresses, and sometimes other individualized comments, into a standard form letter. The only "hands on" part is signing the letters, putting them in envelopes (which the computer already has addressed), affixing stamps and dropping them into the mail.

As part of its startup costs, the new firm should budget for an effective publicity and advertising campaign. Becoming known to the public is essential, and justifies this heavy, one-time cost. An established firm budgets and chooses its advertising based upon

D DOVER REALTY COMPANY

1776 Twelfth Street, Waltham, Xxxxx 12345   (908) 555-4321

Mr. James R. Patton
3318 Martin Avenue
Waltham, XXXXX 12345

Dear Mr. Patton:

   I and my associates have joined together to found Dover Realty, Inc.
We will be having an open house at our new offices on Saturday, April 18
from 3PM to 9PM and I would like to extend to you and your family my invitation to visit us at that time.

   Dover Realty is the result of our philosophy that a real estate company
should offer dedicated, sincere service to the people whom it represents.
I and all my new associates understand how important buying or selling a home
is to a family such as yours and we believe that a real estate professional's
best measure of success is the satisfaction and confidence of everyone he works
with.

   I have been listing and selling homes in the Marlowe Hills area for over
five years, and our other sales associates, Ken Marlowe, Nancy MacConnell,
Rupert DePlane and Margaret Sayers bring the same kind of experience to our
new firm. We offer every service that a buyer or seller may need. We constantly monitor and evaluate all information available concerning the markets in
which we specialize, and pride ourselves on our up-to-date knowledge. We intend
to offer the highest possible standard of professional service.

   If you are considering buying or selling a home, please consider our
service. If not, then we hope that you will remember us when the need arises
in the future. In any event, I hope that it will be possible for you to visit
with us at our open house on the 18th.

   Very Sincerely,

   George Reich
   Senior Sales Associate

Figure 15-1.   Sample Cold Mailing – New Firm

a continuing program of evaluation of its needs. While adjustments are made from time to time, its advertising will follow a fairly well-established pattern. The new firm will switch into this pattern as it becomes established. Any firm, new or established, must consider the effectiveness of every dollar spent, and make sure that the limited funds available for marketing and advertising are used to the best possible advantage.

IDENTIFICATION OF THE FIRM

The firm should adopt a symbol that it can use on all its advertising, letterhead paper, and signs. Such a symbol is called a logotype, or *logo*. All of us are familiar with several of these, and when we see one we immediately think of the company that uses it – and we think of its products. Familiar examples are the Coca-Cola® red and white circle, the arches of McDonald's® restaurants, and a tiger who likes sugar-coated cornflakes. An objective of almost any business is to create a symbol as easily recognized as these. Of course, except for participants in franchise programs, real estate brokerage firms don't need a nationally known symbol. But each should try to create a symbol which becomes well known in its locality.

Logo Symbol

A good symbol should be simple and easy to recognize. It also must be versatile: it must look good on letterhead, on business cards, in advertising, and on FOR SALE signs. Throughout this text, we have used a fictitious brokerage firm for our examples, the Dover Realty Company. Its logo can be seen in several of the figures in the book, including the two in this chapter. Note that it is quite simple: little more than a large capital "**D**" with the name of the company next to it. Simplicity is a virtue in the design of a logo. Uncluttered design means instant recognition, provided that the design is memorable enough.

FOR SALE Sign

While our illustrations do not show color, it can be used in the logo and in the firm's FOR SALE sign. One consideration, however, is that the color reproduction costs more, and in any case it cannot be used in newspaper advertising because of prohibitive cost. If the company's sign uses color, certain warnings are necessary. The purpose of the FOR SALE sign is to attract attention, and to be easily visible as a means of identifying not only the real estate for sale, but also the *firm* holding the listing and the *salesperson* who secured it. Colors that blend into the background on which the sign will be placed should be avoided. These include many shades of green and brown, which are close to the tones of grass and earth and will not stand out satisfactorily from them. Signs that feature a lot of red ought to be avoided as well; for various reasons red, while it stands out well, is an offensive or annoying color to many people.

Figure 15-2. Examples of FOR SALE Sign, SOLD Sign, and Business Card

A great many firms use signs that feature white as the background with lettering and logo of a suitable color, usually with a border of the same color around the edge of the sign. This allows for one-color printing or painting of the signs, since most stock that is used is white to begin with. While it might be thought that a white sign will not stand out against the snow, the lettering on the sign will, and that is what the passers-by are supposed to notice. Against other natural backgrounds, white stands out very well.

The sign shown in Figure 15-2 is a good one. The large logo **D** is an immediate eyecatcher. The rest of the sign includes only the absolutely necessary information: a FOR SALE notice at the top, where it usually is placed, the name of the firm and its telephone number in large letters, and space at the bottom of the sign for the placement of the salesperson's name and telephone. No additional elaboration is necessary or desirable. There is room for all the information to be presented clearly. It is essential that the letters be large enough for someone to read at a distance of up to 30 feet or so; the sign usually is placed close to the front of the lot, and many people walking or driving by may want to stop and take down the names and numbers on it.

Construction of Sign

FOR SALE signs used to be made of metal, designed to be reused again and again. Holes were drilled at top and bottom to allow for the salesperson's placard and the SOLD notice to be bolted on when necessary. The main problem with metal signs is that they deteriorate after a time; they begin to rust, get scratched, or otherwise become messy and unattractive. Also, they're expensive.

Nowadays, many brokerage firms have signs made of tough fiberboard, prepared by a printing specialist rather than a painting shop. These are much less expensive than metal signs, although they are also less durable. Many firms will use a sign only once; when the property is sold the sign is discarded. With the fiberboard sign, the salesperson's information placard (her name and telephone number) is printed on self-stick paper or plastic just like the familiar bumper sticker. When she posts a sign, she attaches her own information sticker to each side; on most signs this should be across the bottom, and the sign should be designed to allow for this space.

When the property is sold, another sticker with the SOLD label is affixed to the sign. It should be located where it will not obliterate either the firm's or salesperson's name and telephone number. SOLD indicators should be of a contrasting color to the sign so that they will stand out. White lettering on a red background is suitable for most; however, if the background of the sign itself is a fairly dark color, red lettering on a white background will stand out better.

Once a property has been sold, the salesperson should try to arrange for the SOLD sign to remain up as long as possible. For this purpose, the brokerage industry considers the property to be "sold" once the seller has agreed to a contract of sale – *not* the much later time when the deal closes and the final "sale" actually occurs. Since it usually takes several weeks from the time of the sale contract to the time of settlement, this means that the firm's sign, the salesperson's name and the SOLD label will be displayed for all those weeks. This is important, because it is well-known in the real estate brokerage business that SOLD signs are one of the most effective forms of advertisement available to the firm and the listing salesperson. They are clear evidence that both operate successfully.

Vandalism and Damage

The worst plague affecting FOR SALE and SOLD signs is vandalism; people remove them, knock them down, mark them up, or otherwise damage them. An advantage of the cheap fiberboard sign is that a vandalized one can be replaced at minimal expense, while a more expensive sign has to be written off at a much higher cost. If the sign isn't vandalized, and weathers well, many salespeople will save it for use later on another property. Some salespeople carry extra used signs with SOLD stickers on them; when one of their listed properties is sold, they simply switch signs and then have a sign available to reuse on a new listing.

Cost, wear and tear, vandalism, and other damage argue against the use of other types of expensive signs. Some firms (particularly those affiliated with franchises) use very large wooden signs set on heavy posts. These are expensive, and may not be worth the extra cost, even though they stand out well. Many of them are so large that they cannot be carried in the trunk of a normal automobile, and one person usually can't install them. They have to be transported to the site by truck, along with an installation crew. A large hole must be dug to accommodate them. When a large sign is removed, another crew and truck will be needed. The hole has to be filled in and maybe even replanted with grass. And all of this has to be paid for by the brokerage firm. Finally, if a large, elaborate sign is damaged or destroyed it will cost a lot to replace or repair it.

By comparison, small signs on wooden or metal stakes can be driven into the ground by one person, with a household hammer. When the time comes to remove it, the small sign can be lifted out of the ground and the hole pressed down with a foot. If it's damaged, stolen or destroyed, the loss is relatively small.

A FINAL WORD: PHILOSOPHY AND POLICY

This book has described the business philosophy and policies the successful real estate brokerage firm uses.

In our economic system, competition and the ups and downs of the real estate and money markets are constant features of the real estate brokerage industry. In recent years, this business has seen dizzying fluctuations in the markets it deals with. Good times and bad have followed one another time and again. It's easy enough to appear to succeed when times are good. But the true test of success is the professionalism, knowledge and dedication it takes to weather the harder times.

In spite of the seeming independence of its participants, real estate brokerage is a field which is extensively regulated by government. Brokers and salespeople must be familiar with several areas of law. Most significant are license law, agency law, and contract law. Several other aspects merit attention as well: environmental regulation, disclosure laws, anti-discrimination law, etc. Real estate salespeople, though they cannot practice law or give legal advice, still are expected to be able to conduct themselves within the law, and to make sure that transactions in which they participate follow the proper legal guidelines.

Brokers and salespeople have to keep up with both the markets for the real estate they list and sell, and the markets for the financing which their customers and clients will need. Mortgage markets can be bewildering, but licensees must be familiar with them, and ready to explain them at any time.

Brokerage is a business, and must be treated as one if it is to be a successful enterprise. In fact, individual salespeople ought to view themselves as single, independent business entities as well: most of the guidelines for operating a traditional business enterprise will work well for the salesperson's career guidance.

This illustrates a peculiarity of the real estate brokerage business. It's important for the firm to retain its own cohesive and consistent identity in the world at large. Realizing this objective is a responsibility which the firm has to leave to its sales force, because they are the ones who consistently contact and work with the public. But at the same time, the nature of the business is that most of the time salespeople operate quite independently of the firm. Their independent contractor status prevents the firm from directing their work closely. This means that the real estate brokerage firm and its sales force have to develop a *symbiotic* relationship: one in which each benefits the other. The firm's policies and management methods have to *encourage* (rather than *direct*) its salespeople to conduct themselves so as to further both their own and the firm's goals and objectives.

All of these facets of the brokerage business point to a single important fact: professionalism and professional attitudes are essential characteristics of everyone involved with a well-run real estate brokerage firm. This is not a business in which slapdash or uninformed performance makes the grade. Professional organizations, such as national, state and local REALTORS® organizations, are dedicated to promoting and encouraging this necessary professionalism.

Within our system, there is ample opportunity for both success and failure. Both will be due to the abilities and skills of the business people operating the firms. Real estate brokerage can be an intensely rewarding business when the people involved are willing to work to make it so. Honest, ethical, and skillful service at a fair price is the keystone to success in this business as it is in so many others. Finally, though it sounds trite, it is true that in this business, as in others, hard work is the primary requirement for success.

We hope that this book has provided an indication of the needs and prospects that will lead to success for its readers.

DISCUSSION QUESTIONS AND PROJECTS

1. How should a new firm choose the geographical area in which it will specialize?

2. How should a new firm select the type of property in which it will specialize?

3. Devise a program of long range (three years or more) goals and objectives that a new brokerage firm might establish. Be sure to include strategy for achieving them.

4. Compare the advertising needs and costs of a new firm and an established one.

5. What are the advantages and disadvantages of advertising on radio or television, from the point of view of a real estate brokerage firm?

6. Secure a sample of a cold mailing piece recently used by a firm in your area. Find out from the firm what the response to it was, and whether they feel it was worthwhile. Could you have made any suggestions for improvement?

7. Assume you are a real estate licensee (if you are not already). Make a list of all the people you think you should keep reminded of your work and availability. How would you accomplish this? Why are these people useful to you?

8. Collect samples of logos and sign designs for several of the firms in your area. Carefully critique them, making suggestions for improvement (with reasons given) for each.

REFERENCES

Hall Institute of Real Estate, *Managing a Real Estate Team*. Hinsdale, IL: The Dryden Press, 1980.

REALTORS® Code of Ethics. Chicago, IL: National Association of REALTORS®, updated periodically.

Statement of Policy and Position on Current Issues. Chicago, IL: National Association of REALTORS®, issued and updated annually in November.

INDEX*

* The terms **broker, brokerage, business, firm, management,** and **salesperson** appear so often in this book that an index listing of the pages upon which they are used would be so long as to be useless. Therefore, for other than general references, the reader should consult the specific terms for which a relationship to, or aspect of, these six terms is sought.